John O. Raum

The History of New Jersey

From its earliest settlement to the present time: including a brief historical account of the first discoveries and settlement of the country. Vol. 2

John O. Raum

The History of New Jersey
From its earliest settlement to the present time: including a brief historical account of the first discoveries and settlement of the country. Vol. 2

ISBN/EAN: 9783337427382

Printed in Europe, USA, Canada, Australia, Japan

Cover: Foto ©ninafisch / pixelio.de

More available books at **www.hansebooks.com**

THE
HISTORY OF NEW JERSEY,

FROM ITS

EARLIEST SETTLEMENT TO THE PRESENT TIME.

INCLUDING

A BRIEF HISTORICAL ACCOUNT OF THE FIRST DISCOVERIES AND SETTLEMENT OF THE COUNTRY,

BY

JOHN O. RAUM,

AUTHOR OF THE HISTORY OF TRENTON; HISTORY OF TRENTON LODGE, No 5, A. F A. M.;
DIGEST OF NEW JERSEY, I. O. O F; MISSION OF ODD FELLOWSHIP,
ETC., ETC., ETC.

IN TWO VOLUMES.

VOL. I.

PHILADELPHIA:
JOHN E. POTTER AND COMPANY,
617 SANSOM STREET.

INTRODUCTORY.

HISTORY has universally conceded that Christopher Columbus was the first successful navigator to the Western Continent, and in furtherance of his discoveries the first colonies were founded, yet it does not concede to him the honor of being the first discoverer, as we have information that I think can be relied on, that Eric of Iceland, made discoveries on this continent as early as the year 986, being five hundred and six years before Columbus landed here; and tradition informs us that the Chinese penetrated within the bounds of the continent in the year 498, nearly one thousand years before the discovery by Columbus.

Although we have no authentic information to sustain the latter, yet we are not prepared fully to reject it, as the Asiatics were, previous to the introduction of the religion of Confucius among the Chinese, a nomadic people, and wandered from place to place, but since the introduction of his religious tenets, they ceased their wanderings, and remained at home, in order that their bones might be entombed with those of their ancestors; and even to this day, those who come to this and other countries, do so with the stipulation, that their bones are to be sent back to their own country.

In support of the discovery by Icelanders, we have the evidence of the researches of the society of Antiquarians of Copenhagen, established in 1837. We have also the evidence of the learned Dr. Wheaton, in his history of the Danes and Norwegians, who, in one passage, says: "Or as they were called Northmen, that there is not the *slightest reason* to believe that the illustrious Genoese was acquainted with the discovery of North

America by the Normans five centuries before his time, however well authenticated that fact now appears to be by the Icelandic records."

And in a lecture delivered in New York City, March 3, 1874, by Rev. Charles Kingsley, Canon of Westminster, England, he stated that "the Northmen discovered the rock bound coast of New England one thousand years ago." One week later, March 10, 1874, Hon. A. M. Waddell, of North Carolina, delivered a lecture in New York on the same subject, in which he brought forth arguments and facts to prove that the first voyage of the Icelanders to Greenland, was in the year 983, which was followed by voyages to North Carolina, which fact was also stated by Humboldt in his "Cosmos," a work of great merit, "and further that the statement of Humboldt was not only true, but less than the whole truth, for in his opinion, the evidence which he was about to offer, established the fact that voyages to, and settlements south of Chesapeake bay were made by a Celtic race before the discovery of Greenland by Eric the Red. Instead then of having been less than four hundred years since the discovery of our continent, it must have been about nine hundred years."

I have introduced these arguments to corroborate the statements made in the opening chapter of this work, that the original discovery of this continent was made by the Northmen, previous to the landing of Columbus.

Preface.

IN presenting to the public a new History of New Jersey, it is only evident propriety, that the indulgence of the reader should be asked to a few preliminary remarks respecting the object had in view in this volume, and the claims which it is conceived it has upon the citizens of the state.

"It is not without reason," says Rollin, "that History has always been considered as the light of ages, the depository of events, the faithful evidence of truth, the source of prudence and good counsel, and the rule of conduct and good manners. * * * *. * * * * It is History which fixes the seal of immortality upon actions truly great, and sets a mark of infamy on vices which no after age can obliterate. It is by History that mistaken merit and oppressed virtue, appeal in the incorruptible tribunal of posterity, which renders them the justice their own age has sometimes refused them, and without respect of persons, and the fear of a power which subjects no more, condemns the unjust abuse of authority with inexorable rigor. * * * * * History when it is well taught, becomes a school of morality for all mankind."

"All History," says Dryden, "is only the precepts of moral philosophy reduced into examples." He also observes: "The laws of history in general, are truth of matter, method and clearness of expression. The first property is necessary to keep our understanding from the impositions of falsehood, for history is an argument framed from many particular examples or inductions; if these examples are not true, the measure of life which one take from them, will be false, and deceive us in their consequences. The second is grounded on the former; for if the method be confused, if the words of expression of thought be obscure, then the ideas which we receive must be imperfect, and if such, we are not taught by them what to elect, or what to shun. Truth, therefore, is required as the foundation of history, to inform us; dispositions and perspicuity, as the manner to inform us plainly."

Having given the views of two distinguished writers, as to what history should be, let us speak more particularly of the present one.

In preparing this work, the one great object ever before me has been, to present a truthful, impartial and readable narrative of the origin, rise and progress of a state which though not so large as some others, is of equal importance to any other in our glorious Union. Having no ends to gain but those of truth and right; no theories to establish, no partisan views or wishes to gratify; I have honestly endeavored to ascertain what the truth is, and then to set it forth as clearly, and as fully as was possible within the limits to which I was restricted. I have spared no labor in order to be accurate and reliable; I have not neglected to consult any work of value which was within my reach, and having free access at all times to the numerous volumes in the State Library, I have had opportunities to obtain reliable information possessed by very few persons in the state; besides, having been for the last fifteen years, employed in the military department of the state, I have been enabled to obtain reliable information relating to the late rebellion, which will be found fully set forth in the second volume of this history.

Every person should be familiar with the history not only of the country in which he lives and its institutions, but more especially of his own state.

The compiler therefore, thinks it a most fitting time to lay before the citizens of his native state, the many interesting facts and incidents that have occurred from its first formation as a province and state, as well as during the eventful quarter of a century just gone by.

Every Jerseyman may well feel proud that he lives in so favored a state, every foot of whose soil was purchased from the aborigines who inhabited the land prior to the time it was settled by the whites, and that no land was taken up except by purchase.

The great object of the compiler of this work has been to present a truthful, impartial and readable narrative of the origin, rise and progress of every important event in our state. And in order to accomplish this, he has spared no labor or expense to obtain accurate and reliable information, and has not, in the pursuance of this object, neglected to consult any work of value which was within his reach; and in all cases of doubt, has carefully and conscientiously sought to compare and sift conflicting accounts, and to lay before the reader only that which seemed to be the nearest approximation to the truth, which probably under the circumstances, can now be attained.

That a work, covering so large an extent of time, and treating of so vast a variety of subjects, should be free from occasional errors, is not to be expected by any one who knows how exceedingly difficult it is to avoid error in writing on historical subjects, as different authors consulted differ sometimes as to circumstances and dates. With all the care and devotion which I have given this history, I hardly dare flatter myself that here and there errors have not crept in, and escaped observation. I can only hope—which I do with tolerable confidence—that they are few and far between, and that there are none of material consequence to the value and integrity of the history.

With these brief introductory remarks and statements, the present History of New Jersey is submitted to the consideration of the citizens of my native state, with whom I have passed more than half a century; and I trust it may be found valuable for the purpose for which a history is intended, and that a copy may be placed in the hands of every citizen of the state, as the information herein contained can be relied on as authentic, having been collected from the latest and most reliable sources; in full hopes that it may be found useful and interesting, and may become a text book for all matters relating to a state whose citizens have been second to none in their devotion to the interests of the country, in the revolutionary struggle, or any other in which our country has been engaged, and in which they have ever proved themselves no less patriotic than those of any other state in our glorious and prosperous country.

TRENTON, *January* 1, 1877.

Contents.

CHAPTER I.

986—1609.

First discoverers of the Western continent—Opinion of the Indians respecting them—Claims set up for the discovery—Phoenicians, Egyptians and Carthagenians—Tartarians, Siberians and Kamscatkins—Spaniards, Germans, French and English—First colony planted—English charter.   17

CHAPTER II.

1609—1664.

First patent—Extent of land contained therein—Dutch and Swedes—Speech to the Indians in behalf of the Queen of Sweden—Their approval—First name of New Jersey—Surrender of the province by the Dutch.   34

CHAPTER III.

1664—1669.

The Dutch at Delaware bay—Sir Robert Carre—Right of the crown of England to these provinces—Duke of York—First constitution of New Jersey—Inducements to settlers.   54

CHAPTER IV.

1669—1680.

Stratagem of a settler—Penelope Stout—Her rescue—Her descendants—Wampum the chief currency of the country—

Proclamation of the Governor—Division of the Province—
Yorkshire and London purchasers—Meeting of Proprietors.   75

CHAPTER V.

1680—1703.

Settlement of the first or Yorkshire tenth—Settlement of the second or London tenth—First carpenter that came to this country—John Kinsey—His account of the country—Thomas Hooten's account—Mahlon Stacy's account—West Jersey—First Assembly.   98

CHAPTER VI.

1681—1682.

Indian tribes—Modes of burial—Superstitions—Care of the sick—Care of their children—Marriageable ages—Marriage ceremonies—Representatives chosen by the Proprietors—Laws passed by the Governor, council and assembly—Third and last grant by the Duke of York.   120

CHAPTER VII.

1682—1703.

Land grants to settlers—First building at Amboy—First sawmills erected—Bergen settled by the Dutch—Disturbances in the Province—Ferry started at Perth Amboy—First settled preacher in the Province—First ship built in the Province—Prices paid for provisions—Failure of crops—Great distress.   141

CHAPTER VIII.

1703—1707.

Union of the two Provinces of East and West Jersey—Surrender to the Queen—Inconveniences in regard to currency—Conflict between the assembly and Governor, by which he dissolves them—Cornbury assumes to be judge of the qualifications of members—Resistance by the house—Remedies proposed to meet the evils in the Provinces—Queen Anne sustains the assembly, and removes the Governor. 166

CHAPTER IX.

1708—1710.

Lord Lovelace succeeds Cornbury—His conciliatory measures satisfactory to the assembly and people—Paper money established in the Province—Expedition to reduce Canada, and drive out the French—Troops promised from England—The French governor capitulates—Expedition against Port Royal. 188

CHAPTER X.

1711—1776.

Second expedition against Canada—Arrival of transports containing troops from England—Passage of bill permitting Quakers to affirm—Governor Hunter's administration satisfactory to the people—Accession of King George I—Severe storms—Acts for running the division line between New York and New Jersey. 208

CHAPTER XI.

1674—1693.

Quintipartite deed—Twenty-four Proprietors—Borough officers for Bergen and Elizabethtown—Punishment for different crimes—Marriages not to be solemnized until after publication—Militia law—Formation and boundaries of counties—Bergen—Essex—Middlesex—Monmouth. 231

CONTENTS.

CHAPTER XII.

1675.

Page

Continuation of counties—Salem—Gloucester—Somerset—Cape May—Burlington—Hunterdon—Morris—Cumberland—Sussex Warren — Atlantic — Passaic — Mercer -- Hudson—Camden—Ocean—Union.   254

CHAPTER XIII.

1702—1743.

The proprietors cede to the crown their rights of jurisdiction—Lands purchased from the Indians—Population—Habits of the people—Release of Lord Berkeley and Sir George Carteret—Courts—Taxes—Naturalization—First Legislature—Punishment of witches—Trading with the Indians prohibited—Drunkenness —Schools.   285

CHAPTER XIV.

1680—1786.

New Jersey when set off from New York—Extent of East and West Jersey—First purchases—Consideration paid for the lands —First settlement at Burlington—Flood at Delaware Falls—Religious institutions—Places of public worship—First courts in Trenton—United States government offices removed to Trenton.   302

CHAPTER XV.

1744—1757.

Mutiny of New Jersey troops—Troubles between the Governor and the two houses—The Indians favor the French and oppose the English—Plan of union proposed—Not satisfactory

CONTENTS.

to the English, or the people of the Provinces—Virginia raises troops, and places them under command of Colonel George Washington. 328

CHAPTER XVI.

1758—1775.

French and English wars—New Jersey raises double the number of men called for—Governor Bernard pacifies the Indians—Five colonial governors appointed by the crown in as many years—The French surrender their possessions on this side of the water—Parliament undertakes to tax the American colonies—Stamp act passed—Its repeal. 356

CHAPTER XVII.

1760—1775.

Disgust excited by the restrictions on trade—The colonies oppose the right of Parliament to tax them in any way—Petitions and remonstrances—The colonists refuse to purchase imported goods from England—Angry discussion between the governor and assembly—Destruction of tea—Battle of Lexington—Washington appointed commander-in-chief—Minute men raised in New Jersey. 383

CHAPTER XVIII.

1775—1776.

Appointment of Provincial Treasurer—Committee of safety—Acts preparing for war—Delegates to Continental Congress—Provincial Governors of New Jersey—Governor Franklin's Proclamation—Governor Livingston's prediction—Virtual declaration of Independence—Governor Franklin's arrest—Opposition to the measures of Congress. 405

CHAPTER XIX.

1775—1776.

Page.

Our people divided on the war question—First blow at Lexington—Opposition to the claims of the British Parliament—Capture of the Hessians—Death of Colonel Rahl—Washington recrosses the Delaware. 427

History of New Jersey

CHAPTER I.

986—1609.

First discoveries of the Western continent—Opinion of the Indians regarding them—Claims set up for the discovery—Phenicians, Egyptians, and Carthagenians—Tartarians, Siberians, and Kamschatkans—Spaniards, Germans, French, and English—First colony planted—English charter.

THE first visit to the western continent, of which we have any knowledge, was made in the year 986, by Eric, of Iceland, who, in consequence of his florid countenance, was termed the *Red*—and also to distinguish him from another of the same name. He emigrated from Iceland, and made his first landing at Greenland, at which place he formed a settlement. He was the first original discoverer from any foreign nation or country,* of which we have any definite knowledge.

In the year 994, Biarne, son of one of the settlers who accompanied Eric on this first voyage, returned to Norway, and gave a flowing account of the discoveries he had made south of Greenland. And on the return of Biarne, to Greenland, Lief,

---

*An account of his discovery was published in 1837, by a Society of Antiquarians, at Copenhagan.

the son of Eric, bought Biarne's ship, and with a crew of thirty-five men, embarked on a voyage still further south than had been explored by Biarne, in the year 1000. Sailing some time to the southwest, he came to a country covered with slaty rock, which he called HELLULAND, meaning slate land.

They next proceeded in a southerly course, and having sailed for some time, found a low, flat coast, studded with cliffs of white sand, behind which were woods of extensive growth. This section of country they called MARKLAND, meaning WOODED LAND.

They next sailed south and west, and finally arrived at a promontory, which extended to the east and north, around which they sailed some time, when their course was turned westward, and sailing in that direction, they passed between an island and some main land, when they entered a bay into which flowed a river, at which place they concluded to winter.

And having built their winter houses, they discovered abundance of vines, and from this circumstance they called the country VINELAND.

The particular location of this part of the country was, for a long time, in doubt, but the Antiquarian Society above mentioned, have recently, after a long examination and all the evidence obtained by them, determined it to be at the head of Narragansett Bay, in Rhode Island. The promontory described as extending east and north, corresponds with that of Barnstable and Cape Cod, and the islands on the west as those of Nantucket and Martha's Vineyard, in Massachusetts.

In the year 1002, Thorwald, brother of Lief, visited Vineland, at which place he remained two years, and was finally murdered by the natives. Before his death, he coasted around the promontory now called Cape Cod.

The place where he met his death and was buried, was Gurnet Point, at the north side of the entrance to Plymouth harbor, Massachusetts. This was called by his crew, KRASSAMES or cross-land, because over the grave of Thorwald, they erected a cross at the head and foot.

In the year 1007, three ships sailed from Greenland to Vineland. One under the command of Thorfin Karlesfue, a Norwegian of royal descent, and Snorre Thorbrandsen, who was also of distinguished lineage. Another commanded by Biarne Grimalfson and Thorhal Gamlasen. And the third by Thorward and Thorhall. These three ships had one hundred and sixty men, and carried all kinds of domestic animals, for planting and sustaining a colony. They sailed from Greenland to Helluland, and passing Markland, arrived at Kilarnes. They then sailed still farther south, keeping close by the shore of the promontory, until they arrived at a trackless beach, where they found long wastes of sand. This they called FURTHUSTANDER, meaning wonder strand or beach. They then passed southerly, sailing by the island discovered by Lief, and from thence they returned to winter at Vineland. The bay into which they sailed was called, by them, *Hopsvatn* or *Hop*, which in English is *Hope*, the same place in Rhode Island now called *Mount Hope*, afterwards celebrated as the residence of King Philip, the celebrated Indian warrior.

Thorfin was successful in almost all his enterprises, but after a time he returned to Greenland, and finally went to Iceland and settled there.

There is no doubt but that the learned society above mentioned has correctly located Vineland. Markland is supposed to be what is now Nova Scotia, and Helluland, Newfoundland and the coast of Labrador.

The first effectual and most important discoveries were made in 1492, by Christopher Colen, or Columbus, a native of Genoa, a fortified seaport city of Northern Italy, in the Sardinian States, on the coast of the Mediterranean.

Columbus made four voyages to this continent; in the first of which he was accompanied by Amerigo Vespucci, or Vespucius, a native of Florence, a celebrated city in Italy, and capital of the Grand Duchy of Tuscany.

Vespucius made three other voyages, one in 1497 and another in 1498, under the patronage of Spain, and another in 1501, in the service of Portugal. In the first of these he discovered the Carribee Islands, and in the latter, with three ships, he arrived at, and discovered the eastern portion of the continent of America, in five degrees of south latitude.

HISTORY OF NEW JERSEY.

In 1497, John Cabot and his son Sebastian, and three hundred men, with two caravals, freighted by the merchants of London and Bristol, sailed under a patent of Henry VII. of England. The first year he touched at Labrador, and the next year at Newfoundland. The first was discovered on the 24th of June, and called by them *Prima Vista*, meaning in Italian, *first sight*. A few days afterwards they discovered a smaller island, which they called St. Johns, from the fact that the island was discovered on St. John the Baptist's Day, June 24th.

They then sailed westerly and northerly, to the latitude of sixty-seven and a half degrees, expecting to find a passage to India, but being disappointed, they turned back and sailed along the coast southward to Florida, and from thence returned to England. It was upon the discoveries made by this voyage, that the English founded their claim to the eastern portion of North America.

Gasper de Cortereal, a Portuguese nobleman, followed in the year 1500, and surveyed six or seven hundred miles of the coast of Labrador.

After Americus Vespucius had made his first voyage, he coasted a great part of the continent which Columbus had not seen, at the expense of the Castilian and Portuguese kings. Although Americus was not the first discoverer, yet the name being a more common and fitting one, it was adopted as the name of the newly discovered continent. It might, with more propriety, have been called *Cabotia* or *Sebastiana*, from the fact that Sebastian Cabot discovered more of the continent than both Columbus or Vespucius, yet Columbus, as the first effectual discoverer, deserved the name, both as being the first finder as well as for his modesty in not naming it after himself.

Gasper de Cortereal sailed again, a few years after his first voyage, but never returned; and it was supposed he was murdered by the natives, in revenge for having carried off a number of the natives as slaves on his first voyage. Two expeditions which sailed in search of him, were never heard of afterwards.

The discoveries of Columbus having conferred more benefit than those previously made, we desire to speak of him more particularly.

He had early in life applied himself to the study of astronomy and geography in his own country, and being possessed of an unusual desire to understand the state and condition of all countries upon the face of the globe, as well as to make new discoveries for the benefit of mankind and science, and not for any advantage pecuniarily or otherwise, that might accrue to himself, as his modesty forbade his assuming honors even where they were his just due.

In order to accomplish his cherished object, and open up new countries to the world, he settled at Lisbon, a city of Western Europe, and capital of the kingdom of Portugal, and the province of Estremadura, on the right bank of the Tagus, near its mouth in the Atlantic ocean.

His principal object in settling there was in consequence of that nation having pushed their discoveries farther at that time than any other nation had. While here he employed nearly all his time in drawing maps and charts, and preparing himself for future enterprises. He married and settled in Lisbon, was of a good family, a grave and temperate man, of considerable learning, studious in mathematics, and from his youth was brought up to understand navigation.

Columbus was moderately tall and long visaged, his complexion a good red and white, light eyes, and cheeks somewhat full, neither too fat nor too lean. In his youth he had fair hair, which turned grey before he was thirty years of age. He was moderate in eating and drinking, always dressed in a plain and modest manner, naturally grave, but affable to strangers, and pleasant even among his domestics, strict and devout in religious matters, and though a seaman, was never heard to curse or swear.

What were his particular motives to search after this new world, are not certainly known. It has by some been attributed to information he had received; others to his skill in the nature of the globe, that made him conclude it probable that there must be a tract of land to the westward of Spain, and that it was not to be imagined the sun, when it set in the horizon, gave light to no other body.

Whatever gave rise to the project, he resolved to attempt a discovery, and being unable to do it at his own expense, he first offered his services to the Genoese, next to the King of Portugal. Not meeting with encouragement from either, he sent his brother Bartholomew to England to offer his service to Henry VII. His proposal was approved by King Henry, but the brother on his return being taken by pirates, and Columbus receiving no answer, left Portugal and went to Spain. On his application to Ferdinand and Isabella, King and Queen of Castile and Arragon, he succeeded so well that in the year 1492, they provided him with money, and entrusted him with three small ships for the expedition. He also obtained a grant from them as admiral of the western seas. All civil employments, as well as governments in the continent or world to be discovered were to be wholly at his disposal, and besides the revenues of the posts of admiral and viceroy, he was to enjoy a tenth of all the profits arising by future conquests.

His little squadron, manned only with ninety men, set sail from Palos for the Canaries the 3d of August, 1492, and arriving at those islands the 12th, sailed from thence on the 1st of September on his grand design. He had not sailed a fortnight to the westward before his men began to murmur at the enterprise. They observed the wind constantly set from east to west, and apprehended there would be no possibility of returning if they missed the land they were made to expect. On the 19th observing birds to fly over their ships, and on the 22d weeds driving by them, they began to be better satisfied, concluding they were not far from land.

They continued their course several days further westward, and meeting with no land, the seamen mutinied to that degree that they were almost ready to throw the admiral overboard and return home, when happily for him they saw more birds, weeds, pieces of boards, canes, and a shrub with the berries upon it, swim by them, which made them conjecture there must be islands thereabout.

On the 11th of October, about 10 o'clock at night, the admiral first discovered a light upon the island of Guanahani,*

---

* A bay or harbor, or sea of water.

or St. Salvador, as he named it, in consideration that the sight of it delivered him and his men from the fear of perishing. This is one of the Bahama islands, about fifteen leagues long, in north latitude fifteen degrees.*

Day appearing, the ships came to anchor very near the island. The natives crowded the shore, and beheld the ships of these new comers with astonishment, taking them for living creatures.† The admiral believing there was no great danger to be apprehended from them, went ashore in his boat with the royal standard, as did the other two captains, with their colors flying, and took possession of the country in the name of the King and Queen of Spain, with great solemnity. The Indians meanwhile stood gazing at the Spaniards without attempting to oppose them. The admiral ordered strings of glass beads, caps, and toys to be distributed among them, with which they seemed greatly delighted.

The principal ornament about them was a thin gold plate in the form of a crescent, hanging from the nose over the upper lip. The admiral, by signs, asked them from whence they had received their gold plates. At which they pointed to the south and southwest.

---

* The sailor who first discovered land expecting some great reward from the King of Spain, when he found out his disappointment, in his rage renounced Christianity and turned Mohammedan.

† One of the River Indians, in his speech at the treaty of Albany, 1754, relates the surprise of their forefathers at the sight of the first ship that came up the North river in the same manner. His speech, so far as it relates to this subject, was as follows:

"FATHERS, we are greatly rejoiced to see you all here. It is by the will of heaven that we are met here, and we thank you for this opportunity of seeing you altogether, as it is a long while since we had such a one. FATHERS who sit present here, we will give you a short relation of the long friendship which hath subsisted between the white people of this country and us. Our forefathers had a castle on this river. As one of them walked out he saw something on the river, but was at a loss to know what it was. He took it at first for a great fish. He ran into the castle and gave notice to the other Indians. Two of our forefathers went to see what it was, and found it a vessel with men in it. They immediately joined hands with the people in the vessel and became friends."

He rowed in his boats around the island to see if there was anything worth his while to settle there.

Everywhere he went he was followed by the natives, who seemed to admire him, and looked upon his people as something more than human.

From this island he coasted southward about one hundred and eighty leagues, in search of the gold, when he discovered another island, which he called Hispaniola, where his ship struck on a hidden rock and was lost, and he and his crew were taken on board of one of the other vessels. The natives at this island, through fear, fled from him; but taking one of their women, treating her kindly, and then letting her go back among them, she brought numbers to traffic among them, after which they all seemed peaceably disposed, and Columbus, finding there was gold in this island, by the aid of the natives, built a fort, and left thirty-nine men in it, with provisions for an entire year, seeds to sow, and trinkets to trade with the natives.

After discovering a good part of the north and east coast of Hispaniola, trading with the Indians, and near three months' stay in the island, he bent his course homewards, and arrived at Palos, in Andalusia, early in the spring of 1492–3, having performed the voyage in seven months and eleven days. Here the people received him with a solemn procession and thanksgiving for his return, most of his seamen belonging to that port.

The King and Queen were at Barcelona, and when the admiral drew near that city, the court went out to meet him, and received him with the honors due to a sovereign prince. Columbus afterwards made several voyages to America.*

The fame of the discovery, and of the rich cargoes brought to Old Spain, at several times, from the newly discovered country, becoming spread through other countries, gave rise to additional adventurers. The next attempt was made by Sebastian Cabot, a Venetian by extraction, but born in England, and who had given much time to the study of navigation, and was well skilled in cosmography.

---

*He died in the city of Validolid, in Spain, in the spring of 1506, and was buried in the cathedral of Seville, with this inscription on his tomb: "That Columbus had given a new world to Castile and Leon."

He believed in sailing by the northwest, a shorter passage than that lately discovered by the Cape of Good Hope might be found to the West Indies, and Henry VII. fitted out two ships to aid him in making the discovery.

In the beginning of the summer of 1497 he sailed from Lisbon, and steering his course northwest, came upon land about sixty degrees north latitude, supposed to be Greenland, but perceiving that the land still ran north, he changed his course, in hopes of finding a passage in less latitude. About the fiftieth degree he saw that which is now well known by the name of Newfoundland. Here he took three of the natives, and coasted southward, to the latitude of thirty-eight degrees,* but his provisions growing scarce, and expecting no supplies there, he returned to England, where the natives he brought lived a considerable time.†

From this voyage and discovery made by Cabot, the English, under the law of nations, claimed the country—that whatever waste or uncultivated country is discovered, it is the right of that prince who had been at the charge of the discovery. This, from universal law, gave at least a right of pre-emption, and was good against all but Indian proprietors.

We have seen in the discovery of North and South America, that inhabitants were found at the places touched at. How these people originally came there, is a question not easily solved.

---

*Maryland.

†King Henry VII. commissioned John Cabot (5th of March, in the eleventh year of his reign) and his three sons to sail in quest of unknown lands, and to annex them to the crown of England, with this clause: " Which before this time have been unknown to all Christians." His first design was to discover a northwest passage to Cathay or China. In this voyage he sailed very far eastward, on the north side of Labrador. In his next voyage, which was made in company with his son Sebastian, in 1497, he steered to the south of Labrador, and fell in with the island of Baccalaos, or Newfoundland, and took possession both of that island and all the coast of the northeast part of America as far as Cape Florida, which he also claimed in the name of the King of England. Sebastian drew a map of the whole coast of North America. This map was hung up in His Majesty's privy-gallery at Whitehall, and was destroyed by fire at the burning of the gallery in King William's reign.

All therefore, that can be done, is to give a short view of the most probable conjectures that have been hitherto offered.*

It is not unlikely the new world was known to the Phenicians, even a considerable time before the days of Plato, who, in all likelihood, found but few (if any) inhabitants there. That they contributed towards the planting of it, we have found some reason to believe, as they are supposed to have made three voyages thither; that colonies from other nations crossed the Atlantic, and landed in America, cannot be well denied. Neither the Egyptians nor Carthagenians are supposed void of some traditional knowledge of America, since they are believed† to have communicated such knowledge to other nations, which, if we admit the truth of the above, it would naturally follow that some of the ancient Egyptians and Carthagenians had been here, and contributed towards the peopling of this continent, as well as the Phenicians.

The author of *de Mirabilibus Audit*, supposed to be Aristotle, expressly asserts that the Carthagenians discovered an island beyond Hercules' pillars, abounding with all necessaries, to which they frequently sailed, and several of them had fixed their habitations there; but, adds he, the Senate would not permit their subjects to go thither any more, lest it should prove the depopulation of their own country.

It has been said that several of the original American nations *rent their garments*, the more effectually to express their grief on any melancholy. The Hebrews, Persians, Greeks, Sabines, and Latins, according to various authors, did the same, from whence some imagine that those Americans deduced their origin from one or more of those nations, but this is two slender a foundation upon which to build such a belief.‡ Menasseh Ben Israel

---

*Voltaire says: "If we are not astonished that the discoverers found flies in America, it is absurd to wonder that they should meet with men."—[Univ. Hist.

†Perizonias and Cellarius seem to have inferred from thence, that the new world was not entirely unknown to the remoter ages of antiquity.

‡William Penn, in his letter to the committee of the Free Society of Traders, in London, in 1683, gives a short sketch of his opinion, touching the

concluded that the Israelites were the progenitors of the aboriginal Americans.

Though the Phenicians, Egyptians, and Carthagenians might have planted some colonies, yet the bulk of the inhabitants must certainly have deduced their origin from another part of the world. Had the Phenicians and Egyptians peopled even a considerable part of America, it would scarcely have been taken so little notice of by the ancients, even supposing those nations had industriously endeavored to conceal their western discoveries, for in such case there must have been a constant communication kept open between America, Egypt, and Phenicia, and a very extensive trade carried on. So that many particulars relating to the new world, must necessarily have transpired; nor could even the sailors themselves, who navigated the Phenician ships, have omitted divulging many accounts of what they observed on this continent, some of which would undoubtedly have been transmitted to us.

We are inclined to the belief that the inhabitants of this continent were descended from a people who inhabited a country not so far distant as Egypt and Phenicia, the most probable of which is the northeastern part of Asia, particularly Tartary, Siberia, and the peninsula of Kamschatka, which was probably the tract through which many Tartarian colonies passed into America, and peopled the most considerable portion of it.

California, the most western of our states, being contiguous to, and no very great distance from the northeastern part of Asia, and east of Kamschatka, is a tract approaching to America.

It is also supposed that Asia and America were formerly connected by an isthmus, which might have been destroyed by an earthquake.

The latter supposition may be supported by the authority of those writers who have rendered parallel cases creditable—such as the disjunction of Britain from Gaul, and Spain from the African continent.

---

origin of the Indians here, whom he imagines to be descended from the Jews; that after the dispersion of the ten tribes, they emigrated through the eastermost parts of Asia, to the westermost parts of America.

A communication between Asia and America seems to agree with truth, not only from what has been advanced by Reland and other writers, but from the discoveries made by the Russians, given in their public prints of the year 1737, in which we find that some of the Czarina's subjects touched at several islands, which lie at a distance in the eastern direction from Japan and Kamschatka, and consequently between those countries and America.

As early as 1749, Leonard Enler, professor of mathematics, and member of the Imperial Society of Petersburgh, conceived the idea that the northwestern cape of Asia, discovered by Capt. Behring, was not thirty degrees off the last known headland of California.

M. de Guignes informs us, in a memoir upon the ancient navigations of the Chinese to America, that though they have always been believed to have been confined within the bounds of their own country, yet they penetrated into America in the year 458 of the Christian era, and that Christopher Columbus was not the first who attempted discoveries towards the west. That long before him the Arabians, while they were masters of Spain and Portugal, enterprised the same thing from Lisbon, but after having advanced to the far west, they were obliged to put back to the Canaries. There they learned that formerly the inhabitants of these islands had sailed towards the west for a month together, to discover new countries.

Thus we see that the most barbarous people without the knowledge of the compass, were not afraid to expose themselves to the open sea in their slight, small vessels, and that it was not so difficult for them to get over to America as we imagine.

In a history of Kamschatka, published in 1765, and translated into English by J. Grieve, M. D., we find a particular description of the customs and ways of living of the inhabitants there, which agrees in several particulars, and upon the whole seems not very different from the original customs of the North American Indians.

In 1524, John Verrazzano, a Florentine, sailed to America and proceeded along the coast from Florida to the fiftieth degree of north latitude, and entered the harbor of New York.

In 1534, James Cartier commanded a fleet fitted out in France under direction of the French King for the purpose of making further discoveries in America, and arrived at Newfoundland in May of that year. He thence sailed northerly, when he found himself in a broad river or gulf, which he named St. Lawrence, as it was discovered by him on the day of the festival of that Saint. He sailed up the St. Lawrence until he came to a swift fall. This country he called New France, and his was the first attempt of the French to form a settlement in America.

In 1539, the Spaniards made an attempt to form by conquest a settlement within the limits of the United States. Fernando de Soto, Governor of Cuba, sailed from Havana with nine vessels, nine hundred men besides sailors, two hundred and thirteen horses, and a herd of swine, and landed at Espirito Santo, in Florida. He expected to find mines and plenty of gold, but was disappointed. The natives opposed him, and he was often deluded by them.

He crossed the Alleghany mountains, and wintered in the Chickasaw country. Then crossed the Mississippi river. He wandered about, and was exposed to many hardships. Famine overtook him, and he suffered severely from the opposition of the natives. He finally died near the mouth of the Red river.

Those of his men that remained, passed down the Mississippi river and arrived at Panuco, in Mexico, in September, 1543. More than half of his men perished during the expedition of four years in the wilderness.

In 1562, during the civil war between the Protestants and Catholics in France, Admiral Coligny formed a project of carrying a colony of Protestants to America that they might enjoy religious freedom. He easily obtained permission of the French King, who was anxious to get rid of his Huguenot or Protestant subjects.

The admiral fitted out two ships, and under the command of John Ribault, they landed within the limits of South Carolina, built a fort and garrisoned it with twenty men, after which he returned to France.

After he had left, the company mutinied and killed their captain for his severity.

They suffered the most extreme privations, and were so reduced in circumstances that they were compelled to leave, and fitting out a vessel they embarked with such things as they could. After having been out several weeks their provisions were exhausted, so that they were obliged to kill and eat one of their number who offered himself as a victim to satisfy their hunger.

They were a few days afterwards picked up by an English vessel and carried to England.

In 1564, Laudoniere, a Frenchman, carried a colony to Florida, where he erected a fortification on the river May, which he called Fort Caroline.

The following year, Ribault, who was sent to supersede Laudoniere, arrived in Florida with seven vessels. He took all the best men from the fort and started on an expedition against the Spaniards, leaving Laudoniere in the fort without adequate means of defense. At the same time, Melandez, under King Philip II. of Spain, was on his way to Florida with a fleet and army for the purpose of driving out the Huguenots and settling it with Catholics. He massacred Ribault and all his company, except Laudoniere and a few others who escaped to France. Melendez built three forts on the river May, and garrisoned them with Spanish soldiers. He then proceeded south, and discovered the harbor of St. Augustine where he built a city, the oldest city within the limits of the United States, east of the Mississippi river.

In 1579, Sir Humphrey Gilbert, under the patronage of Queen Elizabeth, made an attempt at colonization in America. In his first attempt he was unsuccessful, and was obliged to return. In his second attempt, he reached Newfoundland, and took possession of the country in the name of his sovereign. He sailed southwesterly to the mouth of the Kennebec. There he lost the largest of his three vessels, and all the crew perished. He then set his face toward England, but his little bark sunk upon the voyage, and he was heard of no more.

Although the English had very early made the discovery of

North America, a considerable time elapsed before any advantages accrued.

In 1584, Sir Walter Raleigh was the first Englishman who attempted to plant a colony in it.*

In this year he obtained a patent from Queen Elizabeth, for him and his heirs, to discover and possess forever, under the crown of England, all such countries and lands as were not then possessed by any Christian prince, or inhabited by Christian people. Encouraged by this grant, Raleigh and others fitted out ships at different times, and the first colony they settled was at Roanore,* in Virginia, but after various attempts at forming a settlement there, they met with such discouragements that it was some time afterwards before many improvements were made.

In 1606, without regard to Raleigh's patent, King James granted a new patent of Virginia, in which was included what is now the New England States, New York, New Jersey, Pennsylvania, and Maryland. From Queen Elizabeth's time, 1584, to the time this patent was granted, the whole country bore the name given it by Raleigh, it is said in honor of his virgin mistress, the Queen of England, while others assert it was because of its virgin soil, never having been settled before. The persons to whom this last patent was granted were Sir Thomas Gates, Sir George Somers, Richard Hakluyt, clerk, Edward Maria Wingfield, Thomas Hanham, Richard Gilbert, Esqs., William Parker, George Popham, Lord Chief Justice of England, and others. The extent of the land granted was from thirty-four to forty-five degrees of north latitude, with all the islands lying within one hundred miles of the coast.

Two distinct colonies were to be planted by virtue of this patent, and the property to be vested in two different bodies of adventurers. The first was to belong to Somers, Hackluyt, and Wingfield, under title of the London Adventurers or London

---

* That is, a regular colony under grants. Sir Amigell Wadd, of Yorkshire, Clerk of the Council to Henry VIII. and Edward VI., and author of a book of travels, was the first Englishman that made discoveries in America.

† Now Roanoke.

Company, and was to reach from thirty-four to forty-one degrees, with all lands, woods, mines, minerals, &c.

The other colony was to reach from the end of the first to forty-five degrees, and granting the same privileges to Hanham, Gilbert, Parker, and Popham as he had to the others. This was called the Plymouth Company. Both parties were privileged to take in with them as many partners as they chose, and all others were forbidden to plant within the bounds granted to them without first obtaining their license therefor. One-fifth part of all gold and silver mines, and the fifteenth part of all copper mines, were reserved to the use of the crown.

Under this grant the London Company fitted out several ships, with artificers of every kind, and everything necessary for a new settlement, and at once set out for America and planted a colony there.

In 1623, there were so many complaints of bad management, that on inquiry a *quo warranto* was issued against the patent, and after a trial had in the king's bench it was declared forfeited, after which Virginia came under the immediate direction of the crown.

The Plymouth Company also attempted to make a settlement the same year that their patent was granted, but met with poor success until about the year 1620, when another colony arrived from England, under command of Capt. Miles Standish. They arrived at Cape Cod, in the latitude of forty-two degrees, and having turned the cape, found a commodious harbor opposite the point, at the mouth of the bay, at the entrance to which were two islands well stocked with wood. Here they built a town which they called Plymouth. This greatly augmented the colonies in New England. Multitudes of dissenters, thinking this a good opportunity of enjoying liberty of conscience, offered their services to the Plymouth Company, and the grand patent having been delivered up to the king, other patents were granted to Lord Musgrave, the Duke of Richmond, the Earl of Carlisle, Lord Edward Gorges, and new colonies were planted in divers places.

Under the commission given to John Cabot and his son Sebastian, they were authorized to discover the isles, regions and provinces of the *heathen and infidels*, which had been unknown to all the nations of Christendom, in whatever part of the globe they might be placed." And therefore wherever they landed, they took possession of the country in the name of the King of England. In the charter granted to Sir Walter Raleigh by Queen Elizabeth of England, in 1584, he was empowered to discover, occupy, and govern " remote, heathen, and barbarous countries" which had not been in possession previously of any Christian prince or people. The ships sent out by Raleigh under this commission were commanded by Amidas and Barlow.

In 1585, and again in 1609, they endeavored to establish settlements in Virginia, in both of which they were unsuccessful.

The patent granted by King James, in 1606, for Virginia, extended from the southern boundary of North Carolina to the northern boundary of Maine, and it was divided into two districts, called North and South Virginia. The southern they called the London Company, and was granted to Sir Thomas Gates and his associates, while the northern was granted to Thomas Hanham and his associates, and was styled the Plymouth Company.

CHAPTER II.

1609—1664.

Extent of lands contained in first patent—Dutch and Swedes—Speech to the Indians in behalf of the Queen of Sweden—Their approval—First name of New Jersey—Surrender of the Province by the Dutch.

IT is evident from the foregoing, that the colonies of New York, New Jersey, Pennsylvania, and Maryland, were included in the great patent last mentioned, but after it had become void, the crown was at liberty to regrant the same to others, but it does not appear that any part of those provinces were settled by virtue thereof; neither was any distinct discovery of them made until many years afterwards.

New Jersey, Pennsylvania, and the other adjacent lands, notwithstanding the ancient right of the crown of England, had two pretenders—the Dutch and Swedes.

The claim set up by the Dutch, was under color of a discovery in the year 1609, by Henry Hudson, an Englishman, commander of a ship called the Half Moon, and fitted out from Holland, by the East India Company, for the purpose of discovering, by a northwest passage, a nearer way to China.

In this voyage, he sailed up as far as New York City, and continuing his course up the river, by him called Hudson's river, as far as Albany.

Returning to Amsterdam some time after, the Dutch pretended to have purchased the chart he had made of the American coast, and having obtained a patent from the States, in the year 1614, to trade in New England, they settled in New York, which place they called New Netherland.

New York City was called by them New Amsterdam, and the island they called Manhattan.

The Dutch kept possession until Sir Samuel Argole, governor of Virginia, disputed their title upon the ground that the country having been discovered by an Englishman, in right of his master he could not suffer it to be alienated from the crown without consent of the King. He therefore compelled the Dutch colony to submit to him, and to hold it under the English. But some time after, a new governor arriving from Amsterdam, they not only neglected to pay their usual acknowledgment to the governor of Virginia, but in the year 1623, they fortified their colony by building several forts.

On the Delaware* they built one near Gloucester, in the province of New Jersey, which they called Fort Nassau; a second one on the Hudson river,† near Albany, which they called Fort Orange, in the province of New York; and a third on Connecticut river,‡ which they named the Hirsse of Good Hope.

These settlers, being merchants, at the same time they built their forts, erected trading-houses at Forts Nassau and Orange.

As the Hudson river lay near the sea, and the navigation being esteemed by them less difficult than the Delaware, their settlements were chiefly built on both sides of the former river, at the entrance of which the town, called by them New Amsterdam, was built, so that by the time the Swedes came to America, they had abandoned the lands adjacent to the Delaware, and wholly settled upon the Hudson river.

The manner in which the Dutch had taken possession of the country, and had built their forts, was communicated to King Charles I.; such pressure, by his embassadors at the Hague, was brought to bear upon him, that the States were compelled to disown having given any authority for what the Dutch had

---

*Called by them South River.
†North River.
‡Called Fresh River.

done, when the whole blame was laid upon the East India Company.

King Charles then gave a commission to Sir George Calvert, afterwards made Lord Baltimore,* to possess and plant that part of America, now called Maryland; and to Sir Edmond Locyden or Ployden, to plant the northern parts toward New England.

The Dutch, being afraid of the power of the English, manifested at once their willingness to leave their plantations, provided the English would give them £2500 as compensation for the amounts they had expended.

Soon after this, King Charles, being involved in trouble, was unable to give to his colonies the support they needed. They therefore not only relinquished their first proposals, but furnished the natives with arms, and taught them the use of them, that by their assistance they might dispossess the English and render themselves secure.

In the year 1626, during the reign of Gustavus Adolphus, the first settlement by the Swedes here began to be agitated in their own country. In this year William Useling, an eminent merchant of Stockholm, in Sweden, having learned of its fertile lands, abounding in all kinds of fruits, with all the necessaries of life, gave his countrymen a glowing account of the country, and endeavored to persuade his people to settle a colony here.

---

* "About the year 1620, while George Calvert, afterwards Lord Baltimore, was Secretary of State to James I., he obtained a patent for him and his heirs to be absolute lord and proprietor (with the royalties of a Count Palatine) of the province of Avalon, in Newfoundland, which was named by him from Avalon in Somersetshire, wherein Glastenberry stands the first fruits of Christianity in Britain, as the other was in that part of America. There he built a fine house in Ferryland, and spent twenty-five thousand pounds in advancing this new plantation. After the death of King James, he went twice in person to Newfoundland. Finding his plantation very much exposed to the insults of the French, he was at last forced to abandon it, whereupon he went over to Virginia, and after having viewed these parts, came to England, and obtained from King Charles, who had as great regard and affection for him as King James, a patent to him and his heirs, for Maryland, that King naming it in honor of his beloved Queen, Henrietta MARIA." [Biogr. Britania, Art. George Calvert.

Through the influence of Useling, his monarch issued a proclamation at Stockholm, exhorting his subjects to contribute to a company for the accomplishment of this purpose. This was called the West India Company, and was confirmed by that Prince. The General Assembly raised sums of money to carry on the intended settlement, to which the King, his lords of the council, the chief of his barons, knights, coronets, the principal officers of his army, bishops, clergy, and many of the common people of Swedeland, Finland, and Liffland contributed, and persons of responsibility were chosen to see that the proposition was put in execution.

The persons who composed this commission were an admiral, a vice-admiral, merchants, manufacturers, and others, representing the principal interests of the kingdom.

It was proposed to get as many as they should think proper, who would voluntarily accompany them to America, to settle and cultivate a colony there, and in 1627 the Swedes and Finns came over.

They first landed at Cape Inlopen, or Henlopen,* at which they were so well pleased that they called it Paradise Point; after which they purchased from some Indians the land from Cape Inlopen to the Falls of the Delaware,† on both sides of the river, which they called New Swedeland stream. They made presents to the Indian chiefs, for the purpose of obtaining peaceable possession of the lands so purchased; but the Dutch still continuing their pretensions, in 1630, David Peters de Vries built a fort within the capes of Delaware on the west, and about two leagues from Cape Cornelius, at the place sometimes called Lewistown and at other times called Hoarkill.

In 1631, the Swedes also built a fort on the west of the Delaware, to which they gave the name of Christeen.‡ Peter Lindstrom, their engineer, laid out at this place a small town, at

---

* At the entrance of Delaware Bay, in Delaware.

† Where Trenton now stands.

‡ This place is now called Christiana, and is about ten miles from Wilmington.

which they formed their first settlement; it was afterwards demolished by the Dutch.

The Swedes erected another fort on an island called by them Tennecum, about sixteen miles above the town of Christeen, which they called New Gottenburgh.

Their Governor, John Printz, built a fine house with all suitable accommodations; he planted an orchard, and called his settlement Printz's Hall. The principal part of the people also had their plantations on this island.

About this time the Swedes also built forts at Chester and other places. In the same year Chancellor Oxestiern, an ambassador from Sweden, made application to King Charles I. to have the right claimed by the English, as being the first discoverers, yielded up. They also alleged they had purchased the pretence claimed by the Dutch by virtue of prior settlement and buildings here, most of which were destroyed before their arrival.

If this be true, the Dutch did not think proper long to abide by their contract, but gave trouble to the Swedes by encroaching upon their new settlements, and both of them joined together to dispossess the English, who also attempted to settle the eastern side of the Delaware river.

Kieft, a director of the States of Holland, assisted by the Swedes then in the colony, drove the English away, and hired the Swedes to keep them out. The Dutch complained that the Swedish governor, judging this a fitting opportunity, built fort Elsingburgh on the place from whence the English had been driven, and used great freedom with their vessels and all persons bound up the river, making them repair to the fort, and sent persons on board to know from whence they came. The Dutch considered this as using undue authority, especially in a country not their own.

They found the musquitoes so numerous that they were unable to live here, and therefore removing, they named the place Musketoeburgh.

The Dutch seem to have had a very great opinion as regards the land near the Delaware, and were greatly distressed lest they should be dispossessed by the English, who, they complained, had upon several occasions attempted to settle about that river, and thought if they once got a footing there would soon secure every part, so that neither Hollander or Swede would have any thing to say here. In particular they mention Sir Edmond Ployden, as claiming property in the country under a grant from King James I., who, they allege declined any dispute with them, but threatened to give the Swedes a visit in order to dispossess them.

John Printz continued governor of the Swedes from his arrival until about the year 1654, when he returned to Sweden, having first deputed his son-in-law, John Papegoia, governor in his stead, who also some time after returned to his native country, and left the government to John Rysing. He renewed the league of friendship with the English and Dutch in the neighborhood, and formally with the Indians. For this purpose a meeting was held with the sachems or Indian Chiefs at Printz's Hall, on Tenneeum Island, where a speech was made them in behalf of the Queen of Sweden, expressing the desire of the Swedes to renew their friendship. The Indians had before made complaint that the Swedes had introduced much evil amongst them, because many of the Indians, since their coming, were dead; but the Swedes now making them considerable presents, which were received and divided among them, one of their chiefs, whose name was Noaman, made a speech, rebuking the rest for having spoken evil of the Swedes and done them harm, telling them that they should do so no more; that the Swedes were a good people, and thanking them for their presents, promised for the future that a more strict friendship should be observed between them. That as formerly they had been but one body and one heart, they should be henceforth as one head, in token of which he waves both his hands as if tying a strong knot; promising also that if they heard of any mischief plotting against the Swedes, although it were midnight, they would give them notice, and desired the like notice from the Swedes if they understood harm was intended them. The Swedes then desiring the Indians in general would give them some signal that they all assented to what was said, they gave a general shout of approbation, and in the conclusion were entertained by the Swedes with victuals and drink. This league was kept faithfully on the part of the Indians.

The Swedish ships sent to succor this new colony, was obstructed in their intended voyage by the Spaniards, and they being unable for want of money to keep their forts in repair, gave their more powerful neighbors, the Dutch, opportunities, with less danger, to make encroachments upon them.

Accordingly, the Dutch this year who inhabited the neighborhood of Virginia and New Sweden, gave great disturbance to the Swedes, and tried to regain the forts they had formerly possessed.

But by means of the Swedish governor and Peter Stuyvesant, who commanded under the Dutch at New Amsterdam, it was apparently settled; yet, in the year following, the Dutch fitted out several vessels from New Amsterdam, with six or seven hundred men, who in the summer, under the command of Stuyvesant, came up the Delaware and established their first quarters at Elsingburgh, where they took some of the Swedes prisoners.

They next sailed towards a fort called Holy Trinity, and having landed their men at a point near the place, and entrenched themselves, they soon after went up to the fort and demanded a surrender, and threatened what they would do in case of refusal. After this, by treaty or otherwise, they gained possession of the land, took down the Swedish flag and hoisted their own, securing all places with their soldiers, and sent the Swedes they had taken prisoners on board their vessels.

This acquisition was deemed of considerable importance because this fort was considered as the key of New Sweden.

On the 2d of September, they besieged Christiana, fort and town; destroyed New Gottemburg, with such houses as were outside of the fort; plundered the inhabitants of what they had, and killed their cattle.

The Swedes endeavored to pursuade the Dutch to desist from their acts of hostility, but to no purpose. After a siege of fourteen days they, being in want of ammunition, were obliged to surrender upon the best terms they could obtain, which were " that all the great guns should be restored, and that they could march out of the fort with their colors flying, and drums beating," which was a great gratification to the Swedes.

The officers and other principal inhabitants among the Swedes, were carried prisoners to New Amsterdam, and taken from thence to Holland. The common people, consenting to submit to the rule of the Dutch, were allowed to remain in the country.

From this time until 1664, New Sweden and New Netherland continued in possession of, and under the government of the Dutch, who, on Manhattan Island, at the mouth of the Hudson river, had built a city called by them New Amsterdam (New York), and the river they sometimes called the Great river.

About one hundred and fifty miles up they built a fort, and called it Orange (Albany), from which place they drove a profitable trade with the Indians, who came overland as far up as Quebec, to deal with them.

The first bounds of New York, were Maryland on the south; the mainland, as far as could be discovered, westward; the river of Canada (St. Lawrence), and New England, eastward. But the limits of this province, by the grants afterwards, were reduced into a much narrower compass.

The province now called Nova Cæsaria or New Jersey, was so called in compliment to Sir George Carteret, one of the proprietors and a Jerseyman.*

We are not informed of the precise time when the first English settlements were made in this State, though it is supposed that the Danes, or Norwegians, who came over with the Dutch colonists, and first commenced a settlement at New York about the year 1618, were the first to commence a settlement at Bergen, in this State. As early as 1614, an attempt was made to form a settlement at Jersey City, that point being fortified.

In 1623, the Dutch West India Company sent a ship with settlers and articles of trade, under command of Capt. Cornelius Jacobse Mey. He entered the Delaware bay, and gave his own name to its northern cape. He then sailed up the river as far as Gloucester, and built fort Nassau. This was undoubtedly the first attempt to establish a settlement in this State. Great induce-

---

*It is said for some little time, at first, to have borne the name of New Canary. The Indian name was Scheyichlie.

ments and advantages were offered by the Dutch West India Company to all who would undertake to establish a settlement on the eastern shore of the Delaware. Charters were granted to individuals, giving them exclusive title to large tracts of land, subject only to Indian claims.

This being considered a great privilege, quite a number took advantage of it, and sent over agents to purchase lands for them. They formed an association to settle the lands, but when De Vries, their agent, arrived here, he found none of the Europeans who preceded him, and the fort (Nassau) he found had fallen into the hands of the Indians. He immediately erected a fort, landed his passengers, and returned to Holland.

On the 28th of August, 1609, Henry Hudson entered Delaware bay, under the patronage of the Dutch East India Company. The water being shoal, he found the navigation rather difficult, and therefore did not proceed in that direction but a short distance. With his vessel, the Half Moon, he followed the eastern shore of our State, and anchored within Sandy Hook, on the 3d of September, 1609, and on the 5th he sent his boat ashore for the purpose of exploring and sounding the waters within Sandy Hook. His men landed and proceeded some distance into the woods of Monmouth county.

They were well received by the natives, who presented them green tobacco and dried currants, which existed there in great quantities.

When Captain Mey had entered Delaware bay, in 1623, he gave his own name to its most northern cape, which is still retained. He next explored the bay and river, and having landed, he built a fort at *Techaaco*, upon Timber creek, called at that time by the natives *Sassachon*. This creek is located in the county of Gloucester, and empties into the Delaware river.

The Dutch having obtained possession of the country on the Delaware, the governor of the colony appointed directors to govern the settlements.

Johannes Paul Jaquet was the first director; next to him was Peter Alricks, Hinojossa, and William Beckman. The patents to the lands granted by these directors are still part of the titles of the present owners. The Dutch, at this time, also obtained large tracts on the eastern part of New Jersey, and formed other settlements between the Delaware and Hudson rivers.

The English never relinquished their claim, but held it as being the prior discoverers to the Dutch, but the latter, assisted by the Swedes, resisted all attempts of the English to form settlements here. They destroyed their trading houses, confiscated their goods, and imprisoned the English settlers, which caused long and angry controversies between the New England and Dutch governments.

King Charles the II., fearing the ill consequences, should a Dutch colony be allowed in his dominions, determined to dispossess them, and in order to accomplish his purpose, gave a patent to his brother, the Duke of York, in which were included the provinces of New York, New Jersey, and all other lands thereunto appertaining, with power to govern the same.

The reign of the Duke was not sufficiently enterprising to insure success, and therefore the interest he had in his newly acquired possessions did not avail him much; besides, he had a strong aversion to the Dutch; he was therefore compelled to resort to military stratagem to hold possession of his provinces.

Before there was any formal declaration of war with Holland, Sir Robert Carre was sent to America, with a small fleet and some land forces, to put the Duke in possession of the country. His commission was dated April 26th, 1664, and it was sometime after this that a formal declaration of war with Holland was made. The Dutch in this country, being unprovided for defence against a royal squadron accompanied by land forces, rendered the expedition a safe and easy one.

Col. Richard Nicholls, George Cartwright, and Samuel Meverike joined with Carre in this commission to dislodge the Dutch.

They arrived at the Hudson river in the latter part of 1664, and the time of their arrival was so soon after the date of the patent of the Duke of York, that the Dutch had but very little notice* of their design, and therefore no time to prepare for their defence.

---

* The first notice they had was from Thomas Willet, an Englishman, about six weeks before their arrival.

The land forces consisted of three hundred men, under command of Col. Nicholls.

The Dutch Governor,* an accomplished soldier, who had lost a leg in service, was totally unprepared for this sudden and unexpected attack, and being aware also of the defects in the title by which the Dutch held the lands, and their present incapacity for defence, was easily prevailed upon to surrender.

When the English arrived at New Amsterdam, they issued the following proclamation, which was circulated through the country, in order to show the design they had in view in coming into the country.

"By His Majesty's Command:

"Forasmuch as His Majesty hath sent us by commission, under his great seal of England, amongst other things, to expel or to reduce to His Majesty's obedience all such foreigners as have, without His Majesty's leave and consent, seated themselves amongst any of his dominions in America, to the prejudice of His Majesty's subjects and the diminution of his royal dignity, we, His Majesty's Commissioners, do declare and promise that whosoever, of what nation soever, will, upon knowledge of this proclamation, acknowledge and testify themselves to submit to His Majesty's government, as his good subjects ought to do, shall be protected by His Majesty's laws and justice and peaceably enjoy whatsoever God's blessing and their own honest industry have furnished them with, and all other privileges with His Majesty's English subjects. We have caused this to be published, that we might prevent all inconveniences to others; if it were possible, however, to clear ourselves from the charge of all those miseries that anyway may befall such as live here, and will not acknowledge His Majesty for their sovereign. Whom God preserve."

Immediately upon notice of the arrival of the English in the bay, Stuyvesant, the Dutch Governor, dispatched the following letter:

---

* Peter Stuyvesant.

"Right Honorable Sirs:

"Whereas we have received intelligence that, about three days since, there arrived an English man-of-war, or frigate, in the bay of the North river, belonging to the New Netherlands; and since that three more are arrived, by what order or pretence is unknown to us; and having received various reports concerning their arrival upon this coast, and not being apt to entertain any prejudice intended against us, have, by order of the commander in chief of the New Netherlands, thought it convenient and requisite to send the worshipful, the bearer hereof, that is to say, the worshipful John Declyer, one of the chief council; the Rev. John Megapolensis, minister; Paul Lendelvandergrist, mayor of this town, and have joined with them Mr. Samuel Megapolensis, doctor in physick, whom by these presents I have appointed and ordered, that with the utmost respect and civility, they do desire and entreat of the commander in chief of the aforesaid men-of-war or frigates, the intent and meaning of their approach, and continuing in the harbor of Naijacly, without giving any notice to us, or first acquainting us with their design, which action hath caused much admiration in us, having not received timely knowledge of the same, which, in respect to the government of the place, they ought, and were obliged to have done; wherefore upon the considerations aforesaid, it is desired and entreated from the general of the aforesaid men-of-war or frigates, as also from our before deputed agents, whom we desire your honors civilly to treat, and to give and render unto them the occasion of your arrival here upon this coast, and you will give an opportunity (that after our hearty salutes and well wishes of your health) to pray that you may be blessed in eternity, and always remain, right honorable sirs, your honors' affectionate friend and servant,

"P. Stuyvesant.

"By order and appointment of the governor and commander in chief of the council of New Netherlands, the 19–29th of August, 1664.

"Cornelius Ruyven, *Secretary.*"

To this letter, Col. Nicholls sent the following answer:

"*To the honorable the governor and chief council of the Manhatans :**

"RIGHT WORTHY SIRS:

"I received a letter by some worthy persons entrusted by you, bearing date the 19–29th of August, desiring to know the intent of the approach of the English frigates, in return of which I think fit to let you know, that His Majesty of Great Brittain, whose right and title to these parts of America is unquestionable, well knowing how much it derogates from his crown and dignity, to suffer any foreigners, how near soever they be allied, to usurp a dominion, and without His Majesty's royal consent, to inhabit in these or any other His Majesty's territories, hath commanded me, in his name, to require a surrender of all such forts, towns, or places of strength, which are now possessed by the Dutch under your command. And in His Majesty's name, I do demand the town, situated upon the island, known by the name of Manhatoes, with all the forts thereunto belonging, to be rendered unto His Majesty's obedience and protection into my hands. I am further commanded to assure you, and every respective inhabitant of the Dutch nation, that His Majesty being tender of the effusion of Christian blood, doth, by these presents, confirm and secure to every man his estate, life, and liberty, who shall readily submit to his government; and all those who shall oppose His Majesty's gracious intentions, must expect all the miseries of a war which they bring upon themselves. I shall expect your answer by those gentlemen, Colonel George Cartwright, one of His Majesty's commissioners in America, Captain Robert Needham, Captain Edward Groves, and Mr. Thomas Delavall, whom you will entertain and treat with such civility as is due to them and yourselves, and you shall receive the same from, worthy sirs, your very humble servant,

"RICHARD NICHOLLS.

"Dated on board His Majesty's ship, the Guinea, riding before Naijack, the 20–30th of August, 1664."

Stuyvesant having now obtained full information from the Eng-

---

*The Indian name by which New York island was formerly called.

lish general himself, of the nature of his business with him, returned the following answer:

"That they were so confident of the discretion and equity of His Majesty of Great Britain, that were His Majesty truly informed of their right, he would not have given such an order. That the Dutch came not into these provinces by violence, but by virtue of a commission from the States General in 1614, when they settled the North river, near fort Orange, and to avoid the invasions and massacres commonly committed by the savages they built a little fort there. That afterwards, in the year 1662, and at the present time, by virtue of a commission and grant to the governor of the West India Company, and another in the year 1656, of South river, to the burgomasters of Amsterdam, they had peaceably governed and enjoyed these provinces. That they were the first discoverers; had purchased the land of the natives—princes of the country; and had continued in the uninterrupted possession thereof. That they made no doubt that if His Majesty of Great Britain, were truly informed of these passages, he was too judicious to give any order that the places and fortresses in their hands should be given up, especially at a time when so strict a friendship subsisted between His Majesty and the States General. That the offering of any act of hostility and violence against them, would be an infraction of the treaty which subsisted between His Majesty of Great Britain and the States General. That as to the threats in the conclusion of General Nicholls' letter, he had nothing to answer, only that they feared nothing but what God should lay upon them."

Upon the receipt of this answer, Col. Nicholls determined that there was nothing to be gained by delay, and accordingly resolved to assert the rights of his master, and immediately issued an order to Capt. Hyde, to the following effect·

"Whereas, the governor and council of the Dutch plantation upon the Manhatoes, in Hudson's river, have, in answer to a summons, returned their resolutions to maintain their right and title of the States' General and West India Company, of Holland, to their forts, towns and plantations in these parts of America, I do therefore, in protection of His Majesty's service, recommend to Captain Hugh Hyde, commander in chief of the squadron, to prosecute, with the advice of the captains under his command, His Majesty's claim and interest, by all ways and means, as they shall think most expedient, for the speedy reducing the Dutch under His Majesty's obedience, and for so doing this shall be their warrant.

"Given under my hand the 24th of August, 1664, on board his majesty's ship the Guinea.

"RICHARD NICHOLLS."

The Dutch governor being convinced by the above order, and the preparations he had seen going on, that the English were determined to carry out their threats, Stuyvesant thought it best, before hostilities actually commenced, to propose one more expedient, and on the 4th of September, he addressed another letter to Nicholls, as follows:

"MY LORD:

"Upon our letter the day before yesterday, and the communication by words of mouth by our deputies, touching the just right and possession, without dispute of my lords, the States General of the united provinces, as also of our discovery of the news from Holland, which makes us not to doubt but that the King of Great Britain and my lords, the said States are at this hour agreed upon their limits. This had given us hope, my lord, to avoid all dispute, that you would have desisted from your design, or at least have given time, that we might have heard from our masters, from which expectation we have been frustrated by the report of our said deputies, who have assured us by word of mouth, that you persist on your summons and letter of 20—30 August, upon which we have no other thing to answer, but that following the order of my lords, the States General, we are obliged to defend our place. However that in regard that we make no doubt, that upon your assault and our defence there will be a great deal of blood spilt, and besides it is to be feared greater difficulty may arise hereafter. We have thought fit to send unto you Mr. John de Decker, counsellor of state; Cornelius Van Riven, secretary and receiver; Cornelius Steenwick, mayor; and James Coussea, sheriff, to the end of finding some means to hinder the spilling of innocent blood, which we esteem, my lord, not to be your intention. Praying that you will please to appoint a place and hour, and send or cause your deputies to meet there, with full commission to treat and seek out the means of a good accommodation, and in the mean time to cause all hostility to cease. Upon which, after recommending you to the protection of God, we remain, my lord, your thrice affectionate friend and servant,

"P. STUYVESANT."

To this letter Col. Nicholl's replied in an answer directed to the honorable the governor of the Manhatoes, as follows:

"RIGHT WORTHY SIR:

"In answer to yours of the 4th of September, new style, by hands of John de Decker, counsellor of state; Cornelius Van Riven, secretary and receiver; Cornelius Steenwick, burgomaster, and James Cousseau, sheriff, I do think it once more agreeable to the King's intentions, and my duty to his strict commands, to propose and receive all ways and means of avoiding the effusion of Christian blood; of which sincere intention, I suppose you are already fully satisfied, and shall have no cause to doubt it for the future; as also, that I do insist upon my first summons and message to you, for a speedy surrender of the towns and forts now under your command, into His Majesty's obedience and protection. You may easily believe that in respect of greater difficulties which are ready to attend you, I should willingly comply with your proposition to appoint deputies, place, and time to treat of a good accommodation. But unless you had also given me to know, that by such a meeting you do intend to treat upon articles of surrender, I do not see just cause to defer the pursuance of His Majesty's commands. My first demand, and my last answer, of reducing your towns and forts to His Majesty's obedience, which, why you call acts of hostility, I see no reason.

"However, since you have given yourself and messengers this new trouble, I shall also take this fresh occasion to assure you that I heartily wish health, peace, and prosperity to every inhabitant of your plantations, and particularly to yourself, as being your affectionate humble servant.

"RICHARD NICHOLLS.

"Gravesend, 25th August, 1664."

Stuyvesant, finding Nicholls grew more resolute in his enterprise, and the country in general upholding him, after having tried in vain what other expedients he could, was compelled, at last, to surrender the fort and province under his government to the English, and commissioners were thereupon appointed to treat upon the articles. Those on the part of the English were Sir Robert Carre, Knight; Colonel George Cartwright; John Winthrop, Esq., Governor of Connecticut, and Samuel Willis, one of his council; Captain Thomas Clarke, and Captain John Punctown, commissioners from the general court of Massachusetts.

The persons named by Governor Stuyvesant were John de Decker, Nicholas Varlett, commissary, concerning matters of traffic; Samuel Megopolensis, Cornelius Steenwick, Stephen Courtland, and James Coussea.

The following articles of this treaty were agreed upon the 27th of August, 1664, old style, and were signed and confirmed by Colonel Nicholls and Governor Stuyvesant, and subscribed by the commissioners, and contained twenty-four articles:

The first gave to the States General, or the West India Company, free enjoyment of all farms and houses, except such as were in the forts, with liberty within six months to transport all arms and ammunition that belonged to them, or to be paid for the same.

2. All public houses were to continue for the use they were for at the time.

3. All people were to continue free denizens, to enjoy their lands, houses, goods, ships, wheresoever they were in the country, and to dispose of them as they please.

4. If any inhabitant desired to remove himself, one year and six weeks was allowed him from the date of the treaty to remove himself, his wife, children, servants, and goods, and to dispose of his lands.

5. Any officer of state or public minister who desired to go to England, should be transported, freight free, in His Majesty's frigates.

6. Any people were allowed freely to come from the Netherlands, and plant in the country, and Dutch vessels were freely allowed to come hither, and any of the Dutch were allowed freely to return home, or send any sort of merchandise home in their own vessels.

7. All ships from the Netherlands were allowed to transport goods into the colony for six months next ensuing from the time of the coming of the English.

8. They were allowed to enjoy liberty of conscience in matters relating to religion, in divine worship, and Dutch discipline.

9. They were guaranteed that no Dutchman then in the colony, or Dutch ship, should, on any occasion whatever, be pressed to serve in war against any nation whatsoever.

10. No soldiers were to be allowed to be quartered upon them without their being satisfied and paid for by the officers, and if the fort at present was inadequate to lodge all the soldiers, the burgomaster, by his officers, was to appoint some houses capable to receive them.

11. The Dutch were to enjoy their own customs concerning their inheritances.

12. All public writings and records which concern the inheritances of any people, or the reglement of the church, or poor, or orphans, were to be carefully kept in the hands they then were, and such writings as particularly concern the States General, were to be sent to them at any time they might demand them.

13. No judgment that had passed any judicature should be called into question, and those who thought justice had not been done them, were allowed to apply to the States General, and the other party were required to answer them for the supposed injury.

14. Any Dutch residing in the colony desiring at any time to travel or traffic in England, or any place or plantation, in obedience to His Majesty of England, or with the Indians, was to receive, upon his request to the governor, a certificate that he is a free denizen of the place, whereupon he was to have liberty so to do.

15. In case there was a public engagement of debt by the town of Manhatoes, and a way agreed upon for the satisfying of the engagement, the same plan was to be adhered to until the engagement was satisfied.

16. Inferior officers and magistrates were to continue as they then were until the customary time of election, when they were to choose new ones, who were to take the oath of allegiance to His Majesty of England before he could enter upon the office.

17. All differences of contracts and bargains made before that time, were to be determined according to the manner of the Dutch.

18. In case the West India Company, of Amsterdam, owe any sums of money to any persons here, it was agreed that recognition and other duties payable by ships going for the Netherlands be continued six months.

19. The officers, military, and soldiers, were to march out with their arms, drums beating, and colors flying, lighted matches, and if any of them will plant, they were to have fifty acres of land set out to them, and if any of them will serve any as servants, they were to continue with all safety, and become free denizens afterwards.

20. In case the King of Great Britain and the States of Netherland should at any time agree that this place and country be re-delivered into the hands of the said States, whenever His Majesty sent his commands to re-deliver it, it should immediately be done.

21. The town of Manhatans were allowed to choose deputies, who should have free voices in all public affairs.

22. Those who had any property in any houses in the fort of Aurania, should, if they please, slight the fortifications there, and then enjoy all their houses as all people do where there is no fort.

23. If any of the soldiers desire to go into Holland, and if the company of West India, in Amsterdam, or any private persons here, will transport them into Holland, they should have a safe passport from Colonel Richard Nicholls, Deputy Governor under His Royal Highness; and the other commissioners to defend the ships that shall transport such soldiers, and all the goods in them, from any surprisal or act of hostility to be done by any of His Majesty's ships or subjects.

24. The copies of the King's grant to His Royal Highness, and the copy of His Royal Highness' commission to Colonel Richard Nicholls, testified by two commissioners more and Mr. Winthrop to be true copies, were to be delivered to Mr. Stuyvesant, the present governor, on Monday next, by eight o'clock in the morning, at the old Milne, and these articles consented to and signed by Colonel Richard Nicholls, Deputy Governor to His Royal Highness, and that within two hours after the fort and town called New Amsterdam, upon the island of Manhatoes, shall be delivered into the hands of the said Colonel Richard Nicholls by the service of such as shall be by him thereunto deputed by his hand and seal."

The articles having been agreed on, the fort and city of New Amsterdam were surrendered to the English. Some of the houses were then built of brick and stone, and in part covered with red and black tile. The land being high, it made an agreeable prospect to those that visited it from the sea. Most of the Dutch inhabitants remained, and took the oath of allegiance to the English government, and they and their posterity remained loyal subjects so long as they were under the crown of Great Britain; but after we had made an effort to throw off the British yoke, they espoused the cause of the country, and fought for freedom.*

---

* In the year 1751, as some workmen were digging down the bank of the North River, in New York, in order to build a still-house, a stone wall was discovered, between four and five feet thick, and near eight feet under ground, supposed to have been the breastwork of a battery.

CHAPTER III.

1664—1669.

The Dutch at Delaware Bay—Sir Robert Carre—Right of the Crown of England to these Provinces—Duke of York—First Constitution of New Jersey—Inducements to settlers.

THIRTEEN days after the surrender of New Amsterdam, Col. Nicholls marched up the country to Orange fort, and having taken it without much resistance, he gave it the name of Albany.* Previous to his taking this fort, he, with the other commissioners, sent Sir Robert Carre,† with the ships under his command, on an expedition into Delaware bay and river, to compel the submission of the inhabitants there. The commission granted was as follows:

"Whereas, we are informed that the Dutch have seated themselves at Delaware bay, on His Majesty of Great Britain's territories, without his knowledge and consent, and that they have fortified themselves there and drawn a great trade thither, and being assured if they be permitted to go on, the gaining of this place will be of small advantage to His Majesty. We, His Majesty's commission, and by instructions to us given, have advised and determined to endeavor to bring that place and all strangers there, in obedience to His Majesty, and by these do order and appoint that His Majesty's frigates, the Guinea, and the William, and Nicholas, and all the soldiery which are not

---

*After the Duke of York's Scotch title.

† Pronounced Carr.

in the fort, shall, with what speed they can conveniently go thither, under the command of Sir Robert Carre, to reduce the same, willing and commanding a l officers at sea and land, and all soldiers to obey the said Sir Robert Carre, during this expedition.

"Given under our hands and seals, at the fort of New York, upon the isle of Manhatoes, the third day of September, 1664.

"RICHARD NICHOLLS.
"GEORGE CARTWRIGHT.
"SAMUEL MEVERICK."

This commission was deliverd to Sir Robert Carre, with full instructions as to the manner he was to conduct the expedition upon his arrival in Delaware bay, which were as follows:

"Instructions to Sir Robert Carre, for the reducing of Delaware bay, and settling the people there under His Majesty's obedience.

"When you are come near unto the fort, which is possessed by the Dutch, you shall send your boat on shore to summons the governor and inhabitants to yield obedience to His Majesty, as the rightful sovereign of that tract of land, and let him and them know that all the planters shall enjoy their farms, houses, lands, goods, and chattles, with the same privileges, and upon the same terms which they do now possess them; only that they change their masters, whether they be the West India Company or the city of Amsterdam. To the Swedes you shall remonstrate their happy return under a monarchial government, and His Majesty's good inclination to that nation, and to all men who shall comply with His Majesty's rights and titles in Delaware without force of arms. That all cannon, arms, and ammunition which belongs to the government shall remain to His Majesty.

"That the acts of parliament shall be the rule for future trading.

"That all people may enjoy liberty of conscience.

"That for six months, next ensuing, the same magistrates shall continue in their offices, only that they and all others in authority must take the oath of allegiance to His Majesty, and all dublic acts be made in His Majesty's name.

"If you find you cannot reduce the place by force, or upon these conditions, you may add such as you find necessary, on the place; but if these, nor force will prevail, then you are to despatch a messenger to the governor of Maryland, with a letter to him, and request his assistance, and of all other English who live near the Dutch plantations.

"Your first care, after reducing the place, is to protect the inhabitants from injuries, as well as violence of the soldiers, which will be easily effected if you settle a course for weekly or daily provisions by agreement with the inhabitants, which shall be satisfied to them, either out of the profits, customs or rents belonging to their present master, or in case of necessity from hence.

"The laws for the present cannot be altered as to the administration of justice between the parties.

"To my Lord Baltimore's son you shall declare, and to all the English concerned in Maryland, that His Majesty hath, at his great expense, sent his ships and soldiers to reduce all foreigners in those parts to His Majesty's obedience, and to that purpose only you are employed. But the reduction of the place being at His Majesty's expense, you have commands to keep possession thereof for His Majesty's behoof and right, and that you are ready to join the governor of Maryland upon His Majesty's interest on all occasions, and that if Lord Baltimore doth pretend right thereto by his patent, (which is a doubtful case,) you are to say that you only keep possession till His Majesty is informed and satisfied otherwise. In other things, I must leave you to your own discretion, and the best advice you can get upon the place."

Carre having received this commission, immediately set sail with the ships under his command. On his arrival against New Castle, (then called New Amstel,) the Dutch and Swedes, following the example of New Amsterdam, their capital, at once capitulated and surrendered their fort. The articles were signed and sealed by the English commanding officer, and six of the principal inhabitants of the place on behalf of themselves and others, and were as follows:

"Articles of agreement between the honorable Sir Robert Carre, Knight, on the behalf of His Majesty, of Great Britain, and the burgomasters on behalf of themselves, and all the Dutch and Swedes inhabiting on Delaware bay and Delaware river.

" 1. That all the burgesses and planters will submit themselves to His Majesty without any resistance.

" 2. That whoever, or what nation soever, doth submit to His Majesty's authority, shall be protected in their estates, real and personal, whatsoever, by His Majesty's laws and justice.

" 3. That the present magistrates shall be continued in their offices and jurisdictions to exercise their civil power as formerly.

" 4. That if any Dutchman, or other person, shall desire to depart from this river, it shall be lawful for him so to do with his goods, within six months after the date of these articles.

" 5. That the magistrates and all the inhabitants (who are included in these articles) shall take the oath of allegiance to His Majesty.

" 6. That all people shall enjoy the liberty of their consciences in church discipline, as formerly.

" 7. That whoever shall take the oath is from that time a free denizen, and shall enjoy all the privileges of trading into any of His Majesty's dominions as freely as any Englishman and may require a certificate for so doing.

" 8. That the scout, the burgomaster, sheriff, and other inferior magistrates, shall use and exercise their customary power in administration of justice, within their precincts for six months, or until His Majesty's pleasure is further known.

" Dated October 1st, 1664."

Thus it will be seen in all the early conquests made by the crown of Great Britain, the rights of conscience, and protection of the civil powers of the governments conquered were, in all cases, rigidly maintained.

New Amsterdam, Fort Orange, and the inhabitants on the Delaware or South river, being reduced, the whole country was in the possession of the English, and things having assumed a quiet posture about New York, Richard Nicholls was commissioned the 24th of October, 1664, by Cartwright and Meverick, to repair to Delaware bay and govern the place.

He was authorized to depute such officers, civil and military, and adopt such other measures as he should think proper, until the pleasure of the King should be further known.

In this way things rested until 1668, when Nicholls and his council at New York gave the following directions for a better settlement of the government on the Delaware.

"That it is necessary to hold up the name and countenance of a garrison in Delaware with twenty men and one commissioned officer.

"That the commissioned officer shall undertake to provide all sorts of provision for the whole garrison, at the rate of five pence per day, viz.: wholesome bread, beer, pork, pease or beef, that no just complaint be made of either. That the soldiers, (so far as conveniently they may,) be lodged in the fort, and keep the stockadoes up in defence. That the civil government be continued till further orders.

"That to prevent all abuses or oppositions in civil magistrates, so often as complaint is made, the commissioned officer, Capt. Carre, shall call the scout,* with Hans Block, Israel Holme, Peter Rambo, Peter Cock, Peter Aldrick, or any two of them, as councellors to advise, hear, and determine, by the major vote, what is just, equitable, and necessary in the case and cases in question.

"That the same persons also, or any two or more of them, be called to advise and direct what is best to be done in all cases of difficulty, which may arise from the Indians, and to give their council and orders for the arming of the several plantations and planters, who must obey and attend their summons upon such occasion.

"That two-thirds at least of the soldiers remain constantly in and about New Castle at all hours.

"That the fines or premunires and light offences be executed with moderation, though it is also necessary that ill men be punished in an exemplary manner.

"That the commission officer, Capt. Carre, in the determination of the chief civil affairs, whereunto the temporary before-

---

* A civil officer, corresponding with a constable of the present day.

mentioned councellors are ordained, shall have a casting voice where votes are equal.

"That the new appointed councellors are to take the oath to his Royal Highness.

"That the laws of the government, established by his Royal Highness, be shewed and frequently communicated to the said councellors and all others, to the end that being therewith acquainted, the practice of them may also in convenient time be established, which conduceth to the publick wellfare and common justice.

"That no offensive war be made against any Indians, before you receive directions from the governor for your so doing.

"That in all matters of difficulty and importance, you must have recourse by way of appeal, to the governor and council at New York."

The above instructions were dated April 21st, 1668, and in less than two months after their promulgation, the government at New York received information that some of the tribe of the Mantas Indians, on the Delaware, had murdered the servants of one Tomm.

Peter Aldricks and Peter Rambo, arriving soon after at New York, confirmed the news, and further informed the government that it was the desire of the Indians in those parts, that selling strong liquor to them should be absolutely prohibited upon the whole river, as they attributed the murders above mentioned as having occurred in consequence of a drunken frolic.

This was no doubt the case, as the Indians on the Delaware always manifested a peaceable disposition toward the English settlers.

The governor and Colonel Lovelace wrote to Carre, authorizing him to convene those in commission with him for the management of civil affairs, and having advised with them to make all necessary rules and give orders for the government of both Christians and Indians, and if the murders and restraining the Indians from strong drink might be attended with difficulties, Carre was ordered, after having consulted with the Indians as to the best method of proceeding, to send a statement of the matter to the council at New York.

Another disturbance soon followed, which seemed likely to prove a matter of some consequence against the newly established government, but it was prevented by the vigilance of the administration. A Swede, at Delaware, represented that he was the son of Coningsmarke, the Swedish general. He went from one place to another, spreading rumors to disturb the civil peace and laws, and endeavored to enlist in his favor a party strong enough to incite an insurrection, and thereby throw off the English allegiance.

Henry Coleman, a native of Finland, and an inhabitant at Delaware, associated with him, left his habitation, cattle, and corn, and being well versed in the Indian language, they kept constantly among them, and by that means their designs were at first suspected.

The governor issued a proclamation, calling upon Coleman to surrender within fifteen days, to answer what should be alleged against him, and in case of non-compliance, his estate should be forfeited to the King.

We are not informed whether Coleman, in obedience to the proclamation, gave himself up or not, but Coningsmarke being a vagrant, more effectual measures were resorted to to capture him, and he was very soon in custody, and all the rest that had anything to do with the plot were compelled to give security for their conduct, and an account of their estate was ordered to be taken.

The governor, in a letter to Carre, tells him:

"That as for the poor, deluded sort, I think the advice of their own countrymen is not to be despised, who, knowing their temper well, prescribed a method for keeping them in order, which is severity, and laying such taxes on them as may not give them liberty to entertain any other thoughts but how to discharge them. I perceive the little Domine hath played the trumpeter to this disorder. I refer the quality of his punishment to your direction."

On the 18th of October, 1669, a council assembled at New York, at which the governor, Thomas Delaval, Ralph Whitfield, and Thomas Willet, the secretary, were present. This council assembled for the trial of those who had violated the laws, at which the affair of Coningsmarke was first taken into consideration. It was adjudged that Coningsmarke, commonly called the Long Finne, deserved to die, yet, in regard that many concerned with him in the insurrection might also be involved in the premunire, if the rigor of the law should be extended, and amongst them diverse simple and ignorant people, it was thought fit to order that the Long Finne should be severely whipt, and stigmatized with the letter R, with inscription in great letters on his breast; that he received that punishment for rebellion, and afterward to be secured till sent to Barbadoes or some other remote plantation to be sold. It was further ordered, that the chief of his accomplices should forfeit to the King one-half of his goods and chattels, and a smaller mulct laid on the rest, to be left at the discretion of the commissioners appointed to examine the matter.

In pursuance of this sentence, the Long Finne was brought, fettered, from Delaware, and put prisoner in the Stadt House at York, on the 20th of December, and there confined an entire year, when a warrant was signed, and he, in pursuance of it, was transported for sale to Barbadoes.

At this council the case of an Indian who had committed a rape on a Christian woman, was considered, and it was decreed that he should be put to death if he could be found, and ordered that application be made to the sachems of his tribe to deliver him up, that justice might be executed upon him. He had been once before taken and condemned to death at Delaware, but escaped by breaking jail.

A man by the name of Douglass, at Hoarkill, after this gave the new settlers a great deal of trouble by his seditious practices, but he was apprehended, sent to jail, and afterwards taken to New York, where he was tried and sent eastward, and ordered not to return to the government any more.

Francis Lovelace succeeded Nicholls in the government in May, 1667, and continued governor until the colony was given up to the Dutch in the summer of 1673. Nicholls had remained governor since the Dutch surrendered, being about two years and a half.

In February, 1669, Governor Lovelace gave a commission, and letters of instruction were sent to Hoarkill,* authorizing Hermanus Fredericksen to be scout, Slander Matson, Otto Walgast and William Cleason to be commissaries† to keep good order there, and to try all matters of difference under ten pounds; while all matters above that, and all criminal matters, were to be tried at New York.

He also appointed Captain Martin Prieger to collect the customs for all European goods imported at the Hoarkill, and on the furs and peltry exported from thence, ten pound per cent.

"The right of the Crown of England to these provinces having been indisputably established, King Charles II., by letters patent, bearing date March 20th, 1664, for the consideration therein mentioned, granted unto James, Duke of York, his heirs and assigns, all that part of the main-land of New England, beginning at a certain place, called or known by the name of St. Croix, near adjoining to New Scotland, in America; and from thence extending along the sea coast, unto a certain place called Pemaquie, or Pemaquid, and so up the river thereof to the furthest head of the same, as it tendeth northward; and extending from thence to the river of Kimbequin, and so upwards by the shortest course to the river Canada, northwards; and also all that island, or islands, commonly called by the

---

* This part of the colony was called Hoarkill or Hoernkill from the creek which winds like a horn. It was so named by the Dutch, but when the English came in possession they called it Lewistown. Hoarkill or Lewistown was situated at the mouth of Delaware bay, and was the general resort for pilots waiting to convoy vessels up the river. Where this creek was described as being deep and sandy in 1669, and 1765, it was described as a mowing marsh, and the channel through which vessels used to pass, was diminished to about a hundred yards breadth at the mouth. It contained two islands, one of which, two hundred years ago, was very small, and the other, but half a league in circumference, had in less than a hundred years increased, the one about ten, and the other about thirty times their former size.

† Justices of the peace.

several name or names of Matowacks or Long Island, situate and being towards the west of Cape Cod, and the narrow Higansetts, abutting upon the land between the two rivers, there called or known by the several names of Connecticut and Hudson's rivers; together also with the said river called Hudson's river, and all the land from the west side of Connecticut river to the east side of Delaware bay, and also several other islands and lands in the said letters patents mentioned; together with the rivers, harbors, mines, minerals, quarries, woods, marshes, waters, lakes, fishings, hawking, hunting and fowling, and all other royalties, profits, commodities, and hereditaments to the said several islands, lands and premises belonging or appertaining."

The Duke of York, being thus seized, did by his deeds of lease and release, bearing date the 23d and 24th of June, 1664, in consideration of a competent sum of money, grant and convey unto John Lord Berkely, Baron of Stratton, one of the King's privy council, and Sir George Carteret, of Saltrum, in the county of Devon, knight, and one of the privy council,* and their heirs and assigns forever, all that tract of land adjacent to New England, and lying and being to the westward of Long Island and Manhattas Island, and bounded on the east part by the main sea, and part by Hudson's river, and hath upon the west Delaware bay or river, and extendeth southward to the main ocean as far as Cape May, at the mouth of Delaware bay, and to the northward as far as the northermost branch of the said bay or river of Delaware, which is in forty-one degrees and forty minutes of latitude, and crosseth over thence in a straight line to Hudson's river, in forty-one degrees of latitude, which said tract of land is hereafter to be called Nova Cæsaria or New Jersey; and also all rivers, mines, minerals, woods,

---

* Smollet informs us that Sir George Carteret was Governor of Jersey, and held it for King Charles II. in the troubles of 1649; expelled the House of Commons in 1669, for confused accounts, as Chamberlain; and Clarendon says he was Treasurer of the Navy, and Vice-Chamberlain of the King's household.

fishings, hawkings, huntings, and fowlings, and all other royalties, profits, commodities, and hereditaments whatsoever to the said lands and premises belonging or in anywise appertaining, with their and every of their appurtenances, in as full and ample manner as the same is granted to the said Duke of York by the before recited letters patents.

Lord Berkely and Sir George Carteret, in consequence of this conveyance, being now the sole proprietors of New Jersey, for the better settlement of the same, agreed upon a certain constitution of government, which gave general satisfaction, and in consequence thereof the eastern parts of the province were rapidly peopled.

This constitution gave the governor, with the advice and consent of his council, power to appoint a deputy to act in case of his death or removal.

2. Also, power to appoint six councellors at least, and twelve at most, or any even number between six and twelve, with whom he was to advise.

3. In case the proprietors failed to appoint a secretary of the province, the governor had the power to appoint. This officer was to enter in books all public affairs, record and enter all grants of land from the lords to the planters, and all conveyances of lands, house or houses made by the landlord to any tenant for a longer term than a year, and to do all other things directed by the lords proprietors, or ordained by the governor, council, and general assembly for the good and welfare of the said province. He was also termed register.

4. A surveyor-general was to be chosen by the proprietors, and in case of their failure to appoint, the governor was to choose. His business was to lay out and bound all lands that were granted by the lords to the planters, and all other lands within the province, either by himself or by deputy, and certify the same to the register, to be by him recorded. The governor and council, or deputy governor and council, had power to remove for cause the register or surveyor-general.

5. All officers were required, before entering upon the duties of their office, to swear or subscribe, in a book kept for that purpose, the oath of allegiance to the crown, and fidelity

to the interests of the lords proprietors of the province. And such as subscribed and did not swear, and violated his promise in that subscription, was liable to the same punishment as though he had sworn and broken his oath.

6. All who were or became subjects of the King of England, and who swore or subscribed allegiance to the King, and faithfulness to the lords, shall be admitted to plant and become freemen of the said province.

7. No person qualified as aforesaid, should at any time be molested, punished, disquieted, or called in question, for any difference in opinion or practice in matters of religious concernments, who do not actually disturb the civil peace of said province; but that all and every such person and persons may, from time to time, and at all times, freely and fully have and enjoy his and their judgments and consciences, in matters of religion, throughout the said province, they behaving themselves peaceably and quietly, and not using this liberty to licentiousness, nor to the civil injury or outward disturbance of others.

8. The general assembly were empowered to constitute and appoint such and so many ministers or preachers as they should think fit, and to establish their maintenance, giving liberty besides to any person or persons to keep and maintain what preachers or ministers they please.

9. They were to choose from among themselves twelve deputies or representatives, to join with the governor and council, for making such laws, ordinances, and constitutions, as they may think necessary for the present good and welfare of the province. But so soon as parishes, divisions, tribes, and other distinctions are made, that then the inhabitants or freeholders of the several respective parishes, tribes, divisions, and distinctions, were to meet annually, on the first day of January, and choose freeholders for each respective division, tribe, or parish, to be deputies or representatives of the same. A majority of representatives shall, with the governor and council, be the general assembly of the province.

THEY WERE TO HAVE POWER,

1st. To appoint their own time of meeting, and to adjourn from time to such times and places as they should think convenient.

2d. To enact and make all such laws, acts, and constitutions, as shall be necessary for the well government of the province, and, if thought necessary, to repeal them. All laws were to be in reason, and agreeable to the laws and customs of His Majesty's Kingdom of England, and not against the interests of the lords proprietors, nor any of the concessions, and especially that they be not repugnant to the article for liberty of conscience.

These laws were to be in force one year and no more, unless confirmed by the lords proprietors, after which they were to be in continual force, until expired by their own limitation.

3d. They were by law to constitute all courts with the limits, powers, and jurisdictions of the same, as also the several offices, and number of officers belonging to each court, with their respective salaries, fees, and perquisites, their appellations and dignities, with the penalties that shall be due to them, for the breach of their several and respective duties and trusts.

4th. To lay equal taxes and assessments, equally to raise moneys or goods upon all lands, except such as belong to the lords proprietors before settling.

5th. To erect within the said province such and so many manors* with their necessary courts, jurisdictions, freedoms, and privileges as to them shall seem meet and convenient; as also to divide the said province into hundreds,† parishes, tribes, or such other divisions or distinctions and districtions as they shall think fit, and to distinguish them by such names as they may think proper, and to appoint so many ports, harbors, creeks, and other places, for the convenient loading and unloading of goods and merchandise out of ships, boats, and other vessels, as they shall judge most conducive to the general good of the province.

6th. To erect, raise, and build within the said province, or any part thereof, such and so many forts, fortresses, castles, cities, corporations, boroughs, towns, villages, and other places of strength and defence, and to incorporate with charters and priv-

---

* Manor, meaning the land belonging to a nobleman or lord, or so much land as a lord or great personage formerly kept in his own hands for the use and subsistence of his family.

† Meaning a circuit or county, supposed to contain about a hundred families.

ileges as to them shall seem good, and to fortify and furnish with such provisions and proportions of ordnance, powder, shot, armor, and all other weapons, ammunition, and habiliments of war, both offensive and defensive, as shall be thought necessary and convenient for the safety and welfare of the province.

7th. To constitute trained bands and companies, with the number of soldiers, for the safety, strength, and defence of the province, and of the forts, castles, cities, &c.; to suppress all mutinies and rebellions; to make war, offensive and defensive, with all Indians, strangers, and foreigners, as they shall see cause; and to pursue an enemy as well by sea as by land, if need be, out of the limits and jurisdiction of the said province, with the particular consent of the governor, and under his conduct, or of our commander-in-chief, or whom he shall appoint.

8th. To give to all strangers, as to them shall seem meet, a naturalization, and all such freedoms and privileges within the province, as to His Majesty's subjects do of right belong, they swearing or subscribing as aforesaid, who shall be considered in the said province the same as the King's natural subjects.

9th. To prescribe the quantities of land which shall be from time to time allotted to every head, free or servant, male or female; and to make or ordain rules for the casting of lots for land and laying out of the same.

10th. The general assembly was to make provision for the support of the governor, and for defraying all necessary charges for the support of the government; to collect the lords' rents, without charge or trouble to them.

11th. To enact, constitute, and ordain all such other laws, acts, and constitutions, as shall or may be necessary for the good prosperity and settlement of the province.

THE GOVERNOR WITH HIS COUNCIL

was to see that all courts established by the laws of the general assembly, and all ministers and officers, civil and military, executed their several duties and offices respectively, according to the laws in force, and to punish them for swerving from the laws, or acting contrary to their trust, as the nature of their offences should require.

2d. To nominate and commissionate the several judges,

members, and officers of courts, whether magisterial or ministerial, and all other civil officers, coroners, &c.; and to revoke their commissions, powers, and authority at pleasure.

3d. To appoint courts and officers in cases criminal, and empower them to inflict penalties upon offenders against any of the laws in force in the province, as the said laws shall ordain; whether by fine, imprisonment, banishment, corporeal punishment, or to the taking away of member or of life itself, if there be cause for it.

4th. To place officers and soldiers for the safety, strength, and defence of the forts, castles, cities, &c., and to revoke their commissions at pleasure; prosecute war, pursue an enemy, suppress all rebellions and mutinies, as well by sea as land, and to exercise the whole militia. But he was to appoint no military forces but what were freeholders in the province, except by consent of the general assembly.

5th. Where he saw cause after condemnation, he had power to reprieve until the case was presented, with a copy of the whole trial, proceedings, and proofs, to the lords, who would either command execution of the sentence or pardon the offender.

6th. In case of death or removal of any of the representatives within the year, he was to issue summons or writ, commanding the freeholders to choose others in their stead.

7th. To make warrants and seal grants of lands, according to the concessions and prescriptions, by the advice of the general assembly.

8th. To act and do all things that would conduce to the safety, peace, and well government of the province.

And for the better security of all the inhabitants in the said province, they are not to impose, nor suffer to be imposed, any tax, custom, subsidy, tollage, assessment, or any duty whatsoever, upon any color or pretence, upon the said province and the inhabitants thereof, other than shall be imposed by the authority and consent of the general assembly.

2d. To take care that the lands are quietly held, planted, and possessed seven years, after its being duly surveyed by the surveyor-general or his order.

3d. To take care that no man, if his cattle stray or range, or graze on any ground within the province not actually appropriated or set out to particular persons, shall be liable to pay any tresspass for the same, provided he do not purposely suffer his cattle to graze on such lands.

And that the planting of said province may be more speedily promoted, we do hereby grant unto all persons who have already adventured into the said province of New Cæsaria, or New Jersey, or shall transport themselves or servants before the first day of January, 1665, to every freeman that shall go with the first governor where he embarks (or shall meet him at the rendezvous he appoints for the settlement of a plantation, there armed with a good musket, bore twelve bullets to the pound, with ten pounds of powder and twenty pounds of bullets, with bandaliers and matches convenient, and with six months' provisions) for his own person arriving there, one hundred and fifty acres of land, English measure; and for every able man-servant that he shall carry with him, armed and provided as aforesaid, and arriving there, the like quantity of land; and for every able man-servant he or she shall send, armed and provided as aforesaid, and arriving there, the like quantity of one hundred and fifty acres of land, English measure; and for every weaker servant or slave, male or female, exceeding the age of fourteen years, which any one shall send or carry, arriving there, seventy-five acres of land; and to every Christian servant, exceeding the age aforesaid, after the expiration of their time of service, seventy-five acres of land for their own use.

2d. To every master or mistress that shall go before the 1st day of January, 1665, one hundred and twenty acres of land; and for every able man-servant that he or she shall send or carry, armed and provided as aforesaid, and arriving within the time aforesaid, the like quantity of one hundred and twenty acres of land; and for every weaker servant, male or female, exceeding the age of fourteen years, arriving there, sixty acres of land; and to every Christian servant, to their own use and behoof, sixty acres of land.

3d. To every free man or free woman that shall arrive in the said province, armed and provided as aforesaid, within the second year, from the 1st day of January, 1665, to the 1st day of January, 1666, with an intention to plant, ninety acres of land, English measure; and for every able man-servant that he or she shall carry or send, armed and provided as aforesaid, ninety acres of land, like measure.

4th. For every weaker servant or slave aged as aforesaid, that shall be so carried or sent hither within the second year, forty-five acres of land of like measure; and to every Christian servant that shall arrive the second year, forty-five acres of land of like measure, after the expiration of his or their time of service, for their own use and behoof.

5th. To every free man and free woman arriving in the third year, with the intention to plant, from January, 1666, to January, 1667, and provided as aforesaid, three score acres of land, and the same quantity to every able man-servant; and for every weaker slave aged as aforesaid, thirty acres of land; and to every Christian servant, thirty acres of land, after the expiration of their time of service.

And that the lands may be more regularly laid out, and all persons the better ascertained of their titles and possessions, the governor, council, and general assembly (if any be) are to take care and direct that all lands be divided by general lots, none less than two thousand one hundred acres, nor more than twenty-one thousand acres in each lot, excepting cities, towns, &c., and the near lots of townships; and that the same be divided into seven parts, one-seventh part to us, our heirs, and assigns, the remainder to persons as they come to plant the same, in such proportions as is allowed.

2d. That the governor, or whom he shall depute, in case of death or absence, if some be not before commissionated by us as aforesaid, to give to every person to whom land is due, a warrant, signed and sealed by himself, and the major part of his council, and directed to the surveyor-general or his deputy, commanding him to lay out, limit, and bound, (the number of) acres of land, (as his due proportion,) is for such a person, in such allottment, according to the warrant.

3d. We also grant convenient portions of land for highways and streets, not exceeding one hundred feet in breadth in cities, towns, and villages, &c., and for churches, forts, wharffs, keys, harbors, and for public houses, and to each parish, for the use of their ministers, two hundred acres, in such places as the general assembly shall appoint.

4th. The governor is to take notice, that all such lands laid out for the uses and purposes aforesaid, in the next preceding article, shall be free and exempt from all rents, taxes, and other charges and duties whatsoever, payable to us, our heirs or assigns.

5th. That in laying out lands for cities, towns, villages, boroughs, or other hamlets, the said lands be divided into seven parts, one-seventh part whereof to be by lot laid out for us, and the rest to be divided to such as shall be willing to build thereon, they paying after the rate of one penny or half-penny per acre, (according to the value of the land) yearly to us.

6th. That all rules relating to the building of each street, or quantity of ground to be allotted to each house within the said respective cities, boroughs, and towns, be wholly left, by act as aforesaid, to the wisdom and discretion of the general assembly.

7th. That the inhabitants of said province, have free passage through or by any seas, bounds, creeks, rivers, or rivulets, &c., in the said province, through or by which they must necessarily pass, to come from the main ocean to any part of the province.

8th, and lastly. It shall be lawful for the representatives of the freeholders to make any address to the lords, touching the governor or council, or any of them, or concerning any grievance whatsoever, or for any other thing they shall desire, without the consent of the governor and council, or any of them.

Given under our seal of our said province, the 10th day of February, in the year of our Lord 1664.

BERKELEY,
G. CARTERET.

This was the first constitution of New Jersey, and it continued entire, till the province became divided in 1676.

I have not given it entire, only the main points contained therein.

Sir George Carteret, then the only proprietor of the eastern division, confirmed and explained the concessions, with few additions.

The county of Bergen was the first settled place. A great many Dutch being already there when the province was surrendered, remained under the English government. A few Danes were also concerned in the original settlement of the county, from whence they derived the name of Bergen, after the capital of Norway.

The manner of their original settlement was singular. They had but small lots where their dwellings were, and these were built contiguous in the town of Bergen; their plantations, from whence their subsistence was obtained, being at some distance from their residences.

The reason for building thus, was from fear of the numerous Indians in the early days of their settlement,* about forty or fifty years previous to the surrender of the Dutch to the English.

In 1664, John Bailey, Daniel Denton, and Luke Watson, of Jamaica, Long Island, purchased of certain Indian Chiefs, who at that time inhabited Staten Island, a tract or tracts of land, on part of which the city of Elizabeth now stands, and for which (on their petition) Governor Richard Nicholls, granted a deed or patent to John Baker, of New York; John Ogden, of Northampton; John Bailey, and Luke Watson, and their associates, dated at Fort James, in New York, the 2d of December.† This was before Lord Berkely and Sir George Carteret's title was known, and by this means this part of the province had some few very early settlements.

Shrewsbury was first settled by emigrants from Connecticut in 1664, and Middletown by the English in 1666, and it is supposed that there were Dutch and English settlers at both these places before that time.

About 1669 these places were a great resort for industrious reputable farmers; the English from the west end of Long Island, removed here in great numbers, and most of them fixed about Middletown, from whence by degrees, they extended their settle-

---

* Morton, in his memorial published in 1620, tells us that the Hollanders had a large trade on Hudson's river previous to that time.

† This is what is commonly called the Elizabethtown grant.

ments to Freehold, and its immediate vicinity. To Shrewsbury there came many families from New England.

There were very soon four towns in the province—Shrewsbury, Middletown, Elizabeth, and Newark; and these, with the surrounding country, were in a few years plentifully inhabited by the accession of the Scotch, of whom there came a great many; as well as from England, together with the Dutch who remained, as well as settlers from the neighboring colonies.

Lord Berkeley and Sir George Carteret in 1669, appointed Philip Carteret governor, and gave him power, with the advice of a majority of council, to grant lands to all such as by the concessions were entitled thereto. In these concessions there was no provision for bargaining with the Indians.* But when Governor Carteret arrived, he thought it prudent to purchase from the Indians their right in the land.

It is worthy of remark here that all the lands in New Jersey were first purchased from the Indians before they were settled.

The sums paid for the lands, to the Indians, were inconsiderable in comparison with the damage a neglect might have occasioned.† For though the Indians about the English settlements,

---

* This was supplied in 1672, by particular instructions directing the governor and council to purchase all lands from the Indians and be reimbursed by the settlers as they made their purchases.

† We are informed that Richard Hartshorn, a considerable settler at Middletown, who came over in this year (1669), had like to have experienced some disadvantages from this neglect in the patentees of that town. "The Indians," says he "came to my house and laid their hands on the post and frame of the house, and said that house was theirs, they never had anything for it, and told me if I would not buy the land, I must be gone. But I minded it not, thinking it was Davis' land, and they wanted to get something of me; they at last told me they would kill my cattle and burn my hay, if I would not buy the land nor be gone; then I went to the patentees, which were James Grover, Richard Stout, John Bound, and Richard Gibbons. They told me it was never bought, nor had the Indians anything for it. Nicholls desired of them and the Indians also, only to have leave to set a trading house; and at that time, they did not intend any one should have the land, but keep it for the use of the country; always giving leave for any man to trade with goods, and not otherwise. But I told them I would not live on those terms, and not only so, but it was dangerous, for the Indians threatened to kill my

were not at this time considerable as to numbers they were strong in their alliances, and besides of themselves could easily annoy the plantations; and there having been several skirmishes between the Dutch and Indians, in which some blood had been spilled, fear was entertained in regard to obtaining their friendship.

The governor therefore thought it best, and so ordered that all new comers were either to purchase of the Indians themselves, or if the lands were before purchased, they were to pay their proportion.

The plan adopted by him answered his expectation, as the Indians parted with the lands to their own satisfaction, they became a jealous, shy people, serviceable and good neighbors. Frequent reports of their coming to kill the white people disturbed their repose, yet no instance ever occurred of their doing them any injury in the early settlements.

---

cattle. They told me no man had power to buy but the patentees, and they would buy it. Thus it continued some months. I considered the thing as well as I then was capable, and went to Gravesend and bought William Goulder out, and when I came back the Indians were at me and I did. James Grover, Richard Stout and Samuel Spicer, were at Wakecake when I bought Wakecake and paid for it, I being then a patentee as well as the rest."

CHAPTER IV.

1669—1680.

Stratagem of a Settler—Penelope Stout—Her Rescue—Her Descendants—Wampum the chief Currency of the Country—Proclamation of the Governor—Division of the Province—Yorkshire and London Purchasers—Meeting of Proprietors.

IN the Dutch skirmishes with the Indians, the English from Long Island, together with such as were settled among the Dutch, used to join the latter in frequent excursions up the rivers to annoy the Indians.

There is a tradition that in one of these expeditions up a Jersey river, one of the company, of more curiosity or boldness than the rest, went at some distance in the country to discover an Indian town, which at last he did, by coming upon it before he was aware of his situation. He there found quite a number seated together. At the instant he saw them, they saw him. He was surprised, but quickly recollecting himself, took a paper out of his pocket, and with it boldly went up, telling them it was proposals from the government at New York, and read at random such things as came into his head. By this stratagem he got off without molestation, and having acquainted the inhabitants at New York as to what he had seen, notified the government there that if they would send a party against the Indians he would act as pilot for them. A party was accordingly sent, and coming upon the Indians in the night, some of them found means to get to windward of their little town, and setting fire to it, burnt it down. Their wigwams being built close together, and made of flags, bushes, and other light combustible matter, covered with the bark of trees, so that the fire burnt with great violence. The Indians, notwithstanding their surprise, armed with their bows and arrows, fought with dexterity and courage, but being overpowered by numbers, many of them were destroyed.

nother tradition informs us that while New York was in possession of the Dutch, about the time of the Indian war in New England, a Dutch ship coming from Amsterdam was stranded on Sandy Hook, but the passengers succeeded in getting to shore. Among them was a young Dutchman, who had been sick during most of the voyage. He was taken so sick after landing that he was unable to travel, and the other passengers being afraid of the Indians, would not stay till he recovered, but made such haste as they could to New Amsterdam. His wife, however, would not leave him. The rest promised to send on for him as soon as they arrived. They had not been long gone before a party of Indians, coming down to the water and hastily coming to the spot, discovered them, and soon killed the man, cutting and dreadfully mangling the woman, so that they left her for dead. She had strength enough, however, after they had gone, to crawl up to some logs not far distant, and getting into an old hollow one, lived there several days, upon what she could pick off from the tree. The Indians had left some fire on the beach, which she managed to keep together, and by that means she kept herself warm. She remained in this manner several days. On the seventh day she saw a deer pass with some arrows sticking in it, and soon after appeared two Indians, one an old man, the other a young man. She was glad to see them, hoping they would soon put her out of her misery. Accordingly one made towards her, to knock her in the head, but the elderly man prevented him. They had quite a dispute in reference to her, the old man insisting on keeping her alive, while the other wanted to dispatch her at once. After they had debated the point for a considerable time, the first hastily took her up, and tossing her upon his shoulder, carried her to his wigwam at Middletown, where he dressed her wounds and soon cured her. After some time the Dutch at New Amsterdam, hearing of a white woman among the Indians, concluded it must be her, and some of them came to her relief. The old man who had preserved her, gave her choice either to stay or go. She preferred the latter, and was taken to New York among her countrymen. In New York she married Richard Stout, being at that time in her twenty-second year, he being in his fortieth year, and an Englishman of good family. They settled at Middletown. The old Indian who saved her life used frequently to visit her. At one of his visits she observed him to be more pensive than common, and sitting down, he gave three pensive sighs.

She then took the liberty of asking him what the matter was. He told her he had something to tell her in friendship, though at the risk of his own life, which was, that the Indians were that night to kill all the whites at Middletown, and advised her to go off to New Amsterdam. She asked him how she could get off, and he told her he had provided a canoe, at a place which he named.

Having left her, she sent for her husband out of the field, and told him what the Indian had communicated to her, and he not believing it, she told him the old man had never deceived her, and that she with her children would go. Accordingly, going to the appointed place, she found the canoe and paddled off.

When they were gone, her husband began to consider the matter, and sending for five or six of his neighbors, they set themselves upon their guard, and about midnight they heard the dismal war-whoop. Presently there came up a company of Indians.

The inhabitants expostulated with them, and told them if they persisted in their bloody design, they would sell their lives very dear.

Their arguments prevailed, and the Indians desisted and entered into a league of peace, which they kept inviolate. From this woman, thus miraculously saved, is descended a numerous posterity of the name of Stout, at present inhabiting New Jersey.

She retained her scars throughout a long life, had several children, and lived to the age of one hundred and ten years, and before her death saw her offspring multiplied to five hundred and two, in about eighty-eight years.

Her maiden name was Penelope Vanprinces, and she was born in Amsterdam, about the year 1602.

When the Indians had killed her first husband, and as they thought, her too, they stripped them of their garments and left them on the beach for dead. Penelope, however, revived, although her skull was fractured and her left shoulder so injured that she was never after able to use it like the other; besides, she was so cut across the body that her bowels protruded, and she was obliged to keep her hand upon her wound.

At the time this affair occurred, there were supposed to be about fifty families of white people and five hundred Indians inhabiting this part of New Jersey.

Carteret did not arrive in his province as governor of New Jersey till the latter part of the summer of 1665, until which time the province was under Nicholls' jurisdiction.

On the arrival of Carteret, he summoned a council, granted lands, and administered the government on the plan of the general concessions, and took up his residence at Elizabeth Town, to which it is said he gave the name after Elizabeth, wife of Sir George Carteret. He brought with him about thirty people, some of them servants. They brought goods proper for the planting of a new colony, and the governor soon after sent persons into New England and other places for the purpose of publishing the proprietors' concessions and to invite people to settle there, upon which many soon came, some of whom settled at Elizabeth Town, others at Woodbridge, Piscataway, and Newark.

The ship that brought the governor remained about six months, then returned to England, and the following year made another voyage.

Sundry other vessels were from time to time sent by the proprietors with people and goods to encourage the planting and peopling the lands. Thus the province of East New Jersey increased in settlement, and continued to grow till the Dutch invasion in 1673, when they, having got possession of the country, some stop was put to the English government, but the treaty afterwards between King Charles II. and the States General, at London, 1673-4, put all general difficulties of that kind out of dispute.

In the sixth article, we find the following:

"That whatever country, island, town, haven, castle, or fortress, hath been, or shall be taken by either party from the other since the beginning of the late unhappy war, whether in Europe or elsewhere, before the expiration of the times above limited for hostility, shall be restored to the former owner in the same condition it shall be in at the time of publishing this peace."

Though the inhabitants were at variance among themselves, there was also a considerable number of settlers arriving between the years 1665 and 1673, after which time they increased rapidly.

But the Elizabethtown purchasers and others, setting up a right, differing in some respect from that of the proprietors, and other incidents, having fallen out, some of which were of considerable consequence, while others were so small in their nature, that one would think they might easily have been settled; yet, being nourished by a more vindictive spirit than was necessary on all sides, they occasioned much disturbance among the settlers.*

In the summer of 1672, Carteret went to England, and left Captain John Berry, his deputy, to govern the province during his absence.

In 1674, he returned and found the inhabitants more disposed to peace and union among themselves. He brought over with him the King's proclamation, with a new commission and instructions from Sir George Carteret, whereupon he immediately summoned the people, and published them, which for a time had a good effect towards restoring proprietary authority, and the public peace. He remained governor until his death in 1682.

---

* We do not propose to enter particularly into these disturbances, which in several instances went to disreputable lengths. Governor Andross, of York, in 1680, undertook to dispute the commission of Governor Carteret, of Jersey, and sending to Elizabethtown, an armed force, seized and carried him prisoner to New York.

During his time the councils and general assemblies, as well as the supreme courts, sat at Elizabethtown. The secretary's office, and nearly all the other public offices were located there, and the residences of most of the officers of the government were also there.

In September, 1671, an extraordinary council was held at New York, composed of the principal officers of the two provinces. There were present at this council, Governor Francis Lovelace, together with the mayor and secretary of New York, Major Steenwick, Governor Philip Carteret, and Capt. James Carteret, of New Jersey.

The cause of the assembling of this extraordinary council, was the arrival of William Tomm and Peter Alricks, from Delaware, with particulars of the Indian murders before mentioned; that two Christians, (Dutchmen) had, as there related, been murdered by some Indians at the Island of Matinicunk,* on the Delaware. Alricks being present at the council, imparted to them of what nation these murderers were; that they consisted of about fifty or sixty persons, and that the outrages committed on the river for the last seven years, had been traced to them; that the Indians, who were their confederates, (as it was supposed they would be in case of war), numbered about one thousand persons, besides women and children.

That two of the sagamores, (a King or Chief) of the nation of the murderers, promised their best assistance to bring them to justice, or procure them to be knocked in the head, if sustained by the government, and that many other Indians he met on the road, severely disapproved the murder, were very sorry for it,

---

* The upper island situated partly between Burlington and Bristol, afterwards taken up by a proprietary right, by Robert Stacy, and by him given to Burlington, and in 1682 confirmed by a proprietary law, for the use of a free school, forever. It is detached from the main channel by a small channel occasioned by the waters of Assiscunk creek. When Gookin, a former governor of Pennsylvania, was about obtaining a grant of the islands in the Delaware river, it is said the lords of trade excepted this island in their report to the King and council, as having been already occupied, and therefore not on a footing with the other islands. It is inconsiderable as to value, compared with many others, yet long possession and some improvements, have rendered it useful to Burlington.

and offered every assistance in their power in apprehending the murderers.

Alricks further stated, that it was proposed by the Sachems, (chiefs) as the best scheme to set upon this nation, to cause a kintecoy, (act of rejoicing or merriment), to be held, and that in the midst of their mirth one should be hired to knock them in the head; and adding, as his own opinion, that the best time to fall upon them was about the 25th of October, because after that their usual custom was to go a hunting, and then they could not easily be found. But the immediate danger now was of their destroying the corn and cattle of the Christians, and that the murders were owing to Sashiowycan, who, having a sister dying, expressed great grief for her, and said the Mannetta hath killed my sister and I will go kill the Christians; and taking another with him, they together executed the barbarous acts.

The council, after having considered this information, came to the conclusion that Thomas Lewis, then bound with his sloop for New Castle, should delay his voyage for three or four days, at which time Alricks and Henry Courturier would be ready to go with him; that in the mean time, general instructions should be given to take with them. That the Governor of New Jersey and Capt. James Carteret, (who were then present,) should, with as much expedition as possible, order a general assembly to be called in that government, (according to their custom on all emergent occasions,) to know the strength of the people and their readiness, as well as how far they were willing to contribute towards the prosecution of a war against the Indians.

That a frequent correspondence be kept between the two governments, and that nothing be done in this Indian war without mutual advice and consent of both the governors, unless extraordinary opportunity should offer, where advantage against the enemy might suddenly be taken before notice could be given.

These resolutions having been duly considered, the next step was to transmit instructions to William Tomm, (who was one of the commissaries appointed by Carre and the authority at New Castle, or a kind of deputy under them. up the Delaware,) in order that he might consider how a war could be prosecuted to the best advantage, as it required time to get things in order.

All the scattering frontier plantations were immediately to thresh out or remove their corn, and so dispose of their cattle that they should receive the least damage by the effect of the war. Next he was to order that no one, on pain of death, should sell any powder, shot, or strong waters to the Indians, and that in the meantime the inhabitants were to carry (if such a thing was practicable) a seeming complacency with the nation to whom the murderers belonged, either by treaty or traffic, in order to avoid suspicion of the designs that were sought to be accomplished.

It was also directed that if they would deliver up the murderers, or their heads, the English were at liberty to assure them there would be no disturbance.

Governor Lovelace also wrote to Carre to be vigilant in making preparations for the war, and as directions could not be specific, the whole was left to his prudent management, with the advice of his commissaries.

The next council held upon the subject was in November, at Elizabethtown.

Governor Lovelace, Carteret, and a number of other persons were present.

The season was now thought to be too far advanced to begin the war, but the magistrates were authorized to treat with the neighboring Sasquehana Indians, or others, to join together against the murderers, as well as such that harbored them, and to promise a reward for their apprehension, provided caution were used to create no sudden jealousy. But this proved unnecessary, as the Indians, uneasy about the murder, were not averse to a full revenge, as it afterwards proved.

In December, a party of them meeting at Rambo's, sent for Tomm and others, and promised within six days to bring in the murderers, dead or alive. Accordingly, two Indians sent by the sachems to take them, coming to Tashowycan's wigwam in the night, one of whom was his particular friend, he asked him if he intended to kill him; he answered no, but the sachems have ordered you to die. He demanded what his brothers

HISTORY OF NEW JERSEY.

said, and being told they also said he must die, he then, holding his hands before his eyes, said, kill me. Upon this, the other Indian (not his intimate friend) shot him in the breast. They took his body to Wickaco, and afterwards hung it in chains at New Castle. The English gave the sachems for this five matchcoats.

The other murderer, hearing the shot, ran naked into the woods, and it was never afterwards known what became of him, but it was supposed he perished either from the effects of hunger or cold.

The Indians, upon this death, summoned many of their young men, and in the presence of the English, told them that now they saw a beginning of punishment, and all that did the like should be served in the same way.

Thus ended an affair which, to the settlers from the formidable body of the Indians, looked extremely discouraging.

In 1672 the inhabitants at New Amstell (New Castle) and the Hoarkills suffered considerable loss by the Dutch privateers plundering their effects. As a reparation, they were empowered by the government to lay an imposition, and power was given to the magistrates to levy and receive upon each anchor of strong liquors disposed of among them, the real value of four guilders in wampum.*

Wampum was the chief currency of the country. Great quantities had been formerly brought in, but the Indians had carried so much away, it had at this time (1673) grown scarce, and this was thought to be owing to its low value. To increase

---

*Eight white wampums, or four black, passed at this time as a stiver (Dutch two cents, or one penny sterling); twenty stivers made what they called a guilder (about thirty-eight cents, or one shilling and nine pence sterling). The white wampum was worked out of the inside of the great conques into the form of a bead, and perforated to string on leather. The black, or purple, was worked out of the inside of a mussel, or clam-shell; they were sometimes worn as broad as one's hand, and about two feet long; these the Indians called belts; they were commonly given and received at treaties, as seals of their friendship. For smaller matters a single string was given. Every bead was of a known value, and a belt of a less number was made to equal one of a greater, by as many as were wanting fastened to the belt by a string.

its value, the governor and council at New York issued a proclamation, in 1673, that instead of eight white and four black, six white and three black wampums should pass in equal value as a stiver or penny, and three times as much the value in silver. This proclamation was published at Albany, Eusopus, Delaware, Long Island, and parts adjacent.

Mention was made that Sir George Carteret, by his instructions to Governor Carteret, confirmed the original concessions, with additions and explanations. These were dated July 13th, 1674. Among other things, they directed that the governor and council should allow eighty acres per head to settlers above ten miles from the sea, the same from the Delaware, or other river, navigable with boats, and to those who settled nearer, sixty acres. That the land should be purchased from the Indians, as occasion required, by the governor and council, in the name of the proprietors, who were to be repaid by the settlers with all necessary charges. That all estrays of beasts at land and wrecks at sea should belong to the proprietor, and that all persons discovering any such thing should have satisfaction for their pains and care, as the governor and council might think fit.

About the month of October, 1674, Major Edmund Andross,* arrived in the province, and assumed the government under the Duke of York. He issued a proclamation from New York, on the 9th of November, confirming all former grants, privileges, and concessions heretofore granted, and all estates legally possessed by any under his Royal Highness before the late Dutch government, as also all legal judicial proceedings during that government, and also confirming the known book of laws established and in force under His Royal Highness' government.

Andross being now seated in his government, we leave him to take a view of other matters.

In 1675, a few passengers arrived from England to West Jersey. One-half of the province of New Jersey belonged to

---

* He was afterwards knighted. He bore the unfavorable character of an arbitrary governor, who made the will of his despotic master, (James II.,) and not the law, the chief rule of his conduct.

Lord John Berkeley, which was now about to be sold to John Fenwick, in trust for Edward Byllinge and his assigns.

In this year, Fenwick set sail from London in a ship called the Griffith, to visit the new purchase. After a pleasant passage, he arrived and landed at a rich spot situate near Delaware, which he called Salem, from the peaceable aspect it then bore. He brought his two daughters with him and many servants, two of whom—Samuel Hedge and John Adams—afterwards married his daughters.

Edward Champness, Edward Wade, Samuel Wade, John Smith and wife, Samuel Nichols, Richard Guy, Richard Noble, Richard Hancock, John Pledger, Hipolite Lufever, and John Matlock, were also passengers. These, and others with them, were masters of families.

This was the first English ship that came to West Jersey, and for nearly two years after none followed, owing, probably, to a difference between Fenwick and Byllinge.

This difference having been settled to the satisfaction of both parties by the good offices of William Penn, Byllinge agreed to present his interest in the province of New Jersey to his creditors to satisfy them for the obligations he had incurred, and desired William Penn to join Gawen Lawrie and Nicholas Lucas, two of his principal creditors, they three to act as trustees. Penn was at first unwilling to accept of the trust, but by the importunity of some of the creditors, he was at last prevailed upon to accept it, and with the others accepting the charge, they became trustees for one moiety, or one-half of the province, which, though yet undivided, they were so pressed that they were compelled to sell a considerable number of the shares of their property to different purchasers, who by virtue of their purchases became proprietors according to their number of shares, and they therefore found it necessary that some scheme should be adopted, as well for the better distribution of the land as to promote its settlement, and establish a form of government; concessions for which were mutually agreed upon, and signed by a number of the subscribers.

These concessions gave the proprietors, or a majority of them, under their hands and seals, power to act as commissioners for the time being, with power to order and manage the estate and affairs of the province of West Jersey, and in case of the death of any of them, the remaining to depute others to act in their stead.

They were to take care of the setting forth and dividing all lands, and to take up and contract with the natives, and to divide the said lands into one hundred parts, as occasion should require, the same to be divided into ten equal parts or shares, to be marked on the register, and upon some of the trees belonging to every tenth part, with the letters A, B, and so end with the letter K; and after the same was so marked and divided, they were to grant unto Thomas Hutchinson, of Beverly, Thomas Pearson, of Bonwicke, Joseph Helmsley, of Great Kelke, George Hutchinson, of Sheffield, and Mahlon Stacy, of Hansworth, all of the county of York, who should speedily promote the planting of the province.

They had power to appoint and set out proper places for towns, and to limit the boundaries, taking care that they were regularly built, as the occasion, time, and conveniency of the place would admit of.

And they were to order the affairs of the province in accordance with the concessions, or any other instructions that might be given them by a majority of the proprietors, until such time as other commissioners should be appointed by the inhabitants of West Jersey.

And upon the settlement of the province, the proprietors, freeholders, and inhabitants resident upon the province, were to meet together in some public place, ordered and appointed by the commissioners, on the 25th day of March, 1680, and annually on that day in every year thereafter, at nine o'clock in the morning, and elect from among themselves ten honest and able men fit for government, to officiate and execute the position of commissioners for the ensuing year, to hold said office until such time as ten more shall be elected and appointed.

Each ten of the one hundred proprieties were to elect and choose one, and the one hundred proprieties were to be divided into ten divisions or tribes.

The proprietors were to grant to every person planting or

settling in the province, for his own person arriving, seventy acres of land, English measure; and for every able-bodied man servant he may carry with him, seventy acres of land; and for every weaker servant, male or female, exceeding the age of fourteen years, fifty acres of land; and after the expiration of their time of service they were to have fifty acres of land for their own use, for which they were to pay annually to the proprietors one penny an acre for what shall be laid out in towns, and one half-penny for all others, the first yearly payment to begin within two years after the lands were lain out.

And to those who arrived the second year, fifty acres of land, whether freemen or servants.

And to those arriving in the third year, forty acres of land, provided their intention was to plant in said province.

They were to receive a certificate from the register.

Portions of land were also granted for highways and streets, not under one hundred feet in breadth, in cities, towns, and villages, and for wharves, keys, harbors, and for public houses, in such places as the commissioners should appoint.

They were to see that the courts duly executed the laws of the province, and to displace and punish all officers violating the same, or acting contrary to their duty and trusts. They had also power to reprieve or suspend sentence for the time being, or until the case could be reviewed by higher authority.

All officers were accountable to the commissioners, and they in turn were accountable to the general assembly.

They were not to impose any tax, custom, or subsidy, tollage, assessment, or any other duty whatsoever on the inhabitants, without their consent, other than that which should be imposed by the general assembly.

All officers were to subscribe in a book, that they will truly and faithfully discharge their respective trusts, according to the law of the province, and do equal justice and right to all men, according to their best skill and judgment, without corruption, favor, or affection.

These concessions, comprising forty-five chapters, contained the common law or fundamental rights of the province. For the prevention of fraud, deceit, collusion in bargains, sales, trades, and traffic, and the usual contests, quarrels, debates, and utter ruin, which have attended the people in many nations, by costly, tedious, and vexatious law-suits, and for a due settlement of estates, and taking care of orphans. The powers of the general assembly, when and how they were to be chosen, and all other matters requisite to the government of the province.

The next business of the proprietors who held immediately under Lord Berkeley, was to procure a division of the province, which, after some delay, they succeeded in effecting, after which they wrote the following letter to Richard Hartshorne:

"LONDON, 26th of the sixth month, 1676.

"We have made use of thy name in a commission and instructions, which we have sent by James Wasse, who is gone in Samuel Groome's ship for Maryland, a copy of which is here enclosed, and also a copy of a letter we have sent to John Fenwick, to be read to him in presence of as many of the people that went with him as may be; and because we both expect and also entreat and desire thy assistance in the same, we will a little shew things to thee, that thou may inform not only thyself but friends there; which, in short, is as follows:

"1st. We have divided with George Carteret, and have sealed deeds of partition, each to the other, and we have all that side on Delaware river from one end to the other; the line of partition is from the east side of little Egg Harbor, straight north, through the country, to the utmost branch of Delaware river; with all powers, privileges, and immunities whatsoever; ours is called New West Jersey, his is called New East Jersey.

"2d. We have made concessions by ourselves, being such as friends here and there (we question not) will approve of, having sent a copy of them by James Wasse; there we lay a foundation for after ages to understand their liberty as men and Christians, that they may not be brought in bondage, but by their own consent; for we put the power in the people, that is to say, they to meet and choose one honest man for each propriety, who hath subscribed to the concessions; all these men to meet as an assembly there, to make and repeal laws, to choose a governor, or a commissioner, and twelve assistants, to execute the laws during their pleasure; so every man is capable to choose or be chosen.

"No man to be arrested, condemned, imprisoned, or molested in his estate or liberty, but by twelve men of the neighborhood. No man to lie in prison for debt,* but that his estate satisfy as far as it will go, and he set at liberty to work.

"No person to be called in question or molested for his conscience, or for worshipping according to his conscience, with many other things mentioned in the said concessions.

"3. We have sent over James Wasse, a commission under our hands and seals, wherein we empower thyself, James Wasse, and Richard Guy, or any two of you, to act and do according to the instructions of which here is a copy, having also sent some goods to buy and purchase some lands of the natives.

"4. We intend in the spring to send over some more commissioners† with the friends and people that cometh there, because James Wasse is to return in Samuel Groom's ship for England; for Richard Guy, we judge him to be an honest man, yet we are afraid that John Fenwick will hurt him, and get him to condescend to things that may not be for the good of the whole. So we hope that thou wilt balance him to what is just and fair; that John Fenwick betray him not; that things may go on easy without hurt or jar, which is the desire of all friends; and we hope West Jersey will soon be planted, it being in the minds of many friends to prepare for their going against the spring.

"5. Having thus far given thee a sketch of things, we come now to desire thy assistance, and the assistance of other friends in your parts, and we hope it will be at length an advantage to you there, both upon truth's account and other ways. And in regard to many families, more may come over in the spring to Delaware side to settle and plant, and will be assigned by us to take possession of their particular lots. We do intreat and

---

* Thus it will be seen that among the earliest acts of our forefathers, imprisonment for debt was unknown, and free toleration for worship was strictly enforced.

† A person purchasing ten proprieties became a commissioner, or a number of persons together purchasing ten proprieties, had power to choose from among themselves a commissioner.

desire, that thou, knowing the country, and how to deal with the natives, we say, that thee, and some other friends, would go over to Delaware side as soon as this comes to your hands, or as soon as you can conveniently. And James Wasse is to come to a place called New Castle, on the other side of Delaware river, to stay for thee, and any that will go with him; and you and all to advise together, and find out a fit place to take up for a town, and agree with the natives for a tract of land, and then let it be surveyed and divided in one hundred parts, for that is the method we have agreed to take, and we cannot alter it. And if you set men to work to clear some of the ground, we would be at the charges. And we do intend to satisfy thee for any charge thou art at, and for thy pains. This we would not have neglected, for we know, and you that are there know, that if the land be not taken up before the spring, that many people come over there, the natives will insist on high demands, and so we shall suffer by buying at dear rates, and our friends that cometh over, be at great trouble and charges until a place be bought and divided. For we do not like the tract of land John Fenwick hath bought, so as to make it our first settlement. But we would have thee and friends there to provide and take up a place on some creek or river, that may lie near you, and such a place as you may like; for may be it may come in your minds to come over to our side when you see the hand of the Lord with us. And so we can say no more, but leave the thing with you, believing that friends there will have a regard to friends settling; that it may be done in that way and method, that may be for the good of the whole. Rest thy friends.

"GAWEN LAURIE,
"WILLIAM PENN,
"NICHOLAS LUCAS,
"E. BYLLINGE,
"JOHN ELDRIDGE,
"EDMOND WARNER.'

The proprietors sent over instructions to James Wasse, Richard Hartshorne, Richard Guy, and others, giving them full power, commission, and authority, or any two of them, to act, and do according to the instructions, engaging to ratify and confirm whatever they should do in prosecution of the same. They were to get a meeting with John Fenwick, and the people that went with him (but to conceal from them their business) until they got them together, then they were to show and read the deed of partition with George Carteret; also the transactions between William Penn, Nicholas Lucas, Gawen Laurie, John Eldridge and Edmond Warner, and then read the letter of the proprietors to John Fenwick and the rest, and show him that he had no power to sell any land there, without the consent of John Eldridge and Edmond Warner And if he was willing peaceably to let the land he had taken up of the natives be divided into one hundred parts, that then those that had settled and cultivated ground with him, should enjoy the same without being turned out.

The instructions were quite lengthy, and bore date London, the 18th of 6th month, called August, 1676.

The instrument for dividing the province being agreed upon by Sir George Carteret, on the one part, and the said E. Byllinge, William Penn, Gawen Laurie, and Nicholas Lucas on the other, they together signed a quintipartite deed, dated the 1st day of July, 1676.*

The line of division having been thus far settled, each took their own measures for further peopling and improving their different shares. Sir George Carteret had greatly the advantage over the others in respect to improvements, his part having been already peopled to a considerable extent.

The western proprietors at once published a description of their moiety, upon which many soon removed thither. In order that others might understand the importance of the undertaking, the three principal proprietors published a cautionary epistle.

This epistle contains in its introductory many Christian sentiments. It also sets forth that there is such a province as New Jersey; that the country is wholesome of air, and fruitful of soil, and capable of sea trade; that the Duke of York sold it to Lord Berkeley and Sir George Carteret; that one-half of the

---

* Grants and Concessions, by Leaming & Spicer, p. 61.

said province was sold by Berkeley to John Fenwick, in trust for Edward Byllinge and his assigns; that Byllinge, through the kind offices of William Penn, was willing to present his interest in the province to his creditors, being all he had left to satisfy them, and that he had desired William Penn, a disinterested person, together with Gawen Lawrie and Nicholas Lucas, two of his creditors, to be trustees on behalf of his creditors; both parties had complied with the same, and that they had, after considerable trouble, labor, and cost, succeeded in obtaining a division between Sir George Carteret and themselves as trustees; they therefore divided their half into one hundred parts, lots, or proprieties, ten of which were settled and conveyed to Fenwick, with a considerable sum of money, by way of satisfaction for his interest in the purchase from Lord Berkeley, and by him afterwards conveyed to John Eldridge and Edmond Warner. The ninety remaining parts were to be exposed for sale, on behalf of the creditors of Byllinge, and as a number of friends were concerned as creditors, the trustees made the first offer to them to purchase the lands.

Among some of the purchasers of these lands were two companies, one composed of friends from Yorkshire, the other of friends from London. In 1677, commissioners were sent by the proprietors, with power to buy the land from the natives.

These commissioners were, Thomas Olive, Daniel Wills, John Kinsey, John Penford, Joseph Helmsley, Robert Stacy, Benjamin Scott, Richard Guy,* and Thomas Foulke.

They came over in the Kent, Gregory Marlow, master. This was the second ship from London. They arrived at New Castle the 16th of the sixth month, O. S., and sailed up to Rackoon creek, where they landed their passengers, two hundred and thirty in number. At the time of their leaving London, King Charles II. was pleasuring in his barge on the Thames, and having come alongside of them, and seeing a large number of passengers aboard, he inquired whence they were bound, and having been

---

* Richard Guy came in the first ship. John Kinsey died at Shackamaxon soon after landing, and his remains were interred at Burlington, in ground appropriated for a burying ground.

informed of their destination, he asked if they were all quakers, and gave them his blessing.

At the place where they landed the Swedes had erected some habitations, but they were not sufficient to accommodate all, and some of them were obliged to lay their beds and furniture in cow stalls, and the like places. Snakes were so numerous that they were frequently seen upon the hovels, under which they took shelter.

The commissioners having left before them, landed at Chygoes island,* (afterwards Burlington) their business being to treat with the Indians about the purchase of the lands, and arrange for the settlements. They had Governor Andross' commission as well as that of the proprietors, for the vessel upon which they were had dropped anchor at Sandy Hook, and remained there while the commissioners went to New York to acquaint the governor of their design.

The governor treated them civilly, but learning they had nothing from the Duke of York, refused to surrender the government to them, and clapping his hand on his sword, told them he should defend the government from them till he received orders from the duke, his master, to surrender it. He, however, afterwards told them he would do what was in his power to make them easy till they could send home to get redress. He also granted a commission to the same persons mentioned in the paper produced by them from the proprietors.†

They accepted his commission, and acted as magistrates under him until they received further orders from England, but in matters relating to land, they proceeded according to the method prescribed by the proprietors.

When they arrived at their government they applied to the Swedes for interpreters between them and the Indians. The persons recommended to them were Israel Helmes, Peter Rambo, and Lacy Cock.

By the help of these interpreters, they made a purchase from

---

* From Chygoe, an Indian Sachem, who lived there.

† John Fenwick, having neglected this precaution as to the government of his tenth, was sent for as a prisoner to New York.

Timber creek to Rankokus creek, another from Oldman's creek to Timber creek. After this they procured the services of Henric Jacobson Falconbre as interpreter, and by his assistance they purchased from Rankokus creek to Assanpink creek. But after having agreed upon this last purchase, they found they had not sufficient Indian goods to pay the amount agreed upon, yet they gave them what they had to get the deed signed, but were compelled to agree with the Indians not to settle until the balance was paid.

The deed for the lands between Rankokus and Timber creeks bears date September 10th, 1677; that from Oldman's to Timber creek, September 27th, and that from Rankokus to Assanpink creek, October 10th.

By the consideraton paid for the lands between Oldman's and Timber creek, a judgment may be formed of the rest. "It consisted of thirty matchcoats, twenty guns, thirty kettles and one great one, thirty pairs of hose, twenty fathoms of duffelds, thirty petticoats, thirty narrow hoes, thirty bars of lead, fifteen small barrels of powder, seventy knives, thirty Indian axes, seventy combs, sixty pairs of tobacco tongs, sixty scissors, sixty tinshaw looking glasses, one hundred and twenty awl-blades, one hundred and twenty fish-hooks, two grasps of red paint, one hundred and twenty needles, sixty tobacco boxes, one hundred and twenty pipes, two hundred bells, one hundred jews-harps, six anchors of rum."

In 1703 another purchase was made by the council of proprietors of West Jersey, of lands lying above the falls of Delaware; also another about the same time of lands at the head of Rankokus creek, and several purchases afterwards included the whole of the lands worth taking up in West Jersey, except a few plantations reserved to the Indians.

Among the friends that arrived from Yorkshire in 1677, were Thomas Hutchinson, of Beverly, in the county of York, yeoman; Thomas Pierson, of Bonwicke, in the same county, yeoman; Joseph Helmsley, of Great Kelke, in the same county, yeoman; George Hutchinson, of Sheffield, in the same county, distiller; and Mahlon Stacy, of Hansworth, in the same county, tanner. These were all principal creditors to Edward Byllinge, and to whom several of the other creditors made assignments of their debts, which together amounted to the sum of two thousand four hundred and fifty pounds sterling, and who took in satisfaction of the said sum, seven full, equal, and undivided ninetieth parts of ninety equal and undivided hundred parts of West Jersey, and the same was conveyed to them, their heirs and assigns, by William Penn, Gawen Lawrie, Nicholas Lucas, and Edward Byllinge, by deed bearing date the 1st of the month called March, 1676; and by another conveyance of the same date, from and to the same persons, in satisfaction for other debts to the amount of one thousand and fifty pounds sterling, three other full, equal, and undivided ninetieth parts of the aforesaid ninety equal and undivided hundred parts of West Jersey, were also conveyed.

In the records of the council of proprietors, the following entries relating to the purchases from the Indians are made:

"At a meeting of the council of proprietors at Burlington, the 2d day of November, Anno 1703, present, George Deacon, president; Samuel Jennings, Thomas Gardner, Christopher Wetherill, John Reading. Ordered, that John Wills, William Biddle, Jr., and John Reading, or any two of them, do go up to the Indians above the Falls, and particularly to Caponocus, in order to have the tract of land lately purchased of the Indians marked forth, and get them to sign a deed for the same; as also to receive the residue of the goods as yet unpaid, or so many of them that can be had, and to give him an obligation for the payment of the remaining part next spring. Ordered, likewise, that the persons abovesaid do go to Nimhammoe's wigwam, in order to treat with him, to see the bounds of the land lately purchased of him, to mark the same if it may be, and to pay him what part of the goods is already procured in part toward the said purchase, and to do what else may be necessary towards perfecting purchases of the concerns with the said Indians, and completing of the aforesaid; the said persons also taking with them Thomas Foulke and Andrew Heath, or some other proper person, to be an interpreter between them and the Indians."

At a meeting of the council of proprietors held at Burlington, June 27th, 1703, there were present Mahlon Stacy, Thomas

Gardner, John Wills, George Deacon, Christopher Wetherill, Samuel Jennings, and John Reading. At this meeting the persons appointed to treat with the Indians at the Falls reported, "that they met with the Indians, and made a full agreement with them, with Nimhammoe, for one tract of land adjoining the division line, lying on both sides of the Raritan river; also, with Coponnockous for another tract of land, lying between the purchase made by Adlorde Bonde and the bounds of the land belonging to Nimhammoe, fronting upon Delaware river."

At a meeting of the council of proprietors held at Burlington on the 28th, application was made by many of the proprietors of land that they might be allowed a third dividend or taking up of land in proportion to their particular and respective rights in the province, notice was thereupon ordered to be given that a purchase had been made of lands situate above the Falls of Delaware, and requesting all proprietors who were concerned in the same, or expected to receive benefit thereby, to meet with the council at Burlington, on the 19th day of July next, in order to receive more particular information upon said subject, and concerning said purchase, and upon what terms and conditions it was made, and to deposit their respective proportions of said purchase, and all charges accruing thereby.

In accordance with the above order, the council of proprietors met again on the 19th of July. Present, Samuel Jennings, Thomas Gardner, George Deacon, Christopher Wetheril·, John Hugg, Isaac Sharp, and John Reading, the president being absent.

It was ordered that the proprietors be informed—

First. That the council had made two Indian purchases, amounting to, according to their best computation, the number of one hundred and fifty thousand acres, at the least, the cost whereof to the Indians, with other incidental charges, will amount to about the sum of seven hundred pounds.

Second. That it is the design of the said council to give public notice to the proprietors in England and elsewhere, what purchase is already made, of the opportunity of purchasing more lands that may be sufficient to allow the number of five thousand acres for each dividend to a propriety, and of the cost thereof, which, by as near an estimation as they could make, will be about twenty-four pounds propriety for each dividend, and that if the said proprietors will appoint their agents, and defray their proportionable part of the charges on or before the 20th day of July, 1704, that then they shall receive their respective rights, after the same method that the rest of the proprietors do, at any time after the 18th of October, 1704.

Third. But if the said absent proprietors shall neglect or refuse to pay their parts of the said charge, then that the said Indian purchase already made, shall be taken up by such proprietory residents in these parts that shall deposit their respective parts of the said purchase, which at five thousand for the dividend to a propriety, will amount to about thirty proprieties, which we judge will nearly answer all the proprietors who are or have agents in these parts.

Fourth. It is expected that all such proprietors, who design to be interested for the Indian purchase, do in some short time, advance their particular parts of the said costs, in order to pay the Indians off, according to agreement made with them. Jeremiah Basse, attorney to the West Jersey Society, made a purchase on their behalf, in 1693, of the lands between Cohansick creek and Maurice's river. Many other Indian purchases were before and afterwards made, from time to time, as the lands were wanted, in both East and West Jersey.

CHAPTER V.

1680—1703.

Settlement of the first, or Yorkshire tenth—Settlement of the second, or London tenth—The first carpenter that came to this country—John Kinsey—His account of the country—Thomas Hooten's account—Mahlon Stacy's account—West New Jersey—First Assembly.

Having traveled through the country and viewed the land, the Yorkshire commissioners, Joseph Helmsley, William Emley, and Robert Stacy, on behalf of the first purchasers, chose from the Falls of Delaware down, which was hence called the first tenth. The London commissioners, John Penforde, Thomas Olive, Daniel Wills, and Benjamin Scott, on behalf of the ten London proprietors, chose at Arwaumus, (in and about where the city of Gloucester now is;) this was called the second tenth.

In order to begin a settlement there, Olive sent up servants to cut hay for the cattle he had bought, but when the London commissioners found the others were likely to settle at such a distance, they told them if they would agree to settle near them, they would join in settling a town,* and that they should have the largest share, in consideration that they, (the Yorkshire commissioners,) had the best land in the woods. Being few, and the Indians numerous, they agreed to it.

The commissioners employed Richard Noble, a surveyor, who came in the first ship, to divide the spot.

After he had ascertained the main street, he divided the land

---

* In pursuance of the charter brought with them from England.

on each side into lots, those on the east among the Yorkshire proprietors, the other among the London proprietors.

In order to begin a settlement, ten lots of nine acres each, bounding on the west, were laid out; that done, some passengers from Wickaco, chiefly concerned in the Yorkshire tenth, arrived in the latter end of October.

The London commissioners also employed Noble to divide the part of the island yet unsurveyed, between the ten London proprietors, in the manner before mentioned.

The town thus laid out by mutual consent between the Yorkshire and London commissioners, was first called New Beverly, afterwards Bridlington, but was soon after changed to Burlington, its present name.

Some who came in the ship last mentioned and settled in the neighborhood of Burlington, were Thomas Olive, Daniel Wills, William Peachy, William Clayton, John Crips, Thomas Harding, Thomas Nositer, Thomas Fairnsworth, Morgan Drewet, William Pennton, Henry Jenings, William Hibes, Samuel Lovett, John Woolston, William Woodmancy, Christopher Saunders, and Robert Powell.

John Wilkinson and William Perkins, were likewise with their families passengers, but died on the voyage. Perkins was early in life convinced of the principles of the Quakers. He was from Leicestershire, and was in the fifty-second year of his age when he started with his wife and four children and some servants for this country.

There also came over a man by the name of Marshall, a carpenter by trade, whom they found particularly serviceable in fitting up the habitations of the new comers, but it was late in the fall when they arrived, and the winter was much spent before they had commenced their habitations; during which time they lived in wigwams, built after the manner of the Indians. They were supplied with Indian corn and venison by the natives. These people were not much then corrupted with strong drinks, and in their general conduct they proved themselves very friendly, and rendered every assistance in their power to the English.

They were told that the English sold them the small-pox in

their matchcoats.* This distemper was among them, and a company getting together to consult about it, one of their chiefs said: "In my grandfather's time the small-pox came. In my father's time the small-pox came; and now in my time is the small-pox come." Then stretching his hands towards the skies, said: "It came from thence." To this the rest assented.

Having traced this ship's company into winter quarters, the next in course was the Willing Mind, John Newcomb, comman-

---

* Thomas Budd, who owned a share of a propriety in West Jersey, and was ancestor to a large family there, arrived at Burlington in 1768, in a pamphlet describing the country about nine or ten years afterwards, says:

"The Indians told us in a conference at Burlington shortly after we came into the country, that they were advised to make war on us, and cut us off while we were but few, for that we sold them the small-pox with the matchcoats they had bought of us, which caused our people to be in fears and jealousies concerning them. Therefore, we sent for the Indian Kings to speak with them, who, with many more Indians came to Burlington where we had a conference with them about the matter. We told them we came amongst them by their own consent, and had bought the land of them, for which we had honestly paid them, and for what commodities we had bought at any time of them, we had paid them for, and had been just to them, and had been from the time of our first coming, very kind and respectful to them; therefore, we knew no reason that they had to make war on us, to which one of them, in behalf of the rest, made this speech in answer: 'Our young men may speak such words as we do not like nor approve of, and we cannot help that; and some of your young men may speak such words as you do not like, and you cannot help that. We are your brothers, and intend to live like brothers with you. We have no mind to have war, for when we have war, we are only skin and bones; the meat that we eat doth not do us good; we always are in fear; we have not the benefit of the sun to shine on us; we hide us in holes and corners; we are minded to live in peace. If we intend at any time to make war upon you, we will let you know of it, and the reasons why we make war with you; and if you make us satisfaction for the injury done us, for which the war was intended, then we will not make war on you; and if you intend at any time to make war on us, we would have you let us know of it, and the reason; and then if we do not make satisfaction for the injury done unto you, then you may make war on us; otherwise you ought not to do it. You are our brothers, and we are willing to live like brothers with you. We are willing to have a broad path for you and us to walk in, and if an Indian is asleep in this path, the Englishman shall pass by and do him no harm; and if an Englishman is asleep in this path, the Indian shall pass him by and say: 'He is an Englishman; he is asleep; let him alone; he loves to

der. She arrived from London in November, and dropped anchor at Elsingburg. She brought about sixty or seventy passengers. Some of these settled at Salem, others at Burlington. Among the former were James Nevill, Henry Salter, and George Deacon, with their families.

In this year, also, arrived the fly-boat Martha, of Burlington, (Yorkshire), sailed from Hull the latter end of summer, with one hundred and fourteen passengers, designed to settle the Yorkshire tenth.

---

sleep. It shall be a plain path. There must not be in this path a stump to hurt our feet. And as to the small-pox, it was once in my grandfather's time, and it could not be the English that could send it to us then, there being no English in the country. And it was once in my father's time, they could not send it us then neither; and now it is in my time, I do not believe that they have sent it us now. I do believe it is the man above that hath sent it us.'

"Some are apt to ask, how we can propose safely to live amongst such a heathen people as the Indians, whose principles and practices leads them to war and bloodshed, and ours, on the contrary, to love enemies? I answer, that we settled by the Indians' consent and good liking, and bought the land of them that we settle on, which they conveyed to us by deeds under their hands and seals, and also submitted to several articles of agreement with us, not to do us any injury. But if it should so happen that any of their people at any time should injure or do harm to any of us, then they to make us satisfaction for the injury done; therefore, if they break these covenants and agreements, then in consequence of them, they may be proceeded against as other offenders, viz.: to be kept in subjection to the magistrate's power, in whose hand the sword of justice is committed, to be used by him for the punishment of evil doers, and praise of them that do well.

"Therefore, I do believe it to be both lawful and expedient to bring offenders to justice by the power of the magistrate's sword, which is not to be used in vain, but may be used against such as raise rebellion and insurrections against the government of the country, be they Christians or Indians, (now that these have so far agreed to abide by the laws of civil government,) otherwise, it is in vain for us to pretend to magistracy or government, it being that which we own to be lawful, both in principle and practice. The Indians have been very serviceable to us by selling us venison, Indian corn, pease and beans, fish and fowl, buck-skins, beaver, otter, and other skins and furs. The men hunt, fish, and fowl, and the women plant the corn and carry burthens. There are many of them of a good understanding, considering their education, and in their public meetings of business they have excellent order, one speaking after another; and while one is speaking all the rest keep silent and do not so much as whisper one to the other.

Some masters of families who came in this ship were, Thomas Wright, William Goforth, John Lynam, Edward Leason, William Black, Richard Dungworth, George Miles, William Wood, Thomas Schooley, Richard Harrison, Thomas Hooten, Samuel Saylor, Marmaduke Horsman, William Oxley, William Ley, and Nathaniel Luke, the families of Robert Stacy and Samuel Odas; Thomas Ellis and John Batts,* servants, sent by George Hutchinson, also came in this ship.

"We had several meetings with them. One was in order to put down the sale of rum, brandy, and other strong liquors to them, they being a people that have not government of themselves so as to drink in moderation.

"At this time there were eight kings, (one of them was Okanickon, a noted friend to the English,) and many other Indians. The kings sat on a form, and we on another over against them. They had prepared four belts of wampum, (so their current money is called, being black and white beads, made of a fish-shell,) to give us as seals of the covenant they made with us. One of the kings, by the consent and appointment of the rest, stood up and made the following speech:

"The strong liquor was first sold to us by the Dutch, and they were blind, they had no eyes; they did not see that it was for our hurt. The next people that came among us were the Swedes, who continued the sale of those strong liquors among us; they were also blind, they had no eyes, they did not see it to be hurtful to us to drink it, although we know it to be hurtful to us. But if people will sell it to us, we are so in love with it that we cannot forbear it. When we drink it, it makes us mad. We do not know what we do. We then abuse one another. We throw each other into the fire. Seven score of our people have been killed by reason of the drinking of it, since the time it was first sold us. Those people that sell it are blind—they have no eyes. But now there is a people come to live amongst us that have eyes. They see it to be for our hurt, and we know it to be for our hurt. They are willing to deny themselves the profit of it for our good.

"These people have eyes. We are glad such a people have come amongst us. We must put it down by mutual consent. The cask must be sealed up. It must be made fast. It must not leak by day nor by night—in the light nor in the dark; and we give you these four belts of wampum, which we would have you lay up safe, and keep by you, to be witnesses of this agreement that we make with you, and we would have you tell your children that these four belts of wampum are given you to be witnesses betwixt us and you of this agreement."

* Many that came over as servants succeeded better than some that bought estates. The first, inured to industry and the ways of the country, became wealthy; while the others, obliged to spend what they had in the difficulties

In one of these ships, about this time, arrived John Kinsey, then a young man. His father was one of the commissioners previously mentioned, but dying on his arrival, the care of the family fell to the son. He was afterwards a man of distinction in several public stations, and his son after him, of the same name, held many public offices, and was at one time chief justice of Pennsylvania. There were three of the family bearing the name of John.

Those of the settlers who came here were so much pleased with the country, that they wrote glowing descriptions of it to their friends at home.

John Crips, in writing to Henry Stacy, gave the following account:

"From BURLINGTON, in Delaware river, the 26th of the 8th month, 1677.

"DEAR FRIEND:

"Through the mercy of God, we are safely arrived at New Jersey. My wife and all mine are very well, and we have our healths rather better here than we had in England. Indeed the country is so good, that I do not see how it can reasonably be found fault with. As far as I perceive, all the things we heard of it in England are very true, and I wish that many people (that are in straits) in England, were here.

"Here is good land enough lies void, would serve many thousands of families, and we think if they cannot live here, they can hardly live in any place in the world. But we do not desire to persuade any to come, but such as are well satisfied in their own minds. A town lot is laid out for us in Burlington, which is a convenient place for trade. It is about one hundred and fifty miles up the river Delaware. The country and air seems to be very agreeable to our bodies, and we have very good stomachs to our victuals.

"Here is plenty of provision in the country. Plenty of fish and fowl, and good venison very plentiful, and much better than ours in England, for it eats not so dry, but is full of gravy, like

---

of first improvements, and others living too much on their original stock, for want of sufficient care to improve their estates, had, in many instances, dwindled to indigency and want.

fat young beef. You that come after us need not fear the trouble that we have had, for now here is land divided ready against you come. The Indians are very loving to us, except here and there one, when they have gotten strong liquors in their heads, which they now greatly love. But for the country in short, I like it very well, and I do believe that this river of Delaware is as good a river as most in the world. It exceeds the river Thames by many degrees.

"Here is a town laid out for twenty proprieties, and a straight line drawn from the river side up the land, which is to be the main street, and a market place about the middle. The Yorkshire ten proprietors are to build on one side, and the London ten on the other side; and they have ordered one street to be made along the river side, which is not divided with the rest, but in small lots by itself, and every one that hath any part in a propriety is to have his share in it. The town lots for every propriety will be about ten or eleven acres, which is only for a house, orchard, and gardens, and the corn and pasture grounds is to be laid out in great quantities.

"I am thy loving friend,
"JOHN CRIPS."

Thomas Hooten wrote to his wife under date of 29th of 8th month, 1677.

"MY DEAR:

"I am this present at the town called Burlington, where our land is. It is ordered to be a town for the ten Yorkshire and ten London proprietors. I like the place well. Our lot is the second next the water side. It's like to be a healthful place, and very pleasant to live in. I came hither yesterday, being the 28th of October, with some friends that were going to New York. I am to be at Thomas Olive's house till I can provide better for myself.

"I intend to build a house and get some corn into the ground, and I know not how to write concerning thy coming, or not coming hither. The place I like very well, and believe that we may live here very well. But if it be not made free—I mean as to the customs and government*—then it will not be so well, and may hinder many that have desires to come.

"But if those two things be cleared, thou may take thy opportunity of coming this summer.

"THOMAS HOOTEN."

William Clark wrote to William Penn, Gawen Lawrie, and Edward Byllinge, the proprietors, in the same glowing terms of the new province. His letter was dated New Jersey, 20th 2d month, 1678.

John Crips wrote to his brother and sister under date of Burlington, in New Jersey, upon the river Delaware, the 19th of 4th month, called June, 1678. He also gave a glowing account of the State, in which we find the following passage:

"And this I can truly tell you, if I were now in England with you (and which I should be very glad to see), yet if all I had in the world would but bring me hither, I would freely leave you and my native country, and come to New Jersey again. It's reported the water is not so good as in England. I do not remember that ever I tasted better water in any part of England than in the springs of this place do yield, of which is made very good beer and ale; and here is also wine and cider."

In the 10th month, O. S., 1678, arrived the ship Shield from Hull, Daniel Towers, commander. She dropped anchor at Burlington, and was the first ship that came so far up the Delaware.

Against Coaquanock,† being a bold shore, she went so near in turning that part of her rigging struck the trees. Some on board then remarked that it was a fine place for a town. A fresh gale brought the ship to Burlington. She moored to a tree, and the next morning the people came on shore on the ice,

---

* The customs were those imposed at New Castle upon all comers. The government was at this time administered by virtue of Governor Andross' commission, both which were unexpected and disagreeable, but these objections were soon removed.

† The Indian name for the place where Philadelphia now stands.

so hard had the river suddenly frozen. In her came William Emley, the second time, with his wife and two children, one born on the passage; also two men and two women servants; Mahlon Stacy, his wife, children, and several servants, men and women; Thomas Lambert, his wife, children, and several men and women servants; John Lambert and servant; Thomas Revell, his wife, children, and servants; Godfrey Hancock, his wife, children, and servants; Thomas Potts, his wife and children; John Wood and four children; Thomas Wood, his wife and children; Robert Murfin, his wife and two children; Robert Schooley, his wife and children; James Pharo, his wife and children; Susannah Fairnsworth, her children and two servants; Richard Tattersall, his wife and children; Godfrey Newbold, John Dewsbury, Richard Green, Peter Fretwell, John Fretwell, John Newbold, one Barnes, a merchant from Hull; Francis Barwick, George Parks, George Hill, John Heyres, and a number more.

This same year there also arrived in the province a ship from London, which brought over John Denn, Thomas Kent, John Hollinshead, with their families; William Hewlings, Abraham Hewlings, Jonathan Eldridge, John Petty, Thomas Kirley, and others. Some of these settled at Salem and others at Burlington. About the same time, as well as several years afterwards, the following settlers arrived from England, and settled at Burlington: John Butcher, William Butcher, Henry Grubb, William Brightwin, Thomas Gardner, John Budd, John Bourten, Seth Smith, Walter Pumphrey, Thomas Ellis, James Satterthwaite, Richard Arnold, John Woolman, John Stacy, Thomas Eves, Benjamin Duffeld, John Payne, Samuel Cleft, William Cooper, John Shinn, William Biles, John Skein, John Warrel, Anthony Morris, Samuel Bunting, Charles Read, Francis Collins, Thomas Mathews, Christopher Wetherill, John Dewsberry, John Day, Richard Basnett, John Antrom, William Biddle, Samuel Furnace, John Ladd, Thomas Raper, Roger Higgins, and Thomas Wood.

We have mentioned in a previous chapter the conquest by the Dutch of New York and New Jersey, and the accounts furnished of that affair, though sufficient to authenticate the facts, are defective. Sir George Carteret, in a public declaration to the inhabitants, under date of July 31st, 1674, asserts it positively. The author of the history of New York, on pages 29, 30, 31, says: "A few Dutch ships arrived the 30th of July, 1673, under Staten Island, a few miles distant from the city of New York. John Manning, captain of an independent company, had at that time the command of the fort, and by a messenger sent down to the squadron, treacherously made his peace with the enemy. On that very day the Dutch ships came up, moored under the fort, landed their men, and entered the garrison without giving or receiving a shot. This was in the ship Shield. A council of war was afterwards held at the Stadt House, at which were present Cornelius Evertse, Jun., and Jacob Benks, commodores, and Anthony Colne, Nicholas Boes, Abraham Ferd, Van Zell, captains. All the magistrates and constables from East Jersey, Long Island, Esopus, and Albany were immediately summoned to New York, and the major part of them swore allegiance to the States General and the prince of Orange. Colonel Lovelace was ordered to depart the province, but afterwards obtained leave to return to England with Commodore Benkes. It has often been insisted upon that this conquest did not extend to the whole province of New Jersey, but upon what foundation we are unable to discover. From the Dutch records it appears that deputies were sent by the people inhabiting the country, even so far westward as Delaware river, who, in the name of their principles, made a declaration of their submission, in return for which, certain privileges were granted them, and three judicatories erected at Niewer Amstel, Upland, and Hoarkill. The Dutch governor enjoyed his office but a very short time, for on the 9th of February, 1674, the treaty of peace between England and the States General was signed at Westminster; the sixth article of which restored this country to England."

In 1673, New York and New Jersey were yielded to King Charles II. by the general article of the treaty of peace.

It was to prevent any disputes that might arise upon a plea of the property thus alienated from the first purchasers, that the King, by his letters patent, bearing date June 29th, 1674, granted unto the Duke of York, his heirs and assigns, the several tracts of land in America, which by the former letters patent had been granted to him, and of which New Jersey formed a part. In this year, upon the application of the assigns of Lord Berkeley, the Duke made them a new grant of West New Jersey, and in like manner by an instrument bearing date October 10th, he granted the eastern moiety of New Jersey to the grandson of Sir George Carteret.

We have previously introduced a few letters from some of the first settlers of New Jersey, containing accounts of their several situations, and general sentiments of the country, its general fertility, and healthfulness of its climate. More might be added, but the following is all we propose to introduce in this place.

Mahlon Stacy wrote to his brother Revell and others, in England, under date of 26th of the 4th month, 1680.

"But now a word or two of these strange reports you have of us and our country. I affirm they are not true, and fear they were spoke from a spirit of envy.

"It is a country that produceth all things for the support and sustenance of man, in a plentiful manner. If it were not so, I should be ashamed of what I have before written, but I can stand, having truth on my side, against and before the face of all gainsayers and evil spies. I have travelled through most of the places that are settled, and some that are not, and in every place I find the country very apt to answer the expectation of the diligent.

"I have seen orchards laden with fruit to admiration, their very limbs torn to pieces with the weight, and most delicious to to the taste, and lovely to behold.

"I have seen an apple tree from a pipin kernel, yield a barrel of curious cider, and peaches in such plenty that some people took their carts a peach gathering, I could not but smile at the conceit of it. They are a very delicate fruit, and hang almost like our onions that are tied on ropes.

"I have seen and known this summer, forty bushels of bold wheat of one bushel sown, and many more such instances I could bring, which would be too tedious here to mention. We have, from the time called May until Michaelmas, great store of good wild fruits, as strawberries, cranberries, and hurtleberries, which are like our bilberries in England, but far sweeter. They are very wholesome fruits. The cranberries, much like cherries for color and bigness, which may be kept till the fruit come in again. An excellent sauce is made of them for venison, turkeys, and other great fowl, and they are better to make tarts than either gooseberries or cherries. We have them brought to our houses by the Indians, in great plenty. My brother Robert had as many cherries this year as would have loaded several carts. It is my judgment, by what I have observed, that fruit trees in this country destroy themselves by the very weight of their fruit. As for venison and fowls, we have great plenty. We have brought home to our houses, by the Indians, seven or eight fat bucks of a day, and sometimes put by as many, having no occasion for them; and fish in their season, very plenteous. My cousin Revell and I, with some of my men, went last third month into the river to catch herrings, for at that time they came in great shoals into the shallows. We had neither rod nor net, but after the Indian fashion, made a round pinfold, about two yards over, and a foot high, but left a gap for the fish to go in at, and made a bush to lay in the gap to keep the fish in; and when that was done, we took two long birches and tied their tops together, and went about a stone's cast above our said pinfold. Then hauling these birches' boughs down the stream, where we drove thousands before us; but so many got into our trap as it would hold, and then we began to haul them on shore as fast as three or four of us could, by two or three at a time; and after this manner, in half an hour, we could have filled a three bushel sack of as good and large herrings as I ever saw. And as to beef and pork, here is great plenty of it, and cheap. And also good sheep. The common grass of this country feeds beef very fat. I have killed two this year, and therefore I have reason to know it; besides, I have seen this fall, in Burlington, killed, eight or nine fat oxen and cows on a market day, and all very fat. And though I speak of herrings only, lest any should think we have little other sorts, we have great plenty of most sorts of fish that ever I saw in England; besides several other sorts that are not known there, as rocks, cat-fish, shads, sheeps-head, sturgeons, and fowls plenty, as ducks, geese, turkies, pheasants, partridges, and many other sorts that I cannot remember, and would be too tedious to mention. Indeed, the country, take it as a wilderness, is a brave country, though no place will please all.

"But some will be ready to say, he writes of conveniences, but not of inconveniences. In answer to these, I honestly declare, there is some barren land, as (I suppose) there is in most places of the world, and more wood than some would have upon their lands. Neither will the country produce corn without labor, nor cattle be got without something to buy them, nor bread with idleness, else it would be a brave country indeed; and I question not but all would then give it a good word. For my part, I like it so well, I never had the least thought of returning to England, except on the account of trade.

"MAHLON STACY."

He wrote another letter to William Cook, of Sheffield, dated from the Falls of Delaware,* in West New Jersey, the 26th of the 4th month, 1680, in which he says: "This is a most brave place, whatever envy or evil spies may speak of it. I could wish you all here. Burlington will be a place of trade quickly, for here is a way of trade." After speaking of ships he had fitted out and sent to Barbadoes and the West Indies, he winds up by saying, "I never repented my coming hither, nor yet remembered thy arguments and outcry against New Jersey, with regret. I live as well to my content, and in as great plenty as I ever did, and in a far more likely way to get an estate. Though I hear some have thought I was too large in my former, I affirm it to be true, having seen more with mine eyes in this time since, than ever yet I wrote of."†

---

* Trenton.

† The inhabitants of West Jersey had hitherto either pounded their corn or ground it with hand mills. But about this time Thomas Olive had built his water mill on his plantation, near Rankokus creek, and Stacy had finished his mill at Trenton, on the Assanpink, where the paper mill of Harry McCall now stands. This mill of Stacy's was rebuilt of stone, and continued good until 1843, when it was destroyed by a flood in the Assanpink. These two were the only mills that supplied the country round for several years.

Daniel Wills, in writing to William Biddle, of Bishop's-gate street, London,* from Burlington, under date of 6th of 11th month, 1679-80, says:

"DEAR FRIEND:

"Let every man write according to his judgment, and this is mine concerning this country. I do really believe it to be as good a country as any man need to dwell in. And it is much better than I expected every way for land, I will assure thee. Here is as good by the judgment of men as any in England, and for my part I like the country so well, and it is so pleasant to me that if I had a good estate in land in England, I should not come to live upon it, for through industry here will be all things produced that are necessary for a family as in England, and far more easy, I am satisfied."

Though the passengers who had already come to West Jersey were well satisfied with the country, things in general being found beyond their expectations, yet they labored under one great inconvenience. The governor of New York had at a very early day imposed a tax of ten per cent. on all goods imported into the province, and on exports even something of the kind still existed; five per cent. being demanded of the settlers upon their arrival, or afterwards, at the pleasure of the officer, and that not according to the cost of the goods, but upon the invoices, as shipped in England.

This was an arbitrary act, as neither West Jersey nor the Hoarkill was legally under his jurisdiction.

The settlers bore it patiently till about 1680, although from the first they complained of it, yet by the interposition of their friends in England, the wrong was redressed. Complaint was made to the Duke of York, who referred the matter to the council, where it rested for some time, but at last by the good offices of William Penn, George Hutchinson and others, it was decided in favor of the settlers. Sir John Werden, on behalf of the Duke, wrote to have it discontinued.

---

* William and Sarah Biddle, with their family, removed to West Jersey in the summer of 1681.

The arguments used against this duty or impost were as follows:

"To those of the Duke's commissioners whom he has ordered to hear and make report to him concerning the customs demanded in New West Jersey, in America, by his governor of New York.

"They set forth—

"1st. The fact of the grant of a tract of land in America, by the King, to the Duke of York, consisting of several Indian countries, with power and authority to make laws, and to govern and preserve the territory when planted; provided, the said statutes, ordinances, and proceedings be not contrary, but as near as may be, agreeable to the laws, statutes, and government of the realm of England. It also gave to the Duke of York, whom he terms his dearest brother, his heirs and assigns, authority to make, ordain, and establish all manner of orders, laws, directions, instruments, and forms of government, and magistrates fit and necessary for the territory aforesaid, but with this limitation, so always as the same be not contrary to the laws and statutes of this our realm of England, but as near as may be, agreeable thereto.

"2d. By virtue of this grant the Duke of York for a competent sum of money, (paid by the Lord John Berkeley and Sir George Carteret,) granted, and sold to them, a tract of land, now called by the name of New Cæsaria, or New Jersey, in as ample a manner as it was granted by the King to the Duke."

Under this, they bought the half that belonged to Lord Berkeley for a valuable consideration, and in the conveyance he made them, powers of government were expressly granted, for under no other considerations could they have been induced to purchase, for the reason, that the government of any place, to all prudent men, is more inviting than the soil; because even though the land was good, without good laws, it would not be desirable, and unless they could assure the people of an easy, free, and safe government, both with respect to their spiritual and worldly property, an uninterrupted liberty of conscience, and an inviolable possession of their civil rights and freedoms, by a just and wise government, a mere wilderness would be no encouragement, for it were a madness to leave a free, good, and improved country to plant in a wilderness, and there adventure many thousand pounds, to give an absolute title to another person to tax us at will and pleasure. This single consideration, we hope, will excuse our desire of the government, not asserted for the sake of power, but safety, and not only for ourselves, but others, that the plantation might be encouraged.

3d. That Lord Berkeley and Sir George Carteret, considering how much freedom invites, that they might encourage people to transport themselves into these parts, made and divulged certain concessions containing a model of government. Upon these several went and planted; the country was thus possessed, and the government uninterruptedly administered by said Lord Berkeley and Sir George Carteret, or their deputy, for several years, during which no custom was demanded.

4th. They dealt with said Lord Berkeley upon the faith of these concessions, and the presumption that neither he nor Sir George Carteret would attempt to carry out anything they had not power to do, much less, that they or either of them would pretend to sell a power they never had, since that would not only be a cheat to the people that dealt with them for it, but a high affront to the Duke.

5th. The half of New Cæsaria thus bought of Lord Berkeley, they had disposed of part of their interest to several hundreds of people, honest and industrious, who had come hither with their household goods, and such tools as were requisite for planters to have. Upon their arrival they are saluted with a demand of custom of five per cent., and that not as the goods may be there worth, but according to the invoice as they cost before shipped in England, nor did they take them as they came, but at pick and choose, with some severe language to boot.

"This is our grievance, and for this we made our application to have speedy redress, not as a burden only, with respect to the quantum or the way of levying it, but as a wrong; for we complain of a wrong done us, and ask yet with modesty, *quo jure?* Tell us the title by what right or law are we thus used, that may a little mitigate our pain? Your answer hitherto has been this. That it was a conquered country, and that the King being the conqueror, he has power to make laws, raise money, &c., and that this power *jure regale*, the King hath vested in the Duke, and by that right and sovereignty, the Duke demands that custom we complain of. But suppose the King were an absolute conqueror in the case depending, doth his power extend equally over his own English people as over the conquered? Are not they some of the letters that make up the word conqueror? Did Alexander conquer alone, or Cæsar beat by himself? No! Shall their armies of countrymen and natives lie at the same mercy as the vanquished, and be exposed to the same will and power with their captive enemies?

"Natural right and humane prudence oppose such doctrine all the world over; for what is it but to say that people, free by law under their prince at home, are at his mercy in the plantations abroad; and why? because he is a conqueror there, but still at the hazard of the lives of his own people, and at the cost and charge of the public.

"To conclude this point, we humbly say, that we have not lost any part of our liberty by leaving our country; for we leave not our King nor our government by quitting our soil, but we transplant to a place given by the same King, with express limitation to erect no polity contrary to the same established government, but as near as may be to it."

They insisted upon the equity of their case—

"1st. This very tax of five per cent. is a thing not to be found in the Duke's conveyances.

"2d. New Jersey never paid custom before last peace, and that peace reinvests every proprietor.

"This tax, in plain English, is under another name, paying for the same thing over twice. The lands were bought by us for a valuable consideration here, and is now purchased again of the natives there, too.

"3d. Custom, in all governments in the world, is laid upon trade, but this upon planting is unprecedented."

This custom was taken off as appears by a letter from Samuel Jennings,[*] directed to William Penn, Edward Byllinge, or Gawen Lawrie, under date of the 17th of October, 1680.

---

[*] He, with his family, removed from Coles' Hill, on the upper side of Bucks county, about the third month, 1680.

The western part of New Jersey had now become populous, by the accession of many settlers. Samuel Jennings, arrived the year before, and received a commission from Byllinge to be his deputy. He called an assembly, and with them agreed upon certain fundamental principles of government.

They enacted that there should be a general free assembly for the province, to meet yearly, at a certain day, chosen by the free people of the province, to consider the affairs of the province and make and ordain laws for the good government and prosperity of the free people of the province.

The governor, with the consent of his council, could convene them whenever he might think proper, to consider matters relating to the province.

He was required, with as little delay as the case admitted of, to sign and confirm all acts of the assembly.

He or his council, or any of them, was not to make or raise war at any time, under any pretence whatever, or to raise any military forces within the said province, without the consent and act of the general free assembly.

They were not to make or enact any laws for the province without the consent, act, and concurrence of the general assembly; and in case of violation of the same, if found guilty upon legal conviction, they were to be deemed and taken for enemies to the free people of the province, and the acts were to be void.

The general assembly were not to be prorogued or dissolved before the expiration of one whole year from the day of election, without their own free consent.

They were not to levy or raise any sum or sums of money, or any other tax, without the act, consent, and concurrence of the general assembly.

All officers of State or trust were to be nominated and elected by the general free assembly, and they were to be accountable to that body, or to such as they should appoint.

They were forbidden to send ambassadors, or make treaties, or enter into alliances, upon the public account of the province, without the consent of the assembly.

The general assembly were not to give to the governor any tax or custom for a longer time than for one year.

The liberty of conscience in matters of faith and worship towards God, was granted to all people within the province who should live peaceably and quietly therein; and no one was to be rendered incapable of office in respect to his faith and worship.

Upon the acceptance by the governor, and performance of the proposals therein expressed, the general assembly, proprietors and freeholders of the province of West Jersey, were to accept Samuel Jennings as deputy governor.

These fundamentals, as they were termed, were signed by Samuel Jennings, deputy governor; and Thomas Olive, speaker.

This assembly sat from the 21st to the 28th of November, and passed thirty-six laws, besides the above. Many of these laws were repealed a few years afterwards. Some of them were in substance, as follows:

That it should be the business of the governor and commissioners to see that all courts executed their offices, and to punish such officers as should violate the laws; that lands legally taken up and held, planted and possessed seven years, should not be subject to alteration; that all officers of trust should subscribe to do equal right and justice; that no person should be condemned or hurt, without a trial of twelve men, and that in criminal cases, the party arraigned to except against thirty-five or more upon valid reasons; that in every court, three justices, or commissioners, at least, to sit and assist the jury in cases of law, and pronounce the judgment of the jury; that false witnesses be fined, and disabled from being admitted in evidence, or into any public office in the province; that persons prosecuting for private wrong (murder, treason, and theft excepted,) might remit the penalty or punishment, either before or after condemnation; that juries should be summoned by the sheriff, and none be compelled to see an attorney to plead his cause; that all wills should be first proved and registered, and then duly performed; that upon persons dying intestate, and leaving a wife and child, or children, the governor and commissioners for the time being, were to take security, that the estate should be duly administered, and the administrator to secure two-thirds for the child or children, the other to the widow; where there was no children, one moiety or half the estate was to go to the next of kin, the other half to the widow; always provided, such estate exceed one hundred pounds, otherwise the widow to have the whole; and in cases of leaving children and no provision, the charge of bringing them up to be paid out of the public stock; that felons should make restitution four-fold, or as twelve of the neighborhood should determine; and such as hurt or abuse the person of any, be punished according to the nature of the offence; that whosoever presumed, directly or indirectly, to sell any strong liquors to any Indian or Indians, should forfeit for every such offense, the sum of three pounds; that ten men from Burlington, and ten from Salem, should be appointed to lay out and clear a road from Burlington to Salem, at the public expense; that two hundred pounds should be equally levied and appropriated for the charges of government, upon the several tenths, twenty pounds each; every man to be assessed according to his estate, and all handicrafts, merchants, and others, at the discretion of the assessors. Persons thinking themselves aggrieved had the liberty of appealing to the commissioners of the tenth they belonged to.

Having agreed upon these and other laws, the commissioners next fixed the method of regulating lands.

That the surveyor was to measure of the river Delaware, beginning at Assunpink creek, and from thence down to Cape May; that each and every tenth, or ten proprieties, shall have their proportion of front to the river Delaware, and so far back into the woods as will make or contain sixty-four thousand acres for their first settlement, and for the sub-dividing the Yorkshire and London two-tenths.

To allow three thousand and two hundred acres where the parties concerned please to choose it within their own tenth, to be taken up according to the following rules: One eighth part of a propriety, and so for smaller parts, to have their full proportion of the lands in one place, and greater purchases or shares not to exceed five hundred acres, to one settlement.

That all lands so taken up and surveyed shall be seated within six months after it is so taken up; and if not taken up and seated within the said time, then such choice and survey to be void, and the same lands shall be free for any other purchaser to take up, provided, they shall seat it within one month after it is so taken up.

No person was allowed to take up lands on both sides of the creek, except by consent of the commissioners, for good cause.

No person was allowed to have more than forty perches front on the river or navigable creek, for each and every hundred acres, except it fall upon a point so that it cannot be otherwise avoided, which was to be left to the commissioners.

All lands were to be laid out on straight lines, in order that no vacancies may be left, but that they be joined one seat to another, except the commissioners should order it otherwise.

All persons were to take their just proportion of meadow.

All persons already located were to have liberty to make their settlement their choice.

Every proprietor was to have four hundred acres to his propriety, and so proportionably to lesser quantities for his town lot, over and above his three thousand two hundred acres, which may be taken anywhere within his own tenth, either within or without the town bounds.

No person who had taken up a town lot, had liberty to leave it, and take a lot elsewhere; but he was required to keep the lot he had taken up as his town lot.

Thomas Wright was required to keep his settlement of four hundred acres.

No purchaser was allowed to take up more land within his town bounds than belongs to his town bounds by virtue of his purchase.

No person or persons, (who were not purchasers to whom town lot or lots were given,) were allowed to dispose of, or sell his or their lots of land from their house or houses, and in case they should do so, such sale was void, and the lots were forfeited to the use of the town of Burlington, to be disposed of at the discretion of the commissioners.

No person was allowed to take up any without special order from two or more of the commissioners.

All settlements not agreeable to the commissioners and the aforesaid rules and regulations, were liable to the regulations aforesaid.

The proprietors yet remaining in England were to be notified that it was necessary for the speedy settlement of the province, and for the interest of all concerned therein, to allow to every propriety three thousand two hundred acres, for their first choice, and in case many people should come and desire to settle, they reserved liberty to take up so much land more, not exceeding five thousand two hundred acres; provided that none should take up any proportion of land but as they should settle it.

All public highways were to be set forth at the discretion of the commissioners, in or through any lands taken up, or to be taken up, allowing the owners thereof reasonable satisfaction, at the discretion of the commissioners.

The rules and methods hereby agreed upon were not to make void or disannul any settlements heretofore made in the Yorkshire tenth, who had seated according to a former agreement, who had not taken up more than fifty perches for each hundred acres on the river and navigable creek, and having kept their due breadth and bounds from the same.

These articles were signed and sealed the 5th of December, 1681, by Samuel Jennings, governor; Thomas Olive, Thomas Budd, Robert Stacy, Benjamin Scott, Thomas Gardiner, Daniel Wills, Mahlon Stacy, Thomas Lambert.*

Those who had taken up any lands within the first and second tenth in the province, were required to bring in their deeds and titles to Benjamin Scott and Robert Stacy, Thomas Budd and Thomas Gardiner, on or before the 12th day of January, and all who should, after this date, take up lands within the first and second tenth, were to make application to the same parties, and to make oath that the said lands so taken up actually belonged to them; and the commissioners being satisfied of the same, were to order the surveyor to lay out and survey said lands, and to make return of the same at the next court held at Burlington, that it may be registered.

This was signed by Samuel Jennings, governor; Thomas Olive, Robert Stacy, Thomas Budd, Daniel Wills, Thomas Gardiner, and Benjamin Scott, and dated the 14th of the eleventh month, 1681.

---

* Thomas Lambert purchased and settled Lamberton, now the sixth ward of Trenton.

CHAPTER VI.

1681—1682.

Indian tribes—Modes of burial—Superstitions—Care of the sick—Care of their children—Marriageable ages—Marriage ceremonies—Representatives chosen by the proprietors—Laws passed by the governor—Council and assembly—Third and last grant of the Duke of York.

IT would be vain to undertake to give a particular account of all the different tribes or nations of Indians inhabiting these provinces before the Europeans came among them, there being probably a tribe for every ten or twenty miles, which were commonly described and distinguished by the name of creeks, or other noted places where they resided; thus, there were the Assunpink,* the Rankokas,† the Mingo,‡ the Andastaka, the

---

* Stony Creek, from its gravelly bottom.

† This was called Ankokas, as the Indians did not pronounce the R at all; they were also called Lamikas, or Chichequas, the latter of which was the proper name.

‡ Indian knowledge about the weather were received topics of conversation. Some of their maxims have been found as true as things of that kind generally are. If Jacob Taylor's intelligence be right, they also predicted. "A sachem of this tribe (he says) being observed to look at the great comet, which appeared the 1st of October, 1680, and asked what he thought was the meaning of that prodigious appearance, answered gravely: It signifies that we Indians shall melt away, and this country be inhabited by another people." How this Indian came by his knowledge, without the learned Whiston's astronomical tables, or whether he had any knowledge, is not so material. He will, however, be allowed as good a right to pretend to it, when the event is considered, as the other had in his conjecture concerning the cause of Noah's flood. This, at least, till the regularity of the comets' motions were better known.

Neshaminie, and the Shackamaxon Indians, and those about Burlington were called the Mantas, from the frogs which inhabited the creeks called Manta, or Mantua, in Gloucester; a large tribe resided there.

These and others were all of them distinguished from the Back Indians, who were a more warlike people, by the general name of the Leni Lenapes, or Delawares. The nations most noted from home, that sometimes inhabited New Jersey and the first settled parts of Pennsylvania, were the Naraticongs, on the north side of Raritan river; the Capitinasses, the Gacheos, the Munseys, the Pomptons, the Senecas, and the Maquaas.* This last was the most numerous and powerful. Different nations were frequently at war with each other, of which husbandmen sometimes find to this day remaining marks in their fields.

A little below the falls of Delaware, on the Jersey side, at a place opposite Point-no-point, in Pennsylvania, and several other places, were, until a few years back, banks that had been formerly thrown up for intrenchments against incursions of the neighboring Indians, who, in their canoes, used to go in warlike bodies from one province to another.

It was customary with the Indians of West Jersey, when they buried their dead, to put family utensils, bows and arrows, and sometimes money (wampum) into the grave with them, as tokens of their affection.

When a person of note died far away from the place of his residence, they would convey his bones to his domicil for burial, carrying out the practice of the patriarchs of old. They washed and perfumed their dead, painted the face, and followed to their last resting place the remains, in single or Indian file. Their dead was left in a sitting posture, and the grave was covered pyramidically; thus showing their origin from the Egyptians and other patriarchal countries.

They were careful in preserving and repairing the graves of the dead, and visited them in great solemnity. They were averse to being asked their opinion twice about the same thing.

---

* The Five Nations, before the sixth was added; but few of whom had their residence in New Jersey. They are supposed to have been sometimes, in fishing seasons, among the others here. They were called by the Dutch, Mahaknase.

They abounded in mirthfulness, observed with great care the roots and herbs that grew, and used them for the cure of all bodily diseases, both by outward and inward applications; besides which, they used sweating and the cold bath* for the cure of diseases.

They had an aversion to beards, and would not permit them to grow, but plucked the hair out by the roots. The hair of their heads was black, which they generally kept saturated with bear's grease, particularly the women, who tied it behind in a large knot, sometimes in a bag. They called persons and places by the names of remarkable things, or birds, or beasts and fish.

Thus: Pea-hala, a duck; Cau-hawuk, a goose; Quink-Quink, a tit; Pallupa, a buck; Shingas, a wild-cat; and they observed it as a rule, when the rattlesnake gave notice by his rattle before he approached, not to hurt him; but if he rattled after they had passed, they would immediately return and kill him.

They were very loving to one another; if several of them came to a Christian's house, and the master of it gave one of them victuals and none to the rest, he would divide it into equal shares among his companions. If the Christian † visited them, they would give them the first cut of their victuals; they would not eat the hollow of the thigh of anything they killed.‡ Their chief employment was hunting, fishing, and fowling, and making canoes, bowls, and other wooden and earthen ware, in all which they were, considering their means, very ingenious. They boiled their water in earthen bowls manufactured by themselves.

The chief business of the women was planting corn, parching or roasting it, pounding it into flour in mortars, or breaking it

---

* The mode was first to enclose the patient in a narrow cabin, in the middle of which was a red hot stone, frequently wet with water, producing a warm vapor. The patient, sufficiently wet with this and his own sweat, was hurried to the next creek or river, and plunged into it. This was repeated as often as was necessary, and sometimes great cures were performed. But this rude method at other times killed, notwithstanding the hardy nature of the patients, especially in the small pox and other European disorders.

† They called all white men Christians.

‡ Showing their Jewish origin.

between stones, then making it into bread, and dressing and cooking victuals. Sometimes in their culinary operations they were observed to be very clean, and at other times quite the reverse.

The women also made ropes, mats, hats, baskets, (some of which were very curious.) These were made of wild hemp, roots, and splits of trees.

Their young women were originally very modest and shame-faced, and at marriageable ages distinguished themselves with a kind of worked mat, or red or blue baize, interspersed with small rows of white and black wampum, or half rows of each in one, fastened to it, and then put round the head, down to near the middle of the forehead. Both young and old women would be highly offended at indecent expressions, unless corrupted with drink. They were peculiarly virtuous, and were averse to anything like liberties being manifested toward them. The Indians would not allow of any one mentioning the name of a friend after death.

They would sometimes streak their faces with black when in mourning, but when all went well with them, they painted red. They were great observers of the moon; delighted in fine clothes; were punctual in their bargains, and when any one deceived them, they would not deal with him afterwards. In their councils, they seldom or never contradicted one another till two of them had made an end of their discourse; for if ever so many were in company, only two were allowed to speak to each other, and the rest were required to be silent until their turn came. Their language in discourse was high, lofty, and sublime. Their way of counting was by tens, thus—two tens, three tens, four tens, &c.; and when the number got out of their reach, they would point to the stars, or the hair of their heads. They lived chiefly on Indian corn roasted in the ashes, and sometimes beaten and boiled with water, and made into hominy. They also made an agreeable cake of their pounded corn. They raised beans and peas, but the chief part of their provisions were furnished them from the woods and rivers—hunting and fishing being their chief delight. They pointed their arrows with a sharpened flint stone, and cut their wood with a large stone, the handle of which was made of withes. They ate generally twice a day, morning and evening. Their seats and tables were the ground.

They were naturally reserved; apt to resent insults, and their resentments were retained a long time. They were liberal and generous, kind, and affable to the English. They were uneasy and impatient in sickness, and commonly drank a decoction of roots in spring water; and during sickness ate very sparingly of flesh, and at such times if they ate flesh at all, it must be of the female species. They took remarkable care of the sick while hopes of life remained, but when that was gone some of them would neglect the patient.

Their government was monarchical and successive, mostly on the mother's side, to prevent a spurious issue.*

They washed their children in cold water as soon as they were born, and to make their limbs straight, tied them to a board, and when they travelled they hung it to their backs. The children usually walked at nine months of age.

Their young men married at sixteen or seventeen years of age, provided they had by that time given sufficient proof of their manhood, by a large return of skins. The girls married about thirteen or fourteen, but remained with their mothers to hoe the ground, and bear burdens, &c., for some years after marriage. In travelling, the women generally carried the luggage.

Their marriage ceremony was something after the following: The relations and friends being present, the bridegroom delivered a bone to the bride, she an ear of Indian corn to him, meaning that he was to provide meat, she bread.

It was not unusual with them to change their mates upon disagreement, in which case the children went with the one that loved them best; the man was allowed the first choice if the children were divided, or in case there was but one.

In the year 1682, a large ship of five hundred and fifty tons burden arrived at West Jersey, and got aground in Delaware

---

* The children of the reigning King did not succeed him, but his brother by the mother, or children of his sister, whose sons (and after them the male children of her daughters,) were to reign, for no woman inherited.

bay, where, after laying eight days, she got off and landed her passengers, three hundred and sixty in number, between Philadelphia and Burlington.

Their provisions being nearly exhausted, they sent ten miles to an Indian town near Rankokus creek, for Indian corn and peas. The king of the tribe being there, treated them kindly, and directed such Indians as had provisions to bring them in next morning; they accordingly brought plenty, which being delivered and put in bags, the messengers took leave of the king, who kindly ordered some of the Indians to carry their bags for them to their canoes.

The assembly of West Jersey having, at their last sitting, adjourned to the first of second month, 1682, but being unsuccessful in obtaining a full house, they adjourned to the fourteenth, and then dissolved without doing any business. Another was then called, which sat from the second to the eleventh of the first month following.

Before this time the members had been chosen by the electors of the several tenths indiscriminately, but this assembly declared it to be their judgment, as well as the judgment of those they represented, that the most regular method for preserving the liberty of the people by a free assembly, was that such of the ten proprieties as were now peopled, should each choose ten representatives (and the others also as they became peopled), and also resolved that twenty-four, the speaker being one, should constitute a quorum; they chose the council, justices, and commissioners for laying out land, as well as choosing other officers.

Those chosen were, Thomas Olive, Robert Stacy, Mahlon Stacy, William Biddle, Thomas Budd, John Chaffin, James Nevill, Daniel Wills, Mark Newby, and Elias Farre, councillors; William Biddle, Robert Stacy, Elias Farre, Mahlon Stacy, John Chaffin, Thomas Budd, Benjamin Scott, John Cripps, and Thomas Thackery, justices for Burlington.

James Nevill, George Deacon, Richard Hancock, and Edward Wade, justices for Salem.

Elias Farre, William Biddle, Thomas Budd, Thomas Gardiner, Mark Newby, James Nevill, Thomas Olive, Robert Stacy, Benjamin Scott, and William Cooper, commissioners.

John White, sheriff for Burlington; and Thomas Woodruffe, sheriff for Salem.

Thomas Revell, provincial clerk and recorder for Burlington; and Samuel Hedge for Salem.

Daniel Leeds, surveyor of the province.

Robert Schooley and John Pancoast, constables for Yorkshire tenth; John Bourten and William Brighten, for London tenth; and Thomas Sharp, for the third tenth.

This done, the governor, council, and assembly passed sundry laws, some of which were in substance: that each of the ten proprietors should have liberty to sell as much as five hundred acres of land, within their respective tenths, or take such other expedient as they should judge proper, for defraying public charges for the tenths respectively, for which purpose Mahlon Stacy and Thomas Lambert were appointed for the first, or Yorkshire tenth; Thomas Budd and Thomas Gardiner, for the second, or London tenth; and William Cooper and Mark Newby, for the third, or Irish tenth; and Samuel Jennings and Thomas Budd, for the remaining six tenths.*

They enacted that the fine of three pounds formerly imposed upon those who sold rum and other strong drinks to the Indians, should go one-half to the informer, and the other to be paid into the public stock, at the place where the offence was committed, and that every foreigner offending should pay a fine of five pounds, to be disposed of in the same manner.

That for the more convenient payment of small sums of money, Mark Newby's coppers, called Patrick's half-pence,† were allowed to pass as half-pence current money, provided he gave security to the speaker, for the use of the general assembly for the time being, that he, his executors and administrators, would change them on demand; and further provided that none were obliged to take more than five shillings in one payment.

To prevent clandestine and unlawful marriages, justices were

---

* As it regarded John Fenwick, who owned the other tenth, they seemed to have left him to manage his own concerns.

† These were as their name purports, Irish half-pence, which Newby brought over with him.

to have power to solemnize them, and the parties were first required to publish their intentions fourteen days in some public place appointed for that purpose, and any justice presuming to marry without the consent or knowledge of the parents or trustees of the parties (if such consent could be reasonably obtained), should be fined at the discretion of the general assembly, of which marriage the registrar was to make public entry on the day it was solemnized. The births of children and decease of all persons were also to be entered in the public register of the respective tenths; and for preventing differences between masters and servants, where no covenants were made, all servants were to have, at the expiration of their term of service, according to the custom of the country, ten bushels of corn, necessary apparel, two hoes, and an axe.

All servants of full age, coming into the province without indentures, or other agreements, were required to serve four years from the time the ship landed, and in order to ascertain the same, custom house officers were before appointed, and all under the age of twenty years who came without indentures, were required to be brought to the court within three months after their arrival in the district where the party resided, and the court was to fix the time of servitude.

Where personal estates were insufficient to pay a man's debts, the lands were required to pay it.

To encourage the building a saw mill, one thousand acres of land were required to be sold to William Frampton, to afford him sufficient land for that purpose, and even more, provided the governor and council should deem that quantity insufficient.

The better to settle and confirm the lands, six of the commissioners, with the governor, should (where there was occasion) make an inspection into such as should be taken up, and in case they found them legally located, they might, after public notice in the court, and there being no just reason to the contrary, confirm the same at the next court.

It was ordered that there be four courts held annually, at Burlington and Salem.

The governor was granted twenty pounds, the speaker five pounds, and the clerk five pounds, which was to be raised annually by tax, as follows: nine pounds six shillings and eight pence by the Yorkshire, London, and Salem tenths, each, and forty shillings by the third tenth, the whole being thirty pounds. This was to be delivered to Thomas Budd and Thomas Gardiner in skins, corn, or money, and the remainder of the two hundred pounds, formerly directed to be raised to defray the charges of government, to be collected from the other proprietors.

The representatives of West Jersey continued to be annually chosen, till the surrender of the proprietary government, in 1702.* The council (who were ex-officio), justices of the peace, and therefore inferior offices of government, were chosen by them. The governor was appointed by the proprietors, who governed them by a deputy till the succeeding year, when the assembly, understanding that Byllinge, for some selfish reasons, was disposed to turn Jennings out, who had hitherto been deputy governor, to the general satisfaction of the people, they undertook, by their choice, to continue him governor of the province, pretending they had a right to do it, because, in the constitutions, power was given to six parts out of seven of the assembly to make such alterations for the public good (the laws of liberty, of conscience, of property, of yearly assemblies, of juries, and of evidence, excepted) as they found necessary; and that no advantage might be taken of such judicial proceedings as had not been exactly agreeable to the concessions, they confirmed and ratified them all.

About this time the settlers in many parts were distressed to obtain food. Several got the chief part of what they required to eat by the gun, but as powder and shot were scarce, it was at least a precarious supply. There were at this time many instances of their wants, and sometimes their supplies were received from unexpected sources. It is related of the family of John Hollinshead, who lived near Rankokas, that they were entirely unprovided with powder and shot, and were in con-

---

*In 1699 a law was passed for reducing the number of representatives to ten, for each of the counties of Burlington and Gloucester, five for Salem, and three for Cape May; but as this occasioned dissatisfaction, it was repealed, and the number enlarged as formerly, being Burlington, twenty; Salem, ten; Gloucester, twenty; and Cape May, five.

sequence in great distress. Their youngest son, then a lad of only thirteen, in going through a corn field saw a turkey, and in throwing a stick at it to kill it, a second one came. He killed both of them and carried them home.¹ Soon after, at the house of Thomas Enes, he saw a buck, and telling Enes, the latter set his dogs on it, who followed it to Rankokas creek, which was at that time frozen. The buck in running on the ice slid upon his side, whereupon the dogs seized it. Young Hollinshead then coming up with his knife at once jumped upon it. The buck rose with him on his back and sprung forward, his feet spreading apart slid him gently down on his belly, thereby giving Hollinshead a respite from danger, and an opportunity to kill him. By these means two families were supplied with food, which was a great satisfaction to them in their starving condition.

Sir George Carteret, sole proprietor of East Jersey, died in 1679, and by his will he ordered the province to be sold to pay his debts. This was accordingly done* by his widow and executors, by indenture of lease and release, bearing date the 1st and 2d of February, 1681-2, to William Penn, Robert West, Thomas Rudyards, Samuel Groome, Thomas Hart, Richard Mew, Thomas Wilcox, of London, goldsmith, Ambrose Rigg, John Haywood, Hugh Hartshorne, Clement Plumstead, and Thomas Cooper, who were thence called the twelve proprietors. In this year they published an account of the country, put forth a fresh project for a town, as well as the methods of disposing of their lands.

The plan was a popular one, and gave great satisfaction, especially among the Scotch, from which nation a great many had already arrived in the province. This same year, and for some years succeeding, many more came, among them was

---

* The will is dated December 5th, 1678. He devised to Edward, Earl of Sandwich; John, Earl of Bath; Bernard Grenville, Sir Thomas Crew, Sir Robert Atkins, and Edward Atkins, Esq., and their heirs, among other lands, all his plantation of New Jersey, upon trust and confidence that they and the survivors and survivor of them, and the heirs and executors of the survivor of them should make sale of all the said premises, and out of the money that should upon such sale arise, pay and discharge debts, &c., as therein mentioned.

I

George Keith, who was considered a very skillful business man, and who sometime afterwards became surveyor general.

These twelve proprietors did not long hold the province to themselves, but by particular deeds each took a partner, thereby adding twelve additional proprietors. They were after this time called the twenty-four proprietors. The twelve new proprietors were, James, Earl of Perth;* John Drummond, Robert Barclay, Robert Gordon, Aarent Sonmans, Gawen Lawrie, Edward Byllinge, James Braine, William Gibson, Thomas Barker, Robert Turner, and Thomas Warne.

The grant made to these additional proprietors, by the Duke of York, of East New Jersey, bears date the 14th of March, 1682. This was the Duke's third and last grant of East Jersey, and was more full and expressive than any previously given.

These proprietors published a brief account of the province of East Jersey, for the information of all such persons who are or may be inclined to settle themselves, families, and servants, in that country.

They set forth, that to say anything in praise or much in the description of a country so well known, would be needless. That the late accounts and descriptions of the adjacent countries, West Jersey and Pennsylvania, which are much of the same nature, &c., might suffice. But, considering that in foreign colonies, yea, here in England, every particular country has some excellency in soil, product, or situation, that may affect or delight many persons beyond the places adjacent. We may therefore, for the satisfaction of such, give some brief account thereof.

First. The province or colony lies between thirty-nine and forty-one degrees of latitude, being about twelve degrees more to the south than the city of London, and is bounded southeast by the main sea, east by that vast navigable stream called Hudson's river, which divides this from the province of New York; west by a line of division, which separates this province from West Jersey; and north upon the mainland, and extends itself

---

* From whom Perth Amboy, or Amboy Perth, as it was then called, took its name.

in length on the sea coast and along Hudson's river, one hundred English miles and upwards.

Second. The convenience of situation, temperature of air, and fertility of soil is such, that there is no less than seven considerable towns, viz.: Shrewsbury, Middletown, Bergen, Newark, Elizabethtown, Woodbridge, and Piscataway, which are well inhabited by a sober and industrious people, who have necessary provisions for themselves and families, and for the comfortable entertainment of strangers and travellers, and this colony is experimentally found generally to agree with English constitutions.

Third. For navigation, it hath these advantages—not only to be situated along the navigable part of Hudson's river, but lies also fifty miles on the main sea, and near the midst of this province is that noted bay for ships, within Sandy Hook, very well known not to be inferior to any harbor in America, where ships not only harbor in greatest storms, but there ride safe with all winds, and sail in and out thence as well in winter as summer.

Fourth. For fishery, the sea banks there are very well stored with variety of fish, for not only such as are profitable for transportation, but such also as are fit for food there, as whales, codfish, cole and hake fish, large mackerel, and also many other sorts of flat and small fish. The bay also, and Hudson's river, are plentifully stored with sturgeon, great bass, and other scale fish, eels and shell fish, as oysters, &c., in great plenty and easy to take.

Fifth. This country is also plentifully supplied with lovely springs, rivulets, inland rivers and creeks, which fall into the sea and Hudson's river, in which is also much plenty and variety of fresh fish and water fowl.

Sixth. There is great plenty of oak timber fit for shipping, and masts for ships, and other variety of wood, like the adjacent colonies, such as chestnut, walnut, poplar, cedar, ash, fir, &c., fit for building within the country.

Seventh. The land or soil, (as in all other places,) varies in goodness and richness, but generally fertile, and with much smaller labor than in England, it produceth plentiful crops of all sorts of English grain, besides Indian corn, which the English planters find not only to be of vast increase, but very wholesome and good in its use. It also produceth good flax and hemp, which they now spin and manufacture into linen cloth. There is sufficient meadow and marsh to their uplands, and the very barrens there, as they are called, are not like some in England, but produce grass fit for grazing cattle in summer season.

Eighth. The country is well stored with wild deer, conies, and wild fowl of several sorts, as turkies, pigeons, partridges, plover, quails, wild swans, geese, ducks, &c., in great plenty. It produceth variety of good and delicious fruits, as grapes, plums, mulberries, and also apricots, peaches, pears, apples, quinces, watermelons, &c., which are here in England planted in orchards and gardens; these, as also many other fruits which come not to perfection in England, are the more natural products of this country

Ninth. There is also already great store of horses, cows, hogs, and some sheep, which may be bought at reasonable prices with English moneys or English commodities, or man's labor, where money and goods are wanting.

Tenth. What sort of mines or minerals are in the bowels of the earth, after-time must produce, the inhabitants not having yet employed themselves in search thereof; but there is already a smelting furnace and forge set up in the colony, where is made good iron, which is of great benefit to the country.

Eleventh. It is exceedingly well furnished with safe and convenient harbors for shipping, which is of great advantage to that country, and affords already, for exportation, great plenty of horses, and also beef, pork, pipe staves, boards, bread, flour, wheat, barley, rye, Indian corn, butter, and cheese, which they export for Barbadoes, Jamaica, Nevis, and other adjacent islands, as also to Portugal, Spain, the Canaries, &c. Their whale oil and whale fins, beaver, mink, raccoon, and martin skins (which this country produceth) they transport for England.

Twelfth. The situation and soil of this country may invite many who are inclined to transport themselves into those parts of America, for—

1st. Being considerably peopled, and situate on the sea coast, with convenient harbors, and so near adjacent to the province of New York and Long Island, being also well peopled colonies, may be proper for merchants, tradesmen, and navigators.

2d. It is likewise proper for such as are inclined to fishery, the whole coast and very harbor mouths being fit for it.

3d. Its soil is proper for all industrious husbandmen, and who, by hard labor here, on rack rents, are scarcely able to maintain themselves, much less to raise any estate for their children, may, with God's blessing on their labors, there live comfortably, and provide well for their families.

4th. For carpenters, bricklayers, masons, smiths, millwrights, and wheelwrights, bakers, tanners, tailors, weavers, shoemakers, hatters, and all or most handicrafts, where their labor is much more valued than in these parts, and provisions cheaper.

Thirteenth. They also set forth that the Indian nations are but few compared with the neighboring colonies, and are far from being formidable or injurious to the planters and inhabitants, but are really serviceable and advantageous to the English, not only in hunting and taking the deer and other wild creatures, and catching fish and fowl for food, but in the killing and destroying of bears, wolves, foxes, and other vermin and peltry, whose skins and fur they bring to the English, and sell at less price than the value of the time the Englishman must spend to take them himself.

They then recite the constitution made in 1664, in the time of Lord John Berkeley and Sir George Carteret late proprietors, setting forth the wholesome and liberal provisions made for liberty in the matters of religion, and property in the estates.

They then set forth, if the Lord permit, that they intend to erect and build one principal town, which, by reason of situation, must in all probability be the most considerable for merchandise, trade, and fishery in those parts. It is designed to be placed upon a neck or point of rich land, called Ambo point, lying on Raritan river, and pointing to Sandy Hook bay, and adjacent to the place where ships in that great harbor commonly ride at anchor.

2. The same privileges were allowed for the encouragement of servants, as was provided in the first concessions.

3. Those who desired to purchase lands there, or on quit

rents, should have grants to them and their heirs, on moderate and reasonable terms.

4. Those who desired to transport themselves before purchasing, they would find the terms of purchasing so moderate as to induce them to purchase and settle.

The passage to the province (as the ships run as well in winter as summer, Sandy Hook bay being never frozen), was five pounds per head for masters or servants who are above ten years of age; all under ten, and not children at the breast, pay fifty shillings; sucking children pay nothing. Carriage of goods was usually forty shillings per ton, and sometimes less.

The proprietors at this time were William Penn, Robert West, Thomas Rudyard, Samuel Groome, Thomas Hart, Richard Mew, Thomas Willcocks, Ambrose Rigg, John Heywood, Hugh Hartshorne, Clement Plumsted, and Thomas Cooper. This was before the twelve additional proprietors were taken in.

The following were the proposals for building the town of Ambo Point:

Forasmuch as Ambo Point is a sweet, wholesome, and delightful place, proper for trade, by reason of its commodious situation, upon a safe harbor, being likewise accommodated with a navigable river, and fresh water, and hath by many persons of the greatest experience and best judgment, been approved for the goodness of the air, soil, and situation:

We, the proprietors, purpose, by the help of Almighty God, with all convenient speed, to build a convenient town for merchandise, trade, and fishery on Ambo Point, and because persons that hath a desire to plant there may not be disappointed for want of proposals, we, the proprietors, offer these following:

1st. We intend to divide fifteen hundred acres of land upon Ambo Point into one hundred and fifty lots, to consist of ten acres to the lot, one hundred to be sold in England, and the balance to be reserved for those in America that desired to settle upon them.

2d. The price of each lot was fifteen pounds sterling to those who purchased before the 25th of December, 1682; and to such as purchased afterwards, before the 25th of December, 1683, twenty pounds sterling.

3d. Every lot was to be equally divided, according to the quality of the land, and its situation.

4th. The most convenient spot of ground for a town, was to be divided into one hundred and fifty equal shares, and laid out into streets, according to the rules of art.

5th. Four acres were reserved for a market place, town house, &c., and three acres for public wharfage.

6th. Each purchaser was obliged to build a dwelling-house, and to clear three acres of upland in three years, and upon failure the property was to go back to the proprietors, they repaying the purchase money.

7th. The proprietors were within one year each to build himself a house upon Ambo Point, which should stand in an orderly manner, according to the best and most convenient model.

8th. To encourage carpenters, joiners, brick, and tile makers, bricklayers, masons, sawyers, and laborers of all sorts, they obligated to find them work, and current pay for the same, in money, or clothes, and provision, according to the market price at New York, during one year at least after the 25th of December, 1682, and they were to pay no rent for the land they occupied, so long as they were employed in the proprietors' work.

The province of East New Jersey being now well settled for the time, its situation reduced to a general view, from the accounts then published by Secretary Nicholls, of New York, appears to be thus:

Shrewsbury, near Sandy Hook, adjoining the river or creek of that name, was already a township consisting of several thousand acres, with large plantations contiguous. The number of inhabitants at this time was computed to be about four hundred. Lewis Morris, of Barbadoes, had iron works and other considerable improvements here.

Middletown at this time was supposed to consist of about one hundred families. Several thousand acres was alloted for the town, and several thousand for plantations surrounding it. John Bowne, Richard Hartshorne, and Nicholas Davis, had each well improved settlements here. A court of sessions was held two or three times a year for Middletown and Piscataway, and their jurisdictions.

Several plantations were settled on the north side of Raritan river, below Piscataway. There were also several settlements higher up above the falls, among which were John Palmer, of Staten Island; Thomas Codrington, John Robinson, Messrs. White & Company, and Edsal & Company, of New York; and Capt. Corsen, also had settlements. Some land was likewise located by Millstone river, up the Raritan, and supposed to be near the division line.

Woodbridge at this time had several improved plantations in it, and the surrounding country. Deplairs, the surveyor general, took up land and settled there. This town was considered of greater consequence than the others, being incorporated by royal charter, and here a court-house and prison were built. They numbered about one hundred and twenty families, and in the town and plantations around, many thousand acres. There were several plantations on the north side of the river that divided Elizabethtown and Woodbridge. At the entrance of the creek on the north side, called Carteret's Point, and north of Staten Island, there were other plantations, extending from Elizabethtown to the bounds of New York. Within the Elizabethtown claim, was a partnership settlement between Sir George Carteret and the governor, Philip Carteret. The latter had built a house and resided there. The town at this time consisted of about one hundred and fifty families.

On the north of Milford or Newark river, (called Second river,) was a large tract belonging to Kingsland and Sanford. Higher up the river, another belonging to Capt. Berrie, who divided it; several plantations were soon settled upon it.

Still further up the river was an island which belonged to Christopher Hoogland, of Newark. Above this island was a large tract owned by Jacques Cartelayne, and others, who made some settlements there. These were in the jurisdiction of Newark.

Newark at that time was said to be a compact town, consisting of about one hundred families.

Near the mouth of the bay, upon the side of Overprook creek, adjacent to Hackensack river, several of the rich valleys were settled by the Dutch, and near Snakehill was a fine plantation owned by Pinhorne and Eickne, for half which it is said Pinhorne paid five hundred pounds. On Hackensack river there were other settlements, and on a creek near the river, Sarah Kiersted, of New York, had a tract presented to her by an old Indian Sachem, for services in interpreting between the Indians and Dutch. On this tract there were settled several families. John Berrie, also had a large plantation two or three miles above the tract of Mrs. Kiersted; he lived there and had made considerable improvements upon it. His son-in-law, Smith, lived near him, as well as a man by the name of Baker, from Barbadoes. They had considerably improved their plantations. On the west side of the creek, opposite to Berrie's, there were other plantations, but none north of them.

At Bergen Point (called Constable's Hook), there was a considerable settlement, which was first improved by Samuel Edsall, in Nicholls' time. Other small plantations were improved on Bergen Neck to the east, between the point and a small village of twenty families. Further along, there were sixteen or eighteen families; and opposite New York, about forty families had located. South of this settlement, a few families had settled together, at a place called the Duke's Farm, in honor of the Duke of York, and further up the country was a place called Hobuck,* which was formerly owned by a Dutch merchant, who, in the Indian wars with the Dutch, had his wife, children, and servants murdered by the Indians, and his house and stock destroyed,† but the place was now settled again, and they had erected a mill there.

Along the river side, to the north, the lands were settled by William Lawrence, Samuel Edsall, and Captain Bienfield. At Haversham, near the Highlands, Governor Carteret had taken up two large tracts, one for himself, the other for Andrew Campyne and company. These tracts were at this time (1682) but little improved.

The plantations on both sides of the neck, to its utmost extent, as also those at Hackensack, were at this time under the

---

* Hoboken.

† There were frequent wars or skirmishes between the Dutch and Indians.

jurisdiction of the town of Bergen, and situated about the middle of the neck. A court was held there by selectmen or overseers, comprising four or more in number, as was thought best by the people. These selectmen were chosen annually, to try small causes. This practice had been adopted in all the towns, upon their first settlement. Two courts of sessions were also held here annually, and from which, if the cause exceeded twenty pounds, the party had the right of appeal to the governor, council, and court of deputies or assembly.

Bergen being a compact town, fortifications had been erected against the incursions of the Indians. It contained about seventy families, the principal part of whom were Dutch. Some of these had resided there upwards of forty years.

There were supposed to be at this time about seven hundred families, who had made permanent settlements in the towns of East Jersey, which, computing five to a family, would make the inhabitants about three thousand five hundred, and the plantations outside were supposed to contain half as many more.

Philip Carteret continued to be governor of East Jersey after the quintipartite division, till about the year 1681.* His council, in 1668, consisted of six persons: Nicholas Verlet, Daniel Pierce, Robert Bond, Samuel Edsall, Robert Vanquellin, and William Pardon.

The assembly at this time consisted of double the number which comprised the council.

The first members were Casper Steenmets and Baltazer Bayard, for Bergen; John Ogden, Sen., and John Brackett, for Elizabethtown; Robert Treat and Samuel Swarne, for Newark; John Bishop and Robert Dennis, for Woodbridge; James Grover and John Bound, for Middletown, and the same persons represented Shrewsbury.

The sessions were generally held at Elizabethtown, but some-

---

* His salary was about fifty pounds per year, which was paid in country produce, at prices fixed by law, and sometimes four shillings a day besides, to defray his expenses while the sessions were held. The council and assembly received, while in session, three shillings per day to each member. The rates for public charges were levied at two shillings per head for every male above fourteen years old.

times at Woodbridge, and once or more they were held at Middletown and Piscataway.

Some of the first laws made and published by the legislature at Elizabethtown were in substance as follows: That persons resisting authority should be punished at the discretion of the court; that men from sixteen to sixty years of age should provide themselves with arms, on penalty of one shilling for the first week's neglect, and two shillings for every week after; that for burglary, or highway robbery, the first offence, burning in the hand; the second, in the forehead—in both, to make restitution; and for the third offence, death. For stealing, the first offence, treble restitution, and the like for the second and third offence, with such increase of punishment as the court saw cause, even to death, if the party appeared incorrigible; but if not, and unable to make restitution, they were to be sold for satisfaction, or to receive corporal punishment; that conspiracies or attacks upon towns or forts should be death; that undutiful children, smiting or cursing their father or mother, except provoked thereunto for self-preservation, upon complaint of and proof from their parents, or either of them, should be punished with death; that in case of adultery, the party to be divorced, corporally punished, or banished, or either or all of them, as the court should judge proper; that for night walking, and revelling after the hour of nine, the parties to be secured by the constable, or other officer, till morning, and then, not giving a satisfactory account to the magistrate, to be bound over to the next court, and there receive such punishment as should be inflicted; that thirty pounds should be levied for provincial charges: that is, five pounds to be paid by each town, in winter wheat, at five shillings a bushel; summer wheat, at four and sixpence; peas, at three shillings and sixpence; Indian corn, at three shillings; rice, at four shillings; barley, at four shillings; beef, at two pence half-penny per pound; and pork, at three pence half-penny. That no son, daughter, maid, or servant should marry without the consent of his or her parents, masters, or overseers, without being three times published in some public meeting or kirk near the party's abode, or notice being set up in writing at some public house near where they lived, for fourteen days before, then to be solemnized by some approved minister, justice, or chief officer, who, on penalty of twenty pounds, and to be put out of office, were to marry none who had not followed those directions; that fornication should be punished, at the discretion of the court, by marriage, fine, or corporal punishment, and that no life should be taken but by virtue of some law, and the proof of two or three witnesses.

CHAPTER VII.

1682—1703.

Land grants to settlers—First buildings at Amboy—First saw mills erected—Bergen settled by the Dutch—Disturbances in the province—Ferry started at Perth Amboy—First settled preacher in the province—First ship built in the province—Prices paid for provisions—Failure of crops—Great distress.

DOUBTS having arisen in the minds of the people whether the government of West Jersey had been granted with the soil, and these rumors having been industriously circulated, both here and in England, to the prejudice of the title of the possessors, as well as deterring others from coming over to settle, the assembly, in the spring of 1682, thought it one of their first duties to obviate this, therefore they unanimously resolved, " That the land and government of West New Jersey were purchased together." And in answer to the question, " Whether the concessions agreed upon by the proprietors and people, and subscribed in London and West Jersey, were agreed upon to be the fundamentals and ground of the government of West Jersey, or not?" It was resolved in the affirmative, *nemine contradicente*, only John Fenwick excepted his tenth, which he said, at that time was not under the same circumstances, but now freely consenteth thereto.*
At this assembly Samuel Jennings was appointed governor.†
Before this time he had acted as deputy for Byllinge.

---

* Proprietory records, Secretary's office, Burlington.

† He had for this year a right to take up six hundred acres of land above the Falls, for his salary.

The commissioners and other officers also being chosen, they were duly qualified,* and having agreed that the governor should be chairman or speaker, that he should sit as a member with them, and they together with the council; and that the chairman

---

*The oath of office was as follows:

"I, Samuel Jennings, being elected governor of the province of West Jersey, by the general free assembly thereof, sitting at Burlington, the 11th day of the third month, in the year 1683, do freely and faithfully promise, (according to the best of my ability,) to act in that capacity, according to the laws, concessions, and constitutions, as they are now established in the said province.'

"SAMUEL JENNINGS, *Governor.*"

The engagement and promise of the council elected by the assembly were as follows:

"We, underwritten, being elected and chosen by the general free assembly members of council, to advise and assist the governor in managing the affairs of the government, do solemnly promise, every one for himself, that we will give our diligent attendance from time to time, and him advise and assist to the best of our skill and knowledge, according to the laws, concessions, and constitutions of this province; and do further promise not to reveal or disclose any secret of council, or any business therein transacted, to the prejudice of the public. Witness our hands the 15th day of the third month, Anno, 1683.

"Thomas Budd,   John Skeen,
"John Gosling,   Thomas Olive,
"William Biddle,   Thomas Gardiner,
"Henry Stacy,   James Nevill,
"Elias Farre."

The engagements and promise of the commissioners, justices, and other officers elected, were as follows:

"We, whose names are here underwritten, being by the general free assembly chosen to officiate in our several trusts, commissions and offices for the ensuing year, do hereby solemnly promise that we will truly and faithfully discharge our respective trusts, according to the laws, concessions, and constitutions of the said province, in our respective offices and duties, and do equal justice and right to all men, according to our best skill and judgment, without corruption, favor, or affection. Witness our hands, this 15th of the third month, 1683.

"Thomas Olive, Richard Guy, Andrew Wade, and Andrew Thompson, justices.

"William Biddle, John Gosling, John Skeen, Mahlon Stacy, Thomas Olive, James Nevill, Francis Collins, Thomas Budd, Thomas Gardiner, Mark Newby, commissioners.

"Thomas Revell, recorder; Benjamin Wheat, sheriff; Daniel Leeds, surveyor."

should have a double vote. This assembly passed sundry laws, among which was the following:

"And whereas, it hath pleased God to commit this country and province into the hands of such who, (for the generality of them, are fearing God, and painful and industrious in the promoting and improving the said province, and for the better preventing of such as are profane, loose and idle, and scandalous, from settling amongst us, who are, and will be, not only unserviceable, but greatly burthensome to the province—It is therefore hereby enacted by the authority aforesaid, that all person and persons who shall transport him or themselves into this province, shall, within eighteen months after he or they shall arrive in the said province, procure and produce a certificate, under the hands of such of that religious society to whom he or they did belong, or otherwise from two magistrates (if procurable), or two constables or overseers of the poor, with three or more creditable persons of the neighborhood, who inhabit or belong to the place where he or they did last reside, as may give satisfaction (that is to say), that he or they came not clandestinely or fraudulently away; and if unmarried, that he or she are clear from former engagements in that particular, and also that he or she are such as live soberly and honestly, to the best of their knowledge; and that no justice shall presume to marry any such person or persons who shall come into this province, before such certificate be produced, or that it be laid before the governor or two justices, and give them sufficient satisfaction concerning their clearness; and that all such person and persons who shall settle in the said province, and shall refuse or neglect to produce such certificate as aforesaid, within the said eighteen months, shall be fined, at the discretion of the governor and council of the said province, not exceeding twenty pounds, the same to be levied by distress and sale of the offender's goods, and to be paid into the hands of the treasurer of the said province."

The Scotch had a considerable share in the settlement of East Jersey. Many of them, and a number that afterwards arrived, fixed their habitations about Amboy and up the Raritan. The twelve proprietors appointed Robert Barclay, of Urie, in

Scotland, governor for life, and Thomas Rudyard, a lawyer or attorney of London, deputy governor.

The commission of Barclay was dated at London, the 17th of the fifth month, called July, in the year of our Lord, according to the English account, 1683. He continued to be governor till 1685, when Lord Neil Campbell, also a Scotchman, and uncle to the Duke of Argyle, was appointed governor, and came over to the province. In 1698, Sir Thomas Lane was appointed governor of East Jersey. Barclay died the 3d of October, 1690.

Thomas Rudyard, the deputy governor, arrived at his government the beginning of the year following his appointment. He gave a glowing account of the country soon after his arrival, in which he speaks of the superiority of the province over the neighboring provinces, having both fresh and salt meadows, which were very valuable as contributing so much for the support of stock in winter, which must be supplied in other parts from the store; but he says that where no salt meadows exist, there are no mosquitoes. He speaks also of one thing we have here, which the others are in want of, viz.: vast oyster banks, which furnish, during the winter, a constant supply of fresh victuals to the English, as well as the Indians. Of these, he says, there are many all along the coasts, from the sea, as high up as against New York; so we are supplied with salt fish at our doors, or within half a tide's passage, as well as fresh fish in abundance, in every little brook, such as perch, trout, eels, &c., which we catch at our doors.

At Amboy we are now building some small houses, thirty feet long by eighteen feet broad, such as will entertain workmen, and such as will, go and build larger.

There is plenty of good stone up the Raritan, and oyster shells upon the point, to make lime with. They have durable covering for their houses of shingles; oak, chestnut and cedar are plentiful; the last will endure a man's lifetime.

Five or six saw mills were then being built, and two were already at work, which, when completed, would reduce the price of boards one-half, as well as all other timber for building.

The timber costs nothing, but the workmanship by hand was at London prices, and sometimes more.

His residence was with Samuel Groome, at Elizabeth Town, which was not solitary, as he had little less company than at his house in London.

The people were generally a sober, industrious, professing people, wise in their generation, courteous in their behavior, and respectful to us in office.

Our country here called Bergen is almost entirely inhabited by Dutchmen. At a town called Newark, seven or eight miles from here, is made great quantities of cider, exceeding any we can have from New England, Rhode Island, or Long Island.

Amboy was laid out by Samuel Groome, one of the proprietors, and surveyor general of East Jersey, into one hundred and fifty lots, and a draught was sent home to the other proprietors.

Gawen Lawrie arrived this year as deputy governor of East Jersey, under Robert Barclay, and chose a fresh council, one of whom was Richard Hartshorne.

There had been considerable disturbances in the province, particularly about Middletown and Woodbridge, relating to town affairs,* and the prudent conduct of these officers had contributed largely towards quieting the province.

Gawen Lawrie in writing to the proprietors in London, from Elizabeth Town, under date of the 2d of first month, 1684, gives an account of his visits to different places in the province to lay out a settlement.

He pitched upon a place where a ship of three hundred tons could ride safely within a plank's length from the shore, at low water. Adjoining this he found a piece of marsh ground about twelve perches broad and twenty perches long, with high land on each side. Here he set out lots around this island of one acre each, four poles at the key, and forty poles back, from thence along the river half a mile. These lots were laid out in a pleasant situation, where they could see the ships coming in the bay of Sandy Hook for nearly twenty miles.

---

* In one of these disturbances, Lewis Morris, who was afterwards governor of New Jersey, being a party, was taken prisoner, and confined in a log house. His partizans pried up the logs far enough for him to creep out.

He says "there is no such place in all England for conveniency and pleasant situation. There are sixty lots upon the river, and forty backwards between those and the river, and those backward have a highway one hundred feet broad." Here he laid out a place for a market, with cross-streets from the river to the market, where the town houses were to be built. He then laid out four hundred acres, to be divided into forty-eight parts, thirty six to each proprietor.

The lots in town were sold for twenty pounds, or for half a lot of thirty-six acres, not in the town, forty pounds.

The Scotch proprietors took up sixteen of the lots, and the other proprietors eight lots, and twenty lots were taken up in the town by other people. All were required to build a house thirty feet long, eighteen feet broad, and eighteen feet high to the raising, and to be finished within a year. To pay for laying out, forty shillings a lot, and four pence per annum quit rent. Forty or fifty acres was laid out for the governor's house.

The wharf, between the highway and river, was one hundred feet broad, with a row of trees along the river, before the houses, for shade and shelter. He arranged for the building of two houses for the proprietors, and a house for the governor, forty-six feet long, and eighteen feet broad.

The proprietors had thirty thousand acres of land in different places, which was formerly taken up by Sir George Carteret. Pork and beef sold at two pence per pound, fish and fowl were plenty, and he says there were oysters enough to supply all England. Wheat, four shillings per bushel; Indian wheat, two shillings and six pence per bushel; cider, good and plenty, for one penny per quart; good drink made of water and molasses, about two shillings per barrel, as wholesome as their eight shilling beer in England; good venison, plenty, at eighteen pence per quarter; eggs at three pence per dozen; and all other necessaries of life plenty. Vines, walnuts, peaches, strawberries, and many other things plenty in the woods.

There was laid out for the town, governor's house, and public highways, near about two hundred acres, leaving eighteen hundred acres still to be disposed of.

He established a ferry at Perth,* for men and horses to go and come to Burlington, and Pennsylvania, and New York. He also built a house half-way between there and Burlington, for the entertainment of travellers, and a ferry boat to go to New York, for the purpose of building up the town of Perth, which was a central place.

He says: "Here is a gallant, plentiful country, and good land."

At this time there was but one town in the entire province that had a settled preacher, who followed no other employment, and that was Newark. We are also informed that there was no particular form of religion, but that it was comprised of several sorts, but few of the inhabitants being very zealous, although in every town there was a meeting-house, where public worship was held once a week. There were no public laws in the country for maintaining public teachers, but the towns where they were located provided for their maintenance in their own way.

The richest planters had from eight to ten servants; some of them had as many as a dozen cows, others twenty, and some as many as thirty,—eight or ten oxen, and some had so many horses that they did not themselves know the exact number, for they had them scattered through the country, and kept no more at home than they required for work; they let them run in the woods both winter and summer, and take them only when they wanted to use them.

They had great flocks of swine in the woods, also great flocks of sheep; but these they did not permit to run in the woods, for fear of their being destroyed by wolves.

There were in the towns settled at this time about one hundred houses, but they were not built with much regularity. Every house had connected with it a lot of four acres, so that every one building upon his own lot, made the town irregular and scattered. Their streets were laid out too large, and the sheep in the towns constantly run at large in them.

In consequence of their size, the inhabitants were at no trouble about paving them.

---

* Perth Amboy.

Barnegat was called Burning Hole, and was a celebrated fishing place. There was good land and abundant of meadow near it.

The only fishermen there at that time, that followed that as an occupation, were those who went a whaling on the coasts, although there were all other kinds of fish in abundance everywhere through the country, in all the rivers, and the people generally fished with long sieves or long nets, and were frequently known to catch with a sieve one and sometimes two barrels of good fish, which they would salt up mostly for their own use, and to sell to others.

The first ship built in the province was commenced by Samuel Groome, for trade with the West Indies, but the building of it was discontinued, on account of his death, in 1684. It remained on the stocks for some time before it was completed.

The acres were reckoned according to English measure, sixteen feet to the rood, twenty long, and eight broad. One English butt of wheat, which was eight gallons (English) or Scotch quarts, was required to sow an acre of land, two bushels of barley also to an acre, and two bushels of oats sowed an acre and a-half; an English peck, which was four English quarts, or Scotch shopeus of Indian corn, would plant an acre.

There was at this time but few Indian natives in this part of the country, as they lived mostly in the woods, and had small towns in some places far up in the country.

They planted Indian corn, and depended on shooting deer, and other wild beasts and fowls, for their sustenance. They had kings among themselves to govern them; had no religion, and were always ready to sell their lands. Indian corn sold at two shillings and sixpence per bushel; wheat, four shillings; rye, three shillings; oats, one shilling and eightpence; beef, one penny; pork, twopence; venison, one penny, and mutton threepence per pound, English measure and weight, being a fifth part difference between the money of this country and sterling money, so that wheat being valued here at four shillings the bushel, would be worth but three shillings and threepence sterling, and so of the rest proportionably.

This statement was made by John Barclay and Arthur Forbes,

the truth of which was certified to by Gawen Lawrie, deputy governor, and dated Elizabeth Town, in East Jersey, the 29th of the first month, called March, 1684.

The assembly of West Jersey, at this meeting, the 20th of the third month (May), chose Thomas Olive governor and chairman, or speaker, the governor acting in both these capacities.

The several branches of the Legislature had previously transacted their business in common together. The representatives were returned from their respective first, second, third, and Salem tenths, which were all the tenths settled up to this time. At their first meeting they chose the governor, council, commissioners to lay out land, and all the other officers of their government.

Olive had been twice governor of West Jersey before, and on the last choice he was continued for a year,* but Byllinge, desisting from the claims which the assembly as well as the people had thought unjust, and which had been the cause of their undertaking in opposition to him to choose the governor, he sent this year a fresh commission to John Skeine to be his deputy,† the assembly and people submitted to him, though before they had refused William Welsh in that capacity, while Byllinge continued the claims aforesaid. Skeine died in the twelfth month, 1687, but Dr. Daniel Cox, of London, the greatest proprietor of West Jersey,‡ was, the September previous, appointed to succeed him. He continued in the position till about the year 1690, having appointed Edward Hunloke his deputy. Sometime afterwards a commission was sent to John Tatham, who, in consequence of being a Jacobite,§ being disqualified by his principles, the assembly rejected him, on which the proprietors, in 1692, sent a commission to Andrew Hamil-

---

* His salary was twenty pounds per year.

† Skeine's salary, besides the fees, was said to be thirty bushels of rye.

‡ He owned twenty-two shares of propriety.

§ A partisan or adherent of James II., after he had abdicated the throne, and one who was opposed to William and Mary, and who held with a sect of Christians in Syria and Mesepotamia, that Jesus Christ had but one nature.

ton.* He was accepted, and continued governor of West Jersey while it remained under the proprietary jurisdiction, though with some interruption in 1698, being also some part of the time governor of both East and West Jersey, and Pennsylvania.

In the year 1686, there seems to have been some dangerous persons in East Jersey, if the law passed that year against wearing swords was well founded. According to that, several persons had received abuses, and were in great fear from quarrels and challenges.

To prevent it in the future, no one was permitted, by word or message, to make a challenge, upon pain of six months imprisonment, without bail or main prize, and a fine of ten pounds. Whoever accepted or concealed the challenge, was also to forfeit ten pounds. No person was to wear any pocket pistols, skeins, stilladers, daggers, or dirks, or other unusual weapons, upon pain of five pounds forfeiture for the first offence; and for the second, to be committed, and on conviction, imprisoned for six months, and moreover to pay a fine of ten pounds. No planter was to go armed with sword, pistol, or dagger, upon penalty of five pounds. Officers, civil and military, soldiers in service, and strangers travelling upon lawful occasions, were excepted.

The settlers in both West Jersey and Pennsylvania, about the year 1687, were put to considerable difficulty on account of food, their crops having in great part failed. Several families

---

* His salary, in 1695 and 1696, was two hundred pounds a year, as governor of West Jersey, but the salary, in both East and West Jersey, seems, in some periods, to have been rather occasional. In the latter province, in 1697, provision was made for two hundred pounds, by a law containing the following preamble: "Being sensible of the many great services done by our present governor, Colonel Andrew Hamilton, since his accession to the administration of the government of this province, and taking also into our consideration the great charge that must attend any person in that post, and how little hath yet been done by us answerable to his merit and station, we find ourselves obliged, in point of gratitude, and in testimony of our affection for him, and as a demonstration thereof, to offer, as is hereafter expressed, and pray our governor's acceptance thereof from a poor people, whose good will and regard to him is not to be measured by the value of our offering, but integrity of the offerers." The salary of the governor of East Jersey, in 1694, 1695, and 1696, was one hundred and fifty pounds per annum.

had already spent their last, and were forced to subsist on what was spared by such of their neighbors as were better provided; these were few in proportion to the mouths to be filled. Some near the rivers had lived for weeks upon fish, others were forced to subsist on herbs. While this was the case, a vessel unexpectedly arrived from New England to Philadelphia, laden with corn, which proved a timely supply, for this vessel finding a good market, others soon followed, so that the settlers from this time were amply supplied with food.

In this year, 1687, George Keith, surveyor general of East Jersey, by order of the proprietors there, attempted to run the division line between East and West Jersey. He began with a line from Little Egg Harbor, north by west, and three degrees five minutes more westerly, as the compass then pointed, for a part; the line run by him was sixty miles in length, till he fell upon the corner of John Dobie's plantation, on the south branch of the Raritan. This, by order of the council of proprietors of West Jersey, in or about the year 1721, was traversed by John Chapman, who was esteemed a careful surveyor. Upon the computation, it appeared that the line, at the time he traversed it, was north sixteen degrees and forty-three minutes west, which left a variation of two degrees and twenty-three minutes in thirty-four years. The remaining part of Keith's line was from Dobie's plantation along the rear of that and other tracts and plantations, as they were before patented and surveyed in right of the proprietors of the eastern division of New Jersey, until it intersected that part of the north branch of the Raritan river which descends from a fall of water, at that time known by the Indian name of Allamitung, then running from that point of intersection up the branch or stream of the fall of Allamitung.

Upon the original running of this line, the western proprietors thought too much of their best lands were surveyed to the eastward, and were dissatisfied with it.

In the fall of 1688, the governors of East and West Jersey, on behalf of each division, entered into an agreement that Daniel Cox, governor of West Jersey, on behalf of himself and all the rest of the proprietors of that province, on the one part, and Robert Barclay, governor of the province of East Jersey, on behalf of himself and all the rest of the proprietors of that province, of the other part, to finally determine all differences concerning the deed of partition, and all other disputes and controversies about dividing the lands and settling the bounds between East and West Jersey, agreed that the line of partition ran straight from Little Egg Harbor to the most westerly corner of John Dobie's plantation, as it stands on the south branch of the Raritan river, shall be the bounds, so far, between East and West Jersey, and shall not be altered, but remain as it stands on a printed draught of the proprietors' lands, surveyed in East Jersey, and drawn by John Reed, and since printed here. From thence to run along the back of the adjoining plantations, until it comes to James Dundas' plantation; and from thence, at the most northwesterly part thereof, a line to lie down with a line on the back of those plantations, and to run northeastward, till it touch the north branch of Raritan river, as it is struck upon the map already; but saving the plantations already laid out to be within the line, if they happen to stand a little more westerly than that line is marked.

From the north end of the line, where it touches Raritan north branch, thence forward the largest stream or current of water belonging to the said north branch, shall be the bound or partition; and so continuing the same unto the north end thereof, for the bounds so far.

From the said north end of the branch, a short straight line to run to touch the nearest part of Passaic river, and so following the course of that river, continuing Poquanick river, so long as it runs northerly or northwesterly; these rivers still to be the bounds between both provinces; and if Poquanick river do not run far enough to the latitude of forty-one degrees, then from the said river, a straight line to run northward to the latitude, and that to be the utmost north partition point; and from the said point in a straight line due east, to the partition point on Hudson's river, between East Jersey and New York; provided always, that all plantations and tracts of land laid out and surveyed before the agreement arrives in East Jersey, shall remain to the parties concerned, and the partition shall so run as to include them within East Jersey bounds.

Dr. Cox was to promise and make good the agreements above written, and warrant the title and quiet possession of all the lands so to be appropriated to the proprietors of East Jersey, according to the limits and bounds above mentioned, against all persons that shall or may pretend or claim any interest to any of the said lands as West Jersey proprietors; and Robert Barclay also promised to make good the agreement above written, and warrant the title and quiet possession of lands so to be appropriated to the proprietors of West Jersey, according to the limits and bounds above mentioned, against all persons that shall or may pretend or claim any interest to any of the said lands as East Jersey proprietors. For the faithful performance of which they were mutually to bind themselves, each to the other, in the sum of five thousand pounds, to be well and truly paid on the breach of any of the clauses and covenants before mentioned.

This was signed and sealed in London, September 5th, 1688, by Robert Barclay, and witnessed by David Hewling and Stephen Lucock.

Although there was a desire on the part of both sections to have the line definitely fixed and properly run, as the western proprietors could easily see that East Jersey had the advantage in every step hitherto taken.

The proprietors of West Jersey met at Burlington on the 14th day of the twelfth month, 1687, and resolved to appoint eleven proprietors every year, from among themselves, to be commissioners and trustees. Six of these were to be from the county of Burlington, and four from the county of Gloucester, for the purpose of acting in such affairs as shall generally concern the whole body of proprietors.

These were Samuel Jennings, Thomas Olive, William Biddle, Elias Farre, Mahlon Stacy, Francis Davenport, Andrew Robeson, William Royden, John Reading, William Cooper, and John Wills. They were allowed two shillings per day for each and every day they were engaged, to be paid by the proprietors in proportion to their respective shares in the province.

This was dated the 14th day of the twelfth month, called February, 1687.

The proprietors met at Burlington on the 6th day of the seventh month, 1688, and ratified the above agreement It was ratified by thirty-one of the proprietors of Burlington county, and thirteen of those of Gloucester county, with the exception that the names of Mahlon Stacy and Francis Davenport were excluded, and John Tatham and George Hutchinson were elected in their stead; and in place of William Cooper, Thomas Gardiner, Jun., was elected.

They also changed the number from eleven to nine, five to constitute a quorum.

The latter was agreed upon at Gloucester, the 1st of the first month, 1688, and subscribed by the proprietors.

Upon this agreement was founded the constitution of the council of proprietors of West Jersey.

At a meeting of the proprietors of West Jersey, at Burlington, on the 6th day of the seventh month, 1688, they agreed that every proprietor and person interested in proprieties should pay to the use of Daniel Cox, to any person appointed to receive it, as a reimbursement for the money laid out by him in the Indian purchase lately made in the lower counties, the sum of twelve shillings and sixpence for every thousand acres, and so proportionably to be taken up out of that purchase. The first year to begin the 1st day of April last past, and from that time twelve months, to advance eighteen pence upon every year ensuing, until the time that the money aforesaid be paid for, and the land to be laid out within the bounds of the same purchase, as consideration for the moneys disbursed by the said Daniel Cox, in the said Indian purchase of the whole tract, which, by the surveyor, Andrew Robeson, is computed to be three hundred thousand acres of good land, capable and worthy of improvements, which money being paid, the party so paying shall be acquitted of all other payments in the consideration aforesaid.

The surveyor was not to set out any land within the limits of this Indian purchase, until the money above mentioned be paid and secured as aforesaid.

The lands taken up by order of Dr. Cox, above the falls of

Delaware, every proprietor taking up any part thereof, was to pay Dr. Cox, or his order, twenty-five shillings per thousand acres, and two shillings and sixpence yearly consideration, till the money be paid.

At a meeting of the proprietors, held at Burlington, the 18th of September, 1688, Samuel Jennings was appointed commissioner to examine all deeds, and take a minute of the same, to issue warrants to the surveyor general, for the surveying and taking up of lands for the inhabitants within the county of Burlington, or to any others as occasion should require; and John Reading was appointed to perform the same service within the county of Gloucester, and to all others as occasion should require; and for every warrant for land under one hundred acres, they were to receive the sum of one shilling; and one hundred acres and above, and under one thousand acres, the sum of eighteen pence; and one thousand acres and above, the sum of two shillings and sixpence, the amount to be collected out of the land.

Wherever demand was made of them, the said commissioners were required to deliver to council a copy of their minutes taken by them from time to time, and Andrew Robeson, the surveyor general, was, upon demand of council, required to make return to them of all warrants for land executed by him that had not been previously returned.

Mahlon Stacy, John Day, William Wood, and John Hollinshead were appointed rangers* for the county of Burlington, and upwards, and John Kay, Thomas Sharp, and Israel Helme, Jr., rangers for the county of Gloucester.

No person or persons were permitted to purchase lands from the Indians without the consent of council first obtained; otherwise, they were to be prosecuted as common enemies.

John Skene was appointed by the secretary and register general of the dominion and territories of New England, to receive the records, rolls, and papers of Thomas Revell and John Reading, and made a demand for the same.

---

* In England, a sworn officer of a forest, appointed by the King's letters patent, whose business was to walk through the forest, watch the deer, prevent trespasses, &c., keepers of the parks.

The matter was laid before council, at a meeting held at Burlington, on the 10th day of the eighth month, 1688, whereupon they ordered that all records relating to government, may be delivered according to the secretary's order, except such as relate to lands which they judge to be the proprietor's property, which ought to remain with them.

The council met, pursuant to adjournment, on the eleventh of the eighth month, when it was agreed that all deeds granted only by Edward Byllinge, in and before the year 1682, were adjudged insufficient for the commissioners to grant warrants upon.

Instructions were given to the commissioners in examining deeds and granting warrants for taking up lands.

They were to grant no warrants but upon the production of good deeds, authentic copies, or an extract of the record of such deed under the register's hand.

A particular warrant was to be given for every several deed, or particular purchase.

The president of council was, from time to time, to grant warrants for the commissioners, for the taking up of their own lands.

In the year 1691, Dr. Cox conveyed the government of West Jersey and territories, to the West Jersey Society, consisting of Sir Thomas Lane, knt., Michael Watts, Edward Harrison, Thomas Skinner, James St. Johns, Nicholas Hayward, Mordecai Abbot, Nicholas Battersby, Robert Curtis, John Jurin, Richard Bramhall, Robert Mitchell, Charles Mitchell, James Boddington, John Gunston, Arthur Shallet, John Lamb, William Wightman, Joseph Brooksbank, William Thompson, Henry Harrington, John Love, Thomas Phipps, Isaac Cocks, John Sweetable, Thomas Bromfield, John Norton, Robert Hackshaw, John Bridges, Joseph Paise, Edward Richier, William Dunk, Edward Habberdfield, John Alberson, Edward West, Edward Pauncefort, Obadiah Burnet, Francis Michel, Benjamin Steel, John Slavey, Nehemiah Erwing, John Wilcocks, Richard Mayo, Jonah Netteway, William Brooks, Tracey Pauncefort, Joseph Allen, and Richard Greenaway.

The first settlers of the Yorkshire tenth, in West Jersey, had several of them built upon the low lands, near the falls of Delaware,* in 1676, where they had lived, and been improving about sixteen years.

The Indians had told them that their buildings were liable to be damaged by freshets in the river Delaware, the situation of the place rendering such a thing probable.

They had, however, erected several wooden tenements, with outhouses, which in the spring were accordingly demolished. The snows suddenly melting above caused an uncommon overflow of the river, greater than has ever been known before or since.

This flood came upon the inhabitants so unexpectedly, that many were in their houses, surrounded by the water, from whence they were conveyed by neighbors, in canoes, to the shore opposite. The water continued to rise until it reached the upper stories of some of their houses, when most or all of them gave way, and were dashed to pieces, and many of their cattle were drowned; beds, kettles, and other furniture were afterward picked up on the shores below. The damage occasioned by it was considerable, and the inhabitants were very much alarmed.

Two persons, in one house, who were carried away by the sweeping current, lost their lives before they could be rescued.

By this accident, the inhabitants were taught to fix their habitations on higher ground.

This was called the great flood at Delaware Falls, and occurred in 1692.

In the spring of this year, the proprietors of West Jersey first appointed Col. Andrew Hamilton to be their governor.

Thomas Olive died about this time. He had been a man of importance ever since the first settlement of West Jersey. He came over as one of the London commissioners, in 1677, to buy the lands of the natives, inspect the rights of such as claimed property, to order the lands laid out, and in general, to administer the government, with the other proprietors, of whom there were eight besides himself. He was governor in 1684, in which station he behaved with such prudence and circumspection as to

---

*Trenton.

give general satisfaction. While a common magistrate, he possessed a ready method in transacting business, often doing it to good effect, in the seat of judgment, on the stumps in his meadows. When complaints were made to him which he thought were sudden, and without giving the matter proper consideration, he endeavored to postpone them until cool deliberation had shown them to be justly founded, and then he seldom failed of giving satisfaction to all parties.

He had been imprisoned, and had suffered in other respects on account of his religion in England (being a Quaker), but by his preaching and writings, as well as his public and private conduct, he had gained the general love and esteem of all who had any dealings with him.

In September, 1694, Thomas Gardiner departed this life. He was one of the early settlers at Burlington, and filled several public stations in the government of West Jersey. He was possessed of a good character, and had considerable knowledge of different kinds of business; was an exemplary member of society, and highly esteemed for his religion. His son Thomas was one of the council of proprietors in 1703, to mark out the land purchased from the Indians, and to get a deed for the same.

John Woolston, one of the early settlers at Burlington, who came over in 1677, and had lived at his first place of settlement for over twenty years, enduring the fatigue of a new settlement —who had proved himself a ready friend and neighbor, and a valuable member of society—died in the early part of 1698.

The year 1701 was a memorable one in the history of New Jersey, on account of the disturbances and commotions that agitated several parties here, and the change of government that followed in consequence. Each province had many and different proprietors, who advanced separate schemes and interests, which sometimes interfered one with another.

To facilitate their particular purposes, one party would assume the choice and management of a governor, while another would refuse any but the one nominated by them, and a third would object to proposals from either. They refused to listen to moderate counsels, party discord took place, and instead of peace and order, corruption, for a time, seemed to hold sway;

every expedient to restore union and regularity proved unsuccessful, factions prevailed, and animosities were cherished to that extent, that time seemed only to impart opportunities for accumulating fresh occasions for disgust.

In order to understand these things more fully, we must go back to 1698. Jeremiah Basse, under pretence of a commission he had received from some of the proprietors of East Jersey, with the approbation of the King, superseded Andrew Hamilton, the then governor of both East and West Jersey. But the next year it was ascertained that Basse had not received the approval of the King to his commission, nor had it been granted by enough of the proprietors to make it valid, which induced great numbers of the inhabitants to refuse obedience to him, and to the magistrates and officers appointed by him; and some persons were imprisoned for refusing obedience, others resented it with very great indignation, and the consequence was, feuds and confusion followed.

To endeavor to reconcile matters, and restore peace and harmony to the colony, and to patch up matters for the present, Andrew Hamilton was again appointed governor, and given a new commission from the proprietors, but a great number refused obedience to him, and the magistrates and officers under him, in like manner and for the same reasons that they refused to obey Basse and those he appointed. They had no particular objection to Hamilton, but to the mode of his appointment, as they did not consider it legal, not having received a sufficient number of the proprietors, and being without the sanction of the King.

The disorders in the eastern division, during this time, made such an impression on the minds of many of the people, that they readily hearkened to overtures made for a surrender of the government.*

A considerable part of West Jersey was also, for similar reasons, disposed to a resignation.

The commotions in both, which had been increasing for some

---

* Long before, according to the representation of the lords of trade, October 2d, 1701, "the proprietors of East Jersey did surrender their pretended right of government to King James, in the month of April, 1688, and which was accordingly accepted by him."

years, now seemed to have reached a crisis, and all things seemed to tend towards a surrender of the powers of government, which was brought about in the beginning of the following year.

In the meantime, sundry petitions and remonstrances were sent home, complaining of their grievances and the confusion the colony was in, and praying for redress.

In the year 1702 the surrender was made, by a lengthy instrument signed by both divisions of East and West Jersey, of their pretended right of government, to Her Majesty, in which they recited the letters patent of James, Duke of York, under which he held the said territory, that the present proprietors were unable to govern the same, in consequence of not possessing the legal right so to do, but that it belonged to Her Majesty, in right of her crown of England, to constitute governors of the said provinces, and to give directions for governing the same as she should think fit.

They being desirous of submitting themselves to Her Majesty, were willing to surrender all their pretences to the said powers of government, to the intent Her Majesty may be pleased to constitute a governor or governors of the same provinces, with such powers, privileges, and authorities for the government thereof, and making of such laws there, with the consent of the assembly of the said provinces, and Her Majesty's subsequent approbation thereof, as Her Majesty, in her great wisdom, shall think fit and convenient.

The surrender was signed by forty-seven of the present proprietors of East and West Jersey.

They further state that they have surrendered and yielded up, and by these presents for us and our heirs, do surrender and yield up unto our sovereign Lady Anne, by the Grace of God, Queen of England, Scotland, France, and Ireland, defender of the faith, &c., her heirs and successors, all these the said powers and authorities, to correct, punish, pardon, govern, and rule all or any of Her Majesty's subjects, or others who now inhabit within the said provinces of East and West Jersey, or either of them, and also to nominate, make, constitute, ordain, and confirm any laws, ordinances, and directions, and instruments for these purposes, or any of them, and to nominate or appoint, revoke, discharge, change, or alter any governor or governors, officers, or ministers, which are or shall be appointed, made, or used within the said provinces, or either of them, and to make, ordain, and establish any orders, laws, directions, instruments, forms, or ceremonies of government and magistracy, for or concerning the government of the provinces aforesaid, or either of them, &c., &c.

This was dated the 15th day of April, in the year of our Lord 1702, and signed by the proprietors of the eastern and western divisions.

The Queen's acceptance of the surrender of the government was dated at the court of St. James, the 17th of April, 1702, at which were present the Queen's Most Excellent Majesty, His Royal Highness Prince George of Denmark, the Lord Keeper, Lord President, Lord Steward, Duke of Bolton, Duke of Schlumberg, Duke of Leeds, Lord Great Chamberlain, Earl Marshal, Lord High Admiral, Lord Chamberlain, Earl of Dorset, Earl of Manchester, Earl of Stamford, Earl of Burlington, Earl of Radnor, Earl of Berkely, Earl of Rochester, Earl of Marlborough, Earl of Bradford, Earl of Romney, Earl of Ranalagh, Lord Ferrars, Lord Godolphin, Mr. Comptroller, Mr. Vice Chamberlain, Mr. Secretary Vernon, Mr. Chancellor of the Exchequer, Lord Chief Justice, Sir Charles Hedges, and Mr. Smith.

The following record was made : This day the several proprietors of East and West New Jersey, in America, did, in person, present a deed of surrender, by them executed under their hands and seals, to Her Majesty in council, and did acknowledge the same to be their act and deed, and humbly desire Her Majesty to accept the same, that it might be enrolled in the court of chancery, whereby they did surrender their power of the government of those plantations, which Her Majesty graciously accepted, and was pleased to order, as it is hereby ordered that the same be enrolled in Her Majesty's said high court of chancery, and the said instruments to be delivered to Mr. Attorney-General, who is to take care that the same be enrolled accordingly.

L

Directly after the surrender, Edward Hyde (Lord Viscount Cornbury), grandson of the great Chancellor Clarendon, was ppointed governor of Nova Cæsaria, or New Jersey. His commission bears date December 5th, 1702, being the first year of the reign of Queen Anne.

She issued lengthy instructions to her right trusty, and well beloved Edward Lord Cornbury, our captain-general and governor-in-chief, in and over our province of Nova Cæsaria, or New Jersey, in America. Given at the court of St. James, the 16th day of November, 1702, in the first year of our reign.

He was ordered to repair with all convenient speed to the province, and, being there arrived, to take upon him the execution of the place and trust reposed in him, and forthwith to call together the following persons, whom we do, by these presents, appoint and constitute members of our council in and for that province, viz.: Edward Hunloke, Lewis Morris, Andrew Bowne, Samuel Jennings, Thomas Revell, Francis Davenport, William Pinhorne, Samuel Leonard, George Deacon, Samuel Walker, Daniel Leeds, William Sanford, and Robert Quarry,* Esquires.

At the first meeting of the council, he was with all due solemnity, to cause the commission under the great seal of England, constituting him captain-general and governor-in-chief, to be read and published, and to cause proclamation to be made in the several most public places in the province of his being constituted by the Queen, as captain-general and governor-in-chief. After this he was to take, and then administer to each of the members of council, the oath of office. He was then to communicate to the council such instructions received from the home government as he might deem requisite.

He was commanded to avoid engaging in with any of the parties who had previously, by their enmity to each other,

---

* Quarry was said to belong to the council for five governments at the same time, viz.: New York, New Jersey, Pennsylvania, Maryland, and Virginia. He died about the year 1712. Beverly, in his history of Virginia, represents him as joining with Nicholson, the then governor of that colony, in unfavorable representations against the colonies.

caused divisions in the province, but to endeavor to unite the different conflicting interests.

The members of council were to enjoy freedom of debate and vote, in all affairs of public concern.

Three members of council were to form a quorum, but they were not to act with a quorum of less than five members, except in cases of necessity.

The governor was to transmit to the crown the names of six persons, together with their characters and qualifications, who were inhabitants of the eastern division, and also six of the western division, whom he should esteem best qualified as councillors, and so from time to time as any should die, depart out of the province, or become unfit, in order that the list may be always complete.

All the officers so nominated for council, as also the principal officers, judges, assistants, justices and sheriffs, were to be men of good character, of good estates and abilities, well affected towards the government, and not much in debt.

The council as established was not to be augmented or diminished, and none of the members were to be suspended without good and sufficient cause.

In order the better to consolidate the two divisions of East and West Jersey under one government, he was to call a general assembly for the enactment of laws for the mutual good of the whole. The first general assembly was to sit at Perth Amboy, in East Jersey, and the next one at Burlington, in West Jersey, and the future assemblies were to sit at those places alternately.

The assembly was to be composed of twenty-four representatives, to be chosen, two by the inhabitants householders of the city or town of Perth Amboy, in East New Jersey; two by the inhabitants householders of Burlington, in West New Jersey; ten by the freeholders of East New Jersey, and ten by the freeholders of West New Jersey; and no one was eligible to be elected or sit in the assembly, who did not own one thousand acres of land in his own right, within the division for which he was chosen, and no one was allowed to vote, unless he owned one hundred acres of land in his own right, within the division for which he should so vote.*

Each different matter was to be provided for by a separate law, and none were to be intermixed in the same act, that had no proper relation to each other, or that was foreign to the title of the act.

No one was to be allowed to purchase any lands from the Indians, except the general proprietors.

He was to cause a census to be made of the population of the inhabitants of the province, and to keep an account of all persons born, christened, and buried.

He was to take especial care that God Almighty be devoutly and duly served throughout the government; the book of common prayer, as by law established, be read each Sunday and holy day, and the blessed sacrament administered according to the rites of the church of England. Liberty of conscience was to be extended to all persons except papists.

They were to give due encouragement to merchants and others, and in particular the Royal African Company of England, and the crown recommended unto said company that the province may have a constant and sufficient supply of merchantable Negroes, at moderate rates, in money or commodities. No trading from said province was to be allowed to any place in Africa within the charter of the Royal African Company, otherwise than was prescribed by act of parliament, entitled, " An act to settle the trade to Africa." And they were to report yearly to the commissioners the number of Negroes that were brought into the province and at what rates.

---

* The mode of distribution was changed by royal decree of Queen Anne, on the 3d of May, 1705, by which Perth Amboy was allowed to choose two, Burlington two, Salem two, two by each of the five counties of East Jersey, and two by each of the four counties of West Jersey, still keeping the number at twenty-four. No person was to be chosen or sit in the assembly unless he owned one thousand acres of land in the division, or personal estate to the value of five hundred pounds sterling, either in money, goods or chattels, and no one was allowed to vote unless he had one hundred acres of land, or personal estate in money, goods or chattels amounting to the value of fifty pounds sterling.

Appeals from the courts were to be made to the governor and council, provided the sum or value of the same exceeded one hundred pounds sterling, and in case the parties were then not satisfied they were to be allowed to appeal to the crown, in case the matter exceeded two hundred pounds sterling.

He was, by the assistance of the council and assembly, to find out the best means to facilitate and encourage the conversion of Negroes and Indians to the christian religion.

No person was allowed to keep a press for printing, nor was any book, pamphlet or other matters whatsoever, allowed to be printed without the especial leave or license first obtained from the governor.

CHAPTER VIII.

1703—1707.

Union of the two Provinces of East and West Jersey—Surrender to the Queen—Inconveniences in regard to currency—Conflict between the Assembly and Governor, by which he dissolves them—Cornbury assumes to be judge of the qualifications of members of Assembly—Resistance by the House—Remedies proposed to meet the evils in the Province—Queen Anne sustains the Assembly and removes the Governor.

THE distinction of the two provinces of East and West Jersey were, as to the government, after this time laid aside, and both were united in one under the name of Nova Cæsaria, or New Jersey, and all proceedings after that time were of a more uniform mode than they had been previously.

It was supposed that the surrender would restore peace and harmony in the province; in fact, such was the intention in making it, but in a short time we find them jointly struggling to preserve their privileges against what to them appeared to be the encroachments of the governor, who if his abilities had been equal to his birth and the interest he possessed in the province, he would have proved as formidable an antagonist as any that had come to the colonies, besides his noble birth, being the first cousin of Queen Anne, and son of a family that had received great merit in the revolution for valiant services performed. Having such an interest in the colony, with the disposition to promote harmony, had he not listened to the various factions who meanly sought to trumpet their own animosities, he might have accomplished the restoration of peace and quiet to the then distracted colony, and have laid the foundation for prosperity and greatness to the province, which was the principal aim in sending him hither; but this he utterly failed to accomplish, and his mission to that end proved a fruitless one, and the very work it was expected, and which he was sent to do, had to be done by another.

He was a man of noble birth, and inherited his titles from a long line of ancestors, who had always stood high in his native country, yet he had not the prowess to battle against the different factions he found in the province upon his assuming, by direction of the crown, the reins of government.

He had a large interest in the colonies, and his desire was for peace, but instead of using his own discretion in governing, he had a desire to please all, and by that means involved himself in constant turmoil and difficulties, and in striving to please all, he gave satisfaction to none, whereas had he pursued a different course, he would have rendered greater satisfaction.

Lord Cornbury arrived in New Jersey in the month of August, 1703, and his first act was to publish his commission, both at Amboy and Burlington. He then returned to his government at New York, where he remained but a short time, when he returned to New Jersey, and convened the assembly to meet on the 10th of November at Perth Amboy.* Thomas Gardiner was chosen speaker.†

He was presented and accepted, and then in conformity with the practice of parliament, they made a demand of the particular privileges of assemblies, as follows:

1. That the members, with their servants, shall be free from arrests or being molested in any way, during the session.

2. That they have free access to His Excellency's person, when occasion requires.

---

* The first representatives were Obadiah Bown, Jedediah Allen, Michael Howden, Peter Van Este, John Reid; John Harrison, Cornelius Tunison, Richard Hartshorne, Col. Richard Tounley, for the eastern division; and Thomas Lambert, William Biddle, William Stevenson, Restore Lippincott, John Kay, John Hugg, Jr., Joseph Cooper, William Hall, John Mason, and John Smith, for the western division; Peter Fretwell and Thomas Gardiner, for the town of Burlington; and Thomas Gordon and Miles Forster, for the city of Perth Amboy.

† Son of him whose death was mentioned before.

3. That they may have liberty of speech, and a favorable construction of all debates that may arise among them.

4. That if any misunderstanding shall happen to arise between the council and the house, that in such a case a committee of the council may be appointed to confer with a committee of the house, for adjusting and reconciling all such differences.

5. That these requests may be approved by His Excellency and council, and entered in the council books.

The governor, in answer, told them that he granted the three first, as the just and undoubted right of the house, but rejected the fourth as an innovation, and accordingly ordered an entry of the same in the council books, after which he made an address to the council and general assembly as follows :

"GENTLEMEN :—The proprietors of East and West New Jersey, having, upon very mature consideration, thought fit to surrender to Her Most Sacred Majesty, the Great Queen of England, my mistress, all the powers of government which they supposed were vested in them, the Queen has been pleased to unite these formerly two provinces, now into one, under the name of Nova Cæsaria, or New Jersey Her Majesty has been pleased graciously to honor me with the trust of this government, and has commanded me to assure you of her protection upon all occasions, and you may assure yourselves that under her auspicious reign, you will enjoy all the liberty, happiness and satisfaction that good subjects can wish for, under a most gracious Queen, and the best laws in the universe (I mean the laws of England), which all the world would be glad to partake of, and none are so happy to enjoy but those whose propitious stars have placed under the most happily constituted monarchy. I will not question but that you on your parts, will do all that can be expected from faithful subjects, both for the satisfaction of the Queen, and the good and safety of your country, which must be attended with general satisfaction to all people.

"In order to attain these good ends, I most earnestly recommend it both to you, gentlemen of Her Majesty's council, and you, gentlemen of the assembly, to apply yourselves heartily and seriously to the reconciling the unhappy differences which have happened in this province ; that as the Queen has united the two provinces, so the minds of all the people may be firmly united in the service of the Queen and good of the country, which are all one, and cannot be separated without danger of destroying both.

"Gentlemen, you are now met in general assembly on purpose to prepare such bills to be passed into laws, to be transmitted into England for Her Majesty's approbation, as may best conduce to the settling of this province upon a lasting foundation of happiness and quiet; only I must recommend it to you, that the bills you shall think fit to offer, may not be repugnant to the laws of England, but, as much as may be, agreeable to them. I must recommend to you, gentlemen, in the wording of your bills, to observe the style of enacting by the governor, council and assembly, and likewise that each different matter may be enacted by a different law, to avoid confusion.

"In all laws whereby you shall think fit to grant money, or to impose any fines or penalties, express mention may be made that the same is granted or reserved unto Her Majesty, her heirs or successors, for the public use of this province, and the support of the government thereof.

"Gentlemen, I am farther commanded by the Queen, to recommend it to you, to raise and settle a revenue for defraying the necessary charges of the government of this province, in order to support the dignity of it.

"I am likewise commanded to recommend to your care the preparing one or more bill or bills whereby the right and property of the general proprietors to the soil of this province may be confirmed to them, according to their respective titles, together with all quit rents and all other privileges as are expressed in the conveyances made by the Duke of York, except only the right of government, which remains in the Queen.

"Now, gentlemen, I have acquainted you with some of those things which the Queen is desirous to have done. I shall likewise acquaint you that Her Majesty has been graciously pleased to grant to all her subjects in this province (except papists) liberty of conscience. I must further inform you that the Queen has commanded me not to receive any present from the general assembly of this province, and that no person who may succeed me in this government may claim any present for the future. I am commanded to take care that Her Majesty's orders may be entered at large in the council books, and the books of the general assembly.

"Now, gentlemen, I have no more to offer you at this time, only I recommend to you dispatch in the matters before you, and unanimity in your consultations, as that which will always best and most effectually conduce to the good of the whole."

The governor's speech having been read in the house, the following address was made:

"*May it please your Excellency:*

"I am commanded by this house to return your Excellency our hearty thanks for your Excellency's many kind expressions to them contained in your Excellency's speech, and it is our great satisfaction that Her Majesty has been pleased to constitute your Excellency our governor.

"We are well assured the proprietors, by their surrender of their rights to the government of this province, have put us in circumstances much better than we were in under their administration, they not being able to protect us from the villainies of wicked men, and having an entire dependence on Her Majesty that she will protect us in the full enjoyment of our rights, liberties and properties, do thank your Excellency for that assurance you are pleased to give us of it, and think our stars have been very propitious in placing us under the government and direction of the greatest of Queens, and the best of laws. And we do entreat your Excellency to believe that our best endeavors shall not be wanting to accomplish those things which shall be for the satisfaction of the Queen, the general good of the country, and (if possible) to the universal satisfaction of all the people. With our prayers to the God of Heaven, we shall join our utmost endeavors to unite our unhappy differences, and hope, with the assistance of your Excellency and council, it will not be impossible to accomplish that blessed work. We shall follow the directions given in your Excellency's speech, with what dispatch the nature of the things require, and hope that all our consultations may conduce to the best and greatest ends.

"*Memorandum:* that all the members of this house do agree

to the subject matter above written, though several of them dissent from some of the expressions therein contained."

This address having been presented, the assembly, after regulating the elections complained of, prepared several bills, only one of which, that relating to the purchase of lands from the Indians, which was prepared in accordance with an article in Cornbury's instructions, received the sanction of the governor.

This bill prohibited purchases or gifts of land being made or received from the Indians without license from the proprietors, after December 1st, 1703, under penalty of forfeiting forty shillings per acre. It was also retrospective and made void all Indian bargains, gifts, leases or mortgages, without an English title, unless covered with a propriety right in six months thereafter.

The governor put an end to this session on the 13th of December, by notifying the assembly that the season being far advanced, it was absolutely necessary to conclude their business.

That he wished the several bills before him and them could have been dispatched, but that the matters contained in them were of so great moment, the difficulties so many and the time so short, that it was impossible to finish.

That being now acquainted with the nature of those difficulties, they should come prepared in the spring to remove them, and provide such good laws as might effectually ascertain the rights of the several proprietors, and fully secure every man's property.

These being the points which would most conduce to the peace and welfare of the colony, he recommended the council and assembly to employ their serious thoughts, that the most effectual means to attain those desirable ends might be discovered, and to point out other useful laws, and then he concludes with observing that they would ever find him ready to consent to all such things as should be for the good of the whole.

Great inconveniences were experienced in the year 1704, in consequence of the same coin bearing different values in the provinces on the continent. To remedy this by one general medium, Queen Anne published her proclamation for ascertaining the value of foreign coin in America, by which she reduced all foreign coins to the same current rate within all her dominions in America.

In order to show the just proportion which each coin ought to have to the other, she set forth in this proclamation that Sevill pieces of eight, old plate, weighing seventeen pennyweights twelve grains, should pass at the rate of four shillings and sixpence; Sevill pieces of eight,* new plate, fourteen pennyweight, three shillings and sevenpence one farthing; Mexico pieces of eight, seventeen pennyweights twelve grains, four shillings and sixpence; pillar pieces of eight, seventeen pennyweights twelve grains, four shillings and threepence six farthings; Peru pieces of eight, old plate, seventeen pennyweights twelve grains, four shillings and sixpence, or thereabouts; cross dollars, eighteen pennyweights, four shillings and fourpence three farthings; ducatoons of Flanders, twenty pennyweights and twenty-one grains, five shillings and sixpence; eau's of France, or Silver Louis, seventeen pennyweights twelve grains, four shillings and sixpence; crusadoes of Portugal, eleven pennyweights four grains, two shillings and tenpence one farthing; the silver pieces of Holland, twelve pennyweights and seven grains, five shillings and twopence one farthing; old rix dollars of the empire, eighteen pennyweights and ten grains, four shillings and sixpence; the half, quarters and other parts in proportion to their denominations, and light pieces in proportion to their weight.

From and after the 1st day of January, 1705, no Sevill, pillar, or Mexico pieces of eight, though of the full weight of seventeen pennyweights and a half, was to be accounted, received, taken or paid, within any of the colonies or plantations, at above the rate of six shillings per piece, current money, for the discharge of any contracts or bargains to be made after the said 1st day of January; the halves, quarters, and other lesser pieces of the same coins, to be accounted, received, taken, or paid in the same proportion, and the currency of all pieces of eight of Peru, dollars and other foreign species of silver coins, whether the same or baser alloy, shall, after the said 1st day of January,

---

* Eight to a dollar.

stand regulated according to their weight and fineness, and in proportion to the rate before limited, and set for the pieces of Sevill, pillar and Mexico. So that no foreign silver coin of any sort, be permitted to exceed the same proportion upon any account whatsoever.

This proclamation was dated at Windsor castle, June 18th, 1704, in the third year of the reign of Queen Anne.

Cornbury met the assembly at Burlington, the 7th of September, and his first recommendation to them was to prepare a bill to ascertain the rights of the general proprietors to the soil of the province, and to settle a fund for the support of government. He also took occasion to urge upon them the passage of a law to establish a militia, and also to establish a watch house on the Navesink hills. This was caused in consequence of a French privateer having committed a number of depredations on the settlers at Sandy Hook and the surrounding country.

They took these matters into consideration, but it appears that their acts did not suit the governor, for on the 28th, he abruptly sent for and dissolved them, and issued writs for a new election, and for the new assembly to meet at Burlington, on the 13th of November following.

This election was so managed, that a majority of the members returned were in accord with the governor.

They met at the time, but were divided in their choice for a speaker. The two candidates were Peter Fretwell and John Bowne, the votes for each being equal, they called upon their clerk, William Anderson, to give the casting vote, which he gave to Fretwell, who was accordingly placed in the chair,* then receiving the speech, they, by an address, complimented Cornbury with going through the affairs of government with great diligence and exquisite management, to the admiration of his

---

* The members of this assembly were John Bowne, Richard Hartshorn, Richard Salter, Obadiah Bown, Anthony Woodward, John Tunison, John Lawrence, Jasper Crane, Peter Van Este, Thomas Gorden, John Barclay, and John Royse, for the eastern division; and for the western division, Restore Lippincott, John Hugg, John Kay, John Smith, William Hall, John Mason, Thomas Bryan, Robert Wheeler, Peter Fretwell, Thomas Lambert, Thomas Gardiner, and Joshua Wright.

friends, and envy of his enemies, and passed a bill to raise two thousand pounds,* per annum, by tax, for the support of government, which was to continue two years.

At this session they passed several other laws, among which was one for establishing a militia, by the unnecessary severity of which those conscientiously scrupulous of bearing arms were great sufferers.

On the 12th of December, the governor adjourned them till next year, with more encomiums on their conduct than many of them received from their constituents on their return home, for their servility to the governor was almost universally condemned. During this session they had tamely submitted to the arbitrary will of Cornbury, to deprive them of three of their best members—Thomas Gardiner, Thomas Lambert, and Joshua Wright—under pretence of their not owning sufficient land to qualify them for a seat in the body, though they were well known to be men of sufficient estates.

The assembly again met at Amboy, in 1705, at which those who had composed the previous assembly declared in regard to these men, the members had heretofore satisfied the house of their being duly qualified to sit in the same, and they were then admitted, after the purposes of their exclusion had been fully answered. This session was in October and November, but nothing of much consequence was transacted, and the session which followed at the same place, in October, 1706, also proving unsuccessful, Cornbury again dissolved the assembly.

In the eleventh month of this year, the council of proprietors for the western division, met in accordance with their usual practice.

There were present at this meeting William Biddle, Samuel Jennings, (President) George Deacon, John Wills, William Hall, Christopher Wetherill, and John Kay.

Cornbury sent an order to this council, and proposed certain measures which he desired them to take action upon, but which, for some reasons, they delayed action thereon; but in the spring of the following year, 1707, he sent for the council of

---

*Out of this sum Lieutenant-Governor Ingolsby received six hundred pounds.

proprietors to meet him at Burlington, at which meeting he proposed a number of questions to them, on the same subject as he had previously, and demanded a positive answer to each.

The only satisfaction he received from them, was a summary of their constitution and establishment, a copy of which they sent him, as an answer to the three questions propounded by him to them.*

In their answer they put forth the questions propounded, which were as follows:

1. Who were the council of proprietors of last year, and who were chosen for this year, 1707, and to have the names of them?
2. What are the powers the said council pretend to have?
3. By whom constituted?

They replied, that the persons chosen for the last year to serve the proprietors as agents or trustees, were William Biddle, Samuel Jennings, George Deacon, John Wills, and Christopher Wetherill, for the county of Burlington; and John Reading, Francis Collings, John Kay, and William Hall, of Salem, for the county of Gloucester and below; and for the present year, 1707, William Biddle, Samuel Jennings, Lewis Morris, George Deacon, John Wills, John Kay, John Reading, Thomas Gardiner, and William Hall, of Salem.

In answer to the second question, they state that in the year 1677, the first ship came there from England, which brought the first inhabitants that came to settle in these remote parts. By virtue of Byllinge's right, before she sailed the proprietors met together in London to settle some certain method how the purchasers of land from Byllinge and others should have their just rights laid forth to them, and selected Joseph Helmsley, William Emley, John Penford, Benjamin Scott, Daniel Wills, Thomas Olive and Robert Stacy, as commissioners, empowering them to purchase what lands they could from the Indians, and to inspect

---

* This was delivered to Cornbury in council, on the 30th of the eleventh month. The proprietors then present were Samuel Jennings, William Hall, Thomas Gardiner, John Wills, John Kay, Christopher Wetherill, and Lewis Morris. With this answer, they delivered to the governor and council two papers containing the names of several of the proprietors, declaring the approbation of the council, and one Indian deed.

all rights as any lands were claimed, and when satisfied to order the laying out of the same, which they accordingly did.

Some of them being compelled to return to England, the management of their rights was assumed by the assembly, and so continued until 1687, when they relinquished it, and on the 14th of February of that year, the proprietors met at Burlington and chose and elected eleven persons from among themselves to act for the whole for the next ensuing year, (this was subsequently changed to nine) who accordingly ratified the constitution; since which time the same method had been practised, and no evil results had arisen from it, but on the contrary great advantage had been the result to the proprietors.

The powers of those that are now and have been all along, they are the same with the first that came over from England in 1677. As to the constitution of said agents, trustees or committee, and by whom constituted, it is on certain days in the county of Burlington and Gloucester, yearly and every year, they are chosen by the proprietors.

The above was substantially the report they made to his Excellency.

They concluded by saying: "The above is as good an account as we that are present are able to give, in answer to what was required of us by your lordship, and pray it may find acceptance as such, but if any other thing may seem needful to be answered, we humbly pray it may for this time be suspended, till the whole can be got together."

The writs for the new assembly were returnable to Burlington, April 5th, 1707.

It was soon manifest in this assembly that Cornbury had not the success in elections as in the former choice. His conduct having been arbitrary, the people were dissatisfied.

The assembly chose Samuel Jennings, speaker, received the governor's speech, and soon after resolved themselves into a committee of the whole house to consider grievances. This committee continued sitting from day to day, till at last they passed fifteen resolutions, which they laid before the Queen, together with a petition, on the 8th day of May. They also remonstrated their grievances to the governor.

This remonstrance contained much of a history of the times, and though things were carried to arbitrary lengths, there were not wanting in the province men of discernment to see and lament the unhappy situation of their country, and of spirit to oppose its greatest enemies; several of such were in this assembly, prominent among whom was the speaker.* He had very early known New Jersey, had lived in it through various changes and amid commotions, and had seen great alterations in it. Being largely concerned in public transactions, he knew what belonged to a public character. He had governed the western part of the province for several years, with integrity and reputation. He saw the advantages of a just confidence, and that this was the only way to acquire it. That though the office was in itself respectable, it was the honest execution of it that added to its dignity, produced the intended service, and secured the approbation of a kind but watchful mistress, who desired nothing but the welfare of her subjects, for such Queen Anne was ever found to be.

Jennings was also undaunted, and Lord Cornbury on his part, exacted the utmost decorum. While as speaker he was delivering the remonstrance, the governor frequently interrupted him with a stop, "What's that," &c., at the same time putting on a countenance of authority and sternness, the intention of which evidently was to confound him.

With due submission, yet firmness, whenever interrupted, he camly desired leave to read the passages over again, and did it with additional emphasis upon those most complaining, so that on the second reading they became more observable than at first.†

He at length got through, when the governor told the house to attend him again on Saturday next, at eleven o'clock, to receive his answer.

He did not, however, get ready with it until the 12th, when, sending for the house, he delivered it.

---

* Lewis Morris also now distinguished himself in behalf of privilege, and exercised a large share in the whole conduct of this assembly.

† After the house had adjourned, Cornbury, with some emotion, told those that were with him, that Jennings had impudence enough to face the devil.

The governor was surrogate-general, and before him all wills were admitted to probate, and this was one of the grievances the assembly complained of, as the governor resided at New York, and very seldom came into the province; in fact he admits in his answer, that he had only been there twice during the year, once at Burlington, and once at Amboy. He had, however, appointed a surrogate at Burlington, before whom any of the inhabitants of either division might have their wills proved.

The reply of the governor to the assembly's remonstrance, was a lengthy document, and in it he endeavored to answer the charges made by them.

The assembly did not, however, immediately reply to the governor, having the treasurer's, Peter Fauconier's, accounts to settle, in which they found many articles of an extraordinary nature, several of them having been paid by Cornbury's order merely, and the whole without vouchers. They therefore sent for the treasurer, and he came before them, but refused to produce his vouchers without the governor's commands.

Two members were sent to the governor, to request him to order the treasurer to lay the vouchers before them. The reply of the governor was that he had already ordered it, though he had no legal right to do so, because the lord high treasurer had appointed an auditor-general for the province, and he not being in it, had deputed one to audit the accounts, and that the treasurer was accountable only to the lord high treasurer. But if the house was dissatisfied with any of the articles in the account, and thought proper to apply to him, he would satisfy them. This was not, however, done, and the accounts, extraordinary as they were, remained unsettled till Governor Hunter's administration, several years after.

Several bills of considerable importance were now under consideration, but Cornbury, apprehensive that if he suffered the session to continue much longer it might be productive of something greatly to his disadvantage, so on the 16th he adjourned the house to meet at Amboy the September following.

They did not, however, meet till October, and the first thing they concluded on, was a reply to the answer of the governor to their remonstrance, after which they resolved that they would raise no money till the governor consented to redress the grievances of the country, which, if he did, they would raise one thousand five hundred pounds, for the support of the government for one year.

On the 28th, the house sent a committee to acquaint the governor that having seen his answer to their remonstrance in print, they thought it their duty to make a reply to it, and desired to know when he would admit them to wait on him with it.

The governor replied that he would return them an answer in due time. They waited for his message until the next day, and then concluding that he intended not to give them an opportunity of presenting it, sent a committee with it, and ordered it to be entered in full in their journal.

They told him " it were needless to hunt after imaginary grievances, as real ones in too great numbers present themselves, and though from you we have missed of obtaining that relief that the justice of our complaints entitled us to, yet we do not despair of being heard by Her Sacred Majesty, at whose royal feet we shall, in the humblest manner, lay an account of our sufferings, and however contemptible we are, or are endeavored to be made appear, we are persuaded Her Majesty will consider us as the representatives of the province of New Jersey, who must better know what are the grievances of the country they represent, than a governor can do, who regularly ought to receive information of that kind from them, and we do not doubt that glorious Queen, will make her subjects here as easy and happy as she can.

" When we told Your Excellency, we had reason to think some of our sufferings were very much owing to Your Excellency's long absence from this province, which rendered it very difficult to apply to your lordship in some cases that might need a present help, we spoke truth And notwithstanding all Your Excellency has said of a month's or twelve weeks being here in a year, and the weekly going of a post, we cannot be persuaded to believe that nine months and upwards, in a year, is not a long absence, especially when the seal of the province is carried and kept out of the government all that time, and the Honorable Colonel

Ingolsby, the lieutenant-governor, so far from doing right, that he declined doing any act of government at all. Whether he governs himself by Your Excellency's directions or not, we cannot tell. But sure we are, that this province, being as it were without government for above nine months in a year, we must still think it a great grievance, and not made less so by carrying the seal of the province to New York.

"We are apt to believe, upon the credit of Your Excellency's assertion, that there may be á number of people in the province who will never be faithful to, or live quietly under, any government, nor suffer their neighbors to enjoy any peace, quiet, nor happiness, if they can help it. Such people are pests in all government, have ever been so in this, and we know of none who can lay a fairer claim to these characters, than many of Your Excellency's favorites."

One of the complaints of the assembly was, that some persons under sentence of death for murder, have not only remained until this time unexecuted (they having been condemned not long after Lord Cornbury's accession to the government), but often have been suffered to go at large; one of those persons is a woman that murdered her own child, another a woman that poisoned her husband. The keeping of them so long has been a very great charge. The blood of these innocents cries aloud for vengeance, and just Heaven will not fail to pour it down upon our already miserable country, if they are not made to suffer according to their demerits.

To this Cornbury answered: "Two women that have been condemned for murdering, have not been executed, there having appeared most notorious malice and revenge in some people who were zealous in their prosecutions. The Queen is the fountain of honor, justice and mercy, and as she is so, she may, when she pleases, exert her mercy, either in reprieving or pardoning the criminal. That power of pardoning and reprieving, after condemnation, the subjects of this province, Her Majesty has been pleased to entrust me with, and I am no ways accountable to any person or number of persons whatsoever, for what I do in those matters, but to the Queen's Majesty alone."

To this the assembly again replies:

"What malice and revenge were in the prosecution of the condemned persons, we don't know.

"We never heard of any till now, and hardly can be persuaded to believe it's possible there should be in both instances.

"It is not impossible, there might be malice in the prosecution of the woman who was condemned for poisoning her husband, there not being, as is said, plain proof of the fact, but it was proved she had attempted it before more than once, and there were so many other concurring circumstances as did induce the jury, who were of the neighborhood, and well knew her character, to find her guilty, and it is hardly probable their so doing was an act of malice.

"The woman who murdered her own child, did it in such a manner, and so publicly, that it is unreasonable to suppose there could be any malice in the prosecution of her, and we cannot think, notwithstanding Your Excellency's assertions, that you can or may believe there was. This woman was a prisoner in the sheriff's custody for breach of the peace, and going about some of the household affairs the sheriff employed her in, with a knife in her hand, her child, who was something forward, followed her, crying, upon which the mother turned back to it and cut its throat; but not having cut it deep enough, the child still followed her, all bloody, and crying 'O! mother, you have hurt me,' the mother turned back a second time, and cut it effectually, and then took it up and carried it to the sheriff, or his wife, at whose feet she laid it. How far such a wretch is entitled to the Queen's favor, Her Majesty can best tell, when she is made acquainted with the fact, but sure we are, she never gave Your Excellency the power of pardoning willful murder. Whether Your Excellency has or has not reprieved them, you best know, and are only accountable to Her Majesty for your procedures therein, though we have too much reason to believe, the favorable opinion Your Excellency has so publicly expressed of her, has been a great reason to induce her to make her escape, which she has done."

Cornbury, contrary to all law or custom, assumed to be the judge of the qualifications of the members of the assembly, and dictated to them whether they should be received or not, which they, in their address to the Queen, stigmatized as a direct contradiction to the very nature and being of assemblies, and which, if allowed, would render the liberties, lives and properties of the people entirely at the disposal of the executive, which was never intended by Her Majesty. The house was therefore compelled, in order to sustain its dignity, to take notice of a procedure which would tend to destroy the very being of assemblies by rendering them the tools of a governor's arbitrary pleasure, and the enemies instead of the preservers of the liberties of the country.

Her Majesty's loyal subjects were taken to jails, and there allowed to remain without being admitted to bail. Several of Her Majesty's good subjects were forced to abscond and leave their habitations, being threatened with imprisonment, and no hopes of receiving the benefit of the law, when the absolute will of the governor is the sole measure of it.

They set forth that "one minister of the Church of England was dragged by a sheriff from Burlington to Amboy, and there kept in custody, without any reason having been assigned for it, and was at last hauled by force into a boat by his Excellency, and transported like a malefactor into another government, and there kept in a garrison a prisoner, without any reason being assigned for these violent procedures but the pleasure of his excellency.

"Another minister of the Church of England was laid under the necessity of leaving the province, from the reasonable apprehensions of meeting with the same treatment. No orders of men, either sacred or civil, were secure in their lives, their liberties or estates, under Cornbury's arbitrary rule."

They then go on to say: "If these, and what we have named before, be acts of mercy, gentleness and good nature; if this be doing for the good, welfare and prosperity of the people of this province; if this be the administering laws for the protection and preservation of Her Majesty's subjects, then have we been the most mistaken men in the world, and have had the falsest notion of things, calling that cruelty, oppression and injustice, which are their direct opposites, and these things slavery, imprisonment and hardships, which are freedom, liberty and ease, and must henceforth take France, Denmark, the Muscovian, Ottoman and Eastern empires, to be the best models of a gentle and happy government."

The western proprietors residing in England had resented Cornbury's treatment of the inhabitants, especially in relation to the three members being kept out of the assembly, by which he secured a majority devoted to his measures. They issued a memorial to the right honorable the Lords Commissioners for trade and plantations, dated November 15th, 1704, in which they acknowledge the justness of the commissioners in making the terms of the surrender of government part of Lord Cornbury's instructions relating to the province, and regretted that his Excellency had not given them occasion to acknowledge his due observance of these instructions instead of their having to trouble them with a complaint of his breach of them.

They assert that the instructions in regard to representatives and electors, which was relied upon by them as the chief security of their estates in that province, his Excellency not only violated but totally destroyed that part of the constitution in such a manner as to render all assemblies a mere piece of formality, and only the tools of a governor's arbitrary pleasure.

Their memorial was quite a lengthy document, but as most of the matters contained in it have been before introduced, we deem it unnecessary to quote more at length.

Two days after Cornbury had refused to receive the assembly's reply he sent for them, and though several important bills were unfinished, adjourned the house to the spring of the following year. Not having received the reply in form, he escaped the necessity of attempting to clear up what he could not do with justice and equity. Some of the glaring facts still confirmed the truth of the charges against him. He thought he had a more effectual way of dealing, which was, to lodge a complaint with the Queen, and to accomplish his ends he procured his trusty friend Ingolsby, the lieutenant-governor, with some of the council, to sign and privately transmit an address to her.

This address was signed by Richard Ingolsby, William Pinhorne, R. Mompeson, Thomas Revell, Daniel Leeds, Daniel Coxe, Richard Townley, Robert Quarry, and William Sandford. It set forth, "that the lieutenant-governor and council (although it was signed by only eight of the council out of twenty-four,) while the petition of the West Jersey proprietors alone was signed by eighteen of the proprietors residing in England, and the remonstrance was signed by the speaker in behalf of the majority of the assembly, who adopted it *nemine contradicente*, (without opposition of the minority) of Your Majesty's province of Nova Cæsaria or New Jersey, having seriously and deliberately taken into consideration the proceedings of the present assembly or representative body of this province, thought ourselves bound, both in duty and conscience, to testify to Your Majesty our dislike and abhorrence of the same, being very sensible that the unaccountable honors and pernicious designs of some particular men,* have put themselves upon so many irregularities, with intention only to occasion divisions and distractions, to the disturbance of the great and weighty affairs which both Your Majesty's honor and dignity, as well as peace and welfare, of the country required. Their high encroachments upon Your Majesty's prerogative royal; notorious violations of the rights and liberties of the subjects; manifest interruptions of justice and most unmannerly treatment of his Excellency Lord Cornbury, would have induced us sooner to have discharged our duty to Your Majesty, in giving a full representation of the unhappy circumstances of this Your Majesty's province and government, had we not been in hopes that His Excellency, the Lord Cornbury's, full and ample answer to a most scandalous libel, called the remonstrance of the assembly of Nova Cæsaria, or New Jersey, which was delivered to the governor by the assembly at Burlington in May last, would have opened the eyes of the assembly and brought them back to their reason and duty; but finding that these few turbulent and uneasy spirits in the assembly† have still been able to influence and amuse the judgments of many well-meaning men in that body, as appears by a late *scandalous and infamous libel* called, " The reply of the house of representatives of the province of New Jersey, to an

---

* The assembly representing the whole people.

† He stigmatizes them as few, when they were two-thirds of the entire assembly, representing in the same ratio, the people of the province.

answer made by His Excellency, Edward Viscount Cornbury, governor of the said province, to the humble remonstrance of the aforesaid house. We are now obliged humbly to represent to Your Majesty the true cause which we conceive may lead to the remedy of these confusions.

"The first is owing to the turbulent, factious, uneasy, and disloyal principles of two men in that assembly, Mr. Lewis Morris, and Samuel Jennings, a quaker;* men notoriously known to be uneasy under all government; men never known to be consistent with themselves; men to whom all the factions and confusions in the government of New Jersey and Pennsylvania for many years are wholly owing; men that have had the confidence to declare in open council that Your Majesty's instructions to your governors in these provinces shall not oblige or bind them, nor will they be concluded by them further than they are warranted by law, of which also they will be the judges. And this is done by them (as we have all reason in the world to believe) to encourage not only this government, but also the rest of your governments in America, to throw off Your Majesty's royal prerogative, and consequently to involve your dominions in this part of the world, and the honest, good and well meaning people in them, in confusion, hoping thereby to obtain their wicked purposes.

"The remedy for all these evils, we most humbly propose, is, that Your Majesty will most graciously please to discountenance these wicked, designing men, and show some dislike to this assembly's proceedings, who are resolved neither to support this Your Majesty's government by a revenue, nor take care to defend it by settling a militia.

"The last libel, called 'the reply, &c.,' came out so suddenly,† that as we have yet had no time to answer it in all its particulars, but do assure Your Majesty it is for the most part false in facts, and that part of it which carries any face of truth, they have been malicious and unjust in not mentioning the whole truth,

---

* These two were the most staunch patriots in the assembly, and had the entire confidence of the people.

† Because the governor could not answer it, he at once dissolved the assembly.

which would have fully justified my Lord Cornbury's just conduct. Thus, having discharged this part of our duty, which we thought at present incumbent upon us, we beg leave to assure Your Majesty that whenever we shall see the people of this province labor under anything like a grievance, we shall, according to our duty, immediately apply to the governor, with our best advice for the redress of it, and we have no reason yet to doubt of a ready compliance in him.

"We shall not be particular, but crave leave to refer to His Excellency's representation of them to the right honorable the lords commissioners for trade and plantations.

"The strenuous asserting of Your Majesty's prerogative royal, and vindicating the honor of your governor, the Lord Cornbury, will in our humble opinion, be so absolutely necessary at this juncture, that without your so doing, Your Majesty will find yourself deceived, either in expectation of a revenue for support of the government, or militia for its defence.

"In hopes Your Majesty will take these important things into consideration, and His Excellency the Lord Cornbury, with all the members of Your Majesty's council, into your royal favor and protection, we shall conclude with our most fervent prayers to the Most High, to lengthen your days and increase your glories. And that ourselves in particular, and all others in general, who reap the benefits of Your Majesty's most gentle and happy government, may be, and ever continue, the most loyal and dutiful of subjects to the most glorious and best of Queens."

The grievance of the assembly was duly taken into consideration by Queen Anne, and she was, under the circumstances, compelled to recall Lord Cornbury, and Lord John Lovelace was appointed to succeed him.

The colonists left their own country and came here to avoid oppression and tyrany, and to seek an asylum in a new country, where they could peaceably enjoy their liberties, both civil and religious, but when their governor manifested towards them such acts of unwarranted hostility, their consciences and their love for the good Queen Anne, would not permit them tamely to submit, and they were therefore compelled to remonstrate;

their remonstrance was heard and their wrongs speedily redressed. They intended here to establish a home for the oppressed of all nations, religions and creeds. Their constitution was a liberal one, and guaranteed to them all the rights of freedom, and when efforts were being made to trample those rights in the dust, they wisely remonstrated against them, their petitions were heard and their grievances remedied at once, for had it not been, they had resolved not to tamely submit to what they considered and felt was an unwarrantable interference in their just and established rights, guaranteed to them when they landed on these shores, and these rights they were determined to maintain, peaceably if they could, but by force if they must. Thus in all time showing the spirit which has animated our forefathers.

CHAPTER IX.

1708—1710.

Lord Lovelace succeeds Cornbury—His conciliatory measures satisfactory to the Assembly and People—Paper money established in the Province—Expedition to reduce Canada and drive out the French—Troops promised from England—The French Governor capitulates—Expedition against Port Royal, in Arcadia—Major Sanford expelled from the House for signing a false statement to the Queen.

ON the 5th of May, 1708, the assembly met at Burlington. Samuel Jennings, the speaker, being ill at the time, Thomas Gordon was appointed to succeed him.

They received the speech of the governor, and on the 12th delivered the address of the assembly, which contained the old story of grievances.

This so displeased the governor that he immediately adjourned them to the following September, to meet at Amboy, but in the interval dissolved them, but being himself so soon after superceded, he met them no more.

The business of the last session began by his telling them in his speech, that it was his great desire to see the service of the Queen and the good of the province carried on, supported and provided for, that induced him to call them together, to prepare and pass such laws as were proper, and that he might not be wanting in his duty, he should point out what he thought required their immediate attention.

The first was a bill for the support of government, that the revenue the Queen expected was fifteen hundred pounds per annum, to continue twenty-one years.

Next the reviving or re-enacting the militia bill, which would soon expire.

That he had every session since he had been governor, recommended the passing of a bill or bills for confirming the right and property of the soil of the province to the general proprietors, according to their repective rights and titles, as also to settle and confirm the particular titles and estates of all the inhabitants of the province, and others claiming under the proprietors. That he was still of opinion, such a bill would best conduce to the improvment, as well as peace and quiet of the province. That he had last year recommended the passing of bills for erecting and repairing prisons and court-houses in the different counties; the building of bridges in places where they were wanting, by general tax; and as late experience had taught the necessity of settling the qualifications of jurymen, he desired they would prepare bills for these purposes, and revive such of the acts of assembly, passed in the time of the proprietary government, as would be of use, that they might be presented for the Queen's approbation.

On this occasion the assembly, in their address, declare that they were and always had been, ready and desirous to support the government to the utmost of their poor abilities; that they were heartily sorry for the misunderstanding between the governor and them; that about twelve months ago they had humbly represented to him some of the many grievances their country labored under, most of which, they were sorry to say, yet remained and daily increased; that they found the Queen's good subjects of the province were continually prosecuted by informations upon frivolous pretences, which rendered that excellent constitution of grand juries useless, and if continued would put it in the power of an attorney-general to raise his future upon the ruin of his country; that they found it a great charge to the country, that juries and evidences were brought from remote parts of the province to the supreme courts at Burlington and Amboy.

That it was a great grievance that the practice of the law was so precarious that innocent persons were prosecuted upon informations and actions brought against several of the Queen's subjects, in which the gentlemen licensed to practice the law were afraid to appear for them, or if they appeared, did not discharge their duty to their clients for fear of being suspended, without being convicted of any crime deserving it or reason assigned, as was done at Burlington in May last, to the damage of many of the Queen's good subjects.

That they found the representatives of this Her Majesty's province so slighted and their commands so little regarded, that the clerk of the crown had refused to issue a writ for the electing a member wanting in the house. They hoped he would consider and remove these and many other inconveniences and grievances that the province labored under, which would enable them to exert the utmost of their abilities in supporting Her Majesty's government, and would make them happy under the mild and meek administration of a great and glorious queen.

That they doubted not, were her Majesty rightly informed of the poverty and circumstances of their country and that their livelihoods depended upon the seasons of the year, their most gracious sovereign would pity their condition, and never expect the settlement of any support of government further than from one year to another; that they found the present militia bill so great a grievance to their country, they could never think of reviving or re-enacting it as it now was, though they were heartily willing to provide for the defence of their country, which they hoped might be done with greater ease to the people; that they had been and still were endeavoring to answer Her Majesty's commands, in confirming the right and property of the soil of the province to the general proprietors according to their respective rights and titles, and likewise to confirm and settle the particular titles and estates of all the inhabitants, and other purchasers claiming under the proprietors, but though they had several times met in general assembly, they had not opportunity to perfect it.

They acknowledge the favor of being put in mind of providing prisons, court-houses, and bridges, where such are wanting, which they should take into consideration; that they had a bill for settling the qualifications of juries, prepared last sitting at Amboy, and should now present it, and thanking him for reminding them of reviving their former laws say, they had before appointed a committee for that end, but were impeded by Basse, the secretary, positively refusing to let them have the perusal of them; and that as they had always used their utmost endeavor in the faithful service of the Queen, and for the benefit of the country, so they should still continue to do it with all the despatch they were capable of.

We now part with Lord Cornbury's administration;* at the same time also we part with Samuel Jennings, but not with the same feelings that we part with Cornbury, for his whole energies were devoted to the interests of the people, and was highly esteemed both in his private life and as a legislator.

His indisposition continued for about twelve months, when he died regretted and lamented, for his many social virtues endeared him to the hearts of the people, and he could upon all occasions

---

* At a council held at Amboy, March 28th, 1708, the petition of Edward Viscount Cornbury, late governor of this province, setting forth that he had due to him sundry sums of money, for which he desired warrants to enable him, if the revenue of this province was not able to pay the same, he might demand it of Her Majesty, was read and dismissed.

"Lord Cornbury (says a writer, well informed as to his character,) was no less obnoxious to the people of New Jersey than those of New York. The assembly of that province, impatient of his tyranny, drew up a complaint against him, which they sent home to the Queen. Her Majesty graciously listened to the cries of her injured subjects, divested him of his power, and appointed Lord Lovelace in his stead, declaring that she would not countenance her nearest relations in oppressing her people.

"As soon as my lord was superseded, his creditors threw him into the custody of the sheriff of New York, and he remained there till the death of his father, when succeeding to the Earldom of Clarendon, he returned to England.

"We never had a governor so universally detested, nor any who so richly deserved the public abhorrence. In spite of his noble descent, his behavior was trifling, mean and extravagant.

"It was not uncommon for him to dress himself in a woman's habit, and then to patrol the fort in which he resided (Fort Ann, in New York). Such freaks of low humor exposed him to the universal contempt of the people, but their indignation was kindled by his despotic rule, savage bigotry, insatiable avarice and injustice, not only to the public but even his private creditors, for he left some of the lowest tradesmen in his employment unsatisfied in their just demands." He died in 1723. (History of New York, page 116.)

be fully relied on. His many services have occasioned him to be often mentioned. His religion was that of the Quakers, and he was early in life an approved minister among them, and so continued until his death. Common opinion, apt to limit this sphere of action, will however, allow general rues to have their exceptions, as instances now and then, though perhaps but rarely, occur, where variety of talents have united in the same individual, and yet not interfered. Such, the accounts of these times (stripped of the local uncertainties of faction and party) tell us was the circumstance with regard to Jennings. That his authority, founded on experienced candor, probity, and abilities, enlarged opportunities rendered him not in one capacity or to one society only, but generally useful. It is mentioned that he was of an obliging, affectionate disposition, yet of a hasty, warm temper, and that he notwithstanding managed it with circumspection and prudence, so that few occasions escaped to the disadvantage of his character, or of any cause he engaged in.

That he saw the danger to which his natural impetuosity exposed him ; knew his preservation lay in a close attention to his cooler prospects, and diligently guarding in that spot, experienced the benefit in many trying events; that his integrity and fortitude in all stations were acknowledged ; that his judgment was the rule of his conduct, and this seems to have been but seldom injudiciously founded ; that alive to the more generous emotions of a mind formed to benevolence and acts of humanity, he was a friend to the widow, the fatherless, and the unhappy. Tender, compassionate, disinterested, and with great opportunities, he left but a small estate ; that abhoring oppression in every shape, his whole conduct discovered a will to relieve and befriend mankind, far above the littleness of party or sinister views ; that his sentiments of right and liberty were formed on the revolution establishment, a plan successfully adapted to the improvement of a new country, or any country ; that he was notwithstanding all this sometimes thought stiff and impracticable, but chiefly on account of his political attachments, yet that there were instances where better knowledge of his principles and the sincerity with which he acted, totally effaced those impressions, and left him friends where none were expected. Much of his time was long devoted to the public, with a will to be useful, and for which ample occasion during those times offered. West Jersey and Pennsylvania* and New Jersey, after the surrender, in all about twenty-eight years successively, were repeated witnesses of his sterling conduct in the different positions he held. His constant aim was to study the peace and welfare of mankind, though like many other honest men, he found those who opposed him, and in some instances even met with ungrateful returns for the good he accomplished, and though his endeavors did not always succeed to his mind, he yet survived personal accusations in a great measure, with respect to himself, and the good will of those who approved his course, and as it regarded the public generally, he lived long enough to see it emerging from an unpromising state of litigation and controversy to greater quiet than had been known for many years.

He left three children (daughters), these intermarried with three brothers of the name of Stevenson, whose descendants still reside in New Jersey and Pennsylvania.

In the latter end of 1708, a new assembly was chosen.

The names of the members were Thomas Gordon, Thomas Farmer, Elisha Parker, John Royse, John Harrison, Benjamin Lyon, Gershom Mott, Elisha Lawrence, John Trent, William Morris, Enoch Machelsen, and Mr. Eldridge, for the western division; Thomas Gardiner, Thomas Raper, Hugh Sharp, Nathaniel Cripps, John Kay, John Kaign, Richard Johnson, Nathaniel Breading, Hugh Middleton, and John Lewis, for the eastern.

This assembly met and chose Thomas Gordon speaker, but was dissolved upon the new governor's arrival.

John Lord Lovelace, baron of Hurley, having, as before stated, been appointed to succeed Lord Cornbury, summoned the council to meet him at Bergen, December 20th, 1708, published his commission, and met a new assembly in the spring, at Perth Amboy, and informed them:

"That he was very sensible of great difficulties attending the

---

* He lived some years in Pennsylvania, and held several important offices in that province.

honorable employment in which Her Majesty had placed him, and he hoped they would never fail to assist him to serve the Queen and her people.

"That Her Majesty had shown, in the whole course of her reign, (a reign glorious beyond example), how much she aimed at the good and prosperity of her people, having with indefatigable pains, united her two kingdoms of England and Scotland, and continued the same application to unite the minds of all her subjects. That this was her great care, and ought to be the care of those whom she deputed to govern the distant provinces not happy enough by situation to be under her more immediate government. That, as he could not set before them a better pattern, he should endeavor to recommend himself to them, by following, as far as he was able, her example. That he should not give them any just cause of uneasiness, under his administration, and hoped they would bear with one another.

"That past differences and animosities ought to be buried in oblivion, and the peace and welfare of the country only pursued by each individual. That Her Majesty would not be burthensome to her people, but there being an absolute necessity that the government be supported, he was directed to recommend that matter to their consideration. That they knew best what the province could conveniently raise for its support, and the easiest methods of raising it. That the making a law for putting the militia on a better footing than it at present stood, with as much ease to the people as possible, required their consideration.

"That he should always be ready to give his assent to whatever laws they found necessary for promoting religion and virtue, for the encouragement of trade and industry, and discouragement of vice and profaneness, and for any other matter or thing relating to the good of the province."

The assembly issued an address, in which they told the governor, that they esteemed it their great happiness, that Her Majesty had placed a person of so much temper and moderation over them, and made no question he would surmount every difficulty with honor and safety.

"That Her Majesty's reign would make a bright leaf in history.

That it was the advantage of the present, and would be the admiration of future ages, not more for her success abroad than prudence at home.

"That though their distance had, and might sometimes be disadvantageous to them, yet they experienced the effect of her princely care, in putting an end to the worst administration New Jersey ever knew, by sending him, whose government would always be easy to Her Majesty's subjects here, and satisfactory to himself, whilst he followed so great and good an example.

"That they had no animosities with one another, but firmly agreed to do themselves and their country justice. That they were persuaded none that deserved public censure, would have a share in his esteem, and doubted not of meeting with his hearty concurrence in every measure that conduced to peace and good order.

"That they should support the government to the utmost of their abilities, and most willingly so at a time when they were freed from bondage and arbitrary encroachments, and were convinced that vice and immorality would no more receive the public countenance and approbation."

They assured him all his reasonable desires would be commands to them, and promised it should be their study to make his administration as easy and happy as they could.

This session of the assembly lasted a month, in which business went on with unusual smoothness. The assembly obtained from the governor a copy of the address from the lieutenant governor and council to the Queen, in 1707.

They returned him their thanks for the favor, and requested he would desire the lieutenant governor, and all that signed the address, to attend him at such time as he thought fit to appoint, to prove their allegation, and that the house might have leave to be present, and have opportunity of making their defence, in order to clear themselves from such imputations.

The governor showed a ready inclination to grant this request, and appointed a day for a hearing, but, by the artifices of those concerned, it was evaded from time to time. We are not aware whether they at last gained their point or not.

Most of the inhabitants of New Jersey, now pleased themselves with the prospect of happy times. With a change of governors followed a change of measures and favorites.

Impartiality and candor succeeded trickery and design. The tools of the former administration having nothing but the protection of that to support them, sunk into oblivion.

It was Cornbury's weakness to encourage men that would flatter his vanity, and give in to his humors and measures. Such were sure of his favors, but with Lovelace, the case was different.

Such of the former favorites as yet continued in the council, were not looked upon with that esteem that the other members were, even the confidence which had been usually put in that board, on passing the support bill, was discontinued.

The assembly declared to Lovelace, that though they had entire confidence in his justice and prudence, respecting the disposition of the money for the support of government, they had not the confidence in the gentlemen that were now of Her Majesty's council, and that this was the reason they had altered the former method, and requested that he would favorably represent it to the Queen in their behalf.

The difference of these administrations will appear in a short comparison.

Cornbury, on the subject of support, makes use of the following expressions:

"That I may not be wanting in my duty, in the station the Queen has been pleased to honor me with, I shall put you in mind of those things which I think ought to be immediately provided for; the first of which is providing a revenue for the support of government. The revenue which the Queen expects is fifteen hundred pounds a year, for twenty-one years."

Lord Lovelace, ten months afterwards, upon the same occasion, speaks as follows:

"Her Majesty would not be burthensome to her people, but there being an absolute necessity that the government be supported, I am desired to recommend that matter to your consideration. You know best what the province can conveniently raise for its support, and the easiest method of raising it."

By this difference in the men administering the government,

it may be easily seen that the inhabitants had some reason to promise themselves more happy times than they had experienced heretofore, especially under the administration of Cornbury; but just as things were getting into a good shape, and likely to prove advantageous to the colonists, and to their very great disappointment, Lord Lovelace was suddenly taken away from them by death, for he died within a few days afterwards, and the administration devolved upon the lieutenant governor, Ingolsby, who laid before the assembly the design of the crown respecting an expedition against Canada, under Colonels Nicholson and Vetch.

The assembly immediately voted three thousand pounds for this service, by an emission of paper bills of credit, but did not at this time pass the bills.

The lieutenant governor adjourned them for a few weeks, and then told them he had given them another opportunity of doing their duty to Her Majesty, and what their country required at their hands.

That he found in their votes at the last sitting, a resolution for raising three thousand pounds for Her Majesty's service. That this had now become a debt, and they had only to consider the ways and means of raising it, and that a proper application was made for the paying of their quota of men appointed for reducing Canada.

The assembly prepared three bills: one for raising three thousand pounds, another for enforcing its currency,* and a

---

* Here began the paper currency in New Jersey. The care of the legislature respecting it, in this as well as all the succeeding emissions, being to render the funds for sinking, according to the acts that created it secure, and to prevent the currency failing in value, by changing the bills as they became ragged and torn, and allowing no re-emissions on any account whatsoever, it has from the beginning preserved its credit, and proved of great service to the proprietors in the sale of their lands, and to the settlers, in enabling them to purchase and contract, and pay English debts, and go on with their improvements. The securities, when issued on loan, were double the value in lands, and treble in houses, and five per cent. interest.

The funds for sinking, by tax, the money created for the expedition and other purposes, were mortgages (secured in the acts that made the respective emissions,) on the estates, real and personal, in the province.

Hence they were secured as firmly as the province itself. They were a tnird for the encouragement of volunteers going on the Canada expedition. These bills having received the governor's assent, the house was adjourned to November 1st, to meet at Burlington.

They accordingly met pursuant to their adjournment, but deferred business until December, at which time they sat ten weeks, and passed eighteen bills. They were then adjourned, and afterwards prorogued from time to time, until they were dissolved by Governor Hunter, in 1710.

For a few months before Governor Hunter's arrival, William Pinhorne, as president of the council, exercised the office of commander-in-chief.

In the latter part of the year 1708, Colonel Vetch first applied to the court of Great Britain, for sea and land forces, to reduce Canada.

He, with Colonel Nicholson, obtained a small force from England, with instructions from the several governors on the continent to give them what assistance they could. They had a promise of a fleet of ships of war to follow them in due time. They came over in the beginning of the summer of 1709,* and

---

legal tender to all the inhabitants, in the province and elsewhere, but not to others, except while in the province. The remittances of this province to England, being chiefly from New York and Philadelphia, and these bills not being legal tenders there, they could not operate to the prejudice of English debts, let exchange be what it may, because none were obliged to take them. This was a particularity only belonging to the state of trade of New Jersey, and rendered a paper currency here, free from the objections usually made against it in England.

* Colonels Nicholson and Vetch both appearing at a council held at Amboy, May 30th, 1709, it was concluded that George Riscarricks should be forthwith sent to Weequehala, the Indian Sachem, to acquaint him that the lieutenant-governor, Ingolsby, expected his attendance on that board forthwith, and that Captain Aarent Schuyler should forthwith send for Macotuinst, Cohcowickick, Ohtoffolonoppe, Meskakow, and Teetee, Sachems of the Minisinks and Shawhona Indians, who, appearing soon afterwards, joined in the undertaking, and Ingolsby, governor of New Jersey, G. Saltonstall, governor of Connecticut, and G. Gookin, governor of Pennsylvania, jointly commissioned Colonel Peter Schuyler, on the 23d of May, 1709, to be over these and the other Indians on this expedition, and soon afterwards the three governors joined in a petition to Nicholson, that he would take upon him the chief command of the expedition, after which he bore the name of General Nicholson.

brought with them full instructions from the Queen in reference to the expedition, directed to Colonel Vetch. These instructions were signed by the Queen at the Court of St. James, the 28th of February, 1708-9.

New York was to furnish eight hundred men, New Jersey two hundred, Connecticut three hundred and fifty, and Pennsylvania one hundred and fifty, making fifteen hundred in all.

Colonels Nicholson and Vetch brought over with them four regular companies from England.

The provincial troops were formed into four battalions, with each of which was attached one company of regulars.

All things were to be in readiness by the middle of May, the arms and ammunition were furnished from the magazine at New York. Three months provisions were furnished them. A large storehouse was built to contain the provisions, and six large boats to carry sixty men each for the transportation of the heavier stores by water, and a contract was made with the Five Nations of Indians to make with all speed as many canoes as would be wanted for the expedition. They also engaged the Five Nations, as well as the Indians on the river, to join the expedition, and inducements were held out to all who were willing to go as volunteers.

The governors of New England and Rhode Island were required to raise at least twelve hundred of their best men, and to give encouragement to such as were willing to go as volunteers, and to furnish transports, with three months provisions, and able pilots. Captain Southwick* volunteered with his own galley.†

They were to contract with ship carpenters to build ten or more large flat bottomed boats, to carry sixty men each, for the landing of troops, and also to contract with proper persons for furnishing eight months provision to the troops that were to be left at Quebec or Montreal.

As an inducement to furnish the quota of men required for

---

* He was master of the province galley, belonging to the Massachusetts government.

† A light open boat, used by custom house officers, as well as for pleasure.

the expedition, they were to assure the different governments that such as contributed towards the reduction of Canada should have a preference both with regard to the soil and trade of the country when reduced, to any other of the subjects of the Queen, and she would on her part sanction the same, when the country should be reduced.

Colonel Francis Nicholson offered himself as a volunteer on this expedition, and having in due time arrived in the country and went to work raising the necessary forces on this continent, but in consequence of a difference of opinion having arisen in the ministry at home, the ships of war in accordance with their expectation did not arrive.

They waited without doing anything until winter, when Nicholson returned to England to solicit further assistance, and to send forward what had been proposed.

To do this with more probability of success, they prevailed upon four Indian Sachems of the Five Nations to accompany him to England, to assist in getting up the expedition.* With

---

* Indians in England were at that time a strange sight. These Sachems also met with great consideration on account of the faithfulness and importance of the nation they belonged to, and accordingly were much taken notice of. The English court was at this time in mourning for the death of George, Prince of Denmark; the Queen therefore had under garments of black cloth made for them, and covered with a scarlet mantle edged with gold. They were carried to court in coaches, and introduced in form to the Queen. One of them made a speech, setting forth that they doubted not the Queen was acquainted with their long and tedious war against the French, in conjunction with her children (subjects); that they had been a strong wall for the security of these, even to the loss of their best men, as Quider and Anadagarjaux (Schuyler and Nicholson) could testify; that they were glad an expedition to Canada had been undertaken, and had assisted in the preparations on the lake, whilst Anadiasia (Vetch) at the same time was raising an army at Boston; that as some important affair had prevented the expected fleet, and rendered the design for that season abortive, they were left much exposed, and if the Queen was not still mindful of them, they, with their families, must forsake the country and seek other habitations, or stand neuter, either of which would be much against their inclinations. They concluded by presenting some belts of wampum.

After this they were magnificiently entertained by several of the nobility, and were once present at the review of the guards at Hyde Park, with the

these went over Colonel Schuyler. They sailed early in the year, had several conferences with the lords of trade, and with Nicholson and the forces he brought. They returned in the summer, arriving at Boston.

According to the instructions to the governments on the continent for getting their assistance in readiness, a considerable armament was raised, and set out from Boston on the 18th of September. The fleet consisted of the Dragon, Falmouth, Leostaff and Feversham, men of war; the Star, Bomb, and the Massachusetts province galley,* with transports, in all thirty-six sai'. The forces on board were one regiment of marines from England, two regiments from Massachusetts Bay, one regiment from Connecticut, and one from New Hampshire and Rhode Island, commissioned by the Queen, armed and provisioned in part by her gift, and part by the several colonies, toward which New Jersey contributed three thousand pounds. They arrived at Port Royal, now Annapolis,† in six days from Boston.

After some small cannonading and bombarding, the French governor, Lubercasse, capitulated on the 5th of October, when the fort was given up, and Colonel Vetch, according to instructions, became governor.

The terms of capitulation were, that all the French, numbering four hundred and eighty-one persons, within three miles of the fort, should be under the protection of Great Britain, upon

---

Duke of Ormand at their head. To him they made a speech, and presented him with three skins, to enforce a request that he would forward their business with the Queen.

On their return, at Southampton, Admiral Aylmer, who commanded a fleet there, sent his yacht to bring them on board. They dined with him, and then set sail for America.

* A low, flat built vessel with one deck, and navigated with sails and oars, formerly used in the Mediterranean. It was long and narrow, and carried two masts with lateen (triangular) sails. The largest sort was 166 feet in length, and had 52 oars.

† It was afterwards called Annapolis Royal, but now simply Annapolis, and is a fortified seaport town of Nova Scotia, at the mouth of the Annapolis river, in a fine inlet of the Bay of Fundy, 95 miles west of Halifax. The town was founded in the time of Queen Anne, and was called Annapolis, or "City of Anne."

their taking the oath of allegiance. The other French settlers were left to their own discretion. In case the French made incursions upon the frontiers of New England, the British should make reprisals upon the French in Nova Scotia, by making some of the chief of their inhabitants slaves to their Indians.

Notwithstanding this, the French of L'Acadia soon after committed hostilities, though the Port Royal and Cape Sable Indians desired terms of amity and alliance might be settled with them, which was accordingly done.

On the 14th of October, the men of war and transports sailed again for Boston, leaving a garrison in Port Royal of two hundred marines, and two hundred and fifty of the new raised volunteers from the continent. These were the next year relieved by four hundred of the troops destined for Canada.

Nova Scotia had continued with the French from the year 1662 (except the momentary reduction and possession of it by Sir William Phipps, in 1690,) until now. This acquisition was afterwards confirmed to Great Britain by the treaty of Utrecht.

The design respecting Canada was for this year laid aside. Governor Hunter received a letter from the Earl of Dartmouth, secretary of state, upon the subject of encouraging an attempt upon Port Royal, which the Queen was obliged at present to abandon, by reason of the contrary winds which happened at the time the fleet was about to set sail, as well as other important matters which intervened. She had however, this year caused all necessary preparations to be made for the expedition. He wrote that the Queen, out of her tender care for the good and prosperity of her people in these colonies, intends to pursue her design as soon as the state of her affairs will permit it, being sensible of the great advantages which may be thence expected.

Brigadier Hunter arrived, as governor, in the summer of 1710, and called a new assembly to meet the 6th of December. They chose John Kay, of Gloucester, speaker. They received the governor's speech, which breathed the true spirit, and as it differs so materially with the address of Cornbury, given two years before, and being brief, we give it entire, and in his own words, as follows:

"GENTLEMEN:—I am little used to make speeches, so you

hall not be troubled with a long one. If honesty is the best policy, plainness must be the best oratory. So, to deal plainly with you, so long as these unchristian divisions, which Her Majesty has thought to deserve her repeated notice, reign amongst you, I shall have small hopes of a happy issue to our meeting.

"This is an evil which everybody claims of, but few take the right method to remedy it. Let every man begin at home, and weed the rancor out of his own mind, and the work is done at once.

"Leave disputes of property to the laws, and injuries to the avenger of them, and like good subjects and good Christians, join hearts and hands for the common good.

"I hope you all agree in the necessity of supporting the government, and will not differ about the means. That it may the better deserve your support, I will endeavor to square it by the best rule that I know, that is the power from whence 'tis derived, which all the world must own to be justice and goodness itself.

"There are several matters recommended to you by Her Majesty, to be passed into laws, which I shall lay before you at proper seasons, and shall heartily concur with you in enacting whatsoever may be requisite for the public peace and welfare, the curbing of vice, and encouraging of virtue.

"If what I have said, or what I can do, may have the blessed effect I wish for, I shall bless the hour that brought me hither. If I am disappointed, I shall pray for that which is to call me back, for all power except that of doing good is but a burthen."

The address of the assembly, also being brief, we here insert it, as follows:

"*May it please Your Excellency:*

"We sincerely congratulate your accession to the government of this province, and hope the long wished for time has come, in which the unchristian causes of our divisions will be taken away, which we persuade ourselves you will be as willing, as we conceive you are able to do, by divesting a few designing men of that authority, which they use to the worst purposes.

"We have experienced repeated instances of Her Majesty's care over us, among which one was, the sending the good Lord

Lovelace, who put an end to an administration the then assembly of this province, with great justice, the worst New Jersey had ever known.

"That good man lived long enough to know how much the province had been oppressed, though not to remove the causes. Another instance of Her Majesty's royal favor, we esteem, is the sending Your Excellency to govern us, and we persuade ourselves, your conduct will evince it so to be.

"We hope great things from you, and none but what are just. Let not ill men be put or continued in power to oppress. Let Her Majesty's subjects enjoy their liberties and properties, according to the laws, and let not those laws be warpt to gratify the avarice or resentment of any, and then we may safely leave disputes of property to them; this, we are humbly of opinion, is the greatest honesty, and we make no question you esteem it to be the best policy.

"We always thought it equally reasonable to support a government, and to deny that support to tyranny and oppression. We should be glad our abilities would come up to what we esteem your merits. What we are able to do shall be sincerely done, and in as agreeable manner as we are capable. All your desires, which we doubt not will be reasonable, shall be commands to us, who will be always ready to join in any thing that may conduce to the public benefit, and your own, and hope you may never want will and power to punish wickedness and vice, and encourage true religion and virtue, which if you do, we shall esteem you our deliverer, and posterity shall mention your name with honor."

This address was concurred in by a number of the members who were Quakers, as to the substance of it, but they took exceptions to the style.

This session continued more than two months.

The governor and assembly agreed with great cordiality, but a majority of the council differed from both, although it was composed almost entirely of new members.

Ever since the surrender, the province had been involved in great confusion, on account of the people called Quakers being denied to serve on juries, under pretence that an oath was absolutely necessary. The inhabitants in many parts were chiefly of that persuasion, and juries could not be got without them. The assembly, seeing the confusion that had and would unavoidably follow such refusal, passed a bill for ascertaining the qualifications of jurors, and enabling the people called Quakers to serve on them, &c., and another respecting the affirmation.

The house was anxious to pass a bill to meet the case, but were always opposed by objections from the council, who refused even to submit the matters to a committee.

The assembly also passed a militia act to relieve the Quakers from militia fines, which the council also rejected.

They also took into consideration the charges made to the Queen against a former assembly in Lord Cornbury's time, by lieutenant governor Ingolsby, and eight of the councilmen who sustained the governor in his unwarranted acts in the year 1707.

The address having been read, the question was put whether the said humble address (as it was called) be a false and scandalous misrepresentation of the representative body of this province or not? When it was decided in the affirmative.

The house then resolved to address Her Majesty in justification of the proceedings of the representative body of this province, in the present and former assemblies.

It was also resolved in the affirmative that no person who had signed the above-mentioned false and scandalous representation of the representative body of this province, was a fit member to sit in this house, unless he acknowledged his fault to the house.

Major William Sandford, one of the members of the house at this time, having acknowledged that he signed the above-mentioned address to Her Majesty, was asked if he would acknowledge his fault to this house for the same. His answer was, he signed it, as he was one of Her Majesty's council, and was only accountable to Her Majesty for the same. Whereupon the question was put whether Major Sandford be expelled this house for the same or not, and it was resolved in the affirmative. Whereupon it was ordered that Major Sandford be expelled this house for signing a false and scandalous paper called, the humble address of the lieutenant governor and council to Her Majesty, in the year 1707, and he is expelled this house accordingly.

Pursuant to the resolutions of the house, an address was prepared and sent to the Queen, and a representation to Governor Hunter. This last was a particular answer to the charges.

In this they extolled Governor Lovelace, and stated that had he have lived they would not have been under the necessity of laying their representation before His Excellency.

They also state that they were sorry to have so much reason to say, that it was lately their misfortune to be governed by Lord Cornbury, who treated Her Majesty's subjects here not as freemen who were to be governed by laws, but as slaves, of whose persons and estates he had the sole power of disposing. Oppression and injustice reigned everywhere in this poor, and then miserable, colony, and it was criminal to complain or seem any way sensible of the hardships they then suffered, and whatever attempts were made for their relief not only proved ineffectual, but was termed insolence, and was flying in the face of authority.

Bribery, extortion, and a contempt of laws, both human and divine, were the fashionable vices of that time, encouraged by his countenance, but more by his example, and those who could most daringly and with most dexterity trample upon their liberties, had the greatest share both in the government of this province and his favor.

This usage they bore with patience a great while, believing that the measures he took proceeded rather from want of information or an erroneous judgment, than the depravity of his nature. But repeated instances soon convinced them of their mistaken notions.

His treatment to the Quakers in reference to compelling them to enroll in the militia or pay militia fines, was severely condemned.

That the rights of the general proprietors were invaded in a very high degree, their papers and registers being the evidence, they had to prove their titles to their lands and rents, were violently and arbitrarily forced from them, and they were inhibited from selling or disposing of their lands.

After eulogizing the administration of Governor Lovelace, the review of the address of the lieutenant governor, Ingolsby and the eight councilmen that signed it, and taking the same up *seriatim*, they fully answer every charge therein contained.

The memorial was signed by order of the house of representatives by William Bradford, their clerk, and dated February 9th, 1710.

This representation was kindly received by the governor, and he returned answer, that Her Majesty had given him directions to endeavor to reconcile the differences that were in this province, but if he could not that he should make a just representation to her, and that he did not doubt but that upon the representation he should make, Her Majesty would take such measures as should give a general satisfaction.

The governor accordingly backing the remonstrance to the Queen, all the councillors were removed that were pointed out by the assembly as the cause of their grievances, and their places were supplied by others.

The business of this session having been concluded, the governor prorogued the house.

CHAPTER X.

1711—1776.

Second expedition against Canada—Arrival of transports containing troops from England—Passage of bill permitting Quakers to affirm—Governor Hunter's administration satisfactory to the people—Accession of King George the First—Severe storms—Acts for running the division line between New York and New Jersey.

GOVERNOR Hunter convened the assembly in the summer of 1711, and the business was commenced by his telling them "that Her Majesty's instructions, which he was commanded to communicate, would discover the reason of his calling them together at this time, and that he doubted not the matters therein contained, would be agreeable to them, and the success profitable.

"That the fleet and forces destined for the reduction of Canada, were arrived in good health and condition, and would proceed in a short time. That what was required on their parts, was the levying in each division one hundred and eighty effective private men, beside officers, and to provide for the encouragement, pay, and provisions, as well as transportation over the lakes, and other incidental charges attending the forces.

The assembly at once resolved to encourage this expedition, by raising to the value of twelve thousand five ounces of plate, in bills of credit,* to be sunk, together with the former three thousand pounds, by a subsequent tax, and provided bills

---

* Equal to five thousand pounds currency at that time.

for raising volunteers to go on the expedition and for emitting the money. The governor passed the bills, and dismissed them with thanks for the cheerful dispatch they had given.

This was the second expedition against Canada, and made quite a formidable appearance.

Nicholson's designs having hitherto failed through various disappointments, he now, under the scheme of reducing all Canada, and thereby engrossing the cod fishery, so prevailed on the new ministry that the regiments of Kirk, Hill, Windress, Clayton, and Kaine, from Flanders, Seymour's, Disney's, and a battalion of marines from England, under command of Brigadier Hill, were sent to him on this occasion.

They came in forty transports, under convoy of twelve ships of the line of battle, commanded by Admiral Walker, several frigates, and two bomb vessels. They brought a large train of artillery, under Colonel King, with forty horses and six store ships. They arrived at Boston early in the summer.

By orders from home a congress was held at New London, consisting of all the plantation governors north of Pennsylvania, with Nicholson to arrange the details of the expedition.

Two regiments from Massachusetts, Rhode Island, and New Hampshire, joined the British forces, while the militia of Connecticut, New York, and New Jersey, with the Indians of the Five Nations, under Nicholson, marched by land from Albany to attack Montreal.

The fleet having been retarded at Boston for want of provisions, Admiral Walker wrote to Governor Dudley at Boston: "I concur with the opinion of all the sea and land officers here that the government of this colony have prejudiced the present expedition instead of assisting it."

The fleet, consisting of sixty-eight vessels and six thousand four hundred and sixty-three troops, anchored in the bay of Gaspee, on the south side of the entrance of the St. Lawrence river, to take in wood and water, on the 18th of August, and in the night of the 23d, contrary to the advice of the pilots, they weighed anchor in a fog that was then prevailing, fell in with the north shore, and lost eight transports and eight hundred and eighty-four men upon the island of Eggs.

A council of war was held, and they resolved that by reason of the ignorance of the pilots it was impracticable to proceed, and that advice should be sent to Gen. Nicholson against proceeding to Montreal, which was done, and the fleet returned and anchored in Spanish river,* off Cape Breton, on the 4th of September, 1711, and there, in a council of war, it was resolved not to attempt anything against Placentia,† but to return to Great Britain.

On the 16th of September they sailed for England, and arrived at St. Helens the 16th of October. The Edgar, with the admiral's papers, was blown up. This prevented the expedition from proceeding further, and it was therefore abandoned at a great expense of men and treasure, although having been agitated above three years.

In 1712, Thomas Gardiner, the second of that name, died. He was a resident of Burlington, and has been mentioned several times before. He was a man well acquainted with public business, a good surveyor, and useful member of society. He was several years a member of the council, treasurer of the western division, and the first speaker of assembly after the union of the governments of East and West Jersey.

On the 7th of December, 1713, the governor called the assembly together, and the next day informed them that he was glad to see them after so long absence, and believed they were not sorry to meet him in so good company;‡ that the tender regard Her Majesty had to their quiet, in particular at a time when she had blessed the world with a general peace, called for their pious endeavors, and could not fail of meeting the returns

---

* Spanish river flows along the base of the LaClocke Mountains, and empties into Lake Huron, nearly opposite the central part of the Great Manitoulin islands.

† Placentia, a seaport town of Newfoundland, on the west coast of the peninsula.

‡ Meaning the change of councillors. William Pinhorne, Daniel Coxe, Peter Sonmans, and William Hall, who had signed the memorial to the Queen against the assembly had been suspended, and a mandamus had since arrived appointing John Anderson, Elisha Parker, Thomas Byerly, John Hamilton, and John Reading.

due from the most grateful people to the best and most indulgent princess. That he was persuaded the efforts of such as had been removed from places of trust by the Queen at their request, would be too impotent to destroy the peace, by breaking that mutual confidence or disturbing that harmony that then subsisted between the several branches of the legislature. That full of this confidence, he recommended to their immediate care the providing for past arrears and future support of Her Majesty's government, the discountenancing vice and immorality, the improvement of trade and encouragement for planting and peopling the province. That this could not be better effected than by a law to affirm and ascertain the respective properties of the proprietors and people, if they thought it practicable.

That the gentlemen of the present council, having no views or interests differing from theirs, if they would agree to frequent and amicable conferences with them, or a number of them, upon all matters under deliberation, it would save much time and effectually disappoint all contrivances of their enemies, who, in return for their being at present no councillors, had ridiculously endeavored to persuade some that they were no assembly.

The assembly replied, "That they were indeed glad to meet him in such good company, and as the persons who had hitherto obstructed the welfare of their country were removed, they presumed on the favor oftener than heretofore." They acknowledged themselves under the greatest obligations to the best of Queens, and hoped their actions would demonstrate they were not ungrateful.

Among other bills passed at this session was that entitled, "An act that the solemn affirmation and declaration of the people called Quakers shall be accepted instead of an oath in the usual form, and for qualifying the said people to serve as jurors, and to execute any office or place of trust or profit within this province."

The governor having communicated to the house the instructions of the Queen on that subject, the bill was introduced.

The second enacting clause was thought to be designedly left out by the secretary, who had it to engross. In this shape it passed council without being noticed by them, but on reading it again in the assembly the omission was discovered, and the secretary made his acknowledgment at the bar of the house, when it was again passed over.

This act continued until 1732, and then was supplied by another similar to the one now in force.

Other laws of importance were also passed, and the session was concluded to the mutual satisfaction of all.

In his concluding remarks at the breaking up of the session, the governor said: "I thank you for what has been done this session for the support of this Her Majesty's government, and do not doubt but that you will receive ample thanks from those who sent you for the many good laws that have been passed.

"Some things that in their nature were acts of favor, I have agreed that they should be made acts of assembly, that your share may be greater in the grateful acknowledgment of your country.

"I hope my conduct has convinced the world (I cannot suppose you want any further conviction) that I have no other view than the peace and prosperity of this province. If such a few as are enemies to both are not to be reduced by reason, I shall take the next best and most effectual measure to do it."

Between the years 1713 and 1716 we find no historical matters of interest occurring, as the government under Hunter was conducted with such moderation that nothing occurred to mar the peace of the province, but everything worked in the greatest harmony, and all were not only satisfied but pleased with the administration. The old grievances were amicably healed, and peace was restored.

Governor Hunter met a new assembly at Amboy, in the spring of 1716. This assembly chose Col. Daniel Coxe, speaker, who was presented and accepted, when the governor by speech, informed them that the dissolution of one assembly by the demise of the late Queen, of another by the arrival of a new patent from the present King, constituting him governor of the province, and of a third by reason of a circumstance well known, together with the long sessions at York, and his necessary attendance on the service of the frontiers, had been the occasion of putting off the meeting till now. That on his part he brought with him a firm purpose for the advantage of the subject and the service of the crown, which he says, "I have ever pursued, and now bid a fair defiance to the most malicious to assign one single instance in which I have acted counter to what I now profess, notwithstanding the false and groundless accusations and insinuations to the contrary, from two persons on the other side, who pretended to have been instructed from this, which, though they met with that contempt at home they deserved, I could not without injustice to myself, let pass unmentioned here."

This was the session of the assembly, which should have met at Burlington, but they were convened at Amboy, they therefore determined to remonstrate against the infringement of the usual custom of alternately meeting at each of those places, and accordingly represented to the governor, that in the year 1709 an act was passed entitled, "An act for ascertaining the place of the sitting of the representatives to meet in general assembly," that in March, 1710, the aforesaid act was confirmed, finally enacted, and ratified by her late Majesty, with the advice of her privy council, and transmitted to him (the governor), by the lords commissioners for trade and plantations, the 16th of said month. That they were perfectly willing to pay all due regard and obedience to His Majesty's and the governor's commands, so they could not but think it their duty to maintain the known and established laws of this province. And as that law had the royal sanction, and had gone through all the usual forms both here and in Great Britain which were necessary to confirm and perpetuate it, they were of opinion it was still in force, never having been repealed.

The governor replied, "That His Majesty's instructions, which were laws to him, having restored that affair to the just and equal footing upon which it was put by, and at the time of the surrender of the government by the proprietors, he could not give his consent to any alteration, or give way to anything that might elude the intent and purpose of that instruction without giving juster grounds of complaint against him than he had hitherto given, and that he had reasons of great weight which made it impracticable for him to hold either council or assembly at Burlington at this time."

The dispute being principally founded on the new commission to the governor upon the accession of King George the First to the throne, the assembly thought proper to submit, and transact the business before them at the place where they were then convened.

Matters however did not go on very smooth; the speaker disliked the governor and influenced many of the members.

The governor saw there was no prospect of their carrying out the design of their meeting at that time, and prorogued them. On the 14th of May he again summoned them, this time to meet at Amboy, only nine members appearing. They waited five days, and then presented an address requesting the governor to take such measures as he might think proper to cause the absent members to attend, whereupon he sent warrants to several of them commanding their attendance, as they would answer the contrary at their peril. In obedience to this summons four presently appeared, there being now thirteen present. The governor sent for them, and recommended their meeting at the house and choosing a speaker, (for their speaker was absent among the rest) in order to enable them to send their sergeant-at-arms for those that were still absent.

On the 21st the thirteen met, and the speaker still being absent, they chose John Kinsey speaker. The house being now organized, the governor delivered his address, as follows:

"*Gentlemen :*—The last time you were here upon a like occasion, I told you that I thought fit to approve of whatever choice you thought fit to make of a speaker. I now tell you that I heartily approve of the worthy choice you have made.

"As the conduct of that gentleman who last filled the chair* sufficiently convinced you of a combination between him and his associates to defeat all the purposes of your present meeting, I hope, and cannot doubt, but it will open the eyes of all such as by his and their evil acts and sinistrous practices have been misled and imposed upon, so that for the future here they will not find it so easy a matter to disturb the peace of the country.

"I must refer you to what I said at the opening of the assembly, but harvest drawing near I am afraid you'll hardly have time

---

* Colonel Daniel Coxe.

for more business than what is absolutely and immediately requisite, that is the support of government and the public credit.

"You know that the date of the currency of your bills of credit is near expiring, so there will be wanting a new law to remedy the evil that must attend the leaving the country without a currency for ordinary uses as well as trade.

"ROBERT HUNTER."

The house then went into an examination of the conduct of their late speaker and the absent members, who, on the question, were at different times severally expelled for contempt of authority and neglect of the service of their country, and writs were issued for new elections.*

On the 8th of the following month, and shortly after the exclusion of the speaker, but previous to the expulsion of the other members, the assembly presented the governor the following address:

"*May it please Your Excellency:*

"Your administration has been of a continued series of justice and moderation, and from your past conduct we dare assure ourselves of a continuation of it, and we will not be wanting in our endeavors to make suitable returns, both in providing a handsome support of the government and of such a continuance as may demonstrate to you and the world the sense we have of our duty and your worth.

"The gentleman, our late speaker, has added this one instance of folly to his past demeanor, to convince us and the world that in all stations, whether of a councillor, a private man, or a representative, his study has been to disturb the quiet and tranquillity of this province, and act in contempt of laws and government. We are sensible of the effects it has had and may have on the public peace, and our expulsion of him we hope

---

* The following were the names of the members expelled:—Bergen, Henry Brokholst, David Akerman; Gloucester, Colonel Daniel Coxe (speaker), Richard Bull; Town of Salem, Henry Joyce; County of Salem, William Hall, William Clews; Cape May, Jacob Spicer, Jacob Huling. Spicer was by resolution declared to be incapable of sitting, the others were expelled and declared to be ineligible to be re-elected; a rather summary way to impeach members.

evinces that we are not the partisans of his heat and disaffection to the present government. We are very sorry he has been capable to influence so many into a combination with him, to make effectual his ill purposes. But we hope it is rather the effect of weakness than malice, and that their eyes are now so much opened that they'll return to their duty and join with us in providing for the public credit, and whatever else may make this province happy and Your Excellency easy."

The assembly then resolved, "That the late members whom they had expelled should not sit as members of the house if they should be returned on a new election, during this session of the assembly."

Notwithstanding this, several of the same members were returned, but were refused seats in the house, and the electors were obliged to choose others in their place.

The governor then prorogued them till the 3d of October. In November the same house met at Crosswicks,* in consequence of the small-pox raging at Burlington. The governor opened the business of the session by telling them, "That the support of the government and public credit required their immediate attention; that they knew the funds for the first had expired fifteen months ago, and that the other had suffered much by the obstinacy of some in refusing the payment of taxes, or remissness in others in collecting or putting the laws in execution sufficient (if duly executed) to have answered the end, and in a great measure prevented or remedied that evil; that he doubted not they were now met with a good disposition, as well as in full freedom, all clogs and bars being removed, to pursue to effect the good ends of their meeting, and to make good their engagements and promises in several of their addresses; that the true interest of the people and government were the same, to wit: a government of laws, that no other deserved the name; that this was never separated or separable but in imagination by men of craft, such as were either abettors of lawless power on the one hand, or confusion and anarchy on the other; that the first was not the case of this province, and we had well

---

* The true Indian name of this place is supposed to be Clossweeksung, meaning a separation.

grounded hopes that all endeavors towards the latter had ceased.

This session continued a long while, more than two months, and was a very fruitful one, they having passed sixteen public and private bills, all of which received the governor's assent.

Samuel Smith, one of the members of assembly for Burlington, died in the year 1718. He had sought happiness in the quiets of obscurity, and was against his own inclination called to the assembly, as well as other public stations, all of which he passed through with a clear reputation. In private life he was mild, inoffensive, benevolent, steady and respected.*

This year was remarkable for an uncommon storm of hail. It fell larger than had been remembered ever before in the provinces, killing many wild pigeons and other birds, besides doing considerable damage, destroying dwellings and other property, as well as trees and vegetables.

In the beginning of the summer of 1742 another happened, with a strong gust of wind, accompanied with some rain and hail of very uncommon size. In one house it was said to have broken twenty-eight holes through the roof. The damage to the grain in some places was so great that the farmers refused to sell the stock of the previous year for fear they should be in want for bread. At Amwell a boy was said to have been killed, and others were very much injured.

In the spring of 1758 still another happened. This came from the north, the hail in large stones continuing for eight or ten minutes, and abated gradually. In some places it drifted about six inches thick. It went in a vein of about a mile and a half broad. The destruction of green corn and gardens was very great, and the trees had their young leaves shattered to pieces.

In the spring of 1718 Governor Hunter again met the assembly at Perth Amboy, but at the desire of the members, on account of their private affairs interfering, he adjourned them to

---

* He with five of his brothers, John, Daniel, Joseph, Emanuel, and Richard, and one sister, removed from near Bramham, in Yorkshire, at different times, but mostly in and about the year 1691. Daniel served the public several years faithfully in the assembly, and died in 1742. Richard was for twelve years one of the council, and died the latter part of 1750.

the winter, when again meeting with them he made a speech, setting forth:

"That the revenue had some time since expired, and that when this came under consideration he desired an augmentation of the officers salaries.

"That in former acts they were so scanty and so retrenched from what they had been, that the officers were not enabled to perform their respective duties.

"That the assembly of New York had passed an act for running the division line between this province, and that upon supposition another for the same purpose would be passed here; that the justice due the proprietors and the disturbances among the people made such a law an immediate necessity; that he had formerly recommended their providing for an agent at the court of Great Britain, and now repeated it, that the lords commissioners for trade had in several of their letters complained of the want of one, and that this was the only province in His Majesty's dominions that had none.

"That by means of this omission, their business in England stood still; that what could not be delayed without danger or loss to the public since his administration, had been negotiated by persons employed by him, at his own very great expense, which he hoped they would consider; that as to projects of trade, he had no reason to change his opinion since they last met, that to this subject he referred them on what he then spoke.*

The assembly said in their address, "That they were not

---

* "As for the measures of advancing, or rather for giving, a being to trade amongst you, the generality of you has shown such aversion to solid ones, and others such a fondness for imaginary or ruinous ones, that without a virtue and resolution of serving those you represent against their inclination, your endeavors will be to little purpose. But if anything of that nature fall under deliberation, I cannot think of a better guide than a just inspection into the trade in other provinces where it is in a good and flourishing condition, the means by which it became so can be no mystery; where it is otherwise, or has decayed, you will find the true cause of such decay conspicuous. And it is but a rational conclusion that what has formed trade, or that on which it depends, credit in one place cannot but be the most proper means either to begin it or preserve it in another."

insensible that the present circumstances of the government as well as of the country, made their meeting necessary, notwithstanding the rigor of the season ; that they were not unmindful that the revenue was expired, nor of their duty in a reasonable support; that they were willing to pass an act for running the division line betwixt this province and New York, but conceived the expense of that affair belonged to the proprietors of the contested lands; that they were very sensible an agent for the province at the Court of Great Britain was very necessary, but were sorry the circumstances of the province were such that they could not make a suitable provision for so useful an officer, and that they would readily come into any measures that might be effectual to promote the trade and prosperity of the province."

This session passed eleven public and private bills, among which was the one for running and ascertaining the division line between New Jersey and New York, but this act was never put in execution further than fixing the north partition point. This was done by indenture made the 25th of July, 1719, between R. Walter, Isaac Hicks, and Allave Jarret, surveyor general, on the part of New York; John Johnston, and George Willocks, on behalf of East Jersey; Joseph Kirkbride, and John Reading, on behalf of West Jersey; and James Alexander, surveyor general, on behalf of both East and West Jersey. These commissioners and surveyors, duly authorized, met at the place appointed, and after many observations of the latitude, unanimously by deed fixed the north partition point on the northwest branch of the Delaware, which they found to be that branch called the Fish Kill.

After this had been done, the West Jersey commissioners thought there was nothing further for them to do; the others though greatly interested in having it settled, left it an uncertainty until 1764, when, by acts of assembly of both colonies, it was referred, to be finally settled and determined by commissioners to be appointed by the crown.

Another act passed at this time was that for running and ascertaining the line of division between East and West New Jersey.*

---

* This was a straight line from the most northerly point or boundary on the northermost branch of the Delaware river, to the most southerly point of a certain beach or island of sand, lying next to and adjoining the main sea on

The beginning of the summer of this year afforded a fair prospect of a plentiful harvest; much was expected from a great crop in the ground. A day or two in the beginning proved good weather, but before the grain was secured, showers of rain and a few hours sunshine constantly succeeded each other. Clouds, at first small in appearance, spread widely and rain filled the furrows. The intervals of sunshine encouraged opening the shocks, but were not long enough to dry them. After several weeks came two days and a half of fair weather. What could be dried and saved was now done. The rain then began again, and continued day after day as before, alternate rain and sunshine, for nearly three weeks, so that single ears of corn standing grew. Thus it continued till the grain was gradually reaped. Several lost their corn entirely, others saved but little. This was what they called the wet harvest.

We have now, in the year 1720, come to the end of Governor Hunter's administration. He resigned in favor of William Burnet, (son of the celebrated Bishop Burnet). He at once returned to England, after having occupied the position of governor of the province for ten years.

Governor Burnet had a ready art of obtaining money; few loved it more. This foible, it is said, drew him into schemes, gaming, and considerable losses. His address here was engaging and successful. He assented to most of the laws the people wanted, and filled the offices with men of character.

He had before, as early as the year 1705, been appointed lieutenant governor of Virginia, under George, Earl of Orkney, and while on his voyage thither was taken prisoner to France.

The assembly at the sessions last mentioned fixed for salary and incidental charges, six hundred pounds per annum. For two years this had been the accustomed support since the surrender, except once in Lord Cornbury's time, five hundred pounds was provided in the succeeding administrations.

This was continued until Lewis Morris became governor of

---

the north side of the mouth or entrance of Little Egg Harbor. All the lands, islands and waters eastward of this line, was to be forever known as the eastern division, while those on the west were to be the western division of the province.

New Jersey, separate from New York, when it was augmented to one thousand pounds per annum and sixty pounds house rent, with five hundred pounds additional the first year, for expenses attending the voyage, &c.

Soon after his arrival Governor Burnet met the assembly, when but little business was thought necessary, neither did they very well agree. That house had been continued a long time, and were now dissolved, and writs issued for a new election.

The members returned were convened early in the spring of 1721, and chose Dr. John Johnston speaker.

The members of council named in the instructions to Governor Burnet were Lewis Morris, Thomas Gordon, John Anderson, John Hamilton, Thomas Byerly, David Lyell, John Parker, John Wiles, John Hugg, John Johnston, Jr., John Reading, and Peter Bard.

The members of this house of assembly were John Johnston and Andrew Reading, for Perth Amboy ; John Kinsey and Moses Rolph, for the county of Middlesex ; Robert Lettis Hooper and Thomas Leonard, Somerset ; Josiah Ogden and Joseph Bonnel, Essex ; William Provost and Isaac Vangezon, Bergen ; William Lawrence and Garret Schank, Monmouth ; John Allen and Jonathan Wright, town of Burlington ; William Trent and Thomas Lambert, county of Burlington ; Samuel Cole and John Mickle, Gloucester ; John Mason and Thomas Mason, town of Salem ; Isaac Sharp and Bartholomew Wyatt, county of Salem ; Humphrey Hughes and Nathaniel Jenkins, Cape May.

Governor Burnet delivered the following address :

"*Gentlemen*:—The choice which the country has made of you to represent them, gives me a happy opportunity of knowing their sentiments. Now, when they have been fully informed of mine in the most public manner, I have no reason to doubt that after so much time given them to weigh and consider every particular, you bring along with you their hearty resolutions to support His Majesty's government in such an ample and honorable manner as will become you to offer, and me to accept ; and in doing this, I must recommend to you not to think of me* so

---

* Whether an alteration in sentiment or instructions, or both, was the cause, must be left to conjecture ; but while Burnet was governor of Massachusetts

much as of the inferior officers of this government, who want your care more, and whose salary have hitherto amounted to a very small share of the public expense. I cannot neglect this occasion of congratulating you upon the treasures lately discovered in the bowels of the earth, which cannot fail of circulating for the general good, the increase of trade, and the raising the value of estates. And now you are just beginning to taste of new blessings; I cannot but remind you of those which you have so long enjoyed, and without which all other advantages would but have increased your sufferings under a Popish King and a French government.

"You can ascribe your deliverance from these to nothing but the glorious revolution begun by King William the Third, of immortal memory, and completed by the happy accession of his present majesty King George to the throne of Great Britain, and his entire success against his rebellious subjects at home, and all his enemies abroad.

"To this remarkable deliverance, by an overruling hand of Providence, you owe the preservation of your laws and liberties, the secure enjoyment of your property, and a free exercise of religion, according to the dictates of your conscience. These invaluable blessings are so visible among us, and the misery of countries where tyranny and persecution prevail so well known, that I need not mention them to raise in your minds the highest sense of your obligations to serve God, to honor the King, and love your country.

"W. BURNET."

The assembly, through John Johnston, their speaker, delivered the following address to the governor:

"*May it please Your Excellency:*

"We gladly embrace this opportunity to assure Your Excellency that our sentiments and those we represent, are one and

---

Bay his conduct was different. There he insisted for several years with the greatest firmness on an indefinite support, and pursued it through the plantation boards, privy council, and even to the parliament itself, where his death prevented its coming to a conclusion; but his course was entirely different here, as he appears to manifest more interest in the subordinate officers of the province than for himself.

the same, cheerfully to demonstrate our loyalty to our sovereign King George, and submission to his substitute, and readiness to support his government over us in all its branches, in the most honorable manner the circumstances will allow, which we hope Your Excellency will accept of, though it fall short of what the dignity of His Majesty's governor and the inferior officers of the government might expect were the province in a more flourishing condition.

"We thankfully acknowledge Your Excellency's congratulation, and doubt not when the imaginary treasures (except Mr. Schuyler's) becomes real, the country will not be wanting in their duty to His Majesty in making Your Excellency and the officers of the government partakers of the advantage. We doubt not but Your Excellency will extend your goodness to countenance any proposal that may tend to the public utility.

"We hope Your Excellency will excuse us in falling short of words to express our thankful acknowledgments to God Almighty and those under him, who have been instruments in working deliverance to that glorious nation to which we belong from popery, tyranny, and arbitrary power, wishing it may always be supplied with great and good men, that will endeavor their utmost to maintain His Majesty's royal authority, and assert and defend the laws, liberties and properties of the people against all foreign and domestic invaders.

"We beg Your Excellency to believe the sincerity of our thoughts, that there are none of His Majesty's subjects that entertains hearts more loyal and affectionate, and desire more to testify their duty, gratitude and obedience to their sovereign King George, his issue, and magistrates of their respective degrees, than doth the representatives of His Majesty's province of New Jersey.

"JOHN JOHNSTON, *Speaker*."

Sundry bills were prepared during this session, among these one whose title is too singular to be omitted. It was, "An act against denying the divinity of our Saviour Jesus Christ, the doctrine of the Blessed Trinity, the truth of His holy Scriptures, and spreading atheistical books."

This bill did not pass, but was rejected on its second reading.

Assemblies in the colonies rarely troubled themselves with these subjects, perhaps never before or since. It probably arose from the inclination of the governor, who had a turn that way, and who had written a book to unfold some part of the Apocalypse.

The sessions continued nearly two months. The support of the governor was settled at five hundred pounds per year, for five years.

After this when several other bills had been passed, the governor dismissed them with the following speech:

"*Gentlemen:*—I have so many reasons to thank you for your proceedings in this affair, that should I mention them all, time would not suffice me. Two I cannot but acknowledge in a particular manner: the acts for the cheerful and honorable support, and for the security of His Majesty's government in this province.

"I cannot but say that I look upon the latter as the noblest present of the two, as I think honor always more than riches. The world will now see the true cause of our misunderstandings in the last assembly, and that we met in the innocency and simplicity of our hearts; that the enemy had sown such seeds of dissension among us that defeated all our good purposes, and made us part with a wrong notion of one another.

"It has pleased God now to discover the truth, and no man in his sober senses can doubt that the hand of Joab was then busy, as it is now certain that it has been at this time.

"It is a peculiar honor to me to be thus justified in all my conduct by the public act of the whole legislature, and God knows my heart that I am not fond of power, that I abhor all thoughts of revenge, and that I study to keep a conscience void of offence towards God and towards man.

"After the publication of the acts, I desire you to return to your house, and after having entered this speech in your minutes, to adjourn yourselves to the first day of October next, that though it is not probable we should meet so soon, it may not be out of our power if occasion should be.

"May 5th, 1722.   W. BURNET."

Governor Burnet, after this, continued to preside over New

York and New Jersey until 1727, when he was removed to Boston, and was succeeded by John Montgomerie, Esq., who continued in the position until his death, which happened July 1st, 1731, when the government devolved on Colonel Lewis Morris until August 1st, 1732.

He was succeeded by William Cosby, who also occupied the position until his death in 1736. The government then devolved on John Anderson, Esq., president of council.

Anderson died about two weeks afterwards, and was succeeded by John Hamilton, Esq., (son of Andrew Hamilton, governor in the time of he proprietors). Hamilton governed nearly two years.

In the summer of 1738, a commission arrived appointing Lewis Morris, Esq., as governor of New Jersey, separate from New York. He continued in the office until his death in 1746. He was succeeded by President Hamilton, it being the second time he occupied the office by virtue of his being president of council.

Upon the death of Hamilton, which occurred soon after, he was succeeded by John Reading, Esq., the next oldest councillor, who continued to exercise the office until the summer of 1747, when Jonathan Belcher, Esq., arrived in the province. He continued in office ten years, and died in the summer of 1757.

Upon the death of Belcher, John Reading succeeded him, by virtue of being president of council. This was also the second time he had acted as governor, by virtue of his position in council.

Francis Bernard, Esq., arrived as governor in 1758, but in two years afterwards he was removed to Boston, and was succeeded in 1760 by Thomas Boone, Esq., and the next year he was removed to South Carolina, and was succeeded here by Josiah Hardy, Esq., in 1761.

Hardy was afterwards removed and appointed consul at Cadiz, &c., and in the spring of 1763 he was succeeded by William Franklin, Esq., the last royal governor.

At the breaking out of the war in 1776, he was known to be so wholly wedded to the crown as to be an enemy of the people of the province.

P

On the 30th of May, 1776, he summoned the members of the legislature to meet the provincial congress, which was then in session. They passed a resolution declaring that the proclamation of William Franklin, late governor, ought not to be obeyed.*

Congress soon after declared him to be an enemy to the liberties of the country, and discontinued his salary as governor. Colonel Nathaniel Heard, who commanded the militia of Middlesex county, was directed to arrest him, and take his parole in writing that he would not attempt to exercise any special authority in the province, and in case he should refuse to sign it to put him under strong guard, and keep him in close custody.

He refused to sign the parole, whereupon Colonel Heard surrounded his house with a guard of sixty men, and despatched a messenger to the congress asking further instructions. He was commanded to bring the late governor to Burlington.

The fact of his arrest and confinement by the provincial congress was then reported to the continental congress, at that time in session at Philadelphia, and they asked for instructions as to what disposition should be made of him, at the same time recommending that he be removed to some other province. They directed that he should be examined, and if, in their opinion, it was thought necessary that he should be confined, then the continental congress would direct in what way he should be imprisoned.

He was accordingly arraigned before the provincial congress on the 21st of June, and refused to answer any questions put to him by that body. He also denied the authority of that body over him, and denounced them in severe terms for having usurped the authority of the King in the province. He was accordingly ordered into close confinement, under a guard commanded by Lieutenant Colonel Bowes Reed.

An order was received from the continental congress on the 25th of June, directing that he should be sent under guard to Governor Trumbull of Connecticut, who was requested to take his parole. Immediately after his release, Franklin sailed for England.

Although born in Philadelphia, and the son of one of the

---

* This resolution was passed by a vote of thirty-five to eleven against it.

greatest patriots of the war, the great Benjamin Franklin, he yet remained loyal to the British government, and was a conspicuous enemy to American independence. His father refused all intercourse with him during the war, solely on the ground of the steps he had taken in reference to the struggle.

The governor wrote his father a letter under date of July 22d, 1784, proposing a reconciliation. The old patriot replied: "Nothing has ever hurt me so much and affected me with such keen sensations as to find myself deserted in my old age by my only son; and not only deserted, but to find him taking up arms against me in a cause wherein my good fame, fortune and life were all at stake." Governor Franklin died in England, November 17th, 1813, in the eighty-third year of his age, having resided there thirty-seven years.

We have no knowledge that they ever became reconciled, for Benjamin Franklin held the liberties of his country dearer than his own life, as was evidenced by the bold stand he took during the war, even in the presence of those he knew to be open and avowed enemies.

As before stated, Governor Burnet commenced his administration in the year 1720, and during his time some of the most remarkable acts of the assembly were those for the support of the government, for which they made liberal provision. Five hundred pounds per annum for five years was voted as the salary of the governor, and at the same time they authorized the issue of bills of credit to the amount of forty thousand pounds, for the purpose of increasing the circulating medium of the province. The act authorizing the latter sets forth in its preamble the fact "that the country had been drained of its metallic currency, and the paper currency of the neighboring colonies never having been made a legal tender, and in consequence of the gold and silver formerly current in this province has been almost entirely exported to Great Britain and elsewhere, and therefore many hardships which His Majesty's good subjects within this colony lie under for want of a currency of money, and that both the neighboring provinces of New York and Pennsylvania, to which the exportation of this province is chiefly carried, have their currency of money in paper bills, and do pay for the produce of this province in no other specie, and which bills of credit of the neighboring provinces being no legal tender here, does expose the inhabitants to numerous vexatious suits for want of bills of credit in this province, by law made and declared a legal tender, as is done in the neighboring provinces."

It further set forth, in order to pay the small taxes for the support of the government, they have been obliged to cut down and pay in their plate earrings and other jewels,

The authorized issue of these were four thousand bills of three pounds each, eight thousand of one pound, eight thousand of fifteen shillings, eight thousand of twelve shillings, eight thousand of three shillings, twelve thousand of one shilling and sixpence, and fourteen thousand of one shilling.

Upon these bills were impressed the arms of Great Britain on the left side, and at the bottom of each and the value of the same, was printed near the top and bottom.

Loan offices were established in the several counties, and the bills were apportioned to them.

To Bergen county, two thousand nine hundred and twenty-pounds. Essex, four thousand eight hundred and ninety-three pounds. Middlesex, four thousand one hundred and sixteen pounds. Monmouth, six thousand and thirty-three pounds. Somerset, one thousand three hundred and seventy-four pounds. Hunterdon, three thousand and twenty-eight pounds. Burlington, four thousand two hundred and eighty-three pounds. Gloucester, three thousand and eighty pounds. Salem, five thousand one hundred and fifty-two pounds, and Cape May, eleven hundred and fifteen pounds.

These bills were to be signed by John Parker, Peter Bard, Robert Lettis Hooper, Esqs., and Mr. James Trent, or any three of them.

The printer was required to take an oath that from the time the letters were set and fit to be put in the press for printing, the bills now delivered by him to the above named persons, until they were printed, and the letters unset and put in the boxes again, that at no time he went out of the room in which the said letters were without locking them up, so as that they could not become at without violence, a false key, or other art then unknown to him; and that no copies were printed off except in his presence, and that all the blotters and other papers whatsoever, printed by the said letters, while set for printing the said letters, to the best of his knowledge, had been delivered to them, together with the stamps for the indents and arms.

The signers were also required to take an oath for the true signing the bills, and that they would sign no more than was authorized by the act.

The commissioner of each county was also required to take an oath that he would faithfully discharge the trust reposed in him for the county for which he was appointed, and also to give bond in the full sum entrusted to him for the faithful discharge of his duty.

The commissioners were created a body politic and corporate for the county in which each were appointed.

The bills were to be lent out by the commissioners to such as should apply for the same, upon their giving as security mortgages on lands, lots, houses, or other valuable improvements lying in the county. The commissioners were first to view the lands and examine the titles.

The bills were to continue current for twelve years, and then to be loaned out at five per cent.

In the year 1730, a similar act was passed authorizing the issue of twenty thousand pounds of credit for sixteen years, in order to increase the revenues of the province, and to take the place of the above loan, which would expire in 1732. For this loan, was received wheat, silver and gold.

In 1735, another act was passed authorizing the issue of bills of credit to the amount of forty thousand pounds for sixteen years. Wheat, gold and silver, as well as mortgages, were to be received for these bills.

In 1740, two thousand pounds in bills of credit were issued for victualling and transporting the troops to be raised in this colony for His Majesty's service on an intended expedition to the West Indies.

In 1746, an act was passed for making current ten thousand pounds in bills of credit to enable the honorable John Hamilton, Esq., commander-in-chief of this colony, or the commander-in-chief for the time being, to defray the expenses of arming and clothing the forces to be raised in this colony for His Majesty's service in the present expedition against Canada.

All these issues, although at one period they were at a heavy discount, were fully redeemed.

The penalty for counterfeiting them was death.

CHAPTER XI.

1674—1693.

Quintipartite deed—Twenty-four proprietors—Borough officers for Bergen and Elizabethtown—Punishment for different crimes—Marriages not to be solemnized until after publication—Militia law—Formation and boundaries of counties—Bergen—Essex—Middlesex—Monmouth.

The original establishment of the government of New Caesaria or New Jersey, was by the proprietors, who claimed to have derived their right from the grant of the Duke of York.

The constitution framed by Berkely and Carteret, engrossed on a parchment roll, and signed by them, bears date January 10th, 1664.

On the 29th of June, 1674, a second grant was made to the Duke of York by Charles II., by the grace of God, King of England, France and Ireland, and defender of the faith; and on the 29th of July of the same year, another grant was made to Lord Berkely and Sir George Carteret.

The commission appointing Philip Carteret, governor of the province, bears date July 31st, 1674.

The quintipartite deed of division between East and West Jersey, was dated July 1st, 1676, in the twentieth year of the reign of King Charles II., between Sir George Carteret, of Saltrum, in the county of Devon, knight and baronet, and one of His Majesty's most honorable privy council of the first part, and William Penn, of Richmansworth, in the county of Hertford, Esq., of the second part; Gawen Lawry, of London, merchant, of the third part; Nicholas Lucas, of Hertford, in the county of Hertford, malster, of the fourth part, and Edward Billinge, of Westminister, in the county of Middlesex, gent., of the fifth part.

This deed recites, that whereas our said sovereign lord, the King's Majesty, in and by his letters patents under the great seal of England, bearing date the twelfth day of March, in the sixteenth year of His Majesty's reign, did give and grant unto his dearest brother James, Duke of York, all that part of the mainland of New England, beginning at a certain place called or known by the name of St. Croix, next adjoining to New Scotland, in America, and from thence extending along the sea coast to a certain place called Pemaquine or Pemaquid, and so up the river to the furthest head of the same as it tendeth northward, and extending from thence to the river of Kenebeque, and so upward to the river Canada, northward; and also all that island or islands commonly called by the several name or names of Matowacks or Long Island, situate and being towards the west of Cape Cod and the Narrow Higansetts, abutting upon the mainland between the two rivers known by the names of Connecticut and Hudson's river, together with the said Hudson river, and all the lands from the west side of Connecticut river to the east side of Delaware bay; also the islands known as Martin's Vineyard or Nantukes, otherwise Nantucket.

This same deed recites that His Royal Highness, the said James, Duke of York, conveyed to John Lord Berkely and Sir George Carteret, all that tract of land adjacent to New England, and lying and being to the westward of Long Island and Manhattan island, part of the said mainland of New England, beginning at St. Croix, mentioned to be granted to His Royal Highness by the said therein and hereinbefore recited letters patent; bounded on the east, part by the main sea, and part by Hudson's river, and hath upon the west Delaware bay or river, and extending southward to the main ocean as far as Cape May at the mouth of Delaware bay; and to the northward as far as the northermost branch of the said bay, or river of Delaware, in forty-one degrees and forty minutes of latitude, and crosseth over thence in a straight line to Hudson's river in forty-one degrees of latitude, which said tract of land was then afterwards to be called by the name or names of New Caesaria or New Jersey.

On the eighteenth day of March, 1673, John Lord Berkeley, in consideration of the sum of one thousand pounds, conveyed unto John Fenwick, one-half of the lands owned by him in New Jersey.

On the ninth day of February, 1674, John Fenwick and Edward Byllinge sold to William Penn, Gawen Lawry and Nicholas Lucas, for one year. And on the tenth day of the same month a tripartite grant of release or confirmation was made between John Fenwick of the first part, Edward Byllinge of the second part, and William Penn, Gawen Lawry, and Nicholas Lucas of the third part.

This last conveyance was for one undivided half-part of New Jersey.

The province was to be divided into two equal parts, separated by a straight line running north and south. That part on the east of this line was to belong to Sir George Carteret, and to be called East New Jersey, while that part on the west, was to be held by William Penn, Gawen Lawry, and Nicholas Lucas, in trust for Edward Byllinge.

They were to pay annually to the Duke of York the sum of twenty nobles, one-half of which was to be paid by Sir George Carteret, and the other half by William Penn, Gawen Lawry and Nicholas Lucas.

After the death of Sir George Carteret, on the first and second of February, 1682, his widow, Elizabeth Carteret, John Earl of Bath, Thomas Lord Crew, Bernard Greenville, Sir Robert Atkins, Sir Edward Atkins, Thomas Pocock, and Thomas Cremer, conveyed the eastern division of New Jersey, in fee simple, to William Penn, Robert West, Thomas Rudyard, Samuel Groom, Thomas Hart, Richard Mew, Thomas Wilcox, Ambrose Rigg, John Heywood, Hugh Hartshorne, Clement Plumsted, and Thomas Cooper.

These twelve proprietors the same year conveyed the land to twelve others, viz: Robert Barclay, Edward Byllinge, Robert Turner, James Brain, Aarent Sonmans, William Gibson, Gawen Lawry, David Barclay, Thomas Barker, Thomas Varne, James Earl of Perth, Robert Gordon, and John Drummond.

The legal year in England began the 25th of March, but the historical year began the 1st of January following; and in Scotland they also began the year on the 1st of January, which accounts for the seeming impropriety of the dates of some of the foregoing, and other ancient records.

In the early days of the province the governor, six councillors and twelve assemblymen, constituted the law making power.

In 1668, we find two burgesses for Bergen, two for Elizabethtown, two for Newark upon Pishawack river, two for Woodbridge, two for Middletown, and two for Shrewsbury.

These met May 26th, 1668, and enacted laws for the punishment of different crimes in the province.

It was at this session enacted that the governor and his council, with the burgesses or deputies of the country, be called the general assembly of the lords proprietors. They were to meet on the first Tuesday of November annually, and the deputies of each town to be chosen on the first day of January annually. Any deputy being absent from the meeting was to pay a fine of forty shillings for every day's absence, unless he gave a reasonable excuse, which was satisfactory to the general assembly when in session, or at any other time to the governor and his council.

Previous to this general assembly the only laws they had were those made by the proprietors themselves, and called the grants and concessions of the lords proprietors. After Carteret's commission as governor, they were governed by his instructions, then by a constitution called the declaration of the proprietors. After the second grant to the Duke of York, and the grant to Sir George Carteret, they were governed by directions, instructions, and orders issued by George Carteret, knight and baronet, vice-chamberlain of His Majesty's household, and one of His Majesty's most honorable privy council, and lord proprietor of the country or province of New Caesaria or New Jersey. But in 1668, Governor Philip Carteret, his council, and the deputies of the several towns, held a general assembly, and enacted laws for the province.

In 1675, an oath of fidelity to the King and the lords proprietors was established.

They were required to swear to the allegiance they owed King Charles as the lawful and rightful sovereign, and that the Pope, neither of himself, nor by any authority of the church, or See of Rome, or by any other means with any other, had any power or authority to depose the king, or dispose of any of His Majesty's kingdoms or dominions, or to authorize any foreign prince to annoy him or his country, &c.

The next general assembly met at Elizabethtown, November 5th, 1675. They were called the governor, council, and deputies, or representatives of the country. They each took the oath, except one from Shrewsbury, who refusing to swear or subscribe, was dismissed.

Previous to the sitting of the general assembly, March 1st, 1682, all the laws enacted by that body were called acts of the general assembly, and were printed as though they were but one act, being distinguished in paragraphs by Roman numerals. But after the session of 1682, they were divided into chapters, and each act was designated by its title. There were at this session eighteen acts passed, the principal one of which was dividing the province into four counties.

Bergen county was to contain all the settlements between Hudson's river and Hackensack river, beginning at Constable's hook, and so extending to the uppermost bound of the province northward between the said rivers.

January 21st, 1709-10, the line was extended to the Pequanock and Passaic rivers, and the sound.

By this act Bergen county was bounded from Constable's hook, along the bay and Hudson's river, to the partition line between New York and New Jersey; thence along the partition line between the said provinces, and the division line of East and West Jersey to Pequanock river; thence down that and Passaic river to the sound, and thence to the place first named.

Its situation on Hudson river, opposite and adjacent to New York, opened an advantageous intercourse with that market. Their lands are generally good for grass, wheat, or any other grain.

In the early days of the province the Schuyler's had here two large parks for deer and other game. The inhabitants of this section of the country being the descendants of the low Dutch or Hollanders, that originally settled there under the Dutch title, preserved the religion of their ancestors, and worshipped after the manner of the Reformed churches in the united provinces. They were in principal, Presbyterians, yet in subordination to the classis of Amsterdam. Their language in general still bears the Dutch accent, nor have they forgot the customs of Holland. The county bordering on New York has an area of about three hundred and fifty square miles. It is bounded on the east by Hudson river, and is intersected by Ramapo, Hackensack, and Saddle rivers, which afford valuable water power. The famous palisades of the Hudson are situated on the east border of the county. The surface is generally uneven, and in the west part mountainous. The soil is fertile, particularly along the valleys of the stream. Magnetic ore and limestone are found. The railroad connecting Jersey City with Binghampton, in New York, traverses the western part of this county. This, the Erie railway, is a broad gauge, double track, between the Atlantic cities and the south, south-west, and north-west. Its connection is 860 miles without change of cars between New York, Rochester, Buffalo, Dunkirk, Salamanca, Corry, Meadville, Akron, Mansfield, Galion, Urbana, Dayton, Hamilton and Cincinnati. The eastern termination is Long Dock, Jersey City.

This county was organized in 1682; reorganized in 1710, but the area was diminished February 7th, 1837, by the formation of Passaic county from Bergen and Essex counties; and again February 22d, 1840, by the formation of Hudson county. This act set off into Hudson county the townships of Bergen, North Bergen, and Harrison. The capital is Hackensack.

The present bounds are, north by Rockland county, New York, east by the Hudson river, south by Passaic and Hudson counties, and east by Passaic county. East and west it is about nineteen miles long; the breadth on the east is fourteen, and on the west nine miles. The central part is generally level and undulating; on the west it is mountainous, and on the east bordering on the Hudson river, are the famous palisades composed of trap-ridge, which extend the whole width of the county. The soil, particularly in the valleys, is fertile, and productive of early summer vegetables—apples, strawberries, and other fruits, the city of New York furnishing an ample market for the productions of the county. There are many small and beautiful farms, with neat cottages, in the Dutch style of architecture, painted white, and being surrounded by shrubbery; they present an air of comfort and thrift. These are principally in the valleys of the Hackensack or Saddle rivers, and on the adjacent hills. The population in 1738, was 4,095; in 1745, 3,006; in 1840, 13,223; in 1850, 14,725, of whom forty-one were slaves; in 1860, 21,618, of whom two were Indians—one male and one female, and in 1870, 30,122, divided in the nine townships, as follows: Franklin, 2,899, of whom seventy-two were colored; Hackensack, 8,038, of whom three hundred and thirty-two were colored; Harrington, 2,664, of whom two hundred and twenty-six were colored; Hohokus, 2,632, of whom two hundred and forty were colored; Lodi, 3,221, of whom one hundred and forty were colored; New Barbadoes, 4,929, of whom three hundred and thirteen were colored; Saddle River, 1,168, of whom sixty-nine were colored; Union, 2,057, of whom seventy-one were colored; Washington, 2,514, of whom one hundred and sixty-nine were colored, making the white population 30,122, and the colored 1,632; total in 1870, 31,754.

In Bergen county are the Schuyler mines. In this county was born the famous Peter Schuyler, who died in 1762, at the age of fifty-two years. He was a younger son of Aarent Schuyler, the discoverer, and first owner of the celebrated mines above mentioned. He had command of the provincial troops against the French in Canada, and was in several campaigns in two wars afterwards, and by judges of military merit, he was allowed to have ranked high. He had qualities besides, that greatly recommended him to his acquaintances, being of a frank, open demeanor, extensive generosity and humanity, and unwearied in his endeavors to accomplish whatever appeared of service to his country. He was taken a prisoner at Oswego when that post was given up to the French, and long detained as such in Canada, where, having letters of credit, he kept an open house for the relief of his fellow sufferers, and advanced large sums of money to the Indians in the French interest, for the redemption of captives, many of whom he afterwards, at his own expense, maintained while there, and provided for their return, trusting to their honor and abilities for repayment, in which way, although he lost much money, he considered it well bestowed. In person he was tall and hardy, rather rough at first view, yet a little acquaintance discovered his sincerity, and that he was ever ready to render any kind office in his power. In conversation he was above artifice, or the common traffic of forms and ceremony. He enjoyed friendship with a true relish, and in every relation what he appeared to be, he truly was.

Franklin township is five miles north and south, and ten east and west. On the north it is bounded by Hokokus township, east by Washington and Midland, south by Saddle river, Chester and Wayne, and west by Pompton and Wayne. On its eastern boundary is Saddle river, and the Ramapo on its west. The soil is well cultivated and productive. Its population in 1750 was 1,741; in 1760, 2,318; and in 1870, 2,899.

Hackensack, formerly a township of this county, was ten miles long, with a width varying from three to five miles. It was bounded north by Harrington, east by the Hudson river, south by North Bergen, in Hudson county, and west by Lodi and New Barbadoes. The famous Palisades were on its east, along the Hudson river. Many of its inhabitants cultivated truck for the New York market. Its population in 1850 was 3,506; in 1860, 5,488; and in 1870, 8,038. Fort Lee, a celebrated military post during the Revolutionary war, was located in this township, on the Hudson river. It is now in ruins, but a village bearing the same name occupies the spot. Below it is a village called Bull's Ferry, named from the ferry that has existed there more than half a century. Below this ferry there stood in the time of the Revolutionary war, a small block house, then in possession of the enemy, which was stormed by General Wayne, but he was unsuccessful in dislodging the enemy, though they were nearly conquered at the time he drew his men off, as it is said they had but a single round left, and had he have continued a few moments longer, would have completely routed them. On the 22d of March, 1871, the townships of Englewood, Palisades, and Ridgefield, were formed from Hackensack township.

Harrington township was much reduced in 1840 by the formation of Washington township, the latter taking off about one-half of its inhabitants. It measures about five miles each way, and is nearly square. Its bounds are Rockland county, New York, on the north, Hudson river on the east, Palisade township south, and Washington on the west. On the east are the famous Palisades, and the Hackensack river divides it on the west from Washington township. Population in 1850, 1,195; in 1860, 1,602; and in 1870, 2,664.

New Barbadoes is north of Lodi, east of Midland, and west of Englewood and Ridgefield townships. It is about five miles long, from north to south, and two wide from east to west. Its population in 1850 was 2,265; in 1860, 3,558; and in 1870, 4,929.

The town of Hackensack is the seat of justice of the county, and lies on the Hackensack river, in New Barbadoes township, about thirteen miles from New York city. Its name is derived from the river. Its extent is more than a mile along two principal streets. It contains nine churches, one of which (the Reformed Dutch) is a handsome stone building. It has two academies, a boarding school, classical institute, and more than three hundred dwellings. Small vessels are constantly plying between this place and New York. At the commencement of the Revolutionary war, it contained only about thirty houses. It now has a population of about 2,000. The first house erected for public worship was in 1696, and the present stone edifice was built in 1791, being the third one on this site.

Saddle river township, before the formation of Passaic county, in 1847, comprised within its limits what is now the township of Manchester. Its form was at that time like a saddle, and from thence it derived its name. It is seven miles long and two miles wide. On its north is Franklin, East Midland, and Lodi, South Lodi, and West Acquackannonck, and Manchester townships, the cities of Paterson and Passaic. In 1850 its population was 823; in 1860, 1,007; and in 1870, 1,168.

Hokokus was formed in 1849, and in 1852 part of it was set off to Washington township. Its population in 1850 was 2,274; in 1860, 2,352; and in 1870, 2,632.

Union was set off from Harrison, Hudson county, and annexed to Bergen county in 1852. Its population in 1860 was 957, and in 1870, 2,057.

Washington was formed in 1840, from the western part of Harrington. It is about seven miles long and five wide. Rockland county, New York, lies on its north, Harrington on the east, Midland south, and Franklin and Hokokus west. Population in 1850, 1,807; in 1860, 2,273; and in 1870, 2,514.

Essex county was first formed in 1682, and contained all the settlements between the west side of Hackensack river, and the partition line between Woodbridge and Elizabethtown, and extended westward and northward to the utmost bounds of the province. The lines were changed in 1709-'10, to begin at the Rahway river where it falls into the sound, and running thence up said river to Robinson's branch; thence west to the division line between the eastern and western divisions, and so follow said division line to Pequannock river where it meets the Passaic river; thence down the Passaic river to the bay and sound; thence down the sound to where it began; Elizabeth being at that time in Essex county.

November 4th, 1741, the lines were again changed, and part of the county was annexed to Somerset.

November 28th, 1822, the easterly bounds were declared to be the middle of the waters of the sound, as far as the limits of the county extended. They were again changed in 1847, when Union county was formed.

Smith, in his History of New Jersey, published in 1800, informs us that "in 1741, Essex county contained the well settled towns of Elizabeth and Newark.* In the latter, the courts for the county were held, and in the former those for the ancient borough. This being an old settled county and good land, was consequently thickly inhabited. Their plantations were too high in value to be generally large, and their improve-

---

* At each of these, there were at that time a public library.

ments were greater than in many other parts. At this time the Presbyterians had seven places of worship, Episcopalians three, Baptists one, and the Dutch Calvinists two."

This county at the present time is about twenty miles long, with an average breadth of about twelve miles.

The county of Passaic, and a small part of Morris, bounds it on the north, Hudson county and Newark bay on the east, Union county on the south, and Morris county on the west. Its population in 1810 was 25,984; in 1820, 30,793; in 1830, 41,911; in 1840, 44,621; in 1850, 73,950; in 1860, 98,877; and in 1870, 143,839.

Belleville township was formed from the eastern portion of Bloomfield in 1839. It is about four miles in length and about two in width.

Acquackannonck, Passaic county, bounds it on the north, Union, Hudson county, from which it is separated by the Passaic river, on the east, Newark on the south, and Bloomfield on the west. It contains extensive manufactories. Population in 1850, 3,514; in 1860, 3,969; and in 1870, 3,644 inhabitants.

The town of Belleville is beautifully situated on the Passaic river, about three miles north of Newark. It was once called Second river, and had a large population as early as 1682. It contains over two hundred dwellings, and several large manufacturing establishments. It is somewhat of a resort in the summer season by persons from New York city and vicinity.

Franklin, formerly called Spring Garden, is a flourishing little manufacturing village, containing about thirty dwellings.

Bloomfield township is five miles long by three wide. On its north is Acqackannonck, Passaic county, Belleville and the city of Newark on the east, Orange on the south, and Montclair and Orange on the west. On the Second and Third rivers, there are numerous manufacturing establishments. The population in 1850 was 3,385; in 1860, 4,790; and in 1870, 4,580. The village of the same name extends about three and a half miles in a northwesterly direction, including West Bloomfield. It was settled in the early part of the colony by New Englanders.

Caldwell was formed from Newark and Acquackannonck in 1798. It is about seven miles long by four wide. On its north is Little Falls and Wayne, in Passaic county, and Pequannock in Morris county, Montclair on the east, West Orange and Livingston on the south, and Hanover and Montville, Morris county, on the west. In the eastern part are the First and Second mountains, and the remainder of the township abounds in hills. The population in 1850 was 2,377; in 1860, 2,688; and in 1870, 2,727.

The town of Caldwell is about ten miles northwest from Newark, and contains about thirty-five dwellings, and a Presbyterian church. Verona is about two miles east from Caldwell, and contains a Methodist church, and about twenty-five dwellings. Fairfield contains a Dutch Reformed church, lies in the northern part of the township, and is a rich agricultural district. Franklin is a thriving village, and lies about a mile west of Caldwell.

Clinton was formed from Elizabethtown, Newark and Orange, in 1834. Its length is about four miles, and breadth about two and a half miles. South Orange and Newark lies on the north of it, and Newark is also on its east, while the township of Union, in Union county, is on its south, and South Orange on the west.

Camptown was a flourishing village, about three and a half miles from Newark, containing about fifty dwellings and three churches, Presbyterian, Episcopal, and what was called a Free Church. The name was derived from the fact that during the Revolutionary war, the American army was for some time encamped here. The population of the township in 1850 was 2,508; in 1860, 3,659; and in 1870, 2,240.

East Orange was formed from part of the town of Orange, March 4th, 1863. Population in 1870, 4,315.

Fairmount was formed March 11th, 1862, from parts of the town of Orange, and the townships of Caldwell and Livingston, and on the 14th of March, 1863, the name was changed to West Orange. It is four miles long by two and a half in width, and in 1870 contained a population of 2,206.

Livingston was formed in 1812, is five miles long and four wide. On the north is Caldwell, on the east West Orange, on the west Chatham and Hanover, in Morris county, and on the south Millburn. It lies ten miles west of Newark, and contains the small settlements of Livingston, Centreville, Moorehoustown, and Northfield. Population in 1850, 1,151; in 1860, 1,323; and in 1870, 1,157.

Millburn was formed from Springfield March 20th, 1857, and February 25th, 1863, part of it was set off to South Orange. Population in 1860, 1,630; and in 1870, 1,675.

Montclair was formed from Bloomfield, April 15th, 1868. The first mountain forms its boundary on the west, and separates it from Caldwell township. Population in 1870, 2,853.

Woodside was formed from the township of Belleville, March 2 4th, 1869 and on the 5th of April, 1871, it was divided between the city of Newark, and annexed to the Eighth ward, and the township of Belleville. Population in 1870, 1,172.

Newark city was first settled in 1666, by emigrants from Connecticut, two years after the first settlement of Elizabethtown. The streets are wide and well laid out. It was originally settled by thirty families from Guildford, a beautiful post borough and township in New Haven county, on Long Island sound; Branford, a post town and seaport of New Haven county; Milford, another post village in the township and seaport of New Haven, on the Wopewang river, as well as from New Haven itself.

Governor Carteret upon his arrival here in August, 1665, sent agents out to New England to publish the concessions, and to invite settlers to the new colony. These towns sent out Captain Robert Treat, John Curtis, Jasper Crane, and John Treat, to view the country, and ascertain more particularly the terms of purchase, and the disposition of the Indians in the vicinity. These agents upon their return, made a favorable report, and were at once deputised to bargain for a township, and select a proper site for a town, as well as to make immediate arrangements for a settlement.

The agents saw at once the advantages to be derived from a settlement where the present city of Newark stands for a town, and accordingly selected that spot.

After everything had been satisfactorily arranged, they set out under the guidance of their agents above named, and after a long and tedious passage, equal to crossing the Atlantic at the present day, they arrived early in the month of May in the Passaic river. Here their further progress was impeded by the Hackensack Indians, who claimed the soil which the Governor had granted, and opposed their landing, unless they were first compensated for the land.

An Indian by the name of Perro laid claim to the land where Newark now stands, and the emigrants were compelled to buy it of him before they were permitted to land.

The land purchased was set forth to be "a parcel of land lying and being on the west side of the Kill Van Coll, beginning at the mouth of a certain creek named Waweayack, (Bound-Brook) upon the side of Newark bay; then running up said creek to the head of a cove; and then in a westerly direction to the foot of the Watchung mountain, running along the foot of said mountain until it meets by an east line a small river coming from the hills into Passaic river, named Jantucuck (Third river); thence running down Passaic river and Arthur Kull bay, till it meets with the mouth of Waweayack, as above said."

This was the original township of Newark, and comprehended Bloomfield, Caldwell, Livingston, Orange, and Springfield, as well as Newark.

The price paid for this land was one hundred and thirty pounds, New England currency, twelve Indian blankets, and twelve Indian guns.

The settlers first located in separate neighborhoods, but being fearful of danger in being thus scattered about in different localities, they determined in 1666 to form one township, with specific rules for government, and "to be of one heart and hand in endeavoring to carry on their spiritual concernments as well as their civil and town affairs, according to God and godly government." They appointed a committee of eleven to order and settle the concernments of the people of the place,

This committee was Captain Robert Treat, Lieutenant Samuel Swain, Samuel Kitchell, Michael Tompkins, Morris Say, Richard Beckly, Richard Harrison, Thomas Blatchly, Edward Riggs, Stephen Freemna, and Thomas Johnson.

These articles specified that "No person could become a freeman or burgess of their town, or vote in its elections, but such as was a member of some one of the congregational churches, nor be chosen to the magistracy, nor to any other military or civil office. But all others admitted to be planters were allowed to inherit and to enjoy all other privileges, save those above excepted."

A number arrived in November of this year from Branford, thereby augmenting the population of the town, so that in June, 1667, the population consisted of sixty-five efficient men, besides women and children.

In the distribution of the lands among the settlers, each man drew by lot six acres as a homestead, the allotments being made in the several localities where they had previously formed a settlement. In parcelling out the lands, the Upper Green, now Washington Square, was reserved for a market place, and the Lower Green, now called the Park, for a military parade ground.

The first magistrates, chosen in 1668, and representatives to the first assembly, were Robert Treat, and Jasper Crane. Mr. Treat was chosen the first recorder, or town clerk. He afterwards removed to Connecticut, of which state he became governor, and shortly after died.

Rev. Mr. Pierson was their first clergyman, and in his old age, his son Abraham was appointed his assistant.

Their first school was established in 1676, and Mr. John Catlin was engaged to instruct the children in as much English reading, writing, and arithmetic, as he could teach. Mr. Catlin was also the first lawyer settled in the town. The first shoemaker was Samuel Whitehead, of Elizabethtown, who was to supply the town with shoes. Newark is now the largest city in the state, and is extensively engaged in manufacturing. The population in 1850 was 38,894; in 1860, 71,941; and in 1870, 105,059. The city is divided into fourteen wards.

The city of Orange is divided into three wards. It was incorporated as a town January 31st, 1860. The present charter creating it into three wards was approved March 3d, 1869, and on the 3d of April, 1872, a supplement was approved by which it was changed to a city. Its population in 1850 was 4,385; in 1860, 8,877; and in 1870, 9,348. East Orange township was formed from part of the town of Orange, March 4th, 1863, and in 1870 contained a population of 4,315. South Orange was set off from Clinton and the town of Orange, March 13th, 1861. Its population in 1870 was 2,963. West Orange was formed from the town of Orange; population in 1870, 2,106.

Middlesex county was formed in 1632, and was the third county in the province. It was to begin at the parting line between Essex county and the Woodbridge line, containing Woodbridge and Piscataway, and all the plantations on both sides of the Raritan river as far as Cheesquake harbor eastward, extending southwest to the division line of the province, and northwest to the utmost bounds of the province.

The lines were changed in 1709-'10. They were again changed in 1713-'14, and again in 1790. Another change was made in 1822, and again in 1838, when Mercer county was formed. The lines were again changed in 1857, at the formation of Union county. The population in 1850 was 28,635; in 1860, 34,812; and in 1870, 45,029.

It is about twenty-four miles long and twelve broad, and has on its north Union county, Staten Island and Raritan bay on the east and southeast, Monmouth and Mercer on the southwest, and Somerset west.

East-Brunswick was formed from Mercer and New-Brunswick n 1860, at which time the population was 2,436, and in 1870 it was 2,861. Spottswood, on the line of the Amboy division of the Pennsylvania Railroad, derived its name from John Johnson, of Spottswood, in Scotland. Herbertsville, or Old Bridge, is on the South river, a branch of the Raritan.

Madison was formed from South Amboy township in 1869, and in 1870 had a population of 1,634. Jacksonville is located at the head of Cheesquake creek.

Monroe was formed from South Amboy in 1838, and in 1850 had a population of 3,001; in 1860, 3,131; and in 1770, 3,253.

New-Brunswick is divided into six wards. Its population in 1850 was 10,008; in 1860, 11,156; and in 1870, 15,058. It was incorporated as a city in 1784. Rutgers College, built of a dark red freestone, and finished in 1811, is located here. This institution was chartered by George III, in 1770, and was called Queen's College in honor of his wife, but did not go into operation until 1781, for want of funds. In 1825 the name was changed, as a mark of respect to Col. Henry Rutgers, one of its distinguished benefactors.

Gordon, in his Gazette, informs us, "That at the close of the 17th century, the place where the city now stands was covered with woods, and called, after the name of its proprietor, 'Prigmore's Swamp.' The first inhabitant of whom any account is preserved, was one Daniel Cooper, who resided where the post road crossed the river, and kept the ferry, which afterward, in 1713, when the county line was drawn, was called Inian's ferry. This ferry was granted by the proprietors, November 2d, 1697, for the lives of Inian and wife, and the survivor, at a rent of five shillings sterling per annum. The first inhabitants were of European origin, from Long Island. About 1730, several Dutch families emigrated from Albany, bringing with them their building materials, in imitation of their ancestors, who imported their bricks, tiles, &c., from Holland. About this time the name of New-Brunswick* was given to the place, which had heretofore been distinguished as 'The River.'"

North-Brunswick contained in 1870, 1,124 inhabitants.

Perth Amboy city is situated at the head of Raritan bay. In 1850 it contained 1,865 inhabitants; in 1860, 2,302; and in 1870, 2,861. It takes its name from James Drummond, one of the proprietors, and Earl of Perth, and Amboy from Ambo, meaning in the Indian language, a point.

The situation for a sea trade, as lying open to Sandy Hook, whence vessels may arrive in any weather in one tide from the sea, and find a safe, commodious harbor, capacious enough to contain many large ships, and was allowed to be as good a port as most on the continent.

Piscataway was incorporated in 1798, so named from some of the first settlers who came from Piscataqua, in Maine, and upon their arrival they called the place New Piscataqua.

New Market, formerly Quibbletown, is a thriving post town. New Brooklyn, Samptown, New Durham, and Raritan Landing, are small villages in the township. The population of Piscata-

---

* German families settling there named it after the Duchy of the same name in Northwestern Germany.

away was in 1850, 2,975; in 1860, 3,186; and in 1870, 2,757.

Raritan township was formed from Piscataway and Woodbridge in 1870, and has a population of 3,460. It is nine miles north and south, and six east and west.

South Amboy township is located on Raritan bay, at the mouth of Raritan river, and has a population of 4,525. This is the termination of the Camden and Amboy division of the Pennsylvania railroad.

There is near this village a superior quality of clay, from which stoneware is extensively manufactured.

South-Brunswick township adjoins Mercer county. Population in 1850, 3,368; in 1860, 3,816; and in 1870, 3,779. Several miles of it in the north part are covered with some notable sandhills.

The village of Kingston is on the line of Somerset county, near Princeton. This was, before the railroads were built, the great thoroughfare between New York and Philadelphia. The passengers were carried through in stages, and as many as fifty stages have been seen here at one time in front of Withington's hotel, loaded with about four hundred passengers. Opposite Withington's hotel, in the early days of the state, Van Tilburgh kept a hotel, which was celebrated as the favorite stopping-place of Washington, as well as the governors, who stopped here in passing from the eastern towns to the capital at Trenton.

Cranberry is in Cranberry township. It was here that David Brainard labored so arduously among the Indians, being attended with remarkable success. Cranberry contains about 1,000 inhabitants. The township was set off from South-Brunswick and Monroe townships in 1872.

Woodbridge is on the northeastern end of the county, and contained in 1850, 5,141 inhabitants, and in 1870, 3,717. It is about ten miles long and nine miles in breadth. Uniontown and Woodbridge are in this township. The town of Woodbridge was first settled by emigrants from England, who came over in 1665, with Governor Carteret. It was at one time a prominent place in the province.

Monmouth county, in 1682, was to begin at the westward bounds of Middlesex county, containing Middletown and

Shrewsbury, and to extend westward, southward, and northward, to the extreme bounds of the province. The lines were altered January 21st, 1709-'10; again March 15th, 1713; again November 28th, 1822, and again February 15th, 1850, at the formation of Ocean county. It is considered one of the best, if not the best, agricultural counties in the state, the farms being under a high state of cultivation. Their marl, which was at one time considered valueless, is now much sought after as a manure. Peat, which is also found in other sections of the county where marl is not, is also used for manufacturing purposes. This is usually mixed with lime, and has been found very efficacious for the purpose of a manure. The population of the county in 1850 was 30,313; in 1860, 39,346; and in 1870, 46,195.

Atlantic township contained in 1870, 1,713 inhabitants. Colt's Neck, originally called Call's Neck, from a Mr. Call, a resident there, is in this township, and is five miles from Freehold, on a neck of land formed by two branches of the Swimming river.

Freehold township was formed in 1798, and contained in 1850, 2,644 inhabitants; in 1860, 3,811; and in 1870, 4,231. The northern and middle part abounds in fertile farms.

The town of Freehold is the seat of justice of the county, and is distant about thirty miles from Trenton. The town contains many large dwellings surrounded by spacious grounds, exhibiting wealth and refinement. The Episcopal is the oldest church in the town, and was used during the Revolution as barracks for the soldiers. It was known in olden times as Monmouth Court-House, from the fact of the courts meeting here. The first court-house erected here stood in front of where the one that was burned down on the 29th of October, 1873, stood. It was built in 1715 of wood, and of antique style, with peaked roof, and clapboarded with shingles. In December, 1727, the court house and jail were destroyed by fire. About the year 1730, another court-house, with the jail under the same roof, was built on the same lot. That building stood over seventy years. It was built of frame, nearly square, smaller than the one which succeeded it, and had a roof shaped very much like that of the old Tenant church, with a small steeple in the centre. This court-house stood here at the time the battle of Monmouth was fought, at which time there was not a dozen houses in the village. The general officers of each army during their occupancy of the place, used the court-house as headquarters. Sir Henry Clinton, Lord Cornwallis, General Knyphausen, and other officers of the English forces, left the court-house suddenly on the morning of the 29th of June, 1778, when it was doubtless taken possession of by Generals Washington, Lafayette, Green, Wayne, Knox, Forman, Morgan, and others, whose names will go down to the latest generation on the page of history.

In 1808 a new court-house was erected, when the old building was removed across the street, and occupied as a barn. In October, 1873, the latter court-house was destroyed by fire, and a new one is now being erected upon the same lot which has been occupied for that purpose one hundred and fifty-eight years.

Holmdel was formed from Raritan in 1857, and in 1860 contained 1,334 inhabitants, and in 1870 1,415. It is seven miles long north and south, and three and a half wide east and west.

Howell was formed from Shrewsbury in 1801, and is ten miles long by seven wide. The New Jersey Southern, and Farmingdale and Squan Village Railroads, pass through the township. The central part contains marl pits of excellent quality, among the principal of which is the Squankum marl. The Hominy hills are located in the northern part, but in other respects it is generally level ground. New Bargain is a small settlement near the middle of the township. Farmingdale is a place of considerable importance, brought into notice through the marl pits located in its vicinity. Howell township contained in 1850 4,058 inhabitants; in 1860, 2,574; and in 1870, 3,371.

Manalapan is considered the most fertile agricultural township in the county. It is purely an agricultural district, and contained in 1850 1,910 inhabitants; in 1860, 2,374; and in 1870, 2,286. Englishtown lies near the centre of the township.

Marlborough contained in 1850 1,564 inhabitants; in 1860, 2,083; and in 1870, 2,231. The Monmouth County Agricultural Railroad passes through the township.

Matawan township was formed from Raritan in 1857, and contained in 1860 2,072 inhabitants, and in 1870 2,839. The village of Matawan, formerly called Middletown Point, is upon a narrow point of land formed by the Matawan creek, three miles from Raritan bay. The first settlers were Scotch, principally from Aberdeen, and it was called by them New Aberdeen. At Mount Pleasant, during the Revolutionary war, lived Philip Freneau, a distinguished poet. He was educated at Princeton college, and enjoyed the friendship of Adams, Franklin, Jefferson, Madison, and Monroe. His patriotic songs and ballads were popular among all classes, possessing merit of a very high order, and were sung with enthusiasm everywhere. He was possessed of fine feelings, though in sentiment he was an infidel, and late in life became addicted to habits of intemperance. He died a miserable death near Freehold, on the 18th of December, 1832, being then in the 80th year of his age.

Middletown township was incorporated in 1798. The first permanent settlement made in this township was in 1666, by Richard Hartshorne, an English Quaker, who settled on the Navesink river. He called his place Portland Point. It was originally settled by Englishmen, from Long Island. Some Dutch and Scotch also settled in the township. The courts used to be held here two or three times a year, for Middletown, Piscataway, and other places. The town of Middletown is about forty-five miles from Trenton. The celebrated Highlands of Navesink are in this township, and extend along Sandy Hook for nearly five miles, on the west of Shrewsbury river. They are about three hundred feet in height, and on Beacon hill is a light-house called the Highland lights, to distinguish them from the one at Sandy Hook. With their new and improved French lights, they can be seen twenty-five miles out at sea.

At Gravelly Point, the British army embarked after the battle of Monmouth, and it is celebrated as being the spot where the unfortunate Captain Joshua Huddy was barbarously murdered.

Millstone township contained in 1850, 1,676 inhabitants; in 1860, 2,356; and in 1870, 2,087.

Ocean township contained in 1860, 3,768 inhabitants; in 1860, 4,346; and in 1870, 6,189. The celebrated watering place, Long Branch, is in this township.

Raritan township, in 1850, contained 4,198 inhabitants; in

1860, 2,979; and in 1870, 3,443. Keyport is situated on Raritan bay, about two miles from Middletown, and twenty-two from New York, and is a place of resort for sea bathing in the summer season. From the town can be had a magnificent view of the bay, Staten Island, the Narrows, Sandy Hook, and the Ocean, which, on a pleasant day, exhibits a scene of great beauty, studded with its myriad sails. There are numerous oyster beds of the finest quality in Chingarora creek, at this place. Population in 1870, 2,366.

Shrewsbury township is level, the southern part being sandy; the soil is fertile, and contains excellent farming land. It was settled by emigrants from Connecticut in 1664. Lewis Morris, of Barbadoes, the uncle of Lewis Morris, Governor of New Jersey, carried on iron works here. The village of Red Bank is pleasantly situated on the Navesink river, two miles from Shrewsbury and five from the ocean. In 1830 it contained but two houses, but is now one of the most thriving villages in the state. It has an extensive trade with New York in vegetables, wood, and oysters. Population in 1870, 2,086.

Upper Freehold township contained in 1850, 2,566 inhabitants; in 1860, 3,198; and in 1870, 3,640.

Wall township was formed from Howell in 1851. Population in 1860, 2,283, and in 1870, 2,669. Squan village is situated on the sea shore, and is a celebrated place for sea bathing, there being several boarding houses there; it is much visited in the summer season. Iron has been considerably manufactured at the Howell furnace. During the Revolutionary war there were extensive salt works at Squan, and on one occasion about one hundred and thirty-five of the enemy landed on a Sunday, and burned all the salt works, as well as destroyed the kettles; they then crossed the river and destroyed the works there. The next day they landed at Shark river, and set fire to two salt works there, but seeing a number of horsemen they retreated, and jumping into boats sank two of them. The pines were infested with robbers, who secreted themselves in caves, and would commit their depredations in the night. The government offered large rewards for their destruction, and they were hunted like wild beasts, and though the most of them were exterminated, the few that was left continued their pillaging until the close of the war.

Eatontown township was formed from parts of the townships of Ocean and Shrewsbury, April 4th, 1873. The village of Eatontown is a mile and a quarter south of Shrewsbury. It derived its name from a family by the name of Eatton, who were among the early settlers, and purchased land here. Tinton Falls is two and a half miles from Shrewsbury, on a branch of the Navesink river, and was named from Tinturn, in Monmouthshire, England, from whence the first settlers came.

CHAPTER XII.

1675.

Continuation of counties — Salem — Gloucester — Somerset — Cape May — Burlington — Hunterdon — Morris — Cumberland — Sussex — Warren — Atlantic — Passaic — Mercer — Hudson — Camden — Ocean — Union.

SALEM COUNTY was named by John Fenwick, and distinguished by his tenth in 1675. The name and jurisdiction was settled by a proprietary law in 1694. The boundaries were fixed in 1709, and altered in 1747. The population in 1810 was 12,761; in 1820, 14,022; in 1830, 14,155; in 1840, 16,024; in 1850, 19,467; in 1860, 22,458; and in 1870, 23,940.

Elisinboro' is the smallest township in the county, containing only seven hundred inhabitants. Printz, the Swedish governor, erected a fort here, at Fort Point, on the eastern bank of Salem river. They called this fortress Helsingberg, from the ancient fortified town of South Sweden of that name, where there are large manufactories of earthenware and iron goods, and from this the name of the township is derived, being originally settled by Swedes. The Indian name of the place was Wootsessungsing. The population is less than it was ten years ago, for in 1850 it was 655; in 1860, 749; and in 1870 but 700.

Lower Alloways creek contained a population in 1830 of 1,222; in 1840, 1,252; in 1850, 1,423; in 1860, 1,471; and in 1870, 1,483. Canton is nine miles from Salem, and Hancock's Bridge is five miles.

Lower Penn's Neck in 1850 contained 1,429 inhabitants; in 1860, 1,506; and in 1870, 1,472. Seven miles from Salem, on the Delaware river, is the small settlement of Kinseyville, (or

Pennsville) from which place there is a ferry to New Castle, Delaware, two miles distant. Fort Delaware is an island opposite this township, which was formed by the sinking of a vessel on a sand bar.

Mannington was at first called East Fenwick; its present name is derived from the Indian word Maneto. Manningtonville is a small settlement in the central part of the township. Mannington township contained in 1850 2,187 inhabitants; in 1860, 2,393; in 1870, 2,351.

Pilesgrove township was named from James Piles, who was in its early settlement, a large landholder there.

Woodstown was early settled by Jackanias Wood, from whom its name is derived. Sharpstown is on the Salem river, and Eldridge's Hill is about one mile from Woodstown.

This township was principally settled by Friends, and in 1726 they erected a meeting-house at Woodstown. The population of the township in 1850 was 2,962; in 1860, 2,024; in 1870, 3,385.

Pittsgrove township was formed from Pilesgrove, and named after Sir William Pitt. It is sixteen miles from Salem. In this township are the small villages of Pittstown (now called Elmer) and Centreville. In 1850 the population was 1,151; in 1860, 1,231; in 1870, 1,667.

Salem is the seat of justice for the county, and is divided into two wards. Its population in 1830 was 1,570; in 1840, 2,006; in 1850, 3052; in 1860, 3,901; and in 1870, 4,555. The first attempt to form a settlement in the state was made at this place in 1641, by some English families from New Haven, Connecticut about sixty in all, who projected their settlement on Salem creek, then called Ferken's creek.

Upper Alloway's creek township contained 2,530 inhabitants in 1850; in 1860, 2,899; in 1870, 3,062. Alloways creek runs through the township. Its name was derived from an Indian chief named Alloways, who lived here upon the arrival of Fenwick in 1675.

Friesburg (or Freastown) derived its name from a German by the name of Freas. Allowaystown and Stockington are in this township.

Upper Penn's Neck is the northermost township in the county, and is situated on the Delaware river. Population in 1850, 2,422; in 1860, 2,901; in 1870, 3,178. Pedricktown is on Oldman's creek, three miles from the Delaware river. Sculltown, (originally called Locktown, from a Mr. Lock) is at the head of navigation on Oldman's creek. Quinton township was formed from Upper Alloway's creek township, February 17th, 1873.

Pennsgrove is at the landing on the Delaware, in Upper Penn's Neck township. Upper Pittsgrove township contained in 1850 1,656 inhabitants; in 1860, 2,082; in 1870, 2,087.

Gloucester county was first laid out in 1677, and in 1709 its boundaries were ascertained by legislative enactment, beginning at the mouth of Pensauken creek; thence up the same to the fork thereof; thence along the line of Burlington county to the sea; thence along the seacoast to Great Egg Harbor river; thence up that river to the fork; thence up the southermost and greatest branch of the same to its head; thence upon a direct line to the head of Oldman's creek; thence down the same to Delaware river; thence up that river to the place of beginning. The population in 1810 was 19,744; in 1820, 23,071; in 1830, 28,431; in 1840, 25,438; in 1850, 14,655; in 1860, 18,444; in and in 1870, 21,562.

The lines were changed by the formation of Atlantic county in 1837, and again upon the formation of Camden county in 1844, and again by the annexation of Washington and Monroe townships from Camden county in 1871.

Clayton township in 1860 contained a population of 2,490, and in 1870 3,674. This township was formed from Franklin in 1858.

Deptford contained a population in 1850 of 3,355; in 1860, 4,213; and in 1870, 4,663. West Deptford township was formed from Deptford in 1871. Woodbury is the seat of justice for the county, and is pleasantly situated on Woodbury creek. Woodbury was first settled by and derives its name from Richard Wood, of Perry, England. This place was settled in 1684. Fort Mercer is on the Delaware, within the limits of West Deptford township, and Fort Mifflin is on an island in the river. Population in 1860 1,534, and in 1870 1,965.

Franklin township was formed in 1820 from Greenwich and Woolwich townships. Population in 1850, 2,984; in 1860, 1,778; and in 1870, 2,188.

Glassborough is in Clayton township, about ten miles southeast of Woodbury. Messrs. Stanger & Co., comprising seven brothers, built glass works here in the time of the Revolution, and from this circumstance the place derived its name. These men were originally from Germany, and had been employed in Wistar's glass works in Salem county. They erected some log buildings, which was the nucleus of the future town. The glass house at Salem is said to have been the first one established in America. The glass works here are extensive.

In 1871, Washington and Munroe townships were set off from Camden county and annexed to Gloucester. Franklinville, formerly called Little Ease, is six miles southeast of Glassboro.' Malaga is at the angle of Gloucester, Cumberland, and Salem counties, on the Maurice river.

Greenwich township contained a population in 1850 of 3,067; in 1860, 2,199; and in 1870, 2,342. Berkeley (or Sandtown), Paulsboro', and Billingsport, the former named after Lord Berkeley, and the latter after Edward Byllinge. are in this township.

Harrison township contained in 1850 a population of 1,984; in 1860, 2,544; and in 1870, 3,038. Mullica Hill* is in this township.

Mantua township in 1860 contained a population of 1,742, and in 1870, 1,897. Barnsboro' and Carpenter's Landing, the latter named from Thomas Carpenter, an old settler, and Harrisonville, formerly called Colestown, are in this township.

Woolwich township was settled at an early period by the Swedes on Raccoon creek, hence they called the name of the first town they located, Swedesboro'.

Battentown is a good sized village, at the southern extremity of Swedesboro', and may be said to be a continuation of that town. Bridgeport, formerly called Raccoon Lower Bridge, is

---

* Mullica Hill derived its name from Eric Molica, a Swede, who purchased a large tract of land, and settled here about the year 1693.

in this township. Woolwich township contained in 1850, 3,265 inhabitants; in 1860, 3,478; and in 1870, 3,760. Woodbury is the seat of justice of the county, and contained in 1860, 1,534 inhabitants, and in 1870, 1,965.

Somerset county was divided from Middlesex by a proprietory law in 1688, at which time it received its name. Its boundaries were limited by the act of 1709; again altered in 1713 and 1741; again in 1790 and in 1838, when Mercer county was formed; and again in 1858. Population in 1850, 19,692; in 1860, 22,057; and in 1870, 23,510. At Baskingridge, in this county, resided William Alexander, Earl of Sterling, one of the early settlers. Theodorus Jacobus Frelinghuysen, ancestor of Theodore Frelinghuysen, was one of the early ministers in this place. He preached in the Dutch church of that village.

The surface of the country is various, the northwest portion being mountainous, and the centre and southeast either level or undulating. The soil of the hills is generally clay or stiff loam, that of the level portions sandy loam, formed of shell, and the mountain valleys are of limestone.

The range of hills about two miles north of Somerville, have been perforated by many mining shafts in search of copper ore. One of these shafts is 1300 feet in length. The ore is said to contain not only a large proportion of copper, but to be worth working on account of the gold it yields. The Bridgewater mineral paint mines are situated near the centre

Somerset county is distinguished as the birthplace of Samuel L. Southard, Peter D. Vroom, Commodore Stockton, William L. Dayton, and Theodore Frelinghuysen. Its capital is Somerville. The Delaware and Raritan Canal passes through this county, and follows the Millstone river to Bound Brook, when it takes a northeasterly course to the Raritan river, at New Brunswick.

Bedminster township is hilly, the soil fertile and well cultivated. It has several small settlements, among which are Lamington, Peapack, Little Cross Roads, Greater Cross Roads, and Pluckamin. The latter was a celebrated place in the Revolutionary war. The American army halted here the day after the battle of Princeton, January 4th, 1777, on their march to

Morristown, and in the winter of 1778-'79, part of the army were encamped at this place. The number of inhabitants in 1850 were 1,826; in 1860, 1,996; and in 1870, 1,881.

Bernards township is on the north branch of the Raritan river, opposite Bedminster. The population of this township was in 1850, 2,267; in 1860, 2,471; and in 1870, 2,369.

Liberty Corners is a post village, eight miles from Somerville. Millington is also a post village, forty miles from Trenton. Vealtown is also a small village. Baskingridge is about forty miles from Trenton. The mansion house of Lord Sterling formerly stood about one mile from this place. It was one of the most splendid in the state, having a fine garden, and a park well stocked with deer. He owned some of the most elegant horses of the day.

The population of Branchburg township was in 1850, 1,143 in 1860, 1,174; and in 1870, 1,251. North Branch is a village of this township.

Bridgewater township contained a population in 1850 of 4,070; in 1860, 4,947; and in 1870, 5,884. Somerville, the county seat, is in this township, and contained in 1850, 1,300 inhabitants. This village is of modern date. Martinsville and Bound Brook are also villages in this township.

Franklin township contained a population in 1850 of 3,062 in 1860, 3,599; and in 1870, 3,912. Weston is a post village on the Millstone river. Middlebush and Griggstown are in this township.

Hillsborough township is on the Millstone river. Its population in 1850 was 3,409; in 1860, 3,488; and in 1870, 3,444. Blackwell's is on the Millstone river, six and a half miles from Somerville. Flagtown, Branchville (or North Branch), and Neshanic, are small villages.

Millstone is on the left bank of Millstone river, and near the Delaware and Raritan Canal, and contains about sixty dwellings. It was founded in 1720, and here the first court-house for Somerset county was built, which was burned by the British in 1779.

Montgomery township contained in 1850, 1,767 inhabitants; in 1860, 1,975; and in 1870, 2,066. Rocky Hill is a post village on the Millstone river, and the Delaware and Raritan

Canal. Plainsville, Harlingen, Blawenburgh, and Stoutsburgh, are in this township.

It was at Rocky Hill that Washington wrote his farewell address to the American army, November 2d, 1783. The dwelling is still standing, and was at that time the residence of Judge Berrian. Congress was at that time in session at Princeton, and the president addressed him in a complimentary manner, to which he replied in the presence of congress and then retired. He was provided with a house at Rocky Hill, where he conferred from time to time with the committees and members of congress, giving them his views on such subjects as were referred to him.

Warren township was formed in 1806, from Bedminster and Bernards. Its population in 1850 was 2,148; in 1860, 2,388; and in 1870, 2,705. In 1778–'9, a part of Washington's army encamped here, in a fertile valley known as Washington's valley.

Cape May was first made a county by proprietory law in 1692, and by another in 1694 its boundaries were better ascertained, and by the act of 1709–'10 they were again fixed. It is the most southerly county in the state, as well as the smallest in population. The Atlantic Ocean bounds it on the east and south, and Delaware bay on the west. This county derived its name from Cornelius Jacobson Mey, who came here in 1623, under the auspices of the Dutch West India Company, with a number of settlers. He explored the coast from Cape Cod to the Delaware, and gave his own name to its northern cape. Its population in 1810 was 3,632; in 1830, 4,936; in 1840, 5,324; in 1850, 6,433; in 1860, 7,130; and in 1870, 8,349.

Cape May city contained in 1870 a population of 1,248. Dennis township was formed in 1826. Dennisville (or Dennis Creek) is a flourishing post village, situated on both sides of the creek of the same name, and seven miles from Cape May Court-House, and called North and South Dennisville. Around this village is an extensive deposit of sound cedar timber in the soil. Ship building and trade in lumber are carried on to some extent.

Lower, the most southern township in the state, was incorporated in 1798. Cape Island is a favorite watering place in the southern part of the township. At the time it first came into notice as a watering place in 1812, there were but few houses there, but it has now increased to considerable importance. During the summer months it is one of the most fashionable places of resort in the United States. It contains five or six churches, one bank, and eleven large and commodious hotels, besides numerous smaller ones. In summer Cape Island has daily communication with Philadelphia, and is thronged by the wealthy and fashionable, principally from that city. It is also largely patronized by residents from New York and the east. While the permanent population is only about one thousand, in the summer season it is increased from ten to fifteen thousand persons. At this place is the finest bathing in the world. Besides the hotels, there are numerous cottages and other houses for summer boarders. In and around the island there are about one hundred houses. The Cape May light-house is about two miles west of the boarding-houses.

Cold Spring is a post village in this township, about ten miles from Cape May Court-House. The name is derived from a remarkable spring near it rising in the marsh, and is overflowed at every tide. Population about 400. This village contains about fifty houses within a radius of a mile. The water of the spring above mentioned flows up from the salt marsh, and is much frequented by visitors at the island. Cape Island received its name from the fact that it is separated from the mainland by a small creek, and the houses are located on both sides of the same, but principally on the north side. Fishing Creek, on the shore of Delaware bay, is six miles southwest of the county seat.

Cape May county is an island. On its east and south is the Atlantic Ocean, west is Delaware bay and West Creek, and north is Tuckahoe river, which runs across its northern extremity.

Middle township was incorporated in 1798, and contained in 1850, 1,884 inhabitants; in 1860, 2,155; and in 1870, 3,443. About one-half of this township is salt marsh or sea beach. It extends across the township from the Atlantic ocean to Delaware bay. Goshen is a post village about five miles northwest of the court house, and contains about twenty-five dwellings. The post village of Cape May Court-House is in the central part of the county, between Great Sound and Jenkins' Sound, and about eighty miles from Trenton, in a straight line. It contained in

1870, 1,348 inhabitants. Upper township was incorporated in 1798, and contained in 1850 1,341 inhabitants; in 1860, 1,552; and in 1870, 1,433.

The village of Tuckahoe is situated on Tuckahoe river. At Beesley's Point a ferry was established as early as 1692, which crossed over Great Egg Harbor river.

The county of Cape May has an area of two hundred and fifty square miles. On the Atlantic coast is a sand beach, which, for the width of from a half to two miles, is covered with grass, affording excellent pasture. It is broken by various inlets, by which the sea penetrates the marshes, forming lagoons, or salt water lakes. The marsh is about four miles wide, and a similar marsh extends across the northern part of the county. Near Dennisville is a deposit of cedar timber in the soil to an indefinite depth, which (although from the growth above it, it is believed to be over 2,000 years old) is still perfectly sound, and a large number of persons are employed in digging it out, and working it into shingles, posts, &c. The soil near the central part is clayey, with a sandy subsoil, and is naturally of a good quality. The county was organized under its present boundaries in 1710, having been previously named from Cornelius Jacobse Mey, a navigator in the service of the Dutch West India Company, who visited Delaware bay in 1623, as previously stated.

Burlington county was first laid out and settled in 1677, and its boundaries were limited by the act of 1709-'10. It was curtailed in 1838, at the formation of Mercer county. The population in 1850 was 43,203; in 1860, 49,730; and in 1870, 53,639.

The county derived its name from the town of Burlington, which was one of the earliest settled towns in West Jersey. The city of Burlington was laid out for a town in 1677, and at that time, and for many years subsequent, the courts were held here, and the legislature of the province met alternately here and at Amboy. The supreme courts were also held here and at Amboy. Burlington is next to the largest city in the county, having at the present time 5,817 inhabitants. It is a port of entry on the Delaware river, nearly opposite Bristol, in Pennsylvania, twenty miles above Philadelphia, and twelve miles southwest of Trenton. The Camden and Amboy division of the Pennsylvania Railroad connects it with New York and Philadelphia. The river here is about one mile wide, and is divided by an island containing three hundred acres, lying nearly opposite the city. The streets are wide, straight, and well shaded with trees, and lighted with gas. The houses are mostly built of brick, and the bank of the Delaware is adorned with many handsome residences and gardens. The city is copiously supplied with good water, raised by means of hydraulic machinery. Burlington College, for males, and St. Mary's Hall, for females, was founded by the Episcopalians in 1846, and had in 1852, one hundred and eighteen students, and a library of twelve hundred volumes. This city is much resorted to during the summer months by the citizens of Philadelphia, with which it communicates by steamboat several times a day. It was originally called New Beverly, then Bridlington, and afterwards by its present name.

The population of Bass River township in 1870 was 807. Beverly township contained a population in 1860 of 2,126, and in 1870, 2,438. Bordentown township and borough contained in 1860 a population of 4,027, and in 1870, 6,041. The Bordentown Female Seminary, under the direction of Rev. John H. Brakeley, is located at this borough. Francis Hopkinson, the celebrated poet of the war, and one of the signers of the Declaration of Independence, resided here. Joseph Bonaparte, Count de Surviliers, ex-king of Spain and Naples, came to this country in 1815, and settled here the following season, and built his palatial residence, now the property of the heirs of Henry Becket. Bonaparte lived here during his stay in this country. He returned to Europe and died there, leaving his possessions here to his nephew. The park and grounds comprise about fourteen hundred acres, which were converted by the count into a place of beauty and elegance. His first residence, which stood on the site of the present one, was destroyed by fire, together with some rare paintings executed by the first masters of the old world, which rendered them of immense value. He had also the busts of the Bonaparte family, carved from the finest Italian marble.

Chester township contained a population in 1850 of 3,061; in 1860, 2,227; and in 1870, 2,586. Moorestown, Chesterville, and Stiles Corners, are in this township.

Chesterfield township contained in 1850 a population of 1,789; in 1860, 1,628; and in 1870, 1,748. Crosswicks and Recklesstown are in this township.

Cinnaminson township contained in 1860 a population of 2,701, and in 1870, 3,112. Bridgeborough, Cinnaminson, Riverside, and Palmyra, are in this township.

Evesham township contained in 1850 a population of 3,067; in 1860, 3,145; and in 1870, 3,351. Evesboro', Marlton, and Milford, are in this township.

Lumberton township contained in 1860, 1,830 inhabitants, and in 1870, 1,718. Lumberton and Hainesport are the principal towns.

Little Egg Harbor township comprises the southeastern section of the county, and contained in 1870 a population of 1,779. Tucker's Beach fronts the township, in the Great and Little Egg Harbor bays. The town of Tuckerton was settled about the year 1699.

Mansfield township in 1850 contained 2,953 inhabitants; in 1860, 2,777; and in 1870, 2,880. Columbus (formerly called Black Horse) and Georgetown, are in this township.

Medford township in 1850 contained a population of 3,022; in 1860, 2,136; and in 1870, 2,189. The town of Medford, on Haynes creek, is in this township.

Mount Laurel township was formed from Evesham, March 7th, 1872. Masonville, Mount Laurel, Hartford, and Fellowship, are post towns; Centretown, Milltown, and Colemantown, are villages.

New Hanover township in 1850 contained a population of 2,245; in 1860, 2,529; and in 1870, 2,536. Jacobstown, Cookstown, Arneytown, Sykesville, Wrightstown, and Pointville, are in this township.

Northampton township in 1850 contained a population of 3,031; in 1860, 2,997; and in 1870, 4,018.

Mount Holly, the county town, is pleasantly situated in the west part of the township, on the Rancocas creek, nineteen miles from Trenton. It derived its name from the hill or mountain in the vicinity of the town, and from the holly trees growing upon its summit   It was first settled by Friends a short time after the settlement of Burlington. It was a place of considerable importance during the Revolutionary war. Stephen Girard at one time resided here.

Pemberton township in 1850 had a population of 2,866; in 1860, 2,672; and in 1870, 2,743. The thriving village of Pemberton is in this township, and contained a population in 1870 of 797; the celebrated Brown's Mills are also here. There are also the villages called Mary Ann, Ong's Hat, Comical Corner, Hanover, and Birmingham.

Randolph township contained in 1870 a population of 450, and was formed from Washington township. March 17th, 1870. Wading River and Lower Bank, are post towns.

Shamong township contains extensive cedar swamps. Population in 1860, 1,008, and in 1870, 1,149. Fruitland and Shamong are post towns.

Beverly township was formed from Willingborough in 1859; Lumberton from Medford, Northampton, and Southampton, in 1860; Bass River township was formed from Little Egg Harbor and Washington, in 1869; Florence from Mansfield, in 1872; and Mount Laurel from Evesham, the same year.

Southampton contained a population in 1850 of 3,545; in 1860, 2,558; and in 1870, 2,374.

Springfield township was settled between 1682 and 1685. Jobstown derived its name from Job Lippincott, who owned considerable land there about the year 1798. Juliustown, the principal village in the township, received its name from Julius Evans. The population of the township in 1850 was 1,827; in 1860, 1,810; and in 1870, 1,761.

Washington township was formed from Northampton, Evesham, and Little Egg Harbor. Pleasant Mills and Green Bank are post towns. Crowleytown, Washington, and Quaker Bridge, are also in this township. It contains an extensive cranberry swamp. There are also large quantities of bog iron ore. The population in 1850 was 2,009; in 1860, 1,008; and in 1870, 1,149.

Westhampton township contained a population in 1850 of

1,507; in 1860, 1,313; and in 1870, 1,369. Rancocas and Smithville are post towns.

Willingborough township contained a population in 1850 of 1,596; in 1860, 643; and in 1870, 750. A portion of Rancocas is in this township.

Woodland township was formed from Pemberton, Shamong, Southampton and Washington, in 1866, and although the largest in the county as to territory, it is the smallest in population, containing in 1870, 389 inhabitants. Shamong, Woodmansie, Mount Misery, and Speedwell, are villages of the township.

Hunterdon county was divided from Burlington by an act of assembly in 1713, and derived its name from Governor Robert Hunter. The boundaries were then fixed, but altered in 1738, and again changed upon the erection of Mercer county in 1838. This county is situated along the Delaware river, above tide navigation, and was, in 1765, the most populous and opulent county in the province. The land is generally good for tillage. This county is very mountainous, and contains diversified hills, table lands, and fertile valleys.

Alexandria township was incorporated in 1798. Mount Pleasant, Little York, Everittstown, Musconetcong, Holland, and Milford, are post towns. On its northern end, bordering on Warren county, is some very fine iron ore. Milford is a thriving village on the Delaware, in a highly fertile and well cultivated region. The township of Alexandria contained in 1850, 3,811 inhabitants; in 1860, 4,088; and in 1870, 3,341.

Bethlehem township was incorporated in 1798, and contains the towns of Bethlehem, Charlestown, Bloomsbury and Junction. The New Jersey Central Railroad runs through the entire length of the township. The population in 1850 was 2,746; in 1860, 1,859; and in 1870, 2,211.

Clinton township was formed from Lebanon in 1838. Its population in 1850 was 2,369; in 1860 including the village of Clinton 2,949; and in 1870, 3,134. This village was formerly called Hunt's Mills, from an early proprietor, in consequence of its valuable water power. It is beautifully diversified with hills, was incorporated as a borough in 1865, and contained in 1870, 785 inhabitants.

Delaware township was formed from a part of Amwell, in 1838. Its population in 1850 was 2,554; in 1860, 2,838; and in 1870, 2,959. Sergeantsville, Head Quarters, Sandbrook, Rosemont, Stockton, Raven Rock and Prallsville are post towns and villages of this township.

East Amwell was formed from Amwell in 1856; in 1860 it contained a population of 1,865; and in 1870, 1,802. The Sourland Mountains are partly in this township and partly in Hillsborough township, Somerset county.

Franklin township contained in 1850 a population of 1,452; in 1860, 1,552; and in 1870, 1,342. Sidney, Pittstown, Quakertown, Oak Grove and Cherryville are post towns.

High Bridge township was formed March 29, 1871, from part of the townships of Clinton and Lebanon. High Bridge is a post village, Readingsburg and Cokesburg are in this township. The south branch of the Raritan river runs through the centre of the township from north to south, and the New Jersey Central Railroad runs across its entire western part.

Kingwood township was formed in 1798. In 1850 the population was 1,799; in 1860, 2,148; and in 1870, exclusive of the borough of Frenchtown, it was 1,942. The borough of Frenchtown was incorporated in 1867, and in 1870 contained a population of 912.

Lebanon township was formed in 1798, and contained in 1850, a population of 2,128; in 1860, 2,495; and in 1870, 3,561 Anthony, Changewater, White Hall, New Hampton and Glen Gardner are post towns.

Raritan township was formed from Amwell in 1838. Its population in 1850 was 3,070; in 1860, 2,270; and in 1870, 3,654; Flemington the county seat is in this township. Its population in 1870 was 1,412. In the vicinity of Flemington are valuable copper mines. Croton and Copper Hill are post villages.

Readington township was formed in 1798. Its population in 1850 was 2,836; in 1860, 3,074; and in 1870, 3,070. The New Jersey Central Railroad runs through the township, near its centre. Whitehouse, Potterstown, White House Station, Readington, Pleasant Run, Stanton, Rowland Mills and Centreville are post villages.

Tewksbury township was formed in 1798. Its population in 1850 was 2,301; in 1860, 2,333; and in 1870, 2,327. New Germantown, Fairmount, Farmersville and Mountainville are in this township.

Union township was formed from Bethlehem in 1853, and contained in 1860, 1,217 inhabitants; and in 1870, 1,051. Perryville and Pattenburg are post towns.

West Amwell township was formed from Amwell in 1856, and contained in 1860, 1,089 inhabitants, and in 1870, 4,872. The town of Lambertville contained in 1850, 1,417 inhabitants; in 1860, 2,699; and in 1870, 3,842. It was incorporated as a town April 13, 1868.

Morris county was incorporated 1738, and its boundaries were then established by law, but were altered by the formation of Sussex in 1753. It was named from Governor Lewis Morris. Morristown is the county seat. Boonton township was formed from Hanover and Pequannock townships in 1867, and in 1870 contained a population of 3,458. Chatham township in 1850, contained a population of 2,469; in 1860, 2,968; and in 1870, 3,715. The Morris and Essex Railroad runs through this township. Chester was formed in 1799, and in 1850 contained a population of 1,334 inhabitants; in 1860, 1,558; and in 1870, 1,743. Hanover was formed in 1700, and in 1850 contained a population of 3,614; in 1860, 3,476; and in 1870, 3,623. Jefferson contained in 1850 a population of 1,358; in 1860, 1,471; and in 1870, 1,430.

Mendham contained a population in 1850 of 1,723; in 1860, 1,660; and in 1870, 1,573. Montville was formed from Pequannock in 1867, and in 1870 contained a population of 1,403. Morris contained a population in 1850 of 4,992; in 1860, including Morristown, 5,985; and in 1870, 5,674. Passaic contained a population in 1870 of 1,624. It was formed from Morris in 1866.

Pequannock, named from the tribe of indians found there, contained in 1850, 4,126 inhabitants; in 1860, 5,438; and in 1870, 1,534. Randolph contained in 1850 2,632 inhabitants; in 1860, 3,173; and in 1870, 5,111. Dover, a thriving post village near the centre of the county, is situated on the Rockaway river and on the Morris canal, about seven miles from Morristown. The inhabitants are extensively engaged in iron manufactures. There are several forges, foundries, rolling mills, spike factories and steel furnaces. The Morris and Essex Railroad passes through the place.

Rockaway contained in 1850, 3,139 inhabitants; in 1860, 3,551; and in 1870, 6,445. In this township is the famous copperas mountain.

Roxbury contained in 1850 2,269 inhabitants; in 1860, 2,865; and in 1870, 3,320. In this township, as well as the adjoining one, Washington, are the celebrated Schooley's Mountains, a great summer resort for invalids.

Washington adjoins Roxbury on the south. Its population in 1850 was 2,502; in 1860, 2,504; and in 1870, 2,484.

Cumberland county was named by Governor Jonathan Belcher, out of respect for the Duke of Cumberland. It was divided from Salem by an act of the assembly in 1747, at which time the boundaries were fixed. Bridgeton, the county town, contains three wards, and is located in Bridgeton township. Its population in 1850 was 2,446; in 1860, 3,595; and in 1870, 6,830. Previous to 1747, it formed a portion of Salem county.

At its formation, it was divided into six townships, since which time Bridgeton, Downe, Landis, and Millville, have been added, making in all ten townships. The population of the county was in 1850, 17,189; in 1860, 22,605; and in 1870, 34,665. This county formed a portion of Fenwick's tenth. In 1868, Cohansey was merged in Bridgeton.

Deerfield is in the northwestern part of the county, seven miles from Bridgeton. The West Jersey Railroad runs through the centre of this township, from north to south. The population in 1850 was 927; in 1860, 1,288; and in 1870, 1,518. Downe is in the southern part of the county, on Maurice river cove, and contained in 1850, 2,341 inhabitants; in 1860, 3,114; and in 1870, 3,385. Mauricetown (on Maurice river), Dividing Creek, and Newport, are the principal towns.

Fairfield was settled principally by emigrants, from the town in Connecticut of the same name. Its population in 1850 was

2,133; in 1860, 2,448; and in 1870, 3,011. Cedarville, Gouldtown, and Fairton, are post towns in this township.

Greenwich is on the Delaware. Its population in 1850 was 1,158; in 1860, 1,265; and in 1870, 1,262. Springtown, Greenwich, and Buena Vista, are in this township.

Hopewell contained a population in 1850 of 1,480; in 1860, 1,757; and in 1870, 1,857. Rosetown and Shiloh, are in this township, though part of the latter is in Stoe Creek township.

Landis was created a township in 1864, from the township of Millville. Its population in 1870 was 7,079. The thriving town of Vineland is in this township. It is a place of considerable note, having increased greater in population than any other city in the state.

Maurice river township contained in 1850, a population of 2,245; in 1860, 2,430; and in 1870, 2,500. Manumuskin, Port Elizabeth, Belle Plain, and Leesburg, are post towns.

Millville* is divided into three wards. Its population in 1850 was 2,332; in 1860, 3,932; and in 1870, 6,101. There are several large glass manufactories here.

Stoe Creek contained a population in 1850 of 1,093; in 1860, 1,267; and in 1870, 1,122. It forms considerable of the boundary between Salem and Cumberland counties.

Sussex county was named by Governor Jonathan Belcher, after the seat of the Duke of New Castle, in Sussex, England. It was divided from Morris by act of assembly in 1753, and is bounded on the west and northwest by the Delaware, and partly on the south by the Musconetcong, and is drained by Flatkill, Paulinskill, and Pequest rivers. It contains an area of about six hundred square miles. Hopatcong lake is on the southeast border. The surface is undulating and hilly. Its principal mountains are the Alamuche, Blue, Hamburgh, Pochuck, Wallkill, and Wawayanda. It contains Franklinite (a compound of iron, zinc, and manganese), red oxide of zinc, and magnetic iron ore are abundant, and extensively worked. Besides these, the county furnishes a great variety of remarkable and interesting minerals to the mineralogist. Limestone is also found in the northwest part. This

---

* So named from its factories or mills.

county joins New York on the northeast, and Pennsylvania on the west, and is the most northern county in the state. Its population in 1850 was 22,989; in 1860, 23,846; and in 1870, 23,168.

Andover contains a population of 1,126. Byram is in the extreme southern part of the county, on Hopatcong lake, and contained in 1850, 1,340 inhabitants; in 1860, 1,202; and in 1870, 1,332. Frankford is near the centre, and contained in 1850, 1,941 inhabitants; in 1860, 1828; and in 1870, 1,776. Greene contained in 1850, 823 inhabitants; in 1860, 1,023; and in 1870, 868. Hardyston contained in 1850, 1,344 inhabitants; in 1860, 1,712; and in 1870, 1,668.

Hampton contains a population of 1,023. Lafayette, is the most central township in the county, and contained in 1850, 928 inhabitants; in 1860, 919; and in 1870, 884. Montague is the most northern township, bordering on New York and Pennsylvania. It contained in 1850, 1,010 inhabitants; in 1860, 983; and in 1870, 932. Newton contains the town of Newton, the seat of justice of the county. It contained in 1850, 3,279 inhabitants; in 1860, including the village, 4,098; and in 1870, 2,403. Sandyston, is the most western township, and borders on Pennsylvania. Its population in 1850, was 1,327; in 1860, 1,480; and in 1870, 1,230. Sparta contained in 1850, a population of 1,919; in 1860, 2,062; and in 1870, 2,032. The Wallkill mountains passes through its centre, from north to south. Stillwater, contained a population in 1850, of 1,742; in 1860, 1,816; and in 1870, 1,632. In 1853 part of Newton township was added to Greene. In 1864, Newton to Andover, Hampton, and town of Newton.

Vernon is the extreme north-eastern township. It is extremely mountainous, the Pochuck, Hamburgh, and Wawayanda mountains passing through its entire length from north to south. Its population in 1850 was 2,619; in 1860, 2,190; and in 1870, 1,979.

Wallpack is on the western part of the county, and forms the boundary between New Jersey and Pennsylvania. Population in 1850, 783; in 1860, 851; and in 1870, 647. This is the smallest township in the county. Wantage is on the north of the county between Montague and Vernon. Population in 1850, 3,934; in 1860, 3,862; and in 1870, 3,636.

On the 20th of November, 1824, Warren county was formed from Sussex. It comprised all the lower part of the county of Sussex, southwesterly of a line beginning on the Delaware River, at the mouth of Flat Brook, in the township of Wallpack, and running from thence a straight course to the northeast corner of Hardwick Church, and from thence in the same course to the middle of the Musconetcong creek. Population in 1830, 18,627; in 1840, 20,366; in 1850, 22,358; in 1860, 28,433; and in 1870, 34,336.

Belvidere the county town, contained in 1850, 1,001 inhabitants; in 1860, 1,530; and in 1870, 1,882.

Blairstown township contained in 1850, 1,405 inhabitants; in 1860, 1,542; and in 1870, 1,379.

Allamuchy township was formed from Independence in 1873. Franklin township was formed from Mansfield and Greenwich, and contained in 1850, 1,565 inhabitants; in 1860, 1,902; and in 1870, 1,655. The Pohatkong mountains are in this township, and the Morris canal passes through it. Frelinghuysen contained in 1850, 1,277 inhabitants; in 1860, 1,297; and in 1870, 1,113. Greenwich contained in 1850, 3,726 inhabitants; in 1860, 2,541; and in 1870, 2,587. Hackettstown contained in 1860, 1,351 inhabitants, and in 1870 2,202. Hardwick, contained in 1850, 727 inhabitants; in 1860, 792; and in 1870, 638. Harmony contained in 1850, 1,565 inhabitants; in 1860, 1,382; and in 1870, 1,405. Hope contained in 1850, 1,755 inhabitants; in 1860, 1,789; and in 1870, 1,542. The Jenny Jump Mountains extend across this township. Independence contained in 1850, 2,621 inhabitants; in 1860, 1,871; and in 1870, 1,766. The Allamuche and Jenny Jump Mountains are in this township. Knowlton, contained in 1850, 1,356 inhabitants; in 1860, 1,557; and in 1870, 1,691. Lopatcong contains 1,150 inhabitants. Mansfield, contained in 1850, 1,615 inhabitants; in 1860, 1,688; and in 1870, 1,997.

Oxford contained in 1850, 1,718 inhabitants; in 1860, 2,350; and in 1870, 2,952. The Scott mountain, and the celebrated Oxford Furnace, are in this township. Pahaquarry, is the extreme northwestern boundary, bordering on the Delaware river, and the state of Pennsylvania. Population in 1850, 460; in 1860, 465; and in 1870, 445. This is the smallest township in the county. Phillipsburg is on the Delaware, directly opposite Easton, in Pennsylvania. The city of the same name is divided into three wards. The population in 1860 was 3,741, and in 1870, 5,932.

The population of Washington township in 1850 was 1,567; in 1860, 2,634; and in 1870, 2,160.

Atlantic county was erected from the eastern part of the county of Gloucester, February 7th, 1837. The population in 1850 was 8,961; in 1860, 11,786; and in 1870, 14,093. Atlantic city is situated on Absecon Beach, and contains 1,043 inhabitants. Buena Vista is in Buena Vista township, and contains 948 inhabitants. Egg Harbor City is between Galloway and Mullica townships, and contained in 1860, 789 inhabitants, and in 1870 1,311. It is a thriving German settlement, in which grapes and strawberries are extensively cultivated.

Galloway contained in 1860, 2,735 inhabitants, and in 1870, 2,860. Egg Harbor is situated on the Great Egg Harbor river, and contained in 1850 2,689 inhabitants, and in 1870 3,585. Hamilton township in 1860 contained a population of 1,945, and in 1870, 1,271. Mays Landing, the capital of the county, is in this township, at the head of navigation on Great Egg Harbor river, about sixty-five miles south of Trenton. It consists of two parts, Mays Landing proper, and Hamilton, about a quarter of a mile up the river, where a dam has been constructed, affording fine water power. Hammonton contains a population of 1,404. Mullica contained in 1850 a population of 2,933; in 1860, 1,600; and in 1870, 2,265. Weymouth is the most southern township, on the Great Egg Harbor river. The population in 1850 was 1,032; in 1860, 823; and in 1870, 810. This is now the smallest township in the county, having been curtailed in forming other townships.

Buena Vista township was formed from Hamilton in 1867; population 948, and contains the towns of Germantown, Landisville, and Buena Vista; the latter contains 948 inhabitants.

Passaic county was formed from Essex and Bergen counties,

February 7th, 1837. Its population in 1850 was 22,569; in 1860, 29,013; and in 1870, 46,416.

Acquackanonck in 1850 contained a population of 2,931; in 1860, 3,235; and in 1870, 4,368. The Morris canal runs through this township. Little Falls contains a population of 1,282.

Manchester contained a population in 1850 of 2,788; in 1860, (when the city of Paterson was not included) 842; and in 1870, 1,166. Paterson city is the capitol of the county. It is situated on the right bank of the Passaic river, immediately below the falls. In the extent of its manufactures, it ranks as the second city in the state, and is the third in population. By means of the Morris canal, it communicates with the Atlantic ports and with the Delaware river. By means of the Erie railway, it communicates with the entire west. Paterson is handsomely laid out, and the scenery in the vicinity of the falls is highly picturesque. There are a large number of cotton mills here, as also silk mills, which are situated near the falls, and are the most extensive in the United States. They employ about seven hundred hands, and manufacture weekly sixteen hundred pounds of silk. There are also two locomotive manufactories, and several mills for the manufacture of carriages, guns, machinery, paper, and other articles. Paterson was founded in 1791, by an incorporated company, with a capital of one million dollars, the object of which was to manufacture cotton cloth. The movement was, however, found to be premature, and was abandoned in 1796. The population in 1840 was 7,596; in 1850, 11,334; in 1860, 19,588; and in 1870, 33,579. The city has nine wards.

Pompton contained a population in 1850 of 1,720; in 1860, 1,591; and in 1870, 1,840. Wayne contained a population in 1850 of 1,162; in 1860, 1,355; and in 1870, 1,521. West Milford is the most northerly and westerly township of the county, and contained in 1850, a population of 2,624; in 1860, 2,402; and in 1870, 2,660. The Bear Foot Mountains extends through the western part of the township. Little Falls township was formed from Acquackanonck in 1868, population 1,282.

Mercer county was erected February 22, 1838, from Hunterdon, Burlington, Somerset, and Middlesex. It was named in honor of Gen. Hugh Mercer, who fell at the battle of Princeton, January 3, 1777. The population in 1850, was 27,992; in 1860, 37,419; and in 1870, 46,386. East Windsor contained a population in 1850, of 2,596; in 1860, 1,913; and in 1870, 2,383. The Borough of Hightstown is in this township, and has a population of 1,347. The Baptists have here a handsome flourishing educational institute.

Ewing township contained in 1850, 1,480 inhabitants; in 1860, 2,979; and in 1870, 2,477. The State Lunatic Asylum is located in this township. Hamilton township, contained in 1850, 2,807 inhabitants; in 1860, 3,773; and in 1870, 5,417. The Soldier's Children's Home is located in this township. It also contains the thriving borough of Chambersburg. Hopewell contained in 1850, 3,698 inhabitants; in 1860, 3,900; and in 1870, 4,276. At Pennington, in this township, are two Seminaries of learning, one under the auspices of the New Jersey Conference of the Methodist Church, and the other conducted and owned by Prof. A. P. Lasher, both of which are excellent educational institutions. Lawrence, in 1850, contained a population of 1,838; in 1860, 2,024; and in 1870, 2,251. At the village of Lawrenceville, in this township, are two superior Seminaries of learning, one for males, conducted by the Rev. Samuel M. Hamel, D. D., and the other for females, by the Rev. Charles Nassau, D. D. Millham contained in 1870, 677 inhabitants. Princeton township contained a population in 1850, of 3,021; in 1860, 3,726; and in 1870, 3,986. The Borough of Princeton contained in 1870, 2,798 inhabitants. At this place is the College of New Jersey, called Nassau Hall, which was incorporated in 1746, and erected in 1757, also a Theological Seminary, for the education of young men for the ministry. In 1856, Nottingham township was merged in Trenton and Hamilton, and in 1859, Washington township was formed from East Windsor.

Trenton the capitol of the State, as well as the seat of justice of the county of Mercer, is beautifully located on the east bank of the Delaware, at the head of tide navigation.

Here is located the State Capitol, built in 1793, enlarged in 1845 and 1865, and again in 1871. The State Prison, State

Arsenal, State Normal and Model schools are also located here. The city has 7 wards. Its population in 1850, was 6,461; in 1860, 17,228; and in 1870, 22,874. Washington contained in 1860, a population of 1,279; and in 1870, 1,294. West Windsor, contained a population in 1850, of 1,596; in 1860, 1,497; and in 1870, 1,428.

Hudson county was erected from the southeasterly part of Bergen county, February 22, 1840. This is the smallest county in area in the state, containing only 75 square miles, though the second in population, and is therefore more compact than any other in the state. Its population in 1850 was, 21,822; in 1860, 62,717; and in 1870, 129,067; having more than doubled in ten years. Bayonne City, contains a population of 3,834. Greenville contains a population of 2,789. Harrison in 1850, contained a population of 1,345; in 1860, 2,556; and in 1870, 2,789. Hoboken contained a population of 2,668 in 1850; in 1860, 9,659; and in 1870, 20,297. In the city of Hoboken are the celebrated Elysian Fields, a place of great resort for the denizens of New York City and other places, being opposite to that city, and about two miles north of Jersey City. It has extensive establishments for the construction of steamers. Several steam ferries connect it with New York city. The scenery in the vicinity of the Elysian Fields is delightful, and it is one of the most pleasant spots that can be conceived for the denizens of a crowded city.

It is divided into four wards, and has more than doubled in population in ten years. This place was the residence of Edwin A. Stevens, Esq., a wealthy citizen, who projected and built the celebrated steam vessel known as Stevens' Battery. This battery cost Mr. Stevens about two million dollars, and was not completed at the time he was removed by death, he however, made ample provision for his executors to complete the same, and present it to the state. The executors in connection with governor Randolph, appointed Major General George B. McClellan, and Captain Newton of New York, two of the most celebrated engineers of the country to complete it, in accordance with the will of Mr. Stevens, by which the highest intelligence and skill was procured to accomplish the object. On the 22d of March

1869, Governor Theodore Randolph, set the above facts forth, in a special message to the legislature, and used the following appropriate language: "A donation of such a magnificent character from a private citizen whose name and reputation have been connected with almost every important public enterprise in the state, and whose skill, industry and ingenuity have given an especial usefulness to unusual wealth, should receive from the legislature a recognition fitted to the reputation of the donor and the munificence of the gift.

"Agreeing with the executors as to the propriety of naming some persons who shall be authorized to confer, as to the probable disposition of the ship, and as to the details of her completion, I will be glad to put myself in communication with the executors as to the persons most acceptable to them and beneficial to the state, not exceeding three in number, as I would recommend.

"I would suggest that the persons thus appointed by the state be authorized to fully confer and advise with the executors as to the mode of completing the Battery, and with the concurrence of this department enter upon such negotiations as to its ultimate disposition as they may deem proper and the legislature hereafter sanction."

On the 1st of April, 1869, in accordance with the above message the legislature passed a joint resolution accepting the vessel when the same should be finished pursuant to the will, and authorizing the governor to appoint three suitable persons as commissioners to hold their offices until said battery shall be finished. These commissioners together with the governor, were empowered by majority vote, to determine to what use the said vessel should be devoted, to inform the executors of such determination, to advise with them as to the details of the completion of the same, and to negotiate for the disposition of said vessel when finished and delivered to the state. The governor and commissioners were annually, or oftener if required, to report to the legislature their proceedings under the resolution. and no contract or agreement for the sale or final disposition of the same was to be valid, until reported to, and ratified by the legislature. The executors of Mr. Stevens were, W. W. Shippen, S. B. Donald, and M. B. Stevens.

March 21st, 1871, the legislature passed a joint resolution authorizing the commissioners to sell for the largest sum that could be obtained, the interest of the state in said Stevens' Battery, with the consent of the governor and chief justice of the state.

Jersey City is divided into sixteen wards, and contained in 1850, a population of 6,856; in 1860, 29,226; and in 1870, 82,546. The population of this city has increased with wonderful rapidity, having more than trebled within the last decade.

On the 2d of April, 1869, the legislature passed an act consolidating the cities of Jersey City, Hudson City, Hoboken, Bergen, the town of Union, and the townships of North Bergen, Union, West Hoboken, Greenville, Bayonne, and Weehawken and part of the township of Kearney, into one city, to be called the City of Jersey City, subject however to a ratification by the people at an election to be held in each place, on the first Tuesday of October of that year. At the election held pursuant to that act, Jersey City, Hudson City, and Bergen, voted in favor, and by the act approved March 17th, 1870, the consolidation was perfected. At the election held in 1872, the township of Greenville voted to come in, and in 1873, an act was passed to that effect. North Bergen in 1850 contained a population of 3,578; in 1860, 6,335; and in 1870, 3,032. The town of Union contains a population of 4,640. Union township contains a population of 6,737. Weehawken contained a population in 1860, of 280; and in 1870, 597. West Hoboken contains a population of 4,132. Weehawken township was formed from Hoboken and North Bergen, in 1859; Bayonne from North Bergen, and West Hoboken, from North Bergen, in 1861; Greenville from Bergen in 1863; Kearney from Harrison, and Union from North Bergen, in 1867.

Camden county was erected from Gloucester, March 13th, 1844, and contained in 1850, 25,422 inhabitants; in 1860, 34,457; and in 1870, 46,193. The city of Camden contained in 1850, 9,479 inhabitants; in 1860, 14,358; and in 1870, 20,045. This city is divided into eight wards.

Center township contained in 1860 1,305 inhabitants, and in 1870, 1,718. Delaware in 1850, contained 2,577 inhabitants; in 1860, 1,602; and in 1870, 1,625. Gloucester city contained a population in 1850, of 2,188; in 1860, 2,320; and in 1870, 3,682.

Gloucester township had a population in 1850, of 2,371; in 1860, 2,320; and in 1870, 2,710. Haddon contained a population in 1870 of 1,926. Haddonfield contained a population in 1870 of 1,075.

Monroe contained in 1860 a population of 1,417, and in 1870 1,663. Washington contained in 1850, a population of 2,114; in 1860, 1,307; and in 1870, 1,567. These two townships were set off from Camden county and annexed to Gloucester, February 28th, 1871.

Newton contained a population in 1850, of 14,087; in 1860, 18,413; these included Camden city, but in 1870, the township, exclusive of the city, contained a population of 8,437.

Stockton contained in 1860 a population of 1,473, and in 1870 2,381. Merchantville contained in 1870, 245 inhabitants.

Waterford contained in 1850, 1,638 inhabitants; in 1860, 1,955; and in 1870, 2,071.

Winslow contained in 1850, 1,540 inhabitants; in 1860, 1,800; and in 1870, 2,050.

Stockton was set off from Delaware in 1859, the same year Monroe was set off from Washington, and parts of Gloucester and Winslow were annexed to Waterford. Center was formed from Union in 1855; Haddon from Newton in 1865. In 1866, Union was merged into Center, and in 1871, part of Newton was annexed to Haddon.

The surface of Camden county is mostly level. The soil in the east part is sandy, and in the west it is a fertile loam, producing great quantities of fruit and vegetables for the Philadelphia markets. Marl is abundant in most parts of the county. The inhabitants in the eastern part are principally engaged in the manufacture of iron and glass.

Camden city, the seat of justice of the county, is situated on the left bank of the Delaware river, immediately opposite Philadelphia, with which it is connected by means of steam ferries. It is the western termination of the Amboy division of the Pennsylvania; also the Camden and Atlantic, and West Jersey Railroads. The city is regularly laid out, with streets intersecting each other at right angles, and contains many handsome dwellings.

Ocean county was erected February 15, 1850, from the southern townships of Monmouth county, including Plumstead, Jackson, Dover, Union, Stafford, and about one third of Howell township; population in 1850, 10,032; in 1860, 11,176; and in 1870, 13,628. Brick township contained in 1850, 1,558 inhabitants; in 1860, 1,385; and in 1870, 2,724. Dover contained in 1850, 2,385 inhabitants; in 1860, 2,378; and in 1870, 3,044. Toms River,* the seat of justice of the county is located on the river of the same name, at the head of navigation, about forty miles from Trenton. Jackson is in the northern part of the county, and contained in 1850, 1,333 inhabitants; in 1860, 1,606; and in 1870, 1,755. Manchester contained in 1870, 1,103 inhabitants. Plumstead contained in 1850, 1,613 inhabitants; in 1860, 2,003; and in 1870, 1,566. Stafford contained in 1850, 1,384; in 1860, 1,436; and in 1870, 1,514 inhabitants. Union contained 1850, 1,759 inhabitants; in 1860, 1,918; and in 1870, 1,923. Mannahawkinsville contained in 1870, 689 inhabitants. Manchester was formed from Dover in 1865; and Eatontown township from Ocean and Shrewsbury in 1873.

Union county was formed from the southern part of Essex county, March 19, 1857, and comprised the townships of New Providence, Springfield, Union, Elizabeth, Westfield, Plainfield, Rahway and Rahway City, and on the 16th of February, 1860, the lines were altered by the annexation of a part of the township of Woodbridge, in Middlesex county. Its population in 1860 was 27,780; and in 1870, 41,859. Clark township contained in 1870, 331 inhabitants. It was formed from the city of Rahway in 1864. Cranford township was formed from Westfield, Springfield, Linden and Clark, in 1871. The village of Cranford, formerly Craneville, from one of its early settlers by the name of Crane, is a beautiful and thriving place, with a number

---

* Toms River derived its name from William Tomm, a man of considerable importance at that day, and who owned a large amount of property on the river now bearing his name. In the early days of the province, courts were not established in each county as we have them now, but men were transported even into another state to be tried. William Tomm was clerk of the court of Uppland, now Chester, in Pennsylvania, and was one of the Swedish emigrants who came over at an early day.

of handsome residences, principally occupied by persons engaged in business in New York.

Elizabeth is one of the most thriving cities in the state. Large sums of money have been expended in paving and improving their streets, and it contains many handsome residences. It is one of the oldest cities in the state, the older portion being poorly laid out, the streets irregular, which was the case with all the older cities in the state. It was named from Lady Elizabeth Carteret, wife of Sir George Carteret. It was at one time the capitol and principal town of the state, and has long been celebrated for its excellent schools, and for its intelligent and polite society. It was settled in 1665, and received its act of incorporation as the borough of Elizabeth, February 8th, 1739, in the thirteenth year of the reign of George II. It was the third settlement made in the state, and the first by the English. The lands were purchased from the Indians residing on Staten Island in 1664, by John Bailey, Daniel Denton, and Luke Watson, of Jamaica, Long Island.

For many years after the settlement of the province, Elizabeth was the largest and most flourishing place in it. All the public offices were here, as well as the residences of most of the officers of the government. The first general assembly met here in 1668, and with few exceptions, they continued their meetings here until 1682. The first inhabitants of the town were composed of emigrants from England, Scotland, New England, and Long Island. The first Presbyterian church is the oldest in the state, having been organized in 1666. The college of New Jersey, the most flourishing in the Union, was commenced in this town, and afterwards removed to Princeton, its present location. Elizabeth is comprised in eight wards. Its population in 1860, was 11,567, and in 1870, 20,832, nearly doubling itself in ten years.

Linden had a population in 1870 of 1,396. New Providence in 1860 had a population of 1,308, and in 1870, 934. Plainfield in 1860, had a population of 3,194, and in 1870, 5,095. Rahway is divided into four wards. In 1860 the population was 7,130, and in 1870, 6,258. This diminution is caused by the formation of Clark and Linden townships. Springfield had a population in 1860 of 1,020, and in 1870, 770.

Summit was formed from New Providence and Springfield townships in 1869, and in 1870 had a population of 1,176. Union had a population in 1860 of 1,812, and in 1870, 2,314. Westfield had a population in 1860 of 1,719, and in 1870, 2,753.

The State of New Jersey contains twenty-one counties, and two hundred and fifty-nine townships, in which are included forty-five cities, towns and boroughs, numbering from five hundred to over a hundred thousand inhabitants. It was one of the original thirteen states, and is separated from New York by the Hudson river, and from Pennsylvania by the Delaware.

It lies between about 38° 44' and 41° 21' north latitude, and between 74 and 75° 20' west longitude, being about 168 miles in extreme length from north to south, and from 37 to 70 miles in breadth, including an area of 7,576 square miles, or 4,849,690 acres of land, of which 1,976,474 are improved; 718,335 are woodland; and the balance is other unimproved land.

The southern and middle portions are mostly flat and sandy, but in the north it becomes hilly, and even rises into low mountains. Some ridges of the Alleghany range cross from Pennsylvania, in a northeast direction, into New York, bearing in New Jersey the local names of Schooley's Mountain, Trowbridge, Ramapo, and Second Mountains. The Blue Mountains cross the extreme northwest portion of the state. Below Raritan bay is a group of hills of from three hundred to four hundred feet high, called Nevisink Hills, washed by an inlet from Raritan Bay, commanding a wide sweep of ocean, and furnishing a beacon to mariners, to whom they are generally the first and last seen of the shore of New Jersey, on their voyages in and out of the port of New York. A range of trap rock, varying from two hundred to five hundred feet high, and known as the Palisades, coasts the Hudson for twenty miles on the northeast of the state. The shores of the Atlantic south of Sandy Hook are lined with a series of inlets and islands, which are constantly changing. The country for some distance back is generally marshy or sandy.

Washed by the Delaware river and bay on the west and south, and by the Hudson river and the Atlantic ocean on the east, New Jersey forms a sort of a peninsula, so to speak. Were it not that its trade is monopolized by New York and Philadelphia, New Jersey has great advantages in position for a commercial state. The Delaware is navigable one hundred and twenty miles from the sea for ocean craft of a smaller kind, and for ships for ninety-six miles; while on the Atlantic side, for more than half its extent, there are numerous inlets and lagoons admitting smaller vessels; and on the northeast, Raritan and Newark bays, and Hudson river, are accessible to vessels of heavy tonnage; so that there is nothing but the circumstances above mentioned to prevent our state becoming a great entrepot of foreign and coasting trade. Besides the rivers mentioned as laving the shores of the state, are a number of smaller streams traversing the interior; the most important of which are the Passaic and Hackensack, emptying into Newark bay, in the northeast; Raritan river, draining the northern and central portions, and pouring its waters into the bay of the same name; Maurice river, in the southwest discharging itself into Delaware bay, and Great Egg Harbor river, emptying directly into the Atlantic ocean. These are severally navigable for coasters, in the order named, ten, fifteen, seventeen, and the last two twenty miles each. Raritan bay and Arthurkill sound cut off Staten Island from New Jersey. This island politically belongs to New York, but by position, to New Jersey. There are a number of low sandy islands along the Atlantic, cut off from the mainland by lagoons. These are generally unfertile and of little value.

The Atlantic shores of New Jersey are renowned the world over for their sea bathing resorts. The most important of these is Cape May, at its southern extremity, which is probably more frequented than any bathing place in America. Its beach slopes gradually, and being covered with a fine, hard, white sand, forms a delightful promenade and drive when the tide is out. Here are about twenty hotels, capable of receiving from two hundred to two thousand guests each; besides smaller hotels and boarding-houses without number. Long Branch, a few miles below Sandy Hook, ranks next in number of its visitors; but Deal, Squan Beach, and Tuckerton are also much frequented. Brown's Mills, twenty miles east of Burlington, situated among the pines, is considered particularly beneficial to consumptive patients.

New Jersey shares with Pennsylvania another still more interesting object in the passage of the Delaware through the Blue Mountains—generally called the Delaware Water Gap, where the river breaks through the mountains, in a gorge about two miles in length, walled in by precipices from twelve hundred to sixteen hundred feet in height, scarcely leaving space for a road between their base and the water.

In Warren county, fifteen miles north of Belvidere, there is a small mountain lake, perhaps two miles in circumference, at an elevation it is said, of near fourteen hundred feet above the level of the Delaware river. It is known to be very deep and plentifully abounds with fish of various kinds. The lake seems to lie almost on the summit of the mountain, and from its immediate vicinity is obtained a magnificent view of the river below, and of the surrounding country for a distance of many miles.

Weehawken heights, near Hoboken, (the commencement of the celebrated Palisades,) are the termination of such a promenade as is seldom offered in the vicinity of any great capitol. They command a near view of New York City and Harlem, and a more remote one of Staten Island and the Narrows, through which may be caught a faint glimpse of the ocean.

It may be noticed that the population in many townships seems to be depreciating, which is not the case, as the difference in population is caused by the frequent changing of township lines.

CHAPTER XIII.

1702—1743.

The proprietors cedes to the crown their rights of jurisdiction—Lands purchased from the Indians—Population—Habits of the people—Release of Lord Berkeley and Sir George Carteret—Consideration money—Courts—Taxes—Naturalization—First Legislature—Punishment of Witches—Trading with the Indians Prohibited—Drunkenness—Schools.

THE proprietaries of New Jersey, wearied out with struggling with the settlers, in the year 1702, ceded to the crown their rights of jurisdiction, upon which Queen Anne joined New Jersey to New York, under the government of Lord Cornbury. The inhabitants of this state, as well as New York, resisted the encroachments of the fraudulent acts of the governor, and in the year 1738, New Jersey petitioned for and obtained a governor of their own, in the person of Lewis Morris. The position of New Jersey gave it superior advantages from depradations by the Indians, as its policy always was to do no act that would have a tendency to exasperate that warlike people; besides, they were always paid for their lands, and could not bring that up as an excuse for any inroads or assaults upon the people of that province. Consequently, the progress of our state was steadily forward, although serious disputes arose in regard to paper money, conveyances of lands to certain claimants by the Indians, the resistance made by squatters to dispossess them of their lands, and other annoying and hostile acts, yet knowing they were in the right, pursued a straight forward course, and were in the end successful.

After the death of Morris, in 1745, Belcher took charge of the difficult post as governor in 1747, but he was not able to manage affairs much better than those who had preceded him. He adopted a conciliatory course in all matters relating to his administration, and favored the founding of the college now located at Princeton.

The state at this time had a population of about 40,000. In 1738, the population had increased to 47,367, of which number about 4,000 were slaves. Dutch manners and habits prevailed to a considerable extent throughout the province, although it was evident that English and French tastes were predominant. The citizens were lively and sociable in manners, and had their weekly evening clubs, and in winter their balls and concerts, in the cities. Their stoops (or porches) were furnished with side seats, which, in the evenings, were well filled with the inmates, old and young of both sexes, who met to gossip or to court, while the cattle wandered about the streets of the then rustic cities.

The habits of the people at that early day were of so sociable a nature, that whole neighborhoods would congregate together in the summer evenings upon their large stoops for social conversation. The mode of building their houses was with the angular zigzag gables fronting the streets, with long projecting gutters, which discharged their unsavory currents of dirty water or melted snows upon the heads of the unwary passer-by. In the interior of their dwellings, Dutch cleanliness, order, and economy prevailed. Their kitchens were usually distinguished by the old-fashioned fire-place, extending across their entire width, taking in logs of wood four feet in length, and leaving room for the grandfather and grandmother to indulge their pipe and mug of cider in the long winter evenings. They lived too with exemplary sobriety, breakfasting on tea without milk, and sweetened by a small piece of sugar passed round from one to the other. They dined on buttermilk and bread, and if to that they added sugar, it was deemed delicious, and sometimes they indulged in broiled and roasted meats. The use of stoves was unknown, and the huge fire-places above mentioned, through which one might almost have driven a wagon, were furnished with ample logs, and were grand and cozy nestling places during the long winter evenings, amid the wail of the snow storms and the roar of the forest trees.

The general prosperity of this colony was proverbial, which was doubtless due to the virtuous and industrious character and habits of our people. Under the English the same simplicity of habits long prevailed, amid which was true enjoyment, of most of which our people have been deprived by the modern habits now prevailing. In those days honesty of purpose characterized the people. One man did not consider himself better than his neighbor on account of his worldly possessions, but all were on an equality. The population of the state in 1750 was about seventy thousand.

William Franklin, son of Dr. Benjamin Franklin, succeeded Gov. Josiah Hardy, in 1763, and was the last royal governor. The same year a treaty of peace was consummated between Great Britain and France, whereby Canada was ceded to the British King. To effect this purpose, William Pitt, the prime minister of England, called upon the colonial governments on this continent to aid in destroying the power of the French in America.

The quota of men called for from this state was five hundred, which was not only furnished cheerfully, but the number was doubled, and in order that they might be raised speedily, a bounty of twelve pounds per man was offered, the pay of the officers was increased, and the sum of fifty thousand pounds was voted to maintain the army. The legislature also directed the erection of barracks at Trenton, Burlington, Elizabeth, New Brunswick, and Amboy. This complement of one thousand men was kept up by the state, during the years 1758, 1759, and 1760, and in the two succeeding years they furnished six hundred men, in addition to which, in 1762, they raised a company of sixty-four men and officers, designed especially for garrison duty, which cost the state an average of forty thousand pounds per annum. Thus they showed their loyalty to the home government, in the readiness to obey the just commands which emanated from Great Britain, and the same spirit was manifest during the entire time they acknowledged the right of that kingdom to govern, and until they resolved, in consequence of its despotic powers, to set up a government for themselves independent of Great Britain.

On the 1st day of July, 1676, New Jersey was divided into

two sections, called East and West New Jersey, Sir George Carteret receiving for his share the easterly section, extending eastward and northward along the sea coast and Hudson's river, from the east side of a certain place or harbor lying on the southern part of the same tract of land, and commonly called or known in a map of the said tract of land by the name of Little Egg Harbor, and William Penn, Gawen Lawrie, and Nicholas Lucas, their heirs and assigns, receiving in severalty as their full part, share, and portion of the said tract of land, in trust for the benefit of Edward Byllinge, as the said undivided moiety was subject, and to be from henceforth called and distinguished by the name of West New Jersey; all that western part, share, and portion of the said tract of land and premises lying on the west side, and westward of the aforesaid straight and direct line drawn through the said premises from north to south, for and in consideration of five shillings to them, the said William Penn, Gawen Lawrie, Nicholas Lucas, and Edward Byllinge, in hand paid by the said Sir George Carteret, the receipt whereof they do here respectively acknowledge, the said Edward Byllinge and they, the said William Penn, Gawen Lawrie, and Nicholas Lucas, by and with the consent, direction, and appointment of the said Edward Byllinge, testified by his being a party hereunto, and by his sealing and executing of these presents.

This westerly part, share, and portion of the said tract of land and premises were, by the consent and agreement of the parties, called by the name of West Jersey, and was all that and only all that part, share, and portion of the said tract of land and premises conveyed by his said Royal Highness, as lieth extended westward, or southward from the west side of the line of said partition, on the Delaware river, and extending to Egg Harbor.

The first general assembly of the state met at Elizabethtown on the 26th day of May, 1668.

Hon. Philip Carteret, governor.

The council consisted of Capt. Nicholas Verlet, Daniel Pierce, Robert Bond, Samuel Edsall, Robert Vanquellin, William Pardon; James Bollen, secretary.

The burgesses consisted of Gasper Stenmetts, Baltazer Bayard, *for Bergen;* John Ogden, John Brackett, *for Elizabethtown;*

Capt. Robert Treat, Samuel Swarne, for Newark, *upon Pishawach river*; John Bishop, Robert Dennes, *for Woodbridge*; James Grover, John Bound, *for Middletown and Shrewsbury.*

The following is an abstract of the laws passed at this first session of the provincial legislature :

"For resisting the authority established by the lords proprietors, as the governor, justices, or any other inferior officers, either in words or actions, fine or corporal punishment, as the court shall judge, upon due examination.

"Every male from sixteen years and upwards, to the age of sixty years, shall be furnished, at their own cost and charges, with good and sufficient arms, and constantly maintain the same, *viz.*, a good serviceable gun well fixed, one pound of good powder, four pounds of pistol bullets, or twenty-four bullets suited to the gun, a pair of bandoleers, or a good horn, and a sword and belt; and if any person or persons shall willfully neglect and not provide himself according to this act, within one month after publication thereof, he shall pay one shilling for the first week's neglect, and for the next week's neglect, and so for every week after, the sum of two shillings, by way of fine, to be levied upon his or their goods and chattels."

In the capital laws, it is enacted :

"That if any person or persons shall maliciously, wittingly, or willingly set on fire any dwelling-house, out-house, store-house, barn or stable, or any other kind of house or houses, corn, hay, fencing, wood, flax, or any other combustible matter, to the prejudice and damage of his neighbor, or any other person or persons whatsoever, he or they shall be committed to prison without bail or mainprize, and make full satisfaction; and if he or they are not able to make satisfaction for the damages sustained by such willful and malicious act, then to stand to the mercy of the court whether to be tried for life or to suffer some other corporal punishment, as the court shall judge, all circumstances being first duly examined and considered of.

"If any person or persons shall willingly and maliciously rise up to bear false witness, or purpose to take away a man's life, they shall be put to death.

"If any man shall willfully or forcibly steal away any mankind, he shall be put to death.

"If any person within this province shall commit burglary, by breaking open any dwelling-house, store-house, ware-house, out-house or barn, or any other house whatsoever, or that shall rob any person in the field or highways, he or they so offending shall, for the first offence, be punished by being burnt in the hand by the letter T, and make full satisfaction of the goods stolen, or the damages that are done; and for the second time of offending in the like nature, besides the making of restitution, to be branded in the forehead with the letter R. And for the third offence, to be put to death as incorrigible.

"And for stealing goods, money, or cattle, or any other beast of what kind soever, to make treble restitution for the first offence, and the like for the second and third offence, with such further increase of punishment as the court shall see cause; and if incorrigible, to be punished with death. And in case they are not able to make restitution for the first, second, and third offences, they shall be sold, that satisfaction may be made.

"If any person be found to be a witch, either male or female, they shall be put to death.

"If any child or children above sixteen years of age, and of sufficient understanding, shall smite or curse their natural father or mother, except provoked thereunto, and forced for their safe preservation from death or maiming, upon the complaint or proof of the said father or mother, or either of them, (and not otherwise), they shall be put to death.

"If any person or persons shall be abroad from the usual place of their abode, and found in night-walking, drinking in any tap-house, or any other house or place at unseasonable times, after nine of the clock at night, and not about their lawful occasions, or cannot give a good account of their being absent from their own place of abode at that time of the night, if required of them, he or they shall be secured by the constable or some other officer, till the morning, to be brought before a justice of the peace or magistrate, to be examined, and if they cannot give them a satisfactory account of their being out at such unseasonable times, he or they shall be bound over to the next court, and receive such punishment as the justices upon the bench shall see cause to inflict upon them.

"That a rate of thirty pounds be levied upon the country for the defraying of public charges, and this rate equally proportioned to each town. That is to say, five pounds for each town, to be paid in manner as followeth: winter wheat at five shillings a bushel; summer wheat at four shillings and sixpence; peas at three shillings and sixpence; Indian corn at three shillings; rye at four shillings; barley at four shillings; beef at two-pence half-penny; pork at three pence half-penny a pound; and this rate to be paid at or before the next general court, into the hands and custody of Mr. Jacob Mollins, of Elizabethtown, which we desire of him to take into his hands for the use of the province, and when received, to disburse and pay to Capt. Bollen the sum of twenty pounds, and the rest as he shall have order to improve for our use."

In order to prevent unlawful marriages, it was ordered that "no person or persons, son, daughter, maid or servant, shall be married without the consent of his or her parents, masters, or overseers, and three times published in and at some public meeting or kirk, where the party or parties have their most usual abode, or set up in writing their purposes of marriage on some public house where they live, and there at least to abide for the space of fourteen days before marriage, which is to be performed in some public place, if possible may be, and none but some approved minister or justice of the peace within this province, or some public officer, where such are not, shall be allowed to marry or admit of any to join in marriage, in their presence, and under the penalty of twenty pounds for acting contrary hereunto, and to be put out of their office, according to the liberty of conscience granted by the lords proprietors in their concessions."

The governor had power to grant his license, under his hand and seal, "to any person or persons that are at their own disposing, or to any other under the tuition of their parents, masters, or overseers, to join in matrimony; provided that the parents, masters, or overseers, are present and consenting thereunto, or that their consent be attested by some public officer, and presented to the governor before the granting thereof, and the others to clear themselves by oath or certificate.*

"That every apprentice and servant that shall depart and absent themselves from their masters or dames, without leave first obtained, shall be judged by the court to double the time of such their absence, by future service over and above other damages and costs which master and dame shall sustain by such unlawful departure.

"Any one having been proved to have transported, or to have contrived the transportation of any such apprentice or servant, shall be fined five pounds, and all such damages as the court shall judge, and that the master or dame can make appear, and if not able, to be left to the judgment of the court.

"Every inhabitant that shall harbor or entertain any such apprentice or servant, and knowing that he hath absented himself from his service, upon proof thereof, shall forfeit to the master or dame, ten shillings for every day's entertainment or concealment, and if not able to satisfy, then to be liable to the judgment of the court.

---

* The following is a copy of a certificate given by Governor Franklin:

By His Excellency William Franklin, Esq., Captain-General and Governor in Chief and over His Majesty's Province of New Jersey, and Territories thereon depending in America.

To any minister or justice of the peace:

WHEREAS, by a mutual Purpose of Marriage between Samuel Opdyke, of the Township of Amwell, and County of Hunterdon, of the one Party, and Susannah Robertson, of the same place of the other Party, of which they have desired my License, and have given Bond, upon condition that neither of them have any lawful Let or Impediment, Pre-Contract, Affinity, or Consanguinity, to their being joined in the Holy Bands of Matrimony. These are therefore to authorize and impower you to join the said Samuel Opdyke and Susannah Robertson in the Holy Bands of Matrimony, and then to pronounce them Man and Wife.

GIVEN under my Hand and the Prærogative Seal, at Burlington, the Seventh Day of December, in the Sixteenth Year of the Reign of our Sovereign Lord GEORGE the Third, by the Grace of GOD of Great-Britain, France and Ireland, King, Defender of the Faith, &c. Annoque Domini One Thousand Seven Hundred and Seventy-Five.

Entered in the Registry of the Prærogative Office.

WM. FRANKLIN.

"Concerning that beastly vice, drunkenness, it is hereby enacted, that if any person be found to be drunk, he shall pay one shilling fine for the first time, two shillings for the second, and for the third time, and for every time after two shillings and sixpence; and such as have nothing to pay, shall suffer corporal punishment, and for those that are unruly and disturbers of the peace, they shall be put in the stocks until they are sober, or during the pleasure of the officer-in-chief in the place where he is drunk."

This session of the assembly was commenced on the 26th and ended on the 30th of May, 1668.

The next session was held at Elizabethtown, on Tuesday, the 3d of November, 1668, at which an act was passed requiring "all the soldiers in every town of the province, from sixteen years old to sixty, to train or be mustered at least four days in the year, and oftener if the chief military officer in the place see it needful, viz., two days in the spring and two days in the autumn, and that there shall be at least ten days between each training day; any chief officer constituted and commissioned for that purpose, wittingly or willfully neglecting the same, shall forfeit for every day's neglect, twenty shillings to the public and every soldier five shillings, and for a half a day, two shillings and sixpence, and for late coming, one shilling.'

Every town within the province was to have a brand-mark for their horses, to distinguish the horses of one town from another; besides which every one was to have and mark his horse or horses with his own particular brand-mark; also, that every town shall have a horn brand-mark, for all cattle from three years old and upward. It was required that there should be an officer appointed by the governor in each town to brand and record every particular man's brand, and the age of each of them, as near as he could, with the color and all observable marks it had before the branding, whether on the ear or elsewhere, with the year and day of the month when branded, and to receive from the owner sixpence for each horse, mare, or colt so branded and recorded; and every one neglecting to have them branded was to be fined ten shillings for every default.

The horses and cattle were to be branded with the same letter in each town; that of Bergen, with the letter B; Newark, with

N; Elizabethtown, with E; Woodbridge, with W; Middletown, with M; Shrewsbury, with S; Delaware, with D; Piscataqua, with P.

The brand was to be fixed on the right buttock of horses, and on the right horn of cattle; the brander to have for cattle, twopence per head. The sale of horses of all kinds was to be recorded in the town book within ten days after the sale, and the recorder was to receive three-pence per head for every such sale, under a penalty of forty shillings for every default.

Every town was required to provide an ordinary for the relief and entertainment of strangers, the keeper of which was to have a license from the secretary, and oblige himself to make sufficient provision of meat, drink, and lodging for strangers; and for neglect in any of the towns, they were to forfeit forty shillings fine to the country for every month's default after publication hereof.

All persons were prohibited receiving or buying any cattle whatsoever of any Indian or Indians, whether swine, neat cattle, or horses, under the penalty of ten pounds.

December 2d, 1675, it was enacted "that whosoever shall profane the Lord's Day, otherwise called Sunday, by any kind of servile work, unlawful recreations, or unnecessary travels on that day, not falling within the compass of works of mercy or necessity, either willfully or through careless neglect, shall be punished by fine, imprisonment, or corporally, according to the nature of the offence, at the judgment of the court, justice or justices where the offence is committed."

Any person falling under the fine of a penal law, no officer was allowed to lay restraint upon his or their arms or ammunitions, plow-irons or chains, horses or cattle, as being so necessary to their livelihood.

Blacksmiths, locksmiths, or any other persons were forbidden to make, mend, or any way repair any Indian gun or guns, upon the penalty of paying for the first offence, after conviction, the sum of twenty shillings, and for the second offence, forty shillings, and for the third offence, to double the whole, and so to continue, which fines to be one-half to the informer, and the other half to the public use.

April 6th, 1676, an act was passed requiring all weights and measures to be sealed, according to the standard of England, and for dry measure, according to Winchester measure.

It was also ordered that the freeholders in every town choose a packer, to see that all meat in barrels for sale be good and merchantable, and well packed and salted, and to contain thirty-two gallons, and put his mark upon the cask or barrel, and to have for his pains of packing and marking of every such barrel, eight-pence.

All leather was to pass under the hand of a sealer, and be approved by him, under a penalty of four-pence per hide.

At a meeting of the general assembly, held at Woodbridge, October 5th, 6th, 7th, and 8th, 1676, it was enacted that there be a "day of public thanksgiving, set apart throughout the whole province, to give God the glory and praise for the signal demonstration of His mercy and favor towards us in this colony, in the preserving and continuing our peace in the midst of wars round about us, together with many other mercies which we are sensible of, which call aloud for our acknowledgment and thanksgiving to the Lord, and oblige us to live to His praise, and in His fear always."

The laws of the general assembly were in force only one year, and consequently at each yearly session the same laws had to be re-enacted, otherwise they lost their vitality.

The salary of the governor was fixed, in the year 1675, at fifty pounds per year, and five shillings was allowed him for a seal. In 1676, the governor was allowed four shillings a day for traveling expenses, the council and deputies, three shillings each per day, traveling expenses, and to continue during the time of their sitting.

In 1679, the salary of the governor was fixed at two shillings per head for every male within the province from fourteen years old and upwards.

A day of thanksgiving was appointed for "next Wednesday come three weeks: that will be the 26th of this instant, November."

In 1681, a law was passed forbidding the sale of rum, brandy, wine, cider, strong beer, or any other intoxicating liquor to the

Indians, under the penalty of twenty pounds for the first offence, and to be doubled for every offence after.

Robert Barclay was appointed governor of East New Jersey for life, July 17th, 1683, and Gawen Lawrie, deputy governor, not exceeding seven years, commission dated July 27th, 1683.

Jeremiah Basse was appointed governor, April 14th, 1698.

The sessions of the general assembly and the courts were held at Elizabethtown up to the 6th day of April, 1686, and all the public records were kept there up to that time, when they were, by act of the general assembly, removed to the town of Amboy Perth, in the county of Middlesex, afterwards called New Perth. The courts were afterwards ordered to be held alternately at the town of Amboy Perth, Piscataway, and Woodbridge.

On the 28th of September, 1692, the legislature finding the act imposing a fine on persons selling liquors to the Indians was ineffectual to prevent that traffic, enacted that the penalty should be "for the first offence, five lashes on the bare back, for the second offence, ten lashes on the bare back, for the third, fifteen, for the fourth, twenty, and so many and no more for every such offence thereafter, to be inflicted by order of the court."

In 1692, an act was passed authorizing the division of the several counties into townships, tribes, or divisions.

In 1693, an act was passed to establish schoolmasters within the province, "for the cultivation of learning and good manners, and for the good and benefit of mankind, which hath hitherto been much neglected within this province."

In 1695, an act was passed regulating schools, in which each town was to choose three men yearly, who were "to appoint and agree with a schoolmaster, and to nominate and appoint the most convenient place or places where the school shall be kept from time to time, that as near as may be the whole inhabitants may have the benefit thereof."

Concessions and agreements of the proprietors, freeholders, and inhabitants of the province of West New Jersey were made on the 25th day of March, 1680, confirming the contract and agreement made on the 2d day of March, 1676, by William Penn, Gawen Lawrie, and Nicholas Lucas, unto Thomas Hutchinson, Thomas Pearson, Joseph Helmsley, George Hutchinson, and Mahlon Stacy.

Samuel Jennings was deputy governor in 1681, from the 25th of September, and was appointed governor the 14th of November, 1681.

The laws of the province of West Jersey were almost precisely the same as those of East Jersey.

The general assembly held their sessions at Burlington.

The courts were held alternately at Burlington and Salem, they being the most populous towns in the province.

In 1682, the legislature granted authority for the erection of public markets for the accommodation of the people; the first market day was to be held at Burlington, to begin and take place the seventh day of the eighth month next ensuing, and at Salem, the seventeenth day of the same month.

"The Seventh day, commonly called Saturday, weekly and every week, shall be the market day at Burlington, to be held there in the place formerly set forth for the market place; and that the market for corn shall begin at the eleventh hour in the morning.

"That the Third day, called Tuesday, weekly and every week, shall be the market at Salem, to be held before the town landing, formerly appointed there for the market place, and that the market for corn shall begin at the eleventh hour in the morning."

For the encouraging learning, and for the better education of youth, it was enacted that the island called Matinicunk, late in the possession of Robert Stacy, with all and every the appurtenances, was given to remain for the use of the town of Burlington for the maintaining of a school for the education of youth within the said town.

In 1683, the assembly gave to Thomas Budd and Francis Collins one thousand acres of land (parts of the land to be purchased of the Indians above the falls), for the building of a market-house and court-house at Burlington

Samuel Jennings was, by the free election and vote of the assembly sitting at Burlington, chosen governor of the province on the 11th of March, 1683. His previous appointment was by the lords proprietors. The assembly gave him six hundred acres of land, to be had and taken up above the falls (after the purchase thereof was made from the Indians), with three years' time to settle the same.*

The first representatives of West Jersey were Thomas Ollive, (speaker), Mahlon Stacy, Joshua Wright, John Lambert, Thomas Lambert,† William Emley, Godfrey Hancock, Daniel Leeds, Thomas Wright, Samuel Borden,‡ Robert Stacy, Thomas Budd, Daniel Wills, Thomas Gardner, John Cripps, John White, John Chaffen, Bernard Devenish, Isaac Meriott, William Peachee, William Cooper, Mark Newbie, Thomas Chackeray, Robert Zane, Samuel Neville, Richard Guy, Marke Reeves, Richard Hancock, John Smith, John Pledger, Edward Wade, George Deacon, Samuel Hedge, Andrew Thompson, Thomas Revell, (clerk).

At the session held at Burlington, July 7th, 1683, it was resolved and unanimously agreed upon by the assembly, that the governor be chairman or speaker, and that he sit as one of the assembly, together with the council, and the chairman to have two votes, or a double vote.

On the 20th day of March, 1684, Thomas Ollive was chosen governor.

September 25th, 1685, John Skene was chosen deputy governor.

November 3d, 1692, Andrew Hamilton was chosen governor.

Previous to 1693, West Jersey had been divided into three counties, Burlington, Salem, and Falls, and these were subdivided into ten-tenths.

At the session of May 12th, 1696, a bill was passed, called a qualifying bill, requiring officers who were not free to take an oath, to sign the following declaration of fidelity and profession of the Christian faith:

"I, A. B., do sincerely promise and solemnly declare, that

---

* All the lands in New Jersey were purchased from the Indians, and none were taken except by purchase.

† From whom Lamberton was named.

‡ From whom Bordentown took its name.

will be true and faithful to William, King of England, and the government of this province of West New Jersey; and I do solemnly profess and declare, that I do from my heart abhor, detest, and renounce, as impious and heretical, that damnable doctrine and position, that princes excommunicated or deprived by the Pope, or any authority of the See of Rome, may be deprived or murdered by their subjects, or any other whatsoever. And I also declare, that no foreign prince, person, prelate, state, or potentate hath, or ought to have, any power, jurisdiction, superiority, pre-eminence, or authority, ecclesiastical or spiritual, within this realm."

THE CHRISTIAN BELIEF.

"I, A. B., profess faith in GOD, the Father, and in JESUS CHRIST, his Eternal Son, the true GOD, and in the Holy Spirit, one GOD blessed forever more; and do acknowledge the Holy Scriptures of the Old and New Testaments to be given by Divine Inspiration."

The tax ordered at this session to be raised for the payment and discharge of the provincial debt was one penny per acre of land cleared, improved, and fenced, meadow only excepted; sixpence upon every hundred acres surveyed and unimproved land; six-pence per head upon all neat cattle from one year old and upwards; twelve-pence per head upon every horse and mare one year old and upwards; six-pence per head for every hog or swine that any person should sell, convey, or dispose of, living or dead; one penny per head for every sheep; and also all persons keeping or owning negroes should pay for every negro of ten years of age and upwards, two shillings and six-pence. Those refusing to pay, or giving in a false account, or concealing and not giving in a negro, were to be fined six shillings; for every head of such beast not given in, ten shillings; for every acre of land improved, two-pence; and for every hundred acres of land unimproved, nine-pence.

Previous to 1694, each tenth chose ten representatives for the provincial assembly, making one hundred representatives in all, which was according to the concessions of the lords proprietors.

After the year 1694, they were chosen by counties. Burlington county comprised two-tenths; Gloucester county, two-tenths; and Salem county, one-tenth. Burlington county had twenty members; Gloucester county, twenty; Salem, ten; and Cape May, five.

In the year 1696 this number was considered superfluous, and the representation was made, for Burlington, ten; Gloucester, ten; Salem, five; and Cape May, three; making in all twenty-eight members.

In the year 1700, the assembly enacted, "that any person or persons that shall break into any house, out-house, or barn, in the day-time or in the night, and shall steal any goods or merchandize to the value of one shilling or upwards, upon being convicted thereof, shall (besides making the restitution of four-fold), for the first offence, receive thirty-nine stripes upon the bare back, and being convicted a second time, shall have burnt with a hot iron upon his, her, or their forehead, a Roman T, added to the above punishment, and being convicted a third time, shall be burned with a hot iron in the cheek with the Roman letter T, suffer a twelve months' close imprisonment, and be kept to hard labor, only having a sufficiency of diet, and corrected by being whipt with thirty-nine stripes on the bare back once in every month during the said term of one year."

After the first offence, if the offender begged transportation, the judge or justice of the Supreme Court was to allow it to him or her. After being transported, in case they returned within seven years, they were to be apprehended, and not only make restitution four-fold, but to receive thirty-nine stripes, and be branded with the Roman letter T on the forehead.

At the session of May 12th, 1701, the law reducing the representatives to twenty-eight was repealed, and the old law allowing them fifty-five re-enacted

On the 15th day of April, 1702, the proprietors of the provinces of East and West Jersey surrendered to Queen Anne all the powers and authorities in them vested in said provinces, previous application having been made to that end August 12th, 1701.

This surrender was signed by twenty-five of the proprietors of

East Jersey, and by thirty-two of West Jersey. The surrender was accepted by the Queen, at the Court of St. James, the 17th day of April, 1702, before the final articles of surrender could have reached England.

On the 16th day of November, 1702, Lord Cornbury (Edward Hyde) was appointed governor of the consolidated province.*

The assembly was ordered to sit alternately at Perth Amboy and Burlington, and to consist of twenty-four representatives, to be chosen, two by the inhabitants, householders of the city or town of Perth Amboy; two by the inhabitants, householders of the city and town of Burlington; ten by the freeholders of East New Jersey, and ten by the freeholders of West New Jersey.

---

* His commission bears date December 5th, 1702.

CHAPTER XIV.

1680—1786.

New Jersey—When set off from New York—Extent of East and West Jersey—First Purchases—Consideration paid for lands—First settlement at Burlington—Flood at Delaware Falls—Religious Institutions—Places of public worship—First courts in Trenton—United States government offices removed to Trenton.

ALTHOUGH the English had very early made the discovery of North America, a considerable time elapsed before any advantages accrued. Sir Walter Raleigh, in 1584, was the first Englishman who attempted to plant a colony in it.*

In this year he obtained a patent from Queen Elizabeth, for him and his heirs, to discover and possess forever, under the crown of England, all such countries and land as were not then possessed by any Christian prince, or inhabited by any Christian people. This was the first patent granted to Sir Walter Raleigh. Encouraged by this grant, Raleigh and other partners, at divers times, fitted out ships, and settled a colony at Roanore,† in Virginia; but, notwithstanding various attempts, they met with

---

* That is, a regular colony under grants. Sir Armigell Wadd, of Yorkshire, a clerk of the Council of Henry VIII and Edward VI, and author of a book of Travels, was the first Englishman that made discoveries in America. [H. Walpole's Anecdotes of Printing, vol. ii, Catalogue of Engravers, pp. 18, 19.]

† Now Roanoke, in Virginia. At that time the country was divided into but two great divisions; the first or southern division was granted to the London company, and the second or northern division, to the Plymouth company. The portion of territory to which the name of Virginia was given, extended rom the thirty-fourth to the forty-fifth degree of north latitude. [Mulford's History, p. 26.]

such discouragements that no great improvements were made until sometime afterwards.

In the year 1606, King James, without any regard to Raleigh's right, granted a new patent of Virginia, in which was included New England, New York, New Jersey, Pennsylvania, and Maryland. From Queen Elizabeth's time to the time of this patent, the whole country bore the name of Virginia, which was given it by Raleigh, in honor of the virgin queen of England, as some say, though others claim that it took its rise from the fact of its never having been settled before—being virgin soil.

The patentees were Sir Thomas Gates, Sir George Somers, Richard Hakluyt, (clerk), Edward Maria Wingfield, Thomas Hanham, and Raleigh Gilbert, Esqs., William Parker, George Popham,* and others. The extent of the land granted was from thirty-four to forty-five degrees north latitude, with all the islands lying within one hundred miles of the coast. Two distinct colonies were to be planted by virtue of this patent, and the property invested in two different bodies of adventurers, the first to belong to Somers, Hakluyt, and Wingfield, under title of the London adventurers, or the London company, and was to reach from thirty-four to forty-one degrees, with all lands, woods mines, minerals, &c.

The other colony was to reach from the end of the first, to forty-five degrees; granting the same privileges to Hanham, Gilbert, Parker, and Popham, under the name of the Plymouth company, with liberty to both companies to take as many partners as they pleased; forbidding others to plant within those colonies without their license; only reserving the fifth-part of all gold and silver mines, and the fifteenth-part of copper, to the use of the crown.

The London company, by virtue of this grant, fitted out several ships, with artificers of every kind, and all things requisite for a new settlement, which sailed for America, and planted a colony there, but in the year 1623, there were so many complaints made of bad management, that on inquiry, a *quo warranto* was issued against the patent, and after a trial had in the

---

* Lord Chief Justice of England.

King's bench, it was declared forfeited;* after which Virginia remained for a long time under the immediate direction of the crown.

In the year the patent was granted, the Plymouth company also attempted to make a settlement, but with no great success until about the year 1620, when they sent fresh recruits from England, under the command of Captain Standish, who arrived at Cape Cod, in the latitude of forty-two degrees, and having turned the Cape, found a commodious harbor, opposite the point at the mouth of the bay, at the entry of which were two islands well stocked with wood. Here they built a town which they called Plymouth. About this time, the colonies in New England were much augmented by multitudes of dissenters, who, thinking this a good opportunity of enjoying liberty of conscience, offered their services to the Plymouth company, and the grand patent being delivered up to the King, *particular* patents were granted to the Lord Musgrave, the Duke of Richmond, the Earl of Carlisle, the Lord Edward Gorges, and new colonies were planted in divers places on this continent.

From what has been said, it is evident that the colonies of New York, New Jersey, Pennsylvania, and Maryland were included in the great patent last mentioned; but that becoming void, the crown was at liberty to re-grant the same to others.

But it does not appear that any part of those provinces were settled by virtue thereof; nor indeed was any distinct discovery of them made until many years afterwards. New Jersey, Pennsylvania, and other lands adjacent, notwithstanding the ancient right of the crown of England, deduced as aforesaid, had two pretenders to them—the Dutch and the Swedes.

The claim the former set up was under color of a discovery made in the year 1609, by Henry Hudson, an Englishman by birth, and commander of a ship called the Half-Moon, fitted out from Holland by the East India company, for the purpose of discovering, by a northwest passage, a nearer way to China.

---

* Other accounts say the patent was dissolved by the King's proclamation in 1624, and that though a quo warranto was issued against it, no determination followed in the courts of justice.

In this voyage he sailed up to the place now called New York, and up the river, which he called *Hudson's* river, and returning sometime after to Amsterdam, the Dutch pretended to have purchased the chart he had made of the American coast, and having obtained a patent from the states in the year 1614, to trade in New England, they settled in New York, which place they called New Netherland, and kept possession until Sir Samuel Argole, governor of Virginia, disputed their title, alleging that the country having been discovered by an Englishman, in right of his master, he could not suffer it to be alienated from the crown without the king's consent. He therefore compelled the Dutch colony to submit to him, and to hold it under the English. Soon after, a new governor coming from Amsterdam, they not only neglected to pay their usual acknowledgment to the governor of Virginia, but in the year 1623, fortified their colony by building several forts: one on the Delaware, (by them called South river), near Gloucester, in New Jersey, which they named Fort Nassau; a second on Hudson's (the North river), in the province of New York, which they named Fort Orange, and a third on Connecticut river, (by them called Fresh river), which they named the Hirsse of Good Hope.

Having examined into the Dutch claim to this continent, let us look for a moment at that set up by their neighbors, the Swedes.

In the reign of Gustavus Adolphus, in the year 1626, an eminent merchant, William Useling, who had visited this country, on his return gave a glowing description of it, applauded its fruitful and fertile lands as abounding with all the necessaries of life, and by many arguments he endeavored to persuade the Swedes to settle a colony here. Literally carried away by the glowing descriptions given by Useling, Gustavus issued a proclamation at Stockholm, exhorting his subjects to contribute to a company associated for the purposes aforesaid.

This company was very soon formed, and called the West India Company, and was confirmed by Gustavus.

In a general convention assembled the year following, large sums of money were raised to carry on the intended settlement, of which the king, the lords of the council, the chief of his barons, knights, coronets, principal officers in his militia, bishops, clergy, and many of the common people of Sweden, Finland, and Liffland, contributed.

In 1627, the Swedes and Finns accordingly came over hither. Their first landing was at Cape Inlopen (now called Henlopen). Here they were so well pleased with the sight presented, that they called it Paradise Point. Sometime after they purchased of some Indians (but whether of such as had the proper right to convey we are not informed,) the land from Cape Inlopen to the falls of the Delaware, on both sides of the river. These falls laid opposite, or rather on the west of the city of Trenton—hence, what is now the city of Trenton was included in that purchase. The Delaware was called by them New Swedeland stream; and they made presents to the Indian chiefs in order to obtain peaceable possession of the lands they had already purchased.

But the Dutch continuing their pretensions, in 1630, one David Petersz de Vries built a fort within the capes of Delaware, on the west, about two leagues from Cape Cornelius, at what is now called Lewistown, which was then called by the name of Hoarkill.

In 1631, the Swedes also built a fort on the west of Delaware, to which they gave the name of Christeen, the ruins of which are still visible. This fort was erected near Wilmington, from which the name of the noted creek, Christiana, is derived.

A small town was here laid out by Peter Lindstrom, their engineer, and here they first settled, but although this settlement was afterwards demolished by the Dutch, yet in 1810, Christiana township, including the village of the same name, numbered 6,698 inhabitants, and in 1820, 8,335 inhabitants.

On an island called Tinicum, sixteen miles above Christiana, and on the Delaware, below the mouth of Darby creek, about six miles below Philadelphia, the Swedes erected another fort, which they called New Gottemburgh.

On the 2d of September, 1655, the Dutch besieged Christiana fort and town, and destroyed New Gottemburgh, together with all the houses that were outside the fort.

From this time till the year 1664, New Sweden and New

Netherland continued in possession and under government of the Dutch, who had built a city on Manhattan Island, at the mouth of Hudson's river, which they named New Amsterdam, (New York) and the river they sometimes called the Great river. About one hundred and fifty miles up they built a fort, and called it Orange (Albany); from thence they drove a profitable trade with the Indians, who came overland as far as from Quebec to deal with them.

The first bounds of New York were Maryland on the south, the main land as far as could be discovered westward, the river of Canada (now St. Lawrence,) northward, and New England eastward.

We have now arrived at that period when, by the grants made, this province was reduced into a much smaller compass.

That province now called New Jersey* was one of these grants set off from New York. It was probably called New Jersey in honor of Sir George Carteret, one of the proprietors, and a Jerseyman.

The Duke of York being seized, did, on the 23d and 24th days of June, 1664, in consideration of a "competent sum of money, grant and convey unto Lord John Berkley, Baron of Stratton, and Sir George Carteret, of Saltrum, in the county of Devon, to their heirs and assigns forever, all that tract of land adjacent to New England, west of Long Island and Manhattan's Island, and bounded on the east by the main sea, a part of Hudson's river; on the west by the Delaware bay and river, extending southward to the main ocean, as far as Cape May, at the mouth of Delaware bay, and north by the northernmost branch of said bay or river of Delaware, which is in forty-one degrees and forty minutes of latitude, in a straight line to Hudson's river, said tract of land hereafter to be called Nova Cæsarea, or New Jersey; and also all rivers, mines, minerals, woods, fishings, hawkings, huntings, and fowlings; and all other royalties, profits, commodities, and hereditaments whatsoever to the lands and premises belonging, or in anywise appertaining, with their and

---

* It is said to have borne for some time the name of New Canary, and afterwards Nova Cæsarea, or New Jersey.

every of their appurtenances, in as full and ample a manner as the same is granted unto the Duke of York by the before recited letters patent.''

Lord Berkley and Sir George Carteret, under this first grant, became sole proprietors, and so continued till the province became divided in 1676. Sir George Carteret then became the sole proprietor of the eastern division. The county of Bergen was the first settled place. A great many Dutch being already there when the province was first surrendered, remained under the English government. A few Danes were probably concerned in the original settlement of this country, from whence came Bergen, after the capital of Norway.

In 1664, John Bailey, Daniel Denton, and Luke Watson, of Jamaica, Long Island, purchased of certain Indian chiefs, inhabitants of Staten Island, a tract or tracts of land, on part of which the town of Elizabeth now stands, and for which, on their petition, Governor Richard Nicholls granted a deed or patent to John Baker, of New York, John Ogden, of Northampton, John Bailey and Luke Watson, and their associates, dated at Fort James, in New York, the 2d of December. This is what is commonly called the Elizabethtown grant.

Numbers of industrious, reputable farmers, most of whom were English residents of Long Island, fixed their residences about Middletown, from whence, by degrees, they extended their settlements to Freehold and thereabouts.

To Shrewsbury there came many families from New England, and there were very soon four towns in the province, Elizabeth, Newark, Middletown, and Shrewsbury, and these, with the country around, were in a few years plentifully inhabited by the accession of the Scotch; and many came from England, besides those of the Dutch that remained in the colony.

After Lord Berkley and Sir George Carteret had appointed Philip Carteret governor of the colony of New Jersey, they gave him power, by advice of a majority of the council, to grant lands to all such as by the concessions were entitled thereto, and though there is no provision in the concessions for bargaining with the Indians,* Governor Carteret, on his arrival, thought it prudent to purchase their rights.

Governor Carteret did not arrive to take charge of the government till 1665, up to which time the province was under Richard Nicholl's administration, then governor of New York.

Governor Carteret, on his arrival, took up his residence at Elizabethtown, which it is said he named after Elizabeth, wife of Sir George Carteret, his brother.

He invited others to settle in the province, by sending ambassadors throughout New England, to which many responded, and soon came and settled, some at Elizabethtown, others at Woodbridge, Piscataway, and Newark.

Thus the province of East New Jersey increased in settlements, and continued to grow until the Dutch invasion in 1673, when they took possession of the country and put a stop to the English government.†

Philip Carteret remained governor till his death in 1682. During his lifetime the general assemblies and supreme courts sat at Elizabethtown.

In 1675, a few passengers arrived from England for West Jersey. One-half of the province at this time belonged to Lord Berkley, while the other half was sold to John Fenwick, in trust for Edward Byllinge and his assigns.

The same year Fenwick sailed from London in a ship called the Griffith, and landed at a rich and pleasant spot near Delaware, which he called Salem, from the peaceable aspect which it bore. He brought his two daughters over with him, besides a number of servants, two of whom, Samuel Hedge and John Adams, afterwards married.

Among the passengers who came with Fenwick, were Edward

---

* This in 1672 was supplied by particular instructions, directing that the governor and council should purchase all lands from the Indians, and be reimbursed by the settlers as they made their purchases.

† Governor Andross, of New York, in 1680, undertook to dispute the title of Carteret as governor of New Jersey. He therefore sent an armed force to Elizabethtown, seized and carried him prisoner to New York, on pretence of his commission not being a good one.

Champness, Edward Wade, Samuel Wade, John Smith and wife, Samuel Nicholls, Richard Guy, Richard Noble, Richard Hancock, John Pledger, Hipolite Lufever, and John Matlock. These, and others with them, were masters of families. This is the first ship that came to West Jersey, and none followed for nearly two years, owing probably to a difference between Fenwick and Byllinge. But this difference was settled to the satisfaction of both parties by the good offices of William Penn.

Articles of concession were agreed upon and signed by a number of inhabitants of West Jersey, which was confirmed by a letter dated "London, 26th of 6th Month, 1676." Article 1st described the boundary of the new concession, as follows: "We have divided with Sir George Carteret, and have sealed deeds of partition each to the other, and we have all that side on Delaware river from one end to the other; the line of partition is from the east side of Little Egg Harbor, straight north, through the country to the utmost branch of Delaware river, with all powers, privileges, and immunities whatsoever; ours is called New West Jersey; his is called New East Jersey."

This, with four additional articles relating to the partition of the colony, was signed by Gawen Lawrie, William Penn, Nicholas Lucas, E. Byllinge, John Eldridge, and Edmond Warner.

In 1677, two companies of Quakers, one in Yorkshire and one in London, made purchase of some of the West Jersey lands, and sent out the following commissioners to purchase the lands of the Indians: Thomas Ollive, Daniel Wills, John Kinsey, John Penford, Joseph Helmsley, Robert Stacy, Benjamin Scott, Richard Guy,* and Thomas Foulke. They fitted out a sailing vessel called the Kent, and landed their passengers, two hundred in number, at Raccoon creek, while the commissioners sailed around to a place they called Chygoes Island,† afterwards Burlington.

---

* Richard Guy came in the first ship; John Kinsey died at Shackamaxon soon after landing; his remains were interred at Burlington, in land appropriated for a burial ground, but now a street.

† From Chygoe, an Indian sachem who lived there.

Their first purchase through their Swedish interpreters, Israel Helmes, Peter Rambo, and Lacy Cock, extended from Timber creek to Rancocas creek, and another from Oldman's creek to Timber creek.

After this they got Henric Jacobson Falconbre to be their interpreter, and purchased from Rancocas creek to Assunpink.*

These commissioners, by mutual consent, laid out and settled New Beverly, which they afterward called Bridlington, but soon changed it to Burlington. The town was divided into tenths between the London and Yorkshire companies.

It has been asserted that the first settlement of Trenton was called by the Indians Littleworth, in consequence of its liability to be destroyed by a flood in the river. My impression, however, is, that the inhabitants never recognized it as the name of the town. Mahlon Stacy, who was one of the first purchasers of land here, in letters written in 1680, dates them from "the Falls of Delaware." Rev. Dr. Cooley, who is supposed to have been the author of a series of articles published some years ago, and from which articles I have obtained considerable information for this and subsequent chapters, stated that he had seen a deed of two lots lying east of Greene street, between Second street (now State) and the Assanpink, which were described as "being in Littleworth." If the inhabitants ever called any part of Trenton by that name it must have been the lowlands between Front street and the creek, as it is but a few years since that was low meadow ground and has been overflowed by freshets within the memory of most of our citizens, and has within a few years been filled up until it has attained its present condition, being made ground. We are not prepared to dispute its being the name of the town at its earliest settlement, but have grave doubts of such being the fact.

The province of Nova Cæsarea, or New Jersey, was included in the original grant made by Charles II. King of England, to his brother James, the Duke of York, on the 20th of March,

---

* Meaning Stony Creek.

1664,* and in June of the same year, the Duke of York conveyed it to Lord John Berkeley and Sir George Carteret, jointly. The province was called Nova Cæsarea or New Jersey from the name of the Isle of Jersey, in the English channel, the country of Sir George Carteret.

On the 6th of August, 1680, the Duke of York relinquished by deed his claim of ownership to the province of West New Jersey; at the same time he reserved the right of government, and accordingly chose Edward Byllinge as governor of that province, and Philip Carteret was chosen governor of East Jersey.

The Quakers of West New Jersey, who were now the proprietors, had established a liberal government, and had placed their civil and religious liberties upon a foundation that promised to stand.

William Penn, with eleven associates, some of whom were already concerned in New Jersey, became the purchasers of Carteret's province. The deeds of lease and release (which are yet in existence), were made to the purchasers on the 1st and 2d of February, 1681-2.

The new proprietors proceeded at once to appoint a governor, and their choice for this office fell upon Robert Barclay, of Urie, in Scotland, a member of their own body.

After the London commissioners, who came over in the Kent, had laid out the town of Burlington, on the Delaware river, the Yorkshire commissioners, consisting of Joseph Helmsley, Robert

---

* Previous to 1752, the year commenced on the 25th of March, consequently the time between the 1st day of January and that day was reckoned with the former year, and was usually expressed by a double date. An instrument, for instance, bearing date January 15th, 1640, according to our calendar, would be expressed January 15th, 1639—40; sometimes only 1639. The day of the month by the new style may be ascertained by omitting ten days in the seventeenth century, eleven days in the eighteenth century, and twelve days in the nineteenth century. The alteration was made in England by a statute passed in 1751, to take effect in January, 1752, which authorized the omission of the eleven intermediate days of the calendar—from the 2d to the 14th of that month.

Stacy and William Emley, chose the purchase from the Assanpink,* or Falls of the Delaware, to Ancocas or Rancocas creek.

In November of this year, two ships arrived with passengers, the "Willing Mind,"† from London, and the "Fly Boat Martha," from Hull, with one hundred and fourteen passengers, who settled on the Yorkshire tract. In 1678, on the 10th of December, the "Shield" arrived from Hull.

This was the first ship that had ever ascended the river as far as Burlington.

She moored to a tree, and the next morning after they arrived the passengers went ashore on the ice.‡ Among the emigrants who came in this vessel were Mahlon Stacy, Thomas Potts, Thomas Lambert, Thomas Neville, and Thomas Wood, with their families; Godfrey Newbold, John Newbold, and Mr. Barnes, merchant, from Hull, Richard Green, and John Heyers.§

Mahlon Stacy took up a tract of land of eight hundred acres, lying on both sides of the Assanpink, but principally on the north side of the creek.‖

Several of the first emigrants settled on the lowlands at the Falls of the Delaware.

The country in the vicinity of the Assanpink was for some time known as the *Falls*, or *Falls of the Delaware*. Mahlon Stacy, in writing to his friends in England, dates his letter from the Falls of the Delaware, in West Jersey, the 26th of the fourth month, 1680.¶

In the year 1681, a law was passed to measure the front of the

---

* This creek is called in the public records, Derwent, St. Pink, Sun Pink, Assunpink, (meaning stony creek, from its gravelly bottom) and Assanpink, its present name

† Some of those who came in this ship settled at Burlington.

‡ Gordon, p. 40.

§ Gordon and Smith's History, p. 109.

‖ This tract lay between the old York road (now Greene street) and the Delaware river, and between State and Ferry streets, and extended into what is now Hamilton township on the south side of the creek. Lambert's purchase was south of Ferry street, Trenton.

¶ Smith's History, p. 114.

river Delaware, from St. Pink to Cape May, in order to divide it into ten proprietaries, each proprietor to have his proportion on the front of the river, and to extend back into the woods, so as to contain sixty-four thousand acres, and each proprietary was to be divided into ten equal parts.*

At this division the first proprietary, or Yorkshire tenth, extended from the Assanpink, where it empties into the Delaware, south to the Rancocas creek, in Burlington county, and east into the woods, so as to contain in each proprietary sixty-four thousand acres of land. At that time the main land extended nearly opposite Cox's mill,† at the mouth of the Assanpink, so as to include the Island of Sand, or Gravelly Island.

The first survey of twenty-five hundred acres was made in June, 1687, and the addition of twenty-five hundred acres was surveyed in 1689, when the lands were taken up. This tract extended north on the Delaware between three and four miles, and back from the river so as to include about five thousand acres; and from the northwestern boundary of Hutchinson's land on the Delaware, the society tract commenced, containing ten thousand acres surveyed in May, 1699. How far the western boundary of this tract extended northerly on the river is not at present definitely known.

The Hutchinson manor-house was on the farm on which the State Lunatic Asylum now stands, formerly owned by John Titus, Esq. All these lands, with most, if not all, the other tracts, were included in what was, as early as 1699, known as the township of *Hopewell*, and which was bounded by the Assanpink on the south, by the line of division between East and West Jersey on the east, and by the present boundary of the township of Hopewell on the north.

At what time this tract of country received the name of Hopewell I am not informed. A part of the plantation belonging to

---

* Leaming & Spicer, p. 436.

† The ruins of Cox's mill are still standing. It was about thirty by thirty-eight feet, and built of stone.

the Dean family was deeded by Jonathan Eldridge, of Burlington, to Moses Petit, of Hopewell, in the township of Nottingham, in 1695.

In 1683, the general assembly gave to Governor Jennings six hundred acres of land, above the *Falls*, in consideration of his necessary charges as governor, "*when the lands shall have been purchased of the Indians.*"* This shows that at the commencement of the seventeenth century the country above the falls had not been purchased or settled.

Very few settlements had been made in the township at the commencement of the last century, with the exception of those made on the lowlands at the Assanpink, in 1676, and which were totally destroyed by the flood in 1692, already mentioned. After this disaster the buildings which were erected in the vicinity of the Assanpink were built on the south side of the creek.

That spot of ground immediately adjoining the creek on the south was called Kingsbury, afterwards Kensington Hill; but when it became a manufacturing place of some note, the name was again changed to Mill Hill, which name it continued to bear until it was incorporated with Bloomsbury and made the borough of South Trenton, and afterwards the third and fourth wards of Trenton.

Mr. Isaac Watson, who came from Nottingham, England, settled on the place late in the occupancy of Mr. Benjamin Van Schoick, and in 1708 built the house which is still standing. The township of Nottingham was so called from the place in England from whence Mr. Watson came. About the year 1700, the settlements were commenced by persons who bought the lands from the original proprietors, or persons who had taken up the lands; and most of the deeds of plantations in the different parts of the township bear date from 1699 to 1710. There was considerable difficulty experienced about the title of lands. Grants of lands had been made at different times to different persons, and when they were surveyed it was found that in some

---

* Leaming & Spicer, p. 471.

cases the same land had been granted to different persons. Some had purchased of those who had taken up the land, whose titles, if they had any, were obtained from the Indians.

Dr. Daniel Cox, being one of the rightful proprietors of the lands in this section of the country, Mr. Thomas Revell was appointed by the purchasers to make such arrangements with Dr. Cox as would secure them in the possession of their land, and from the following it appears that he had attended to the business to their satisfaction :

"August 26th, 1703. We, underwritten, having, at the date of the above, at the house of Ralph Hunt, in Maiden township,* heard read the agreement made the 20th of April, 1703, between Dr. Daniel Cox, Esq., and Thomas Revell, on behalf of the purchasers of the land within Maiden and Hopewell, do hereby declare and signify our full and free assent and consent to the same.

"In testimony thereof have thereto set our hands the day and year above.

"Joshua Anderson,   William Green,
 Ralph and Samuel Hunt, John Burroughs,
 John Banbridge,   Isaac and Joseph Reeder,
 Jonathan Davis,   Theophilus Phillips,
     Robert and John Lanning, and others."†

Notwithstanding the care which the first settlers took to secure good titles for their lands, many of them afterwards had to buy the second time or relinquish them ; and several did give up the lands, with the improvements they had made, and settle in other parts of the country, rather then pay for them again.

The provincial legislature, in 1694, enacted that the inhabitants above the St. Pink, or Derwent (Assanpink), in the province, should belong to Burlington.‡

In May, 1701, Andrew Heath and William Spencer were appointed assessors of the township of Hopewell, and Nathaniel

---

* Lawrence.
† Book of Deeds A A A, p. 8, in secretary of state's office.
‡ Leaming & Spicer, p. 532.

Petit, collector.* These persons lived near the *Falls*, except Mr. Heath, who lived on the farm now owned by Mr. Joseph B. Anderson, in Ewing township.

From the year 1700, the settlement of the township was increased by persons from Long Island, East Jersey, and other parts. Messers. Daniel Howell, Ebenezer Prout, Isaac Reeder, John Burroughs, Charles Clark, Richard Scudder, Robert Lanning, Jacob and John Reeder, William Reed, Simon Sacket, John Deane, John and Abiel Davis, Jonathan Davis, and others, settled in what is now Ewing, as appears from *their* deeds and family records; and in April, 1703, Mr. John Hutchinson (only son and heir of Thomas Hutchinson, who died intestate,) conveyed a lot of land to the inhabitants of Hopewell as a place of burial. The instrument conveying the lands is as follows, and may be found on page 114, A A A, folio 105, at the secretary of state's office, Trenton:

"John Hutchinson, of Hopewell, county of Burlington, &c., to Andrew Heath, Richard Ayre, Abiel Davis, and Zebulon Haston,† of the same county, &c., hath granted to the said Andrew Heath, &c., a piece of land on ‡ the easterly side of the highway leading between the house of the said John Hutchinson and Andrew Heath, &c., containing two acres, in trust for the inhabitants of the said township of Hopewell and their successors, inhabiting and dwelling within the said township, forever, for the public and common use and benefit of the whole township, for the erecting and building a public meeting-house thereon, and also for a place of burial, and for no other use, intent, or purpose whatsoever."

This probably was the first house built for public worship in the township of Hopewell and for Trenton, and probably the

---

* Leaming & Spicer, p. 583.

† Zebulon Haston lived on the place owned by the late Amos Reeder, which was bought by Isaac Reeder in 1707, of Mr. Haston.

‡ This lot has, within the last twenty-five years, been sold by the trustees of the Episcopal Church in Trenton to Ralph Lanning, and lies on an eminence about thirty rods northeast from his dwelling, and north of the State Lunatic Asylum.

first in the state, except that of the Quakers. It was occupied by the Episcopalians until their church was built in Trenton, and occasionally for many years afterwards. A portion of the foundation is still standing, and in it the stone which still consecrates the memory of Samuel Tucker, president of the second provincial congress of New Jersey, and state treasurer, as well as that of his wife, and several prominent citizens of Trenton of that day.

The Friends who had left England, on account of the persecution raised against them for their religion, sought an asylum on the peaceful shores of the Delaware, where they have, undisturbed, enjoyed the privileges of religious, as well as civil freedom. For many years they had no public buildings for worship, but their meetings were held in private houses.

"Governor William Penn, who, in the year 1683, issued an order for the establishment of a post-office, requested Phineas Pemberton carefully to publish the information on the *meeting-house door*, that is, on the door of the *private* house in which the Society of Friends were accustomed to meet. It was usual for Friends settled about the Falls (or Fallsington, in Bucks county), to assemble at the houses of William Yardley, James Harrison, Phineas Pemberton, William Biles, and William Beakes. For the meeting-house at the Falls was not built till 1690, nor the one at Burlington till 1696, nor the one at Bristol till 1710."*

The meeting house in Trenton city was built in 1739. This date was formerly on the building, but when it was repaired, in 1838, in rough-casting it they covered the date completely over, which certainly was an error on their part, as it should have been left as a monument, to designate a period prior to the struggle for American independence.†

The building is located on the corner of Hanover and Montgomery streets. It has been occupied for the same purpose since its erection up to the present time. The door of the entrance to the meeting-house was on the south side of it, facing Hanover

---

* "Friends' Miscellany," vol. vii., p. 29.

† In 1872 this date was again placed on the eastern end of the building.

street, and on the east gable was the inscription above mentioned

It seldom happens but that disasters of some kind befall the settlers of a new country. Change of climate, modes of living, the air, the soil, and other causes, not unfrequently occasion sickness and great mortality among them. This was the case, to a very alarming degree, among the first settlers on James river, Virginia, and also among those who landed on Plymouth rock, in Massachusetts. And many of the inhabitants of the vicinity of the *Falls* were visited with sickness, and were removed by death, by a malignant fever, which prevailed among them in 1687, both in Pennsylvania and New Jersey.*

Phineas Pemberton says, "that on the 16th of 3d month, (that is March 16th), 1687, there was 'a great land flood,' and on the 29th a rupture." This is supposed to refer to the formation of the island at Morrisville, opposite the Trenton bridge, which was at the time separated from the mainland.

The flood here referred to is probably the same as that mentioned by Mr. Smith, as occurring in 1692,† and there appears to be an error in one of the dates, for it is supposed that so great a rise in the waters as to overflow the banks on the Pennsylvania side of the Delaware river, at the falls, must have swept away the settlement on the lowlands, at the mouth of the Assanpink; and yet, this is said not to have occurred till 1692. The lands on the Jersey shore might, however, have been much higher than on the Pennsylvania side, and probably they were, as they were tilled till many years afterward.

Kalm, a Swede, who travelled in this country in 1748, says, "that his landlord in Trenton told him that twenty years before (1728), when he settled there, there was hardly more than *one* house."

In August, 1814, Mrs. Jemima Howell (youngest daughter of Mr. John Burroughs), who was born in the year 1724, informed a citizen of Trenton, that although she could not tell when the

---

* "Friends' Miscellany," vol. vii., p. 31.
† Smith's History, p. 208.

frame church (in Ewing) was built, yet she remembered that she had helped to scrub it, seventy years before. She said she also well remembered when there were but two or three small houses where the city of Trenton is built, and that it was woods from the neighborhood of the frame church to Mahlon Stacy's mill, on the Assanpink, the place lately occupied by Col. Edward B. Bingham, as a paper mill; that they had only a foot-path for many years after, and that the farmers carried their grain to market on pack horses.

Kalm says that in 1748 there were near a hundred houses in Trenton. The probability is, from the description he has given of the town, that he included the buildings on the north and south side of the Assanpink. He also says that there were two small churches—one belonging to the Church of England, and the other belonging to the Presbyterians. As Nottingham and Hopewell were settled almost entirely by Friends, there is reason to suppose that they were among the first to erect places of public worship, which was probably the fact, as their house was built in 1739. Nearly all the first buildings in the original city were on or near the York road (now Greene street), which led from Mahlon Stacy's mills.

When the assembly made the county of Hunterdon in 1714, they enacted that the Court of Common Pleas and Quarter Sessions should be held alternately at Maidenhead (Lawrenceville) and Hopewell, "until a court-house and gaol for the county should be built.*

An act was passed April 9th, 1679, "that the county courts should be held at one time in one town, and another time in another town,"† and accordingly they were held for the county of Hunterdon, in Maidenhead, in the months of June and December, and in Hopewell in March and September, from June, 1713, to September, 1719. The first courts in the county were held at Maidenhead on the second Tuesday of June, 1714, but at what house we are not informed.

---

* Laws and Ordinances, vol. i., p. 100, in State Library at Trenton.
† Leaming & Spicer, p. 116.

HISTORY OF NEW JERSEY. 321

Afterwards they were held at the house of Theophilus Phillips, William Osborn, Mr. Horner, and Daniel Bailey.

In Hopewell they were held first and subsequently at the house of Andrew Heath and the house of Robert Lanning, (the place afterwards owned by the heirs of Nathaniel Lanning).

In September, 1719, the courts were held in Trenton. "It having been represented to the governor that the holding the courts alternately in Maidenhead and Hopewell was attended with inconvenience, in March, 1719, he recommended that the courts should be held and kept in Trenton from the month of September next ensuing."*

The magistrates present at the first court in the county, held at Maidenhead, were John Bainbridge, Jacob Bellerjeau, Philip Phillips, William Greene, John Holcomb, Samuel Greene, and Samuel Fitch. There is a tombstone in the burying ground at Lamberton, containing the name of John Bainbridge which states, "he was a gentleman of great merit, and having the confidence of the people, was called to fill many important offices in the colony." And he was no doubt the ancestor of the Bainbridges in this part of the country, and of the late gallant Commodore Bainbridge.

William Greene and John Reading were the first assessors of Hunterdon, and Ralph Hunt, the first collector—these offices at that time being county instead of township offices, as they now are.

The first grand jurors were William Hixson, Daniel Howell, Robert Lanning, Henry Mershon, Richard Compton, George Woolsey, Joseph Reeder, Jr., Thomas Standling, Richard Scudder, Timothy Baker, John Burroughs, John Titus, Samue Everett, John Ely, and Richard Lanning.

John Muirheid, high sheriff, complained to the court in 1714 and 1717, and in June, 1719, and in March, 1720, that there was no gaol (or jail) for the county.

In 1728-9, John Dagworthy, Esq., high sheriff complained

---

* Laws and Ordinances, p. 223, State Library at Trenton.

X

to the court that the jail was so out of repair that escapes took place daily. "Ordered to be repaired."*

In 1714, the land became the property of Colonel Trent, and in 1719, if not before, the courts were held here part of the time under the act of April, 1676, "directing them to be held in the towns alternately."

In 1824 it was enacted "that the Supreme Court for the county of Hunterdon, be held in July, at Trent's-town."

About the year 1721, a log jail for the county was built at the forks of the road leading from Trenton to Pennington, and from Pennington to the Eight-Mile-Ferry, nearly opposite the residence of the late Jesse Moore, Esq.

From the complaint of the sheriff it appears that neither the jail nor the character of the inhabitants was much credit to the county if the criminals were so numerous and the prison so weak that escapes occurred daily.

Although the sheriff complained to the court of the daily escapes from the jail, there does not appear on the record of the court many criminal cases presented by the grand jury.

They found a bill at one term of the courts against a man "for stealing a *book* called the *New Testament*," and at another court against a man "for stealing a *horse bill*." Besides these, but very few bills were found.

A few years afterwards some of the most interesting trials took place which ever came before this court, in which the Rev. John Rowland was tried for theft, and the celebrated Presbyterian clergyman, Rev. William Tennent, pastor of the Church at Freehold, and Joshua Anderson and Benjamin Stevens, prominent members of the Presbyterian Church at Trenton, were tried for perjury.

The following is an account of that most singular affair:

"About the year 1744, there was an unusual attention to religion in this part of the country. The Rev. William Tennent and the Rev. John Rowland were considerably instrumental in calling the attention of the people to spiritual concerns.

---

* Minutes of the Court, vol. ii.

"Mr. Rowland's popularity and success was very great among all ranks of people, and this drew upon him the enmity of those who disregarded religious truth, and among the number was the Chief Justice of the state.

"The Chief Justice at this time was the son of Lewis Morris, Esq., then governor of the state. He was a member of the council as well as being at the head of the judiciary. The appointment of young Morris to this office was highly reprobated by the people, who opposed the union of the legislative and judiciary, and more especially as this union was in the person of the son of the governor.*

"At this time there was a man traveling about the country by the name of Tom Bell, of notoriously bad character, who had been indicted in most of the middle colonies, yet by his ingenuity and cunning had contrived to escape punishment. It happened one evening, that Mr. John Stockton, of Princeton, met with Bell at a tavern in that place and addressed him as Mr. Rowland. Bell told him his mistake. Mr. Stockton informed him that his error had arisen from his remarkable resemblance to Mr. Rowland.

"This hint was sufficient for Bell. The next day he went into a neighboring town in Hunterdon, where Mr. Rowland had preached once or twice, and introduced himself as the Rev. Mr. Rowland who had before preached for them; and he was invited to officiate for them the next Sabbath.

"Bell received the kindest attention of the family where he staid until the Sabbath, when he rode with the family in their wagon to the church.

"Just before they reached the church, Bell discovered that he had left his *notes* behind, and proposed to the master of the family, who rode by the wagon on a fine horse, to take his horse and ride back, that he might get his notes and return in time for the services. To this the gentleman assented, and Bell mounted the horse, rode back to the house, rifled the desk of his host, and made off with the horse; and wherever he stopped he called himself the Rev. John Rowland.

---

* Mulford's History, p. 345.

"At this time the Rev. Messrs. Tennent and Rowland, with Mr. Joshua Anderson and Benjamin Stevens, were in Maryland or Pennsylvania, on business of a religious nature. Soon after their return to New Jersey, Mr. Rowland was charged with the robbery. At the court, the judge with great severity, charged the jury to find a bill. But it was not until they had been sent out the fourth time, with threats from the judge, that they agreed upon a bill for the alleged crime.

"On the trial, Messrs. Tennent, Anderson, and Stevens, appeared as witnesses, and fully proved an *alibi:* for they testified that on the day the robbery was committed they were with Mr. Rowland, and heard him preach in Pennsylvania or Maryland.

"So Mr. Rowland was acquitted, to the great disappointment and mortification of his persecutors. Their enmity to religion, however, led them industriously to seek occasion, if by any possible means, they might bring disgrace and ruin upon these servants of God.

"There were one or two circumstances which seemed to inspire the hope that their malicious feelings might yet be gratified. The testimony of the man who had been robbed was positive that Mr. Rowland was the robber; and several persons who had seen the man who called himself Rowland, in possession of the stolen horse, corroborated his testimony.

"But Mr. Rowland was out of their power. He had been acquitted.

"Their vengeance, therefore, was directed against those persons by whose testimony Rowland had been cleared, and *they* were accordingly accused of *perjury*, and on *ex parte* testimony, the grand jury found bills of indictment against Messrs. Tennent, Anderson, and Stevens, ' for willful and corrupt perjury.'

" Now the enemies of the gospel and revivals of religion appear to have thought that their end would be easily accomplished and that disgrace would be brought on religion, its ministers, and professors, for Messrs. Anderson and Stevens were pious men. These indictments were removed to the Supreme Court. But Mr. Anderson, living in the county, and feeling his entire innocence of the crime of which he was charged, and being unwilling to lie under the imputation of perjury, demanded a trial at the first Court of Oyer and Terminer.

"He was accordingly tried, pronounced guilty, and sentenced to stand on the court-house steps one hour with a paper on his breast, on which was written in large letters, '*this is for willful and corrupt perjury.*' And the sentence was executed upon him in front of the court-house, which stood on the spot where the Trenton Bank now stands, in Warren street.

"Messrs. Tennent and Stevens were bound over to appear at the next court.

"They attended, having employed Mr. John Coxe, an eminent lawyer, to conduct their defence. Mr. Tennent knew of no person living by whom he could prove his innocence. His only resource and consolation was to commit himself to the Divine will;* and considering it as probable that he might suffer, he had prepared a sermon to preach from the pillory, if that should be his fate. On his arrival at Trenton, he found Mr. Smith of New York, one of the ablest lawyers in America, and a religious man, who had volunteered to aid in his defence; also Mr. John Kinsey, one of the first counselors of Philadelphia, who had come by request of Gilbert Tennent (his brother) for the same purpose.

"Messrs. Tennent and Stevens met these gentlemen at Mr. Coxe's the morning before the trial was to come on.

"Mr. Coxe wished them to bring in their witnesses, that they might examine them before going into court. Mr. Tennent replied that he did not know of any witness but God and his own conscience. Mr. Coxe replied, 'If you have no witnesses, sir, the trial must be put off; otherwise, you will most certainly be defeated. Your enemies are making great exertions to ruin you.'

"'I am sensible of this,' said Mr. Tennent, 'yet it never shall be said that I have delayed the trial or been afraid to meet the justice of my country. I know my innocence, and that God

---

* His affectionate congregation felt deeply interested in his critical situation, and kept a day of fasting and prayer on the occasion.—" Log College."

whom I serve will not give me over into the hands of the enemy. Therefore, gentlemen, go on with the trial.' Messrs. Smith and Kinsey, who were religious men, told him that his confidence and trust in God as a Christian minister of the gospel were well founded, and before a heavenly tribunal would be all-important to him, but assured him that they would not avail in an earthly court, and urged his consent to put off the trial. But Mr. Tennent utterly refused.

"Mr. Coxe then told him that there was a flaw in the indictment, of which he might avail himself. After hearing an explanation from Mr. Coxe, respecting the nature of the error, Mr. Tennent declared that he would rather suffer death than consent to such a course. Mr. Stevens, however, seized the opportunity afforded, and was discharged.

"Mr. Tennent assured his counsel that his confidence in God was so strong, and his assurance that He would bring about his deliverance in some way or other, was so great, that he did not wish them to delay the trial for a moment.

"Mr. Coxe still urged Mr. Tennent to have the trial put off, and considering Mr. Tennent's refusal as manifesting a want of Christian meekness and prudence. But Mr. T. insisted that they should proceed, and left them, they not knowing how to act, when the bell summoned them to court.

"Mr. Tennent had not walked far before he was met by at man and his wife, who asked if his name was not Tennent.

"He told them it was, and asked if they had any business with him.

"The man said they had come from the place in Pennsylvania or Maryland where, at a particular time, Messrs. Rowland, Tennent Anderson, and Stevens had lodged, and in the house where they were; that on the next day they had heard Messrs. Tennent and Rowland preach; that a few nights before they (the man and his wife) had left home, on waking out of a sound sleep, both had dreamed that Mr. Tennent was at Trenton, in the greatest distress, and that it was in their power, and theirs *only*, to relieve him. This dream was twice repeated to them both, and so deep was the impression made on their minds, that they had come to Trenton, and wished to know of him what they were to do.

"Mr. T. took them before his counsel, who, after examining them, and finding the testimony of the man and his wife full and to the purpose, were perfectly astonished. Before the trial began, another person came to Mr. T., and told him that he was so troubled in mind, for the part he had taken in the prosecution, that he could find no rest, till he had determined to come out and make a full confession. Mr. T. sent this man to his counsel. Soon after Mr. Stockton, from Princeton, appeared, and added his testimony.

"On trial, the advocates of the defendant so traced every movement of Mr. Tennent, on the Saturday, Sabbath, and Monday, the time of the theft and robbery by Bell, that the jury did not hesitate to acquit Mr. Tennent.

"Thus was Mr. Tennent, by the remarkable interposition of Divine Providence, delivered out of the hands of his enemies."*

Colonel William Trent was a gentleman of great respectability, and was for several years speaker of the house of assembly of Pennsylvania, and in September, 1723, he was chosen speaker of the house of assembly of New Jersey. In this year William Trent and John Reading were appointed commissioners for the county of Hunterdon. Mr. Trent died December 25th, 1724.† It is supposed by some that he died in Philadelphia, but I believe it is not known to a certainty.

In 1726, the legislative assembly granted to James Trent, the oldest son of William Trent, the exclusive use of the river Delaware for a ferry, two miles above and two miles below the falls. The ferry above the falls has been in use until within the last thirty years, and was a short distance above Calhoun street, while the one below the falls was used until the Delaware bridge was erected in 1804–5. This last ferry was on the direct route between New York and Philadelphia.

---

* "Log College," by A. Alexander, D. D., p. 189.
† Smith's History, p. 419.

CHAPTER XV.

1744—1757.

Meeting of New Jersey Troops—Troubles between the governor and the two houses—The Indians favor the French and oppose the English—Plan of union proposed—Not satisfactory to the English or the people of the provinces—Virginia raises troops and places them under command of Colonel Washington.

AFTER the formal declaration of war by the English, March 24th, 1744, and the matter was laid before the assembly of New Jersey, by President Hamilton, on the 12th of June, they resolved, as stated in a previous chapter, to raise and equip five hundred men for this service. The enterprise met with such favor, that, in less than two months, six hundred and sixty men offered for enlistment. From these five companies were formed for this province, and the sixth was transferred to the quota of New York. These troops under the command of Colonel Philip Schuyler, reached the appointed rendezvous at Albany, on the 3d of September, and found the proposed expedition had been abandoned, in consequence of the failure of England to send forward the forces promised by them; they remained until autumn of the next year, serving to overawe the Indians, and protect the frontier from their incursions and depredations The pay promised by the crown was tardily forwarded, and the troops at the rendezvous became impatient in consequence of the delay. Not so with New Jersey, for the bounties promised them was punctually paid, and the state made ample provision for their comfort. In consequence of the failure on the part of England to pay them, the New Jersey troops mutinied in April, 1747, and determined to leave, with their arms and baggage, unless their arrears were paid up. Colonel Schuyler at once despatched a messenger to President Hamilton, to lay the facts before him, and ascertain what could be done in the matter to avert so dire a disaster. The president recommended to the assembly, to provide for the pay, but the house having expended more than twenty thousand pounds in equipping, transporting and subsisting the troops, declined to make any further appropriations, and they were detained in the service chiefly by the generous aid of the colonel, who supplied the wants of the soldiers, by advancing many thousand pounds from his own private funds. The proposed attack on the French possessions in Canada originated with Governor Shirley of Massachusetts, who prevailed upon the ministry to undertake the expedition. A squadron of ships of war, having on board a body of land forces, commanded by Sir John St. Clair, was, as early as the season would permit, to join the troops of New England at Louisburg, from whence they were to proceed by the St. Lawrence to Quebec. Those from New York, and the more southern provinces were to be collected at Albany, and to march thence against Crown Point and Montreal. So far as this plan was concerned, it was carried out with promptness and alacrity, upon the part of the colonies. The men were raised, and waited impatiently for employment, but neither general, troops, nor orders arrived from England, and therefore the provincial forces continued in a state of inactivity, until the ensuing autumn, when they were disbanded. This affair was one of the thousand instances of incapacity and misrule, which the parent state inflicted upon her dependent American progeny. No further material transactions took place in America during the war, and on the 30th of April, preliminary articles of peace were signed, but hostilities continued in Europe and on the ocean, until October, 1748, when the final treaty was executed at Aix-la-Chapelle, in which the great object of the war was wholly disregarded, the right of the British to navigate the American seas free from search, being unnoticed. The island of Cape Breton, with Louisburg, its capital, so dearly purchased by provincial blood and treasure, was given up under the stipulation, that all conquests should be restored, and the Americans had great cause to condemn the indifference or ignorance, which exposed them to future vexation and renewed hostilities by neglecting to ascertain the boundaries of the French and English territories on the American continent.

President Hamilton, whose health was in a very precarious state at the time the government devolved upon him, died about the middle of the summer of 1747, and was succeeded by John Reading, Esq., the next oldest counsellor, who was soon after displaced by the appointment of Jonathan Belcher, Esq., by the crown. General harmony prevailed between him and the legislature for the space of ten years. In his administration he manifested entire submission to the wishes of the assembly, where they did not interfere with his instructions from the crown. When acts of the assembly did so interfere, he preferred rather to throw himself back on the royal will, than to take issue with them.

He was a man who used few words of his own, but when required to communicate to the house, preferred using those of the ministry, or the petitioner or agent, as the case might be, rarely adding any comments of his own, or expressing any preference upon the subject.

If charged with a failure in his duty, he never resented it in such a way as to create resistance. He was not imperturbable, and though sometimes severely tried by the assembly, by suspension of his salary, he was unmoved.

Two questions arising out of proprietary interests, vexed the whole term of his administration, and though he earnestly endeavored to avoid becoming a party to them, he was made a sufferer in the contests between the council and assembly. There had been no important controversy between the grantees of Carteret and the Elizabethtown claimants, under the Indian title, for more than thirty years. But this peace was occasioned by Carteret not enforcing his title or endeavoring to collect the rents. A large quantity of East Jersey lands, under Carteret's title, had got into the hands of Robert Hunter Morris, and James Alexander, Esquires, both of whom held important offices in the province, the one being Chief Justice, the other Secretary, and both had been members of the council. These gentlemen, with other extensive proprietors, during the life of Governor Morris, and towards the close of his administration, commenced actions of ejectment, and suits for the recovery of quit-rents against many of the settlers.

They immediately resorted to their Indian title for defence, and formed an association consisting of a large proportion of the inhabitants of the eastern part of Middlesex, the whole of Essex, part of Somerset, and part of Morris counties, and by their union and violence, they were enabled to bid defiance to the law, to hold possession of the lands which were fairly within the Indian grant, and to add to their party a great many persons who could not, even under that grant, claim exemption from proprietary demands. The prisons were no longer sufficient to keep those whom the laws condemned to confinement, for in the month of September, 1745, the *associators* broke open the jail of the county of Essex, and liberated a prisoner, committed at the suit of the proprietors; and during several consecutive years, all persons confined for like cause, or on charge of high treason and rebellion for resisting the laws were released at the will of the insurgents, so that the arm of government was in this respect wholly paralyzed. Persons who had long held under the proprietaries were forcibly ejected, others were compelled to take leases from landlords, whom they were not disposed to acknowledge; and those who had courage to stand out, were threatened with, and in many instances, received personal violence.

The council and the governor were inclined to view these unlawful proceedings in the darkest colors, and to treat the disturbers of the peace, as insurgents, rebels and traitors, and to inflict upon them the direst severity of the laws. They prepared and sent to the assembly a riot act, modeled after that of Great Britain, making it felony without benefit of clergy,* for

---

* Benefit of the clergy, in English law, originally, the exemption of the persons of clergymen from criminal process before a secular judge; a privilege which was extended to all who could read, such persons being in the eye of the law, "clerici," or clerks. But this privilege has been abridged and modified by various statutes. [See Blackstone, 4 b. ch. 28.] In the United States no benefit of clergy exists; for our common and public schools contemplates that every person should read and write.

Previous to 1672, the benefit of clergy was prayed for and allowed as in

twelve or more tumultuously assembled together, to refuse to disperse upon the requisition of the civil authority, by proclamation, in form set forth by the act.

The assembly not only rejected this bill, but sought to give a more favorable color to the offences of the associators. The council of the proprietors sent a petition to the king, signed by Andrew Johnson, their president, and dated December 23d, 1748, setting forth, "that great numbers of men taking advantage of a dispute subsisting between the branches of the legislature of the province, and of a most unnatural rebellion at that time reigning in Great Britain, had entered into a combination to subvert the laws and constitution of this province, and to obstruct the course of legal proceedings; to which end they endeavored to infuse into the minds of the people, that neither your majesty nor your noble progenitors, Kings and Queens of England, had any right whatever to the soil or government of America, and that their grants were void and fraudulent; and having by these means associated to themselves great numbers of the poor and ignorant part of the people, they, in the month of September, 1745, began to carry into execution their wicked schemes; when in a riotous manner, they broke open the goal of the county of Essex, and took from thence a prisoner, there confined by due process of law; and have since that time, gone on like a torrent, bearing all down before them, dispossessing some people of their estates, and giving them to accomplices; plundering the estates of others who do not join with them, and dividing the spoil among them; breaking open the prisons as often as any of them are committed, rescuing their accomplices, keeping daily in armed numbers,

---

England. In one instance, the entry of the minutes of the Court of Oyer and Terminer is, "the prisoners being asked if they had anything to say why sentence of death should not be passed on them, according to the verdict found against them, prayed the benefit of clergy; the court being of the opinion that they were entitled to the benefit of their clergy, their judgment is that they be branded in the brawn of the left thumb with the letter T, immediately in the face of the court, which sentence was executed accordingly; and ordered that they be recommitted till their fees are paid, and they each enter into recognizance in one hundred pounds, to be of good behaviour for one year."

and traveling often in armed multitudes to different parts of the province for those purposes; so that your Majesty's government and laws have, for above three years last past, ceased to be that protection to the lives and properties of the people here, which Your Majesty intended they should be.

"These bold and daring people, not in the least regarding their allegiance, have presumed to establish courts of justice, to appoint captains and officers over Your Majesty's subjects, to lay and collect taxes, and to do many other things in contempt of Your Majesty's authority, to which they refuse any kind of obedience.

"That all the endeavors of the government to put the laws in execution, have been hitherto vain; for, notwithstanding many of these common disturbers stand indicted for high treason, in levying war against Your Majesty, yet such is the weakness of the government, that it has not been able to bring one of them to trial and punishment. That the petitioners have long waited in expectation of a vigorous interposition of the legislature, in order to give force to the laws, and enable Your Majesty's officers to carry them into execution. But the house of assembly after neglecting the thing for a long time, have, at last, refused to afford the government any assistance, for want of which your petitioner's estates are left a prey to a rebellious mob, and Your Majesty's government exposed to the repeated insults of a set of traitors."

The assembly knew nothing of this petition of the proprietors, until they had received a copy of it by the agent of the province, and in October, 1749, they sent a counter petition to the King, in which they vindicated their conduct, and declared, "that the proprietories of East New Jersey had, from the first settlement, patented and divided their lands by concession among themselves, in such manner, as from thence many irregularities had ensued, which had occasioned multitudes of controversies and law suits, about titles and boundaries of land. That these controversies had subsisted between a number of poor people on the one part, and some of the rich, understanding and powerful on the other part; among whom where James Alexander, Esq., a great proprietor, and an eminent lawyer, one of your Majesty's council, and surveyor general for this colony, although a dweller in New York, and Robert Hunter Morris, Esq., Chief Justice, and one of your Majesty's council in said colony. That the said Alexander and Morris, not yielding to determine the matter in contest by a few trials at law, as the nature of the thing would admit, but on the contrary, discovering a disposition to harass those people, by a multiplicity of suits, the last mentioned became uneasy (as we conceive) through fear, that those suits might be determined against them, when considered, that the said Chief Justice Morris was son of the then late Governor Morris, by whose commission the other judges of the supreme court acted, and by whom the then sheriffs throughout the colony had been appointed; and should a multiplicity of suits have been determined against the people, instead of a few only, which would have answered the purpose, the extraordinary and unnecessary charges occasioned thereby, would have so far weakened their hands as to have rendered them unable to appeal to Your Majesty in council, from whom they might expect impartial justice. That these are, in the opinion of the house, the motives that prevailed on these unthinking people, to obstruct the course of legal proceedings, and not at any disaffection to Your Majesty's person or government."*

If the council of proprietors, supported by the legislative council, was disposed to aggravate the offences of the insurgents into high treason, it is apparent that the assembly were not less resolved, to consider them of a very venial character, and their conduct, upon this occasion, was highly disingenious. The house could not refuse from time to time, to condemn in strong terms, the conduct of the rioters; but, no representation of the governor or council, could induce them, either to pass the riot act, or to arm the executive with military force, to capture the rioters, guard the prisons, or protect the public peace. If, indeed, the insurgents possessed a colorable title to the lands, and had been oppressed by a multiplicity of suits, which they were disposed to render unnecessary by submission to the law as apparent on the decision of a few; if they had been content

---

* Votes of assembly.

with defending their own possessions, without disturbing those of others, the representations of the assembly might have been less reprehensible. But the title of the insurgents was, on its merits, wholly unsustainable in an English court of justice, where a mere Indian right could never prevail against the grant of the King. The true solution of the course taken by the assembly will be found, most probably, in their sympathy for the rioters, and their hostility towards the leading members of the council, who were large proprietors. The public peace, from this cause, continued unsettled for several years.

The administration of Governor Belcher, was also perplexed by a difference between the council and assembly, on a bill for ascertaining the value of taxable property in each county, for the purpose of making a new apportionment of their respective quotas. Among other property directed to be returned by this " Quota bill," as it was termed, was "*the whole of all profitable tracts of land held by patent, deed, or survey, whereon any improvement is made.*" To this cause the council took exception on two grounds, first, that it was in contravention of the royal instruction prohibiting the governor from consenting to any act to tax unprofitable lands; and second, that it would be gross injustice, by taxing lands according to their quantity, and not according to their quality. Since tracts of lands might, and probably would be deemed *profitable*, when the greater number of acres were wholly unproductive. The council, therefore, proposed to amend the act, by declaring that nothing therein was intended to break in upon the royal instructions, or to warrant the assessors to include any unprofitable lands in their lists. The house roused by this attempt to modify what they deemed a money bill, denied the right of the council to amend such bill, and refused themselves to alter it, so as to remove the objection. The failure to pass the " Quota bill," deprived all the state officers of their salaries during the year.

A few extracts from the messages between the council and assembly, will show the manner in which these bodies treated each other, and also show the form and color of the times. Thus the council, in their address to the assembly, February 19th, 1750, says:

"The assembly in their message, and in their address to his excellency, accuse us of having taken liberties upon us; as to which we think we have taken none, but what were our just right to take. But the liberties the assembly have taken with His Majesty, with his excellency our governor, with the magistrates of this and other counties, and with us, by those papers, and during this and former sessions, (as will appear by their minutes), and by spreading base, false, scandalous, and injurious libels against us, we believe all sober and reasonable men will think unjustifiable—God only knows the hearts and thoughts of men. They have, it seems to us, even not left this province uninvaded, for they take upon them to suggest our thoughts to be *not out of any great regard to His Majesty's instruction, that we have been lead to make our amendment, but to exempt our large tracts of land from taxes*,* when they well knew, that a majority of this house, are not owners of large tracts of land, and those who have such, do declare they never had the least thought of having their lands exempted from taxes, consistent with reason and His Majesty's instructions."

The house, in their democratic pride, did not deign to reply directly to this reproach. But they ordered an entry to be made upon their minutes, declaring—

"That it would be taking up too much time at the public expense, for the house to make any particular answer thereto, nor indeed is it necessary, when considered, that the message itself will discover the council's aim, in having the improved part only, of tracts of land, taken an account of, in future taxation, which, if admitted, would exempt the unimproved parts of such tracts from paying any part of the public tax. So that, should a gentleman be possessed of a tract of ten thousand acres of land, in one tract, worth ten thousand pounds, and only fifty acres of it improved; and a poor freeholder should be possessed of a tract of one hundred acres only, worth but one hundred pounds, and fifty acres of it improved, the poor freeholder must pay as much as the gentleman, and this we may venture to

---

* Some of the council of proprietors were large land holders in the province.

say, (without invading the province of God, which the council are pleased to charge us with,) would be the obvious consequence of the bill in question, if passed in the manner the council insist; and why a poor man, worth only one hundred pounds, should pay as much tax as a gentleman worth ten thousand pounds, will be difficult for the council to show a reason, but at present, we may set it down as a difficult and surprising expedient, indeed to favor the poor."

They accused the council, "instead of making it appear that they had a right to amend the bill, as they have repeatedly resolved they had, unhappily fallen into the railing language of the meanest class of mankind, in such a manner, that had it not been sent to this house by one of the members, no man could imagine that it was composed by a deliberate determination of a set of men who pretend to sit as a branch of the legislature. For towards the close of the above said message, they charge us with having taken liberties with His Majesty, with his excellency our governor, with the magistrates of this, and other counties, and with our having spread false, scandalous, and injurious libels against them, the said council; which they say they believe all sober and reasonable men will think unjustifiable.

"What liberties we have taken with His Majesty, otherwise than to assert our loyalty to him, in our address to the governor, we know not. What liberties we have taken with the governor, unless it be to tell him the true reason of the government being so long unsupported, and to represent the public grievances to him, for redress, we know not.

"What liberties we have taken with the gentlemen of the council, other than to tell them the truth, in modest plain English, we know not. What liberties we have taken with the magistrates of this and other counties, unless it be to inquire into their conduct, upon complaints, and after a fair and impartial hearing, to represent their arbitrary and illegal proceedings, for redress, we know not: and wherein we have been guilty of spreading false, scandalous and injurious libels against the council, we know not.

"Therefore, it will be incumbent on them to point out, and

duly prove some undue liberties we have taken, and libels spread, before any sober and reasonable men will be prevailed on to condemn our proceedings, as unjustifiable; which we think they will not do upon the slender authority of the council's insulting message to this house; which, in our opinion, is so far from being likely to prevail on any sober and reasonable men, to believe the false, scurulous, and groundless charges therein alleged against us. That it will rather discover the council to be men at least under the government of passion, if not void of reason and truth, until they recover the right use of their reason again, it will be fruitless for this house to spend time in arguing with them."

While these important branches of the government, ceased to treat each other with ordinary respect, it was impossible that the public business could be carried on, and the governor wisely dissolved the assembly.

On the 20th of May, 1751, the new house met, and consisted of a majority of new members, and being disposed to despatch the affairs of the province, they passed the quota bill, in a form which dissipated the objections formerly urged against it, classifying lands according to their quality, and making all which could in any way be deemed profitable, liable to taxation, at a rate depending on their actual value.

This difficulty was however scarcely removed, before another, partaking of the same character, arose. In adopting a new act for the support of the government, to the principles furnished by the quota act, the council assumed the right to amend the bill, although such right had always been peremptorily denied them by the house, in relation to all money bills, and in the present case their amendments were unanimously rejected. The assembly in their determination to maintain their point, in this respect, sought to get over the difficulty by making the governor a party to the bill in their favor, and for that purpose, after it had been returned by the council, they sent it up directly to him, that he might place it again before that body, together with his influence, in order to secure its passage. This course, if carried out, would have brought the form of administering the government back to that which it possessed before the alteration made by Governor Morris, when the governor had a seat with, and debated with council. But Governor Belcher declined to receive their bill, and the house being unable to further continue, it was prorogued, and the public treasury still continued empty. It was not until the month of February, 1752, after near four years' delay, that a bill for the support of government received the sanction of the different branches of the legislative powers of the government.

The treaty of Aix-la-Chapelle, which, in Europe, was but a hollow truce, was scarce regarded by the French in America, for, eager to extend their territories and to connect their northern possessions with Louisiana, they projected a line of forts and military positions from the one to the other, along the Mississippi and Ohio rivers. They explored and occupied the land upon the Ohio, buried in many places through the country, metal plates with inscriptions, declaring their claims. They caressed and threatened the Indians by turns; scattered liberal presents, and prepared to compel by force what was refused by kindness.

The enterprise and industry of the French with the Indians, were in strong contrast with the coldness and apathy of the English. After the peace of 1748, the English discontinued their attentions, even to those Indians they had induced to take up arms. They suffered the captives to remain unransomed; their families to pine in want, and utterly disregarded the children of the slain; while the French proved themselves attentive to the interest of their allies, dressed them in finery, and loaded them with presents. They might have exercised a still greater influence over them, had they not sought to convert them to the Roman Catholic faith; for the Indians in their simplicity fancied that the religious ceremonies were arts to reduce them to slavery. By this policy the French had succeeded in estranging the Indians on the Ohio, and in dividing the councils of the Six Nations; drawing off the Onondagoes, Cayugas and Senecas. Their progress with these tribes were rendered still more dangerous by the death of several chiefs, who had been in the English interest, and by the advances of the British in the western country without the consent of the aborigines.

To prosecute the views of territorial acquisition and seduction of the Indians, the French attacked the Twightees, and slew many in order to punish them for adhering to the British, and protecting English traders.

The Ohio company having surveyed large tracts of land upon the Ohio river, with the design of settlement, the governor of Canada remonstrated with the governors of New York and Pennsylvania, upon the invasion of the French territories, and threatened to resort to force, unless the English traders abandoned their intercourse with the Indians. The threats being disregarded, he captured some traders, and sent them to France, whence they retired without redress. He also opened a communication from Presque Isle by French creek, and the Alleghany river to the Ohio, and though the Six Nations forbade him to occupy the Ohio lands, he despised the present weakness of those tribes.

Governor Dinwiddie, of Virginia, learning that the French designed to proceed southward from Fort Venango, on French creek, despatched an agent, for the purpose of gaining intelligence and remonstrating against their designs. For this duty Mr. George Washington, then a young man under twenty years of age, was selected.

He left the frontier with several attendants on the 14th of November, 1753, and after a journey of two months over mountain and torrent, through morass and forest, braving the inclemency of the winter and the howling wilderness, and many dangers from Indian hostility, he returned with the answer of Legardeau de St. Pierre, the French commandant upon the Ohio, dated at the fort, upon Le Boeuff river. The French referred the discussion of the rights of the two countries to the Marquis du Quesne, governor in chief of Canada, by whose orders he had assumed, and meant to sustain his present position. From De la Joncaire, a captain in the French service, and Indian interpreter, Washington received full information of the designs of the French. They founded their claims to the Ohio river, and its appurtenances, on the discovery of La Salle, sixty years before, and their present measures for its defence, had grown out of the attempts of the Ohio company to occupy its banks.

The British ministry understanding the views and operations of the French nation on the American contínent, remonstrated with the court of Versailles. But while that court publicly instructed the governor of Canada to refrain from hostilities, to demolish the fortress at Niagara, to deliver up the captured traders and to punish their captors, it privately informed him, that strict obedience was not expected. Deceived and insulted, the English monarch resolved to oppose force by force, and the American governors were directed to repel the encroachments of any foreign prince or state.

The English force in America, numerically considered, was much greater than that of the French, but divided among many and independent sections, its combined efforts were feeble and sluggish, while the French, directed by one will, had the advantages of union and promptitude, and drew the happiest hopes from the boldest enterprises. To resist them, effectually, some confederacy of the colonies was necessary, and common prudence required that the affections of the Indians towards the English should be assured. A conference between the Six Nations and the representatives of the colonies, was ordered by the ministry, under the direction of Governor De Lancy, of New York. This order was communicated to the assembly of New Jersey, by Governor Belcher, on the 25th of April, 1754. But the house refused on this, as they had upon every other occasion, heretofore, to take part in the Indian treaties, assigning as a reason, that their province had no participation in the Indian trade; they professed, however, their readiness to contribute their assistance to the other colonies, towards preventing the encroachments of the French on His Majesty's dominions, but declaring their present inability to do aught on account of the poverty of their treasury. The reluctance displayed by the assembly upon this subject, together with their rude reply to a remonstrance from the governor, so provoked him that he dissolved them.

The Six Nations, although large presents were made them, were cold to the instances of the confederate council, which met on the

14th of June. Few attended, and it was evident that the affection of all towards the English had diminished. They refused to enter into a coalition against the French, but consented to assist in driving them from the positions they had assumed in the west, and to renew former treaties.

In this convention of the colonies, several plans for political union were submitted, and that devised by Benjamin Franklin, of which the following is an outline, was adopted on the 4th of July. "A general colonial government was to be formed, to be administered by a president-general, appointed and paid by the crown; and a grand council of forty-eight members to be chosen for three years by the colonial assemblies, to meet at Philadelphia the first time at the call of the president. After the first three years, the number of members from each colony was to be in the ratio of the revenue paid by it to the public treasury.

"The grand council was to meet statedly, annually, and might be specially convened, in case of emergency by the president. It was empowered to choose its speaker, and could not be dissolved, prorogued or kept together longer than six weeks at one time, without its consent, or the special commands of the crown. They were, with the president-general, to hold or direct all Indian treaties, in which the general interest of the colonies were concerned, and to make peace and to declare war with Indian nations. To purchase for the crown from the Indians, lands not within particular colonies. To make new settlements on such purchase, by granting lands in the King's name, reserving quit rents to the crown, for the use of the general treasury. To make laws regulating and governing such new settlements until they should be formed into particular governments; to raise soldiers; build forts and equip vessels of war; and for these purposes to make laws and levy taxes. To appoint a general treasurer, and a particular treasurer in each government. Disbursements to be made only on an appropriation by law, or by joint order of the president and council.

"The general accounts to be settled yearly, and reported to the several assemblies. Twenty-five members to form a quorum of the council, there being present one or more from a majority of the colonies. The assent of the president general was requisite to all acts of the council, and it was his duty to execute them. The laws enacted were to be as like as possible to those of England, and to be transmitted to the king in council for approval, as soon as might be after their enactment, and if not disproved within three years, to remain in force. On the death of the president general, the speaker was to succeed him, and to hold his office until the pleasure of the king should be known. Military and naval officers acting under this constitution, were to be appointed by the president, and approved by the council; and the civil officers to be nominated by the council and approved by the president; and in case of vacancy in the civil or military service, the governor of the province in which it happened, was to appoint until the pleasure of the president and council should be ascertained."

This plan was submitted to the board of trade in England, and to the assemblies of the several provinces; Franklin says its fate was singular. The assemblies rejected it as containing too much prerogative, while in England, it was condemned as too democratic. Had it been adopted, the projector might have been famed as the forger of a nation's chains, instead of the destroyer of a tyrant's sceptre. As a substitute, the British ministry proposed that the governors of the colonies, with one or more members of the respective councils, should resolve on the measures of defence, and draw on the British treasury for the money required, to be refunded by a general tax, imposed by parliament on the colonies. But this proposition was deemed inadmissible by the provinces. The "plan of union," as adopted by the congress, was laid before the assembly of New Jersey in October. The house voted that if it should be carried into effect, "it might be prejudicial to the prerogative of the crown, and to the liberties of the people." They instructed their agent at court to petition the king and parliament against its ratification.

Virginia had raised three hundred men, under Colonel Fry and Lieutenant Colonel Washington. The latter marched with two companies to the Great Meadows, in the Alleghany mountains, and having learned that the French had dispersed a party, who had been employed by the Ohio company to erect a fort on the Monongahela river, and who were themselves raising fortifications at the confluence of that river with the Alleghany, and that a detachment was then approaching his camp.

Being convinced of the hostile intentions of this party, Washington resolved to anticipate them. Guided by his Indians, under cover of a dark and rainy night, he surprised the French encampment, and captured the whole party, except one who fled, and Jumonville, the commanding officer, who was killed. Soon after the whole regiment united at the Great Meadows. They were reinforced by two independent companies of regulars, one from South Carolina and the other from New York, forming an effective force of five hundred men.

In consequence of the death of Colonel Fry, the command devolved upon Colonel Washington, who was at this time under age. Having erected a stockade to protect their horses and provisions, they marched to dislodge the enemy at Fort Du Quesne. Their progress was arrested by information of the advance of twelve hundred French and Indians. As the Americans had been six days without bread, and had but a small supply of meat remaining, and fearing the enemy would cut them off from their stores, they resolved to retreat to their stockade, to which they gave the name of Fort Necessity.

Colonel Washington commenced a ditch around this post, but before he could complete it, he was attacked by the French force under Monsieur de Villiars. The troops made an obstinate defence, fighting partly within the stockade, and partly in the ditch, half filled with mud and water, from ten o'clock in the morning until dark, when de Villiars demanded a parley, and offered terms of capitulation. During the night, articles were signed allowing the garrison the honors of war, to retain their arms and baggage, and to return home unmolested. The last clause was not strictly kept, the Indians harassing and plundering the Americans during their retreat. The courage and conduct of Washington on this occasion, was greatly applauded, and laid the foundation for his future greatness. The assembly of Virginia voted their thanks to him and his officers. The French retired to their post on the Ohio.* The French nation strongly reprobated the attack on the part of Jumonville, it having been without summons or expostulation. They declared that while peace prevailed between the two nations, hostility should not have been presumed. The death of Jumonville was called by them an assassination, even in the capitulation of Fort Necessity, the attack upon which, they state to have been made in consequence of the outrage upon their advance party. These allegations were refuted, by a review of the conduct of the French, since the development of their designs upon the Ohio. The capture of the persons and property of the settlers, at Logtown, and of the Indian traders, wherever found in the western country, afforded conclusive evidence of their intention to try the disputed title by force, and they could not, justly, complain of the reply to their argument.†

The French completed Fort Du Quesne, at the confluence of the Monongahela and Alleghany rivers, which is now the thriving city of Pittsburg. They garrisoned it with one thousand regulars, with an ample supply of cannon, provisions, and other munitions, and prepared to occupy the country of the Twightees, with numerous settlers. The Six Nations were now more numerous on the western waters than they were in their ancient location; they were indifferent to the cause of the English, and were divided among themselves, and it was with great difficulty that they maintained their neutrality. Some of them had removed to Canada, preferring the protection of the active and enterprising French commanders. The small body of the English troops on the frontiers was weakened by desertions and demoralized, the Indians who still adhered to their interest retired to Aughwick, in Pennsylvania, and there proclaimed their admiration of the courage of the enemy, and their contempt

---

* Marshall's Washington. Bradford's journal, Review of military operations in North America. London, 1757.

† Colonel Washington, who was ignorant of the French language, was unable to read the articles of capitulation, and was, therefore, obliged to rely on an interpreter, who rendered the word "assasinat," into the word "death," merely.—Wash. Lett.

of the sloth of their friends, and it was with great difficulty that the assembly of Pennsylvania, with all the liberality manifested towards them and their families, and with all its forbearance towards the license of their chiefs, could keep them quiet.

After much delay, however, Great Britain prepared with energy to oppose the growing power of her restless rival on this continent.

They sent forward two regiments of foot from Ireland, commanded by Colonels Dunbar and Halkett, who were ordered to Virginia to be there enforced, and Governor Shirley and Sir William Pepperell were directed to raise two regiments of one thousand men each, to be officered from New England, of which they were to have command. The provinces generally were required to furnish men to be placed at the disposal of the commander-in-chief, who should be appointed to command all the forces of the king, in America, and ample provision was made for their sustenance, transportation and all the necessaries for the soldiers landed or raised within the provinces, which expenses were to be borne by the respective provinces.

Governor Belcher urged the assembly of New Jersey to make liberal provision, but they refused to appropriate more than five hundred pounds for the transportation and subsistence of the troops of this province, in consequence of having previously voted the issue of seventy thousand pounds in bills of credit.

The troops under Major General Braddock, Sir John St. Clair, Adjutant General, and the regiments of Dunbar and Halkett, sailed from Cork on the 14th of January, 1755, and arrived at Alexandria, in Virginia, early in March, from whence they marched to Fredericktown, in Maryland. The governors of New York, Massachusetts, Maryland and Virginia, met at Annapolis to devise a plan of military operations with General Braddock. Three expeditions were determined upon. The first against Fort du Quesne, under General Braddock in person, with the British troops and those of Maryland and Virginia; the second against Forts Niagara and Frontenac, under General Shirley, with his own and Pepperill's regiment; and the third, originally proposed by Massachusetts, against Crown Point, to be executed altogether by colonial troops from New England, New York and New Jersey, under Major General William Johnson.

Before the measures above had been fully matured, Lieutenant Colonel Monckton, a British officer, and Lieutenant Colonel Winslow, a major general of the Massachusetts militia, made an attack against the French, in the province of Nova Scotia, and in little more than a month, with the loss of only three men, they obtained possession of the whole province.

The province of New Jersey, in a continental war, dreaded an attack from Canada by the way of New York, while from the French and Indians on the Ohio, they had no fears. The assembly cordially approved the plan of operations adopted at Annapolis, and particularly the expedition against Crown Point, and at once resolved to raise a battalion of five hundred men, and to maintain which, to issue bills of credit for fifteen thousand pounds, redeemable within five years. The governor nominated Mr. Peter Schuyler, with the rank of colonel, to command this force, and that gentleman's popularity was such that the battalion was not only promptly filled, but a much larger number of men than were required, presented themselves for enlistment.

General Braddock removed his army to Fort Cumberland, on Willis's Creek, where he received his wagons and other necessary supplies; at which place he was reinforced by a considerable body of Americans and Indians, and on the 12th of June he broke up his encampment at this place and passed the Alleghany mountains at the head of two thousand men.

At Little Meadows, he convened a council of war for consultation on future operations. Colonel Washington, who had entered the army as a volunteer aid-de-camp, having a perfect knowledge of the country, as well as the nature of the service, had urged the substitution of pack horses for wagons for the transportation of their baggage. He again urged it upon them, and earnestly and successfully recommended that the heavy artillery and stores should remain with the rear division and follow the army by easy marches, while a body of troops should be chosen, with a few pieces of light cannon and stores, to press forward to Fort du Quesne. For this service, twelve hundred men with twelve pieces of cannon, were sent forward, commanded by General Braddock in person.

Sir Peter Halkett acted as brigadier, having under him Lieutenant Colonels Gage and Burton and Major Spark.

Thirty wagons only, including those with the ammunition, followed. The rest of the army remained under the care of Colonel Dunbar and Major Chapman.

The benefit of these prudent measures was lost by the fastidiousness and presumption of the commander-in-chief, and his strong confidence and reckless temerity were destined to a speedy and fatal reproof.

Having crossed the Monongahela river, and when within seven miles of Fort du Quesne, feeling himself secure and joyously anticipating the coming victory, he was suddenly checked by a destructive fire on the front and left flank, from an invisible enemy.

The van was thrown into confusion, but the main body forming three deep, instantly advanced. The commanding officer of the enemy having fallen, it was supposed that the assailants had dispersed, as the attack was for a moment suspended, but the fire was renewed with great spirit; the English seeing their men falling around them, and unable to see their foe or tell from whence the firing came, broke and fled in utter dismay. Had he have availed himself of the advantage his Indians afforded him, of reconnoitering the woods and passages on the front and flank, as prudently suggested by Sir Peter Halkett, this disaster might have been avoided, but he even sneered at the suggestion. But, in his astonishment at this sudden and unexpected attack, he lost his self-possession, and neither gave orders for a regular retreat, nor for his cannon to advance and scour the woods. His officers behaved admirably, but distinguished by their dresses, and selected by the hidden marksmen, they suffered severely. Every one on horseback, except Washington, was killed or wounded. He had two horses killed under him, and four balls through his coat. Sir Peter Halkett was killed on the spot, and the general himself, having been five times dismounted, received a ball through the arm and lungs, and was carried from the field. He survived only four days. On the first day he did not speak, and at night he only made the remark, "Who would have thought it?" He was again silent, until a few minutes before his death, when he observed, "We shall better know how to deal with them another time," and in a short time after expired.

The defeat was total—the carnage unusually great. Sixty-four out of eighty-five officers, and one-half of the privates, were killed or wounded. Many fell by the arms of their fellow soldiers. Of Captain Stewart's light-horse, twenty-five out of the twenty-nine were killed. The defeat of General Braddock, which was wholly unexpected, produced great consternation throughout all the colonies. Upon the receipt of intelligence of this extraordinary event, as Governor Belcher properly termed it, he summoned the assembly of New Jersey to meet him on the 1st of August, but it was not until the approach of winter that they became fully aware of its disastrous consequences, and began to prepare against them.

The enemy discovering the defenceless state of the frontiers, now roamed fearlessly and unmolested along the western lines of Virginia, Maryland and Pennsylvania, and committed the most appalling outrages and cruelties, which the cupidity and ferocity of the savage could dictate. Their first inroads were in Cumberland county, Pennsylvania, from whence they were soon extended to the Susquehana, and thence through Berks and Northampton counties, across the Delaware into New Jersey.

They were joined by the Shawanese and Delaware Indians, who had hitherto remained faithful to the colonists. They committed depradations the most horrible, laying in waste towns, slaughtering men, women and children; even the settlements of the peaceful Moravians, on the Lehigh, were destroyed, and the inhabitants slaughtered. They made no prisoners, but murdered all who fell into their hands, of both sexes.

The inhabitants of New Jersey, roused by the sufferings of their neighbors, prepared, not only to resist the foe, but to protect their friends. Colonel John Anderson was most conspicuous among the energetic citizens of Sussex county. With four hundred men, whom he collected, he scoured the country, marched to the defence of Easton, and pursued the dastard enemy, unhappily in vain. The governor promptly dispatched troops from all parts of the province to the defence of its western frontier, and the wealthy inhabitants advanced the funds requisite for their maintenance, until the assembly, in the middle of December, took such troops upon the provincial establishment, and recalled their battalion under Colonel Schuyler, from the Northern service, where it was then idle, and placed them also on the frontier. To meet the expenses thus incurred, the house, though greatly chagrined at the rejection, by the king, of their bill for a paper currency, voted ten thousand pounds in such bills, redeemable at the usual period of five years.

The marauding parties of French and Indians hung on the western frontiers during the winter.

To guard against their devastations, a chain of forts and block-houses were erected by Pennsylvania along the Kittatinny or Blue Mountains, from the Delaware river to the Maryland line, commanding the principal passes of the mountains. In New Jersey, forts and block-houses were also erected along the mountains, and at favorable points on the east bank of the Delaware river. Many of the inhabitants left their homes, and all called loudly upon the assembly for additional means of defence; and in the spring, when the Jersey regiment was again to proceed to the north, the house authorized the enlistment of two hundred and fifty volunteers, to supply their place and that of the militia on the frontier.

In enlisting troops for the approaching campaign, the recruiting parties in Pennsylvania and New Jersey gave great offence to the inhabitants by the reception, if not the seduction of their indented servants; and the assembly of the latter province threatened to discontinue the regiment they had furnished, unless the grievance was redressed. Circumstances, however, did not admit the discharge of such recruits to any great extent, of which the house becoming sensible, appropriated fifteen thousand pounds for the maintenance of that regiment for the campaign. Extraordinary inducements were offered at this time for enlistment in the royal regiments. The recruits were exempted from service anywhere but in North America, and were promised a bounty of two hundred acres of land, free from quit rents for ten years, either in the province of New York, New Hampshire, or Nova Scotia, at their option, and in case they should be killed in the service, it was assured to their children.

Parliament voted one hundred and fifteen thousand pounds sterling, to be distributed at the pleasure of the king, among the northern and middle provinces, of which New Jersey received five thousand pounds.

The French, under Montcalm, captured the forts of Ontario and Oswego, and destroyed them in the presence of the Six Nation Indians, they being situated in their country. At the capture of the latter, Colonel Schuyler and half of the New Jersey regiment which formed part of the garrison, were taken prisoners and sent to Canada, from which place they were not released until the end of the campaign, and then on parol, that they would not again enter the field for the period of eighteen months.

The regiment was, however, recruited to its original state of five hundred men at the expense of the province early in the spring.

Discouraged and disconcerted by these events, Loudon relinquished all offensive operations, and disposed his troops for the defence of the frontier. Renewed efforts to increase his force were rendered abortive by the appearance of the small pox at Albany, and the troops on the march from New England, and the army at Lake George, were panic struck by the irruption of an enemy more dreadful than the French, and it became necessary to garrison all the posts with British troops, and to discharge the provincialists, excepting one regiment, raised in New York. Thus terminated for a second time, in defeat and utter dssappointment, the sanguine hopes, formed by the colonists, of a brilliant and successful campaign. Much labor had been employed, and a large amount of money expended, in collecting, by land, from a great distance, troops, provisions, and military stores, at Albany, and in transporting them through an almost unsettled country to Lake George, yet not an effort had been made to drive the invaders even from their outposts at Ticonderoga.

The treaty with Teedyuscung had neutralized the Delaware and Shawanese tribes on the Susquehana, but the country was still exposed to the inroads of the French and western Indians. During the spring and summer months of 1757, the county of

Essex was kept in continual alarm by scalping parties, some of whom penetrated to within thirty miles of Philadelphia, many of whom paid with their lives the just penalty of their temerity. But their sufferings were not to be compared with those of the unfortunate inhabitants. Incessant anxiety pervaded every family in the invested districts; their slumber was broken by the yell of demons, or by dread of attack, scarce less horrible than their actual presence.

They plowed their ground, sowed their seed, and gathered their harvest, in constant fear of the tomahawk and rifle of the savages. Even the women visiting their sick neighbors and relatives, were either shot or captured; and the children driving home the cattle from pasture, were killed and scalped. Many of the wealthiest neighborhoods were deserted, and property of every kind abandoned; extraordinary heroism frequently displayed by men, women and children, in defence of themselves and their homes, and in pursuit of, and combat with the enemy. On the part of the authorities both of Great Britain and the provinces, great want of ability and energy was displayed. Had proper means been taken, much suffering might have been prevented, especially as it regarded non-combatants, who were innocent parties to the war. United counsels, and well directed efforts would have driven the barbarians to their savage haunts, and with the chastisement given them at Kittatining, they would have been compelled to sue for peace. The assembly of New Jersey, however, was not regardless of the danger and suffering of her frontier citizens, and kept on foot, for their protection, a body of rangers, consisting of one hundred and twenty men, under Captain Gardiner, who, although they were unable to prevent occasional irruptions of the foe, gave as much security to the frontier as circumstances would admit.

In the middle of January, Lord Louden summoned the governors of the New England provinces to New York, and in no very good humor, attributed to them the disasters of the late campaign. He told them that "their enterprise against Crown Point had not been timely communicated to the ministry, that their troops were inferior to his expectations, disposed to insubordination, and less numerous than had been promised that the true state of the garrisons had not been reported to him, and the provincial legislatures had given him votes instead of men and money." He concluded this reprimand with a requisition for additional troops from New England, New York and New Jersey. His demands were generally complied with, and in the spring he was placed at the head of a respectable army, thereby giving him no further cause for complaint on this account.

The force he required from New Jersey was one thousand men, but the assembly conceiving five hundred to be their full proportion, refused to do more than complete their regiment, and in answer to the proposal of Governor Belcher, that they should, as New England had done, authorize a draft or conscription, they peremptorily declared, by a vote of twelve to seven, "that they were determined not to oblige or compel any of the inhabitants by force to serve as soldiers."

Early in July, Admiral Holburn arrived at Louisburg with a large squadron of ships and five thousand land forces, and was after many delays joined by Lord Loudon, with six thousand regulars. Much was properly anticipated from this formidable army, but the procrastination of the commander-in-chief doomed the country to severe disappointment. For before his preparations were completed, the French had occupied Louisburg with a superior force, dispatched from Brest, a fortified city and the strongest military post in France; and against which Lord Loudon was not disposed to contend. The enemy was not slow to avail himself of the advantages which might accrue to him by the withdrawal of the British troops from the northern frontiers of New York. Montcalm, at the head of nine thousand men, drawn principally from Crown Point, Ticonderoga, and the neighboring forts, with some Canadians and Indians, invested Castle William on the southern shore of Lake George. This place was garrisoned by three thousand men, including the unfortunate Jersey regiment; was well fortified and supplied with necessaries, but Colonel Monroe was compelled to surrender it within six days after its investment. Montcalm's triumph was stained by the barbarities of his Indian allies, and though he exerted himself to protect his prisoners, the massacre of many will ever be coupled with his name. Major General Webb made strenuous exertions to relieve the fort by arousing the militia of New York and New Jersey. From the latter state one thousand men were immediately dispatched, and three thousand put in readiness to march in case they should be required.

The New Jersey regiment with other prisoners, were released, and returned to New York under parole, not to serve again during eighteen months, and being thus rendered useless, were, at the instance of the assembly, disbanded. This regiment, after the capture of Colonel Schuyler, was commanded by Colonel Parker.

Governor Jonathan Belcher died on the 31st of August, 1757, in the 76th year of his age.

During the preceding two years, his health had been so infirm that he summoned the assembly to attend him at Elizabeth, which gave them considerable dissatisfaction.

The house was opposed to being made a secondary tool of the executive, to go wherever his convenience dictated, but they nevertheless attended Governors Morris and Belcher, when illness prevented these officers from getting to Burlington or Amboy, with great reluctance, and protested at all times against their acquiescence establishing a precedent, and they explicitly refused to adjourn from Burlington to Trenton, on the request of his successor, Mr. Reading, although his health also required their indulgence.

Governor Belcher was a native of New England, and in early youth inherited an ample fortune, which enabled him to visit Europe, and to mingle extensively in the best society, until his lavish expenditure dissipated his wealth.

When he was governor of Massachusetts, his administration at Boston was distinguished by his fondness for ostentation and his imperious deportment, and he finally so disgusted the influential men of that province, by rejecting several respectable persons nominated to the council, that they successfully united to effect his removal. He remained for several years unemployed, until he was appointed to the government of New Jersey. "He was now advanced in age, yet lively, diligent in his station, and circumspect in his conduct, religious, generous and affable. He affected splendor, at least equal to his rank and fortune, but was a man of worth and honor, and though in his last years, under great debility of body from a stroke of the palsy, he bore up with firmness and resignation, and went through the business of his government in the most difficult part of the war with unremitting zeal, in the duties of his office."*

By the death of Mr. Belcher, the administration of the government devolved for the second time on Mr. John Reading, the oldest of the councillors, but, in consequence of his age and infirmity, he at first refused, and finally assumed its duties with great reluctance. For more than a month the government was directed by the whole council, at whose instance, on the application of Lord Loudon, the Assembly voted one hundred rangers to be employed on the frontiers during the winter season.†

---

*Smith's New Jersey, p. 438.

†The captain of this company received six shillings; the lieutenant five; sergeants four; corporals three and six pence, and privates three shillings per day. And each officer and soldier was furnished at the expense of the colony, with a blanket, a half-thick under jacket, a kersey jacket lapelled, buckskin breeches, two check shirts, two pair of shoes, two pair of stockings, a leather cap, and a hatchet. And twenty shillings was allowed to the captain for each private he enlisted.

CHAPTER XVI.

1758—1775.

French and English wars—New Jersey raises double the number of men called for—Governor Bernard pacifies the Indians—Five colonial governors appointed by the crown in as many years—The French surrender their possessions on this side of the water—Parliament undertakes to tax her American colonies—Stamp act—Its repeal.

WITH the opening of the year 1758, a new era dawned upon the colonies, which were aroused by the voice of William Pitt, (Earl of Chatham.)

The enterprise, judgment and firmness which had raised England from the depths of humility, were now employed for the reduction of the American continent. The plan of the campaign was wisely matured and committed for execution to men who had reputations to lose and fortunes to gain. Lord Loudon was recalled. Abercrombie was commander-in-chief, with Amherst for his second, aided by brigadiers Wolf and Forbes. The fleet, consisting of one hundred and fifty sail, was commanded by Boscawen.

The objects designated by the campaign as the places of attack, were Louisburg, the forts on the lakes and Fort du Quesne. Major General Amherst with twelve thousand men, aided by the fleet, laid siege to the first, early in June, and captured it, after an obstinate defence of seven weeks.

General Abercrombie, with seven thousand regulars and ten thousand colonial troops, undertook the expedition against the northern forts. His first attempt was upon the forts at Ticonderoga, which position was strong by nature, and well secured by art, being garrisoned by five thousand men. Here he was repulsed, with the loss of two thousand men, chiefly killed, among whom was Brigadier General Lord Howe, and many other distinguished officers.

Though his force was superior to that of the enemy, he made a hasty retreat, for which imprudence he was compensated by the capture of Fort Frontignac, on the north side of the river St. Lawrence. Although the garrison consisted of one hundred and ten men only, the fort contained a large stock of arms, stores and provisions, designed for the western posts. Nine armed vessels, some of which carried eighteen guns, were also taken. Lieutenant Colonel Bradstreet projected and executed this enterprise.

To Brigadier General Forbes was confided the reduction of Fort du Quesne. He had a detatchment from General Abercrombie's army, still further strengthened by the militia from the south, the whole of which was computed at seven thousand eight hundred and fifty men.*

He was attacked, surrounded by the enemy, and lost above three hundred men, killed and taken prisoners, being himself among the latter, the remainder of whom retired in confusion.†

Colonel Boquet was attacked at Loyal Hannah, in his camp, by a force of twelve hundred French and two hundred Indians, commanded by De Vetri, on the 11th of October. De Vetri was compelled to draw off his force, with considerable loss, after a warm combat of four hours' duration. A second attack was made during the night, but some shells thrown from the camp compelled the enemy to retreat. The loss of Colonel Boquet amounted to sixty-seven rank and file, killed and wounded.

On the 24th of November, the French being unsupported by

---

* The force was as follows:

350 Royal Americans, comprising four companies.

1200 Highlanders, thirteen companies.

2600 Virginians

2700 Pennsylvanians.

1000 Wagoners, comprising the sutlers and followers of the army. Penn. Gazette, 1758.

† This occurred on the 14th of September, 1758.

their Indian allies, abandoned Fort du Quesne, burned it and escaped by the Ohio river, when General Forbes seized the ruined fortifications, hastily repaired and garrisoned them with four hundred and fifty provincial troops, under the command of Colonel Mercer.

The remainder of the army was marched into the interior, and quartered at Lancaster, Reading and Philadelphia.

In the preparations for this campaign, we see the power which an energetic spirit directed by wisdom, may obtain over the mass of mankind. The contributions of the provinces towards carrying on the continental war, had, for the last campaigns, been merely the cold returns of duty, but in this, the people displayed all the zeal with which men pursue their interest when animated by well-founded hopes of success. They were assured their combined forces would be applied to remove the enemy from the frontiers, and instead of being required to furnish a specific quota of troops, each colony was directed to raise as large a force as was in its power, with the greatest possible dispatch, and popular men only were commissioned as officers. This was done in accordance with the recommendations of Mr. Pitt, the prime minister.

Thus inspirited, the assembly of New Jersey, instead of raising reluctantly, five hundred men, doubled that number, and to fill the ranks in season, offered a bounty of twelve pounds per man, increased the pay of the officers and voted a sum of fifty thousand pounds for their maintenance. They at the same session directed barracks to be built at Burlington, Trenton, New Brunswick, Perth Amboy, and Elizabethtown, competent each for three hundred men. This complement of men New Jersey kept up during the years 1758, 1759 and 1760, and in the years 1761 and 1762, in addition to the one thousand men, they furnished six hundred more, besides in the latter year, a company of sixty-four men and officers especially for garrison duty, for which she incurred an average expense of forty thousand pounds per annum.

As has been previously stated, during the war between France and England for the possession of Canada, and to dislodge the French from governing on this continent, New Jersey erected barracks at Perth Amboy for the cantonment of British troops; for the protection of Raritan bay and the Atlantic ocean; at New Brunswick, for the protection of the Raritan river, at Burlington, to protect the Delaware river below that point, at Elizabeth, for the protection of Newark bay, and Staten Island Sound, and the one at Trenton, to protect the Delaware river above Burlington.

In addition to these, forts were built immediately on the rivers in the vicinity of the barracks.

On the 10th of September, 1872, one of these forts was unearthed in the city of Trenton, at the corner of South Warren and Ferry streets, a few rods east of the Delaware river. It was about twenty by forty feet. The walls on the inside were built of stone about two feet in thickness, with a stone bastion or bulwark on each corner and outside the stone wall, facing the river, was a brick wall, and the space between the two was filled with broken stones.

Quite a number of ancient relics were unearthed in this fort, prominent among which were two copper coins of Great Britain, bearing date 1737 and 1739; glass bottles of unique manufacture, also earthen jugs of very singular appearance. The bricks, of which the outer wall was composed, from their appearance, were brought from the old country.

Several bones, evidently of human beings, were also dug up; and these relics of by-gone ages were found in levelling the property preparatory to building. The property now belongs to George B. Consolly.

There is no doubt but that among the ruins of the forts established during the colonial period of this state, many valuable relics may be found, and it would repay our Historical Society to cause excavations to be made in the several localities designated.

On the 13th day of June, 1758, President Reading was superceded by the arrival of Francis Bernard, Esq , who continued to govern the province in unbroken harmony with the legislature, until the 4th of July, 1760. The principal service rendered by this gentleman, was the aid he gave in the pacification of the Indians, at the treaty of Easton, in October, 1758. Upon his transfer to Massachusetts, he was succeeded by Thomas Boone, who continued in office a little more than a year, being removed to South Carolina, and his place in New Jersey was supplied by Josiah Hardy.

Upon his dismissal, and appointment to the consulate at Cadiz, he was succeeded by William Franklin, son of Dr. Benjamin Franklin, who was the last of the royal governors. Thus, in the space of five years, New Jersey had seen five colonial governors appointed by the crown. These frequent changes proved very unacceptable to the colony, which was fully satisfied with the three first we have named, and would have been satisfied to have spared the repeated gift of five hundred pounds usually made to the new governor on his arrival, in consideration of the expense and trouble of his voyage. This present was not made to Governor Franklin. But as the cost of living had considerably increased by the diminution of the value of money, consequent on the increased amount of the circulating medium during the war, the assembly added two hundred pounds to the annual salary, making it twelve hundred pounds.

Great Britain having resolved to annihilate the French power in North America, made adequate preparations for the campaign of 1759. An army of eight thousand men, under General Wolfe, was destined to attack Quebec, while General Amherst, with twelve thousand regulars and provincial troops, should reduce the forts of Ticonderoga and Crown Point, cross Lake Champlain, and by the rivers Richelieu and St. Lawrence, join Wolfe and General Prideaux, assisted by Sir William Johnson, at the head of some friendly Indians, were to capture the fort at the Falls of Niagara, and proceed by Lake Ontario and Montreal, to unite with the other generals. To General Stanwix, was confided the southern department, with orders to watch the western frontier and to erect proper forts for its defence.

This stupendous plan was only partially carried into execution. Quebec was purchased with the life of the gallant Wolfe, who fell at the Plains of Abraham. General Amherst obtained possession of Crown Point and Ticonderoga, but too late in the season to permit him to accomplish the remainder of the plan assigned to him. General Prideaux invested Niagara, but was slain in the trenches by the bursting of a shell. Sir William Johnson succeeding him in command, captured the fort. But it was not until September of the succeeding year, that the great object was entirely gained, when by the union of three British armies before Montreal, the Marquis de Vandreuil was compelled to surrender, by capitulation, the whole of the French possessions to his Britanic Majesty. Thus fell the great power of France in America.

The share of the provincials in this result, gave lustre to the colonial history of the American States. They had kept in the field an average force of twenty-five thousand men during the war; had lost thirty thousand of their young men, and contributed three million five hundred thousand pounds sterling to the payment of its expenses.*

The merit of the victories achieved and of the important posts captured, is due solely to the provincial troops. In all the marches and battles, they were the principal sufferers, and where honor was to be gained, the provincial was distinguished by his fortitude in adversity, and his promptitude and courage in the hour of peril.

In January, 1772, Spain became a party to the war, but the conflict against the united house of Bourbon was of short duration, peace being made with France and Spain on the 3d of November, of the same year. Our interest in the treaty was only so far as it affected the colonies. France surrendered her pretensions to Nova Scotia, and ceded Canada, including Louisiana. Spain yielded Florida. In exchange for this mighty domain, France received the islands of St. Pierre and Miquelon near Newfoundland, with a restricted privilege of the fishery, and the islands of Martinique, Guadaloupe, Mariagalante, Deseada and St. Lucia. Spain obtained the restoration of Havana, which was more than adequate for Florida, which would not have been paid, but with the design of preserving the eastern shore of North America from foreign influence.

---

* Of this sum, parliament reimbursed, at several times, one million, thirty-one thousand six hundred and sixty-six pounds sterling.

Being in exclusive possession of this immense territory, comprehending nearly one-fifth of the globe, Great Britain and her colonies rationally looked forward to its peaceful enjoyment, in full confidence that the aboriginal inhabitants, no longer exposed to dangerous solicitations, nor supported by alien power, would not dare to provoke the resentment of those upon whom they must entirely depend for the gratifications supplied by the whites. But the cupidity of the savage had been highly excited during the late conflict, and as deeply indulged. The present unprotected state of the frontier held forth irresistible temptations to his whetted appetite for plunder. His barbarities had been rather rewarded than chastised. Every treaty brought him rich presents, and his detention of prisoners, whom he had again and again promised to surrender, was overlooked on slight apologies, though obviously done to afford opportunity for new treaties and additional gifts. They beheld the French driven out of the whole country, and themselves in danger of becoming wholly dependent upon a power, which, already commanded by its forts the great lakes and rivers, and they no doubt felt that an immediate and mighty effort was necessary to restrain the tide, which, if unimpeded, would spread itself over the continent, overwhelming all their nations in its course.

A secret coalition was formed among the Shawnees, the tribes upon the Ohio and its tributary waters, and about Detroit, to attack, simultaneously, the English posts and settlements upon the frontier. The plan was deliberately and skillfully projected. The settlements were to be invaded during harvest, the inhabitants, with their corn and cattle to be destroyed, and the outposts to be reduced by famine. The Indians fell suddenly upon the traders, whom they had invited among them, murdered many, and plundered the effects of all to an immense amount. The frontiers of Pennsylvania, Maryland and Virginia were over-run by scalping parties, committing their usual enormities. The out-forts, even the most remote, were assailed about the same time, and all immediately fell into 'the hands of the enemy, except Niagara, Detroit, and Fort Pitt, which, being larger and better garrisoned, were enabled to stand a longer siege.

As, in the preceding Indian contest, the frontier inhabitants were driven in, and the enemy again penetrated into the thickly settled country, but more skill and courage were generally displayed in resisting them. Niagara and Detroit were protected by detachments sent to their relief by General Amherst, while Colonel Boquet, after much fatigue and a bloody battle, succeeded in succoring Fort Pitt. The distressing hostilities continued until October, 1764, when they were terminated by Colonel Boquet, who, with fifteen hundred men, over-ran the Indian country in Ohio, compelling the submission of the tribes, and releasing many white prisoners. The Indians soon after entered into a final and satisfactory treaty with Sir William Johnson, who was authorized for that purpose by the crown.

Governor Franklin, on the approach of the savages to the western frontier of New Jersey, ordered out the militia, remanned the fortifications which had been previously erected, and built several new block houses. Yet some parties of Indians crossed the Delaware, made their way through the lines, and massacred several families. The house met on the 15th of November, when the governor recommended them to provide six hundred men, upon the request of General Amherst, to unite with other forces to invade the Indian country, and to provide more effectually for defence of their own limits. The latter the house undertook, directing two hundred men to be raised for this purpose, and appropriating ten thousand pounds for their support, but they declined to furnish troops for general operations, until a general plan should be formed, and a requisition should be made for aid to the other colonies. At their next session, however, they passed a bill for raising six hundred men on condition that a majority of the eastern colonies should come into the requisition, and when this bill was rejected by the council, and the governor prorogued the house, in order to give them an opportunity to bring in another, they authorized the force required, provided, New York should contribute her full proportion. In this shape the bill passed, and the troops joined the northern army.

A more favorable occasion seemed now to present itself. The war which had grown out of American interests, had been honorably terminated, and it was supposed, that the provinces, grateful for their deliverance, would cheerfully repay the care of a fostering mother. Nor would such anticipations have been disappointed, had the designs of the ministry no other consequences than a single pecuniary burden upon the people.

Towards the end of the year 1763, Mr. Grenville communicated to the colonial agents in London, his purpose of drawing a revenue from America, by means of a stamp duty imposed by act of parliament, and directed them to transmit this intelligence to their respective assemblies, that they might suggest any more preferable duty, equally productive.*

The colonies were considered as integral governments, of which the crown was the head, having exclusive political power within their respective territories, except in cases involving the general interests of the empire, in which, from principles of convenience and necessity, they admitted the supremacy of the British parliament.

While the colonists were willing to pay what was just and right towards the crown, they were unwilling that parliament should impose upon them, and looked upon the proposition as unnecessary, cruel and unjust, and if persisted in determined to resist with all the means in their power.

Mr. Grenville, when forming his American plan of taxation, did not consider all its consequences. But, aware that it would be opposed, he was desirous of trying an old measure under a new aspect, and proposed in distinct terms, to raise a revenue, by taxes or colonial imports. This measure, sufficiently obnoxious in itself, was accompanied by a resolution of parliament, "that it may be proper to charge certain stamp duties in the colonies."

The act of parliament, based on the first proposition was extremely onerous to the American trade, the duties thereby imposed amounting almost to a prohibition of commercial intercourse with the French and Spanish colonies.† It is true, that this

---

* The sum required by Mr. Grenville, was one hundred thousand pounds sterling.

† This act was entitled, "An act for granting certain duties in the British colonies and plantations, in America, for continuing, amending and making

trade, previous to the passage of the act of which we now speak, was unlawful, but it was connived at, and was highly profitable, furnishing to the provinces gold and silver for their remittances to England. The minister in his care to prevent smuggling, did not pause to consider the difference between an advantageous trade in the western hemisphere, and the illicit commerce on the British coast. Converting naval officers into officers of the customs, he nearly destroyed the whole colonial trade with the Spanish and French islands. The preamble to the new impost law, declaring it to be just and necessary, that a revenue should be raised in America, and the resolution to follow it up, with a stamp act, gave an unequivocal and odious character to the law, and sent it forth to the colonies, the pioneer of a system of boundless oppression.

The revenue act became still more unpopular, by the means used to enforce it. The penalties for breach of its provisions, were made recoverable in the courts of admiralty, without the intervention of a jury, before judges dependent upon the crown, and drawing their salaries from forfeitures, adjudged by themselves. The duties were required to be paid in gold and silver, now scarcely attainable, and consequently, the paper currency, more than ever necessary, was rejected and depreciated.

The impressions caused by these measures on the public mind, was uniform throughout America. The legislature of Massachusetts, whose population, essentially commercial, felt most severely the late restrictions, was the first to notice them. That

---

perpetual, an act passed in the sixth year of the reign of his late Majesty, King George II, (entitled an act for the better securing and encouraging the trade of His Majesty's sugar colonies in America), for applying the produce of such duties, and of the duties to arise by virtue of said act, towards defraying the expenses of defending, protecting and securing the said colonies and plantations, for explaining an act, made in the twenty-fifth year of the reign of King Charles II, (entitled an act for the encouragement of the Greenland and Eastland trades, and for the better securing the plantation trade,) and for allowing and disallowing several drawbacks on exports from this kingdom, and thus effectually preventing the clandestine conveyance of goods, to and from the said colonies and plantations, and improving and securing the trade between the same and Great Britain."

body resolved, "That the act of parliament relating to the sugar trade with foreign colonies, and the resolution of the house of commons, in regard to stamp duties, and other taxes proposed to be laid on the colonies, had a tendency to deprive the colonists of their most essential rights, as British subjects and as men— particularly the right of assessing their own taxes, and of being free from any impositions, but such as they consented to by themselves or representatives.

They directed Mr. Manduit, their agent in London, to remonstrate against the ministerial measures, to solicit a repeal of the sugar act, and to deprecate the imposition of further duties and taxes on the colonies. They addressed the assemblies of the other provinces, requesting them to unite in a petition against the designs of the ministry, and to instruct their agents to remonstrate against attempts so destructive to the liberty, the commerce and prosperity of the colonies. The colony of Rhode Island proposed to the provincial assemblies, to collect the sense of all the colonies, and unite in a common petition to the King and parliament.

All the efforts of the American colonies to stay the mad career of the English ministry, proved unavailing. The stamp act was passed with slight opposition by the commons, and unanimity by the Lords.*

Dr. Franklin who had been dispatched to Europe, in November, 1764, as the agent of Pennsylvania, labored earnestly to avert a measure, which his sagacity and perfect knowledge of the American people, taught him was pregnant with danger to the British empire. But, even he does not appear to have entertained the idea that it would be forcibly resisted. He wrote to Mr. Charles Thompson: "The sun of liberty is set, you must light up the candles of industry and economy." To which Mr. Thompson replied; "He was apprehensive that other lights would be the consequence." To Mr. Ingersoll, the agent of

---

* The stamp act was passed on the 22d of March, 1765. It was under the consideration of parliament in March of the foregoing year, but was postponed, it was said, by the exertion of Mr. Allen, chief justice of Pennsylvania, at that time on a visit to London.

Connecticut, the doctor said: "Go home and tell your people to get children as fast as they can." Intimating that the period for successful resistance had not yet arrived.

The ministry desirous of rendering the stamp act as little obnoxious as possible, resolved to appoint the officers of distribution and collection, from among the discreet and reputable inhabitants of the provinces. But, there was no means by which to reconcile the people to a law, every where regarded as the forerunner of political slavery. The stamp officers, either voluntarily or compulsorily, resigned their offices; some were hung or burned in effigy, in several of the provinces, and violent outrages were committed on the person and property of the deputy governor and other officers, at Boston. William Coxe, Esq., who had been appointed stamp officer for New Jersey, voluntarily resigned his office in September, 1765. Subsequently, upon the application of the Sons of Liberty of East Jersey, he published a copy of his letter of resignation, which had been made to the commissioners of the treasury, and declared that he had appointed no deputy, and would never act under the law. Towards the end of November, a number of the inhabitants of Salem county, learning that a Mr. John Hatton was desirous to be employed in the distribution of stamps, compelled him to a similar declaration.

On Saturday, the 5th of October, the ship Royal Charlotte, bearing the stamp papers for New Jersey, Maryland and Pennsylvania, convoyed by a sloop of war arrived at Philadelphia. As these vessels rounded Gloucester Point, all those in the harbor hoisted their colors at half-mast; the bells were muffled, and every countenance assumed the semblance of affliction. At four o'clock in the afternoon, many thousand citizens assembled at the State House to consider the means to prevent the distribution of the stamps. Their deliberations resulted in forcing Mr. Hughes, the stamp officer, most reluctantly to decline the exercise of his office, and in securing the stamps on board of his Majesty's sloop of war, Sabine.

The universal refusal of the colonists to submit to the stamp act, occasioned the entire suspension of legal proceedings. In some of the provinces, however, business was speedily resumed, and in nearly all, the penalties of the act were set at defiance before its repeal. The members of the bar in New Jersey, met at New Brunswick about the middle of February, 1766, to consider the propriety of continuing their practice; and being waited on by a deputation of the Sons of Liberty, who expressed their dissatisfaction at the suspension of law proceedings, they determined at all hazards to recommence business on the first of the ensuing April. At the same time deputies from the self-constituted regulators of public affairs, waited on Mr. White, prothonotary of the county of Hunterdon, who was induced by their politeness, as well as by their energy, to promise that his office should be re-opened at the same period. By law the stamp duty was to commence on the first of November. On the previous day the newspapers generally were put in mourning for their approaching extinction, the editors having resolved to suspend their publication until some plan should be devised to protect them from the penalties for publishing without stamps. The term of suspension was, however, short. On the 7th of November, a half sheet was issued from the office of the Pennsylvania Gazette, without title or mark of designation, headed, "*No stamped* paper to be had," and on the 14th another, entitled, "*Remarkable occurrences.*" Both were in form of the Gazette, which, after the 21st, was again regularly published.*

Associations were formed in every part of the continent for the encouragement of domestic manufactures, and against the use of those imported from Great Britain. To increase their quantity of wool, they determined to kill no lambs, and to use all the means in their power to multiply their flocks of sheep.

The association styled the "*Sons of Liberty*," originated in Connecticut and New York, which very soon extended into New Jersey and other colonies. They bound themselves, among other things, to march to any part of the continent at their own expense, to support the British constitution in America, by which was expressly stated to be understood the prevention of any attempt which might anywhere be made to carry the stamp act into operation.

A corresponding committee of the Sons of Liberty was

---

* Pennsylvania Gazette.

established, who addressed letters to certain conspicuous characters throughout the colonies, and contributed materially to increase the spirit of opposition, and perhaps the turbulence with which it was in some places attended.

On receipt of the intelligence of the passage of the stamp act, several of the colonial legislatures, of which Virginia was the first, asserted the exclusive right of the assemblies to lay taxes and impositions on the inhabitants of the colonies respectively. But the house of representatives of Massachusetts contemplating a still more solemn and effectual expression of the general sentiment, and pursuing the suggestion of Rhode Island, recommended a congress of deputies from all the colonial assemblies to meet at New York on the first Tuesday in October, to consult on the present circumstances of the colonies. Circular letters signed by the speaker, communicating this recommendation, were addressed, respectively, to the speakers of the assemblies in the other provinces. Wherever the legislatures were in session, this communication was immediately acted upon.

It was laid before the assembly of New Jersey on the 20th of June, 1765, on the last day of their session, when the house was there, and the members, as Governor Franklin asserts, determined *"unanimously, after deliberate consideration, against connecting on that occasion,"* and directed a letter to be written at the table, to the speaker of Massachusetts Bay, acquainting him with their determination. The house, at a subsequent session, question,*

---

* June 27th, 1766. The statement of the assembly is curious, and evidently betrays a design to make the best of a circumstance, with the remembrance of which, they were not very content. They say—" This house acknowledges the letter from the Massachusetts Bay; that it was on the last day of the session, some members gone, others uneasy to be at their homes; and do assert, that, the then speaker agreed to send, nay urged, that members should be sent to the intended congress; but changed his opinion upon some " advice " that was given to him; that this sudden change of his opinion displeased many of the house, who seeing the matter dropped, were indifferent about it; and as no minute was made, and no further notice taken of it, the house is at a loss to determine whence his excellency could get the information, that the house took the same into " deliberate consideration," " determined " (as his excellency says from their own words) " unanimously against connecting on that

but do not disprove this statement. But this determination was so highly condemned by their constituents, that the speaker found it necessary, in order to avoid the indignation of the people, and to preserve the public peace, to convene the members by circulars at Amboy, and with them proceed to the nomination of delegates to the convention of New York, consisting of Mr. Ogden, the speaker, Mr. Hendrick Fisher and Mr. Joseph Borden.

This measure was severely reprehended by the governor, and caused an angry contention between him and the assembly.

Delegates from Massachusetts, Rhode Island, Connecticut, New York, New Jersey, Pennsylvania, Delaware, Maryland and South Carolina, assembled at New York, at the time appointed. New Hampshire, Georgia, Virginia and North Carolina were not represented, but the two former gave assurances of their disposition to unite in a petition to the King and parliament.

The assemblies of the two latter not having been in session since the proposition for a congress had been made, had no opportunity to act upon the subject.

This congress adopted a declaration of rights and grievances, upon which they founded a petition to the King, and a memorial to parliament.

---

occasion;" they have recollected the whole transaction, carefully examined their minutes, and can find nothing like it inserted therein; an answer to the Massachusetts letter was written, and if the expressions his excellency mentions, were made use of in it, this house is at a loss to know how they are accountable for it, when it does not appear to be an act of the house; but reflection on this passage, sa'isfies the house that his excellency has more knowledge of the contents of the letter in answer, than the members of the house themselves." It is impossible not to perceive that the members of this assembly, had not that vivid sense of evil resulting from the stamp act, which was displayed in other colonies, particularly, when we consider that this was the first opportunity for expressing their sentiments upon the odious pretentions of parliament. Upon their return to their constituents, however, the members imbibed opinions and zeal more befitting the times; and hence we have additional evidence, that, res'stance to British oppressions, was not produced by the efforts of a few leading and aspiring men, but was the spontaneous act of a high spirited people, well instructed in their rights, and resolutely determined to maintain them.

HISTORY OF NEW JERSEY. 371

In these they claimed the full privileges of English subjects, averred the plenary legislative power of the colonial assemblies, protested against taxation by parliament, and dispensing of the trial by jury; and earnestly pressed upon the attention of the parent state, the burdens imposed by the stamp and other acts, with the utter impossibility of continuing the execution of the former, in consequence of the drain of specie it would produce. A difference of opinion prevailed upon the question, whether the petitions and memorials should be signed and transmitted by the congress, or be sanctioned and forwarded by the provincial assemblies, as their several acts. Messrs. Ruggles of Massachusetts, the chairman of the convention, and Ogden of New Jersey, believing in the propriety of the latter mode, refused to sign with the other delegates; but their conduct was censured by their constituents, and Mr. Ogden, therefore, resigned his seat in the assembly, which was convened by the governor, at his special instance,* that they might consider and adopt the best mode of expressing their sense of the obnoxious measures.

he house received from Messrs. Fisher and Borden their report of the proceedings of the congress, and, unanimously approved them, voting their thanks to those gentlemen for the faithful and judicious discharge of the trust reposed in them. Mr. Courtland Skinner, the newly elected speaker, Mr. John Johnson, Mr. John Lawrence and David Cooper were appointed to correspond with Joseph Sherwood, Esq., the agent of the colony in Great Britain, which was accordingly done, and a long petition was unanimously adopted by the house, setting forth that the stamp act was utterly subversive of the privileges inherent to, and originally secured by grants and confirmations from the crown of Great Britain to the settlers of this colony; that His Majesty's subjects inhabiting the province, are from the strongest motives of duty, fidelity and gratitude, inviolably attached to his royal person and government, and had ever shown, and will show the utmost readiness and alacrity for acceding to the constitutional requisitions of the crown, as they have been from time to time made to this colony. That His

---

* November 27th, 1765.

Majesty's subjects are entitled to all the inherent rights and liberties of his natural born subjects, within the kingdom of Great Britain That it is inseparably essential to the freedom of a people, and the undoubted right of Englishmen, that no taxes be imposed upon them, but with their own consent, given personally, or by their representatives. That the people of this colony are not, and from their remote situation cannot be represented in the parliament of Great Britain ; and if the principle of taxing the colonies without their consent, should be adopted, the people here would be subjected to the taxation of two legislatures, a grievance unprecedented, and not to be thought of without the greatest anxiety. That the only representatives of the people of this colony are persons chosen by themselves ; and that no taxes ever have been, or can be, imposed on them, agreeably to the constitution of this province, granted and confirmed by His Majesty's most gracious predecessors, but by their own legislature. That all supplies being free gifts ; for the people of Great Britain to grant to His Majesty the property of the people of this colony without their consent, and being represented, would be unreasonable, and render useless legislation in this colony in the most essential point. That the profits of trade arising from this colony, centering in Great Britian, eventually contributed to the supplies granted there to the crown. That the giving unlimited power to any subject or subjects, to impose what taxes they please in the colonies, under the mode of regulating the prices of stamped vellum, parchment and paper, appears to us unconstitutional, contrary to the rights of the subject, and apparently dangerous in its consequences. That any incumbrance which, in effect, restrains the liberty of the press in America, is an infringement of the subject's liberty. That the extension of the powers of the court of admiralty, within this province, beyond its ancient limits, is a violent innovation of the right of trial by jury—a right which this house, upon the principles of their British ancestors, hold most dear and invaluable. That, as the tranquillity of this country hath been interrupted through fear of the dreadful consequences of the stamp act, that, therefore, the officers of the government, who go on in their offices for the good and peace of the province, in the accustomed manner, while things are in their present unsettled situation, will, in the opinion of this house, be entitled to the countenance of the legislature; and it is reccommended to our constituents, to use what endeavors lie in their power to preserve the peace, quiet, harmony and good order of the government; that no heats, disorders and animosities, may in the least, obstruct the united endeavors, that are now strongly engaged for repealing the act above mentioned, and other acts affecting the trade of the colonies.

The eleven reasons were at once forwarded to our agent at Great Britain, to be laid before parliament.

On the other side of the Atlantic, Colonel Isaac Barre, in the house of commons, was the champion of the people on this side.

Mr. Charles Townshend, one of the ministers, propounded this inquiry:—"And now, will these Americans, children planted by our care, nourished up by our indulgence, till they are grown to a degree of strength and opulence, and protected by our arms—will they grudge to contribute their mite to relieve us from the heavy weight of that burden which we lie under."

Instantly Colonel Isaac Barre arose to reply. He had before spoken, and was one of the very few who knew how to appreciate the Americans. His words were listened to with the attention they deserved. Taking up Townshend's interrogation, he exclaimed: "*They planted by* YOUR *care!* No; your *oppressions* planted them in America. They fled from your tyranny, to a then uncultivated and inhospitable country, where they exposed themselves to all the hardships to which human nature is liable, and among others, to the cruelty of a savage foe, the most subtile, and I will take upon me to say, the most formidable of any people upon the face of God's earth; yet, actuated by principles of true English liberty, that met all hardships with pleasure, compared with those they suffered in their own country, from the hands of those that should have been their friends.

"*They nourished up by* YOUR indulgence! They grew by your neglect of them. As soon as you began to care for them, that care was exercised in sending persons to rule them in one department and another, who were, perhaps the deputies of deputies to some members of this house, sent to spy out their liberties, to misrepresent their actions, and to prey upon them; men whose behaviour, on many occasions, has caused the blood of those Sons of Liberty to recoil within them—men promoted to the highest seats of justice; some who, to my knowledge, were glad by going to a free country, to escape being brought to the bar of a court of justice in their own.

"*They protected by* YOUR *arms!* Those Sons of Liberty have nobly taken up arms in your defence, have exerted their valor amidst their constant and laborious industry for the defence of a country whose frontier was drenched in blood, while its interior parts yielded all its little savings to your emolument. And believe me—remember, I this day told you so,—that same spirit of freedom which actuated that people at first, will accompany them still; but prudence forbids me to explain myself further. God knows, I do not at this time speak from any motives of party heat; what I deliver are the genuine sentiments of my heart. However superior to me, in general knowledge and experience, the respectable body of this house may be, yet I claim to know more of America than most of you, having seen and been conversant with their country. The people, I believe, are as truly loyal as any subjects the king has, but a people jealous of their liberties, and who will vindicate them, if ever they should be violated. But the subject is too delicate—I will say no more."

Barre's eloquence had its effect, but it was only momentary; the bill passed by a vote of two hundred and forty-five to forty-nine; there was no division or the slightest opposition in the Lords; and on the 22d of March 1765, the royal assent was given, and the stamp act became a law.

Barre's words had been heard in the gallery by an American, who wrote them out, sent them across the Atlantic, and by midsummer, they were as familiar as household words to the Americans, and the name of SONS OF LIBERTY cheered and strengthened the hearts of thousands to dare and do in behalf of their rights. It was on the very night of the passage of the bill, that Dr. Franklin being then in London, wrote to his friend Charles Thompson, the words quoted on a previous page, and received from him, the significant reply also there stated.

The Virginia assembly was in session in May of the same year when the news arrived of the passage of these acts, when Patrick Henry denounced them in the severest terms, and offered resolutions condemnatory of the principles of taxation as adopted by parliament.

Upon them a violent debate ensued, which was protracted for hours. Henry, roused by imputations freely uttered by those who opposed action, exclaimed—"Cæsar had his Brutus, Charles I his Cromwell and George III"—

"Treason!" cried the speaker—"Treason!" echoed from every part of house. "It was one of those trying moments," as Mr. Wirt well says, "which are decisive of character."

Henry faltered not for an instant, but rising to a loftier attitude, and fixing on the speaker an eye of the most determined fire, he finished his sentence with the firmest emphasis,—" and George III *may profit by their example!* If this be treason, sir, make the most of it."*

In Massachusetts, James Otis ably defended the colonists.

The pressure in Great Britain by the people by the injury of their trade to the colonies was so strong that the ministry was compelled to resign, and others were appointed in their places. While efforts were put forth on this side of the Atlantic to obtain redress for American grievances, the colonial agents, the friends of freedom and equal rights, and the merchants interested in the American trade, were not idle in Great Britain.

The refusal to import her manufactures touched her in a vital part. The great diminution for orders for goods, compelled a powerful class of traders to advocate liberal principles, who, under other circumstances, would have gladly sustained any policy which might have had a tendency to lessen their burden of taxation.

The lofty position assumed by the Americans was intolerable. They had long been viewed as men of an inferior race. The arrogant philosophy of Europe had placed them and the animal

---

* Wirt's " Life of Patrick Henry," p. 83.

productions of the country low in the scale of perfectability. By the mass of the vulgar portion of the English, they were ranked with savages and negroes. The colonies, the dependencies of Great Britain, on which she had, for years, poured forth the scourings of her prisons, had denied her supremacy, and refused to submit to her parliament, hitherto deemed throughout her vast empire, politically omnipotent. With the sin of a rebellious temper, they were also charged with ingratitude. Under the pressure of accumulated debt and heavy taxation, the English people envied the display of wealth by the provincialists in the late war, and forgot that its exhibition was made in the common cause, with a generosity which had enforced from English justice, the return of more than a million sterling. Thus supported, the ministry which sought relief for the people, by taxing American industry, would scarcely have been driven from their purpose. But other causes transferred the government to other statesmen, whom consistency required, at least, to reverse measures which they had denounced with unqualified reprobation.

Under the new ministers an inquiry was instituted into the effects of the colonial policy of their predecessors. The merchants and manufacturers gave ample testimony of the paralysis in trade, while Dr. Franklin, as the representative of America, before a committee of the whole house of commons, demonstrated the impossibility of levying the new impositions, and the consequent necessity of the repeal. The majority of parliament was now divided into two parties. The larger one affirmed the right to tax the colonies, but denied the expediency of its present exercise; the other, led by Mr. Pitt, repudiated this right, on the ground that all aids are gifts from the people, and can never be legally obtained without their assent; and that this assent could not be had in parliament, since the colonists were not there represented. A repeal on these principles, however just, according to the English constitution, would not have saved the pride of the nation, and would have destroyed the hopes of future revenue at the will of parliament. Hence the repeal of the stamp act, which took place on the eighteenth of March, by a vote of two hundred and seventy-five, to one hundred and sixty-seven, was accompanied by a declaration of the right of parliament to tax America. It was followed by an act indemnifying those who had incurred penalties on account of stamp duties. The tidings of this event were received in America with joy more temperate than might have been expected from the excitement of the public mind.

At the meeting of the assembly of New Jersey in June, 1766, Governor Franklin congratulated the house on the repeal of the odious stamp act; to which, however, he had been but little accessory, and while he lauded, with the warmth becoming a dependent of the crown, " the tenderness, levity and condescension, the wisdom, justice and equity which His Majesty and the parliament had manifested on this signal occasion," he carefully refrained from reminding the members of the obstacles he had endeavored to raise to their action on the case, and the severity with which he reprehended them for sending delegates to the New York convention, and their approval of its proceedings. The assembly did not fail to use so favorable an opportunity for retaliation, rendered more poignant that the moderation of the province had received the commendation of the ministry ; but the house would have enjoyed its triumph with forbearance, had not the governor by an angry message drawn forth a severe retort.

When the repeal came up in parliament, William Pitt, who was not connected with either the Grenville or the Rockingham ministry, and who was not present when the act was passed, and had taken but little part in public affairs, owing to ill health, now appeared in his place in the house, and strongly advocated its repeal. He said—" It is a long time, Mr. Speaker, since I have attended in parliament : when the resolution was taken in this house to tax America, I was ill in bed. If I could have endured to have been carried in my bed, so great was the agitation of my mind for the consequences, I would have solicited some kind hand to have laid me down on this floor to have borne my testimony against it. It is my opinion that this kingdom has no right to lay a tax upon the colonies. At the same time, I assert the authority of this kingdom to be sovereign and supreme in every circumstance of government and legislature whatsoever. Taxation is no part of the governing or legislative power; and taxes are a voluntary gift and grant of the commons alone. This house represents the commons of Great Britain. When in this house we give and grant, therefore, we give and grant what is our own; but, can we give and grant the property of the commons of America? It is an absurdity in terms. There is an idea in some, that the colonies are virtually represented in this house. I would fain know by whom? The idea of virtual representation is the most contemptible that ever entered into the head of man; it does not deserve a serious refutation. The commons in America, represented in their several assemblies, have invariably exercised this constitutional right of giving and granting their own money; they would have been slaves if they had not enjoyed it.

"The colonies acknowledged your authority in all things, with the sole exception that you shall not take their money out of their pockets without their consent. Here would I draw the line—*quam ultra citraque vequit consistere rectum.*"

A profound silence succeeded these words, and for a time no one seemed disposed to advocate the cause of the late ministry. At length, Grenville* himself, a man of no mean powers, rose and said, "protection and obedience are reciprocal: Great Britain protects America; America is therefore, bound to yield obedience. If not, tell me when were the Americans emancipated?" Looking significantly at Mr. Pitt, he exclaimed, "the seditious spirit of the colonies owes its birth to the factions in this house! Gentlemen are careless what they say, provided it serves the purposes of opposition. We were told, we trod on tender ground; we were bid to expect disobedience; what is

---

*Grenville was the brother-in-law of Pitt, and received at his hands, a "sobriquet that annoyed him not a little. On one occasion, in the course of debate, he had called on the gentleman opposite to him, to say where an additional tax could be laid. "Let them tell me where," he repeated fretfully. "I say, sir, let them tell me where; I repeat it, sir, I am entitled to say to them, tell me where." Pitt, who was in the house that evening, in a whining tone resembling Grenville's, hummed a line of a well known song, "Gentle Shepherd, tell me where." Grenville was in a rage, but the house laughed heartily. The nickname, "Gentle Shepherd," stuck to him, and it was long before it was forgotten.

this but telling America to stand out against the law? To encourage their obstinacy with the expectation of support here? Ungrateful people of America! The nation has run itself into an immense debt to give them protection; bounties have been extended to them; in their favor, the act of navigation, that palladium of British commerce, has been relaxed; and now that they are called upon to contribute a small share towards the public expense, they renounce your authority, insult your officers, and break out, I might almost say, into open rebellion!"

The insinuation was not to be borne for an instant. Every one yielded at once to Pitt, who repelled the attack with characteristic intrepidity, "Sir, a charge is brought against gentlemen sitting in this house, of giving birth to sedition in America. The freedom with which they have spoken their sentiments against this unhappy act, is imputed to them as a crime; but the imputation shall not discourage me. It is a liberty which I hope no gentleman will be afraid to exercise; it is a liberty by which the gentleman who calumniates it, might have profited. He ought to have desisted from his project. We are told America is obstinate—America is almost in open rebellion. Sir, *I rejoice America has resisted;* three millions of people so dead to all the feelings of liberty, as voluntarily to submit to be slaves, would have been fit instruments to make slaves of all the rest. I came not here armed at all points with law cases and acts of parliament, with the statute book doubled down in dog's ears, to defend the cause of liberty, but for the defence of liberty upon a general constitutional principle; it is ground on which I dare meet any man. I will not debate points of law; but what, after all, do the cases of Chester and Durham prove, but that under the most arbitrary reigns, parliament was ashamed of taxing a people without their consent, and allowed them representatives? A higher and better example might have been taken from Wales; that principality was never taxed by parliament till it was incorporated with England."

"We are told of many classes of persons in this kingdom not represented in parliament; but are they not all virtually represented as Englishmen within the realm? Have they not the option, many of them at least, of becoming themselves electors?

Every inhabitant of this kingdom is necessarily included in the general system of representation. *It is a misfortune that more are not actually represented.*

"The honorable gentleman boasts of his bounties to America. Are not these bounties intended finally for the benefit of this kingdom? If they are not, he has misapplied the national treasures. I am no courtier of America. I maintain that parliament has a right to bind, to restrain America. Our legislative power over the colonies is sovereign and supreme. The honorable gentleman tells us he understands not the difference between internal and external taxation; but surely there is a plain distinction between taxes levied for the purpose of raising a revenue, and duties imposed for the regulation of commerce. 'When,' said the honorable gentleman, 'were the colonies emancipated?' At what time, say I in answer, were they made slaves? I speak from actual knowledge when I say that the profit to Great Britain from the trade of the colonies, throughout all its branches, is two millions per annum. This is the fund that carried you triumphantly through the war; this is the price America pays you for her protection; and shall a miserable financier come with a boast that he can fetch a peppercorn into the exchequer at the loss of millions to the nation? I know the valor of your troops; I know the skill of your officers; I know the force of this country, but in such a cause, your success would be hazardous. America, if she fell, would fall like a strong man; she would embrace the pillars of the state, and pull down the constitution with her. Is this your boasted peace? not to sheathe the sword in the scabbard, but to sheathe it in the bowels of your countrymen? The Americans have been wronged, they have been driven to madness by injustice. Will you punish them for the madness you have occasioned? No, let this country be the first to resume its prudence and temper; I will pledge myself for the colonies, that on their part, animosity and resentment will cease. Upon the whole, I will beg leave to tell the house in a few words, what is really my opinion. It is that the stamp act be repealed absolutely, totally and immediately. At the same time, let the sovereign authority of this country over the colonies, be asserted in as strong terms as can be devised, and be made to extend to every point of legislation whatsoever; that we may bind their trade, confine their manufactures, and exercise any power whatsoever, except that of taking their money out of their pockets without their consent."

While the important debate was going on, early in the month of February, Benjamin Franklin was summoned to give his evidence before the house of commons.

The fame of this great man brought together a large attendance in the galleries, and replies to the questions propounded, had a strong influence in settling the question in the minds of the members.

He was asked, whether in his opinion, the people of America would submit to the stamp duty if it was moderated; he answered emphatically—" No, never, unless compelled by force of arms." To the question—" What was the temper of America towards Great Britain before the year 1763?" he replied— "The best in the world. They submitted willingly to the government of the crown, and paid, in their courts, obedience to acts of parliament. Numerous as the people are in the several old provinces, they cost you nothing in forts, citadels, garrisons, or armies to keep them in subjection. They were governed by this country at the expense only of a little pen, ink and paper; they were lead by a thread. They had not only a respect, but an affection for Great Britain—for its laws, its customs and manners—and even a fondness for its fashions, that greatly increased the commerce. Natives of Great Britain were always treated with particular regard; to be an *old England man* was, of itself, a character of some respect, and gave a kind of rank among us."
"And what is their temper now?" it was asked. "O, very much altered," he replied. "Did you ever hear the authority of parliament to make laws for America questioned till lately?" "The authority of parliament," said he, "was allowed to be valid in all laws, except such as should lay internal taxes. It was never disputed in laying duties to regulate commerce." To the question—" Can you name any act of assembly, or public act of your government, that made such distinctions?" he replied—" I do not know that there was any; I think there never was an occasion to make such an act, till now that you have attempted to tax us; *that* has occasioned resolutions of assembly,

declaring the distinction, in which I think every assembly on the continent, and every member in every assembly, have been unanimous."*

The sentiments of Washington were in accordance with those expressed by Franklin. He spoke of the stamp act as "unconstitutional, and a direful attack on the liberties of the colonists." And not long after, when the obnoxious act had been repealed, he thus wrote in a letter to a friend: "The repeal of the stamp act, to whatever cause owing, ought much to be rejoiced at; for had the parliament of Great Britain resolved upon enforcing it, the consequences, I conceive, would have been more direful than is generally apprehended, both to the mother country and her colonies. All, therefore, who were instrumental in procuring the repeal, are entitled to the thanks of every British subject, and have mine cordially."†

On the 22d of February, General Conway, who had opposed from the first, the attempt to enforce the stamp act, now brought in a bill for its total repeal. The debate upon it was long and interesting; but, as Burke said afterwards, "the house by an independent, noble spirited and unexpected majority, in the teeth of all the old mercenary *Swiss* of the state, in despite of all the speculators and augurs of political events, in defiance of the whole embattled legions of veteran pensioners and practised instruments of court, gave a total repeal to the stamp act, and if the scheme of taxing the colonies had been totally abandoned, there would have been a lasting peace to the whole empire."

The repeal in the house of commons passed by a vote of two hundred and seventy-five against one hundred and sixty-seven, and in the house of lords, by a vote of one hundred and five against seventy-one.

Upon the facts of its repeal being made known, the ships which lay in the Thames, displayed their colors in token of appreciation, and the houses were illuminated in all parts of the city of London; salutes were heard, and bonfires kindled in all quarters, and all usual demonstrations on such occasions were manifested.

---

* Franklin's works, vol. 4, p. 106.
† Spark's " Life of Washington," p. 107.

CHAPTER XVII.

1760—1775.

Disgust excited by the restrictions on trade—The colonies opposed the right of parliament taxing them in any way—Petitions and remonstrances—The colonists refuse to purchase imported goods from England—Angry discussion between the governor and assembly—Destruction of tea—Battle of Lexington—Washington appointed commander-in-chief—" Minute men" raised in New Jersey.

ALTHOUGH the joy produced by the repeal of the stamp act, was common to all the colonies, the same temper did not prevail in all. In the commercial cities, the restrictions on trade, excited scarce less disgust than had been created by the stamp act itself; and in the north, political bodies had been formed, which betrayed excessive bitterness in opposition to each other.

The first measures of Massachusetts and New York, demonstrated that the reconciliation with the colonies was not cordial.

In New York, where general Gage was expected with a considerable body of troops, the governor required from the legislature, compliance with the act of parliament, called the "Military Act," which directed the colony, in which any of His Majesty's forces might be stationed, to provide barracks for them and certain necessaries in their quarters. The legislature reluctantly and partially complied with the requisition; but at a subsequent session, when the matter was again brought before them, they determined that the act of parliament could only be construed to require necessaries for troops on a march, and not while permanently stationed in the country; on a contrary construction, they said the colony might be grievously burdened by marching into it, several regiments. They considered these requirements as a tax, and would not admit the power of parliament to levy money by its own authority, and compulsorily, through the colonial legislatures. In April, 1768, Governor Franklin, of New Jersey, made a similar requisition on the legislature, which was fulfilled with alacrity.

The repeal of the stamp act, however grateful to the friends of liberty, to the colonists and to the English merchants trading with them, was not popular with the nation at large. The supremacy of the parliament was maintained by the mass of the people; the hope of revenue from America was too fascinating to be surrendered without further exertion; and the king beheld, with high indignation, the resistance to his authority, and the political principles which his American subjects had displayed. Moved by these considerations, Mr. Charles Townsend, chancellor of the exchequer, in an administration formed by Lord Chatham, a man of splendid and versatile talents, invited the attention of parliament, again to the subject of American taxation. He boasted, "that he knew how to draw a revenue from the colonies without giving them offence," and animated by the challenge of Mr. Grenville, to make his vaunting true, he proposed and carried almost unanimously, a bill imposing certain duties on tea, glass, paper, and painter's colors, imported into the colonies from Great Britain; the proceeds of which were to be appropriated to the support of government in America, so far as should be necessary, and the balance to be paid into the British treasury.

This measure was founded on the erroneous belief, that the colonists objected rather to the mode than to the right of taxation. But though there had been some inaccuracies in expressing their views on the statute regulating trade, there should have been no misapprehension of their determination to resist every attempt to tax them without their consent. The bill of Mr. Townsend had the unequivocal character of a revenue law, and as such, was avowedly enacted; nor were the provincialists slow to declare their sense of its true character.

Petition and remonstrance were again resorted to by the colonial legislatures. The tone, generally taken, was not so high as in the case of the stamp act, but the conviction that the one was as great a violation of public liberty as the other, soon became universal.

On the 11th of February, 1768, the colony of Massachusetts, in addition to her other measures, addressed a circular letter to the assemblies of the respective colonies, stating her own proceedings to obtain redress. Courtland Skinner, Esq., speaker of the house, laid this before the house of representatives of New Jersey, on the 16th of April, whereupon the matter was referred to a committee, consisting of Messrs. Joseph Borden, of Burlington county, John Lawrence, of Monmouth, and Richard Lawrence, of Burlington city, with instructions to draft an answer to the same. The answer, signed by the speaker, says: "Sensible that the law you complain of is a subject in which every colony is interested, the house of representatives readily perceived the necessity of an immediate application to the king, and that it should correspond with those of the other colonies; but as they have not had an opportunity of knowing the sentiments of any other colony, but that of the Massachusetts bay, they have endeavored to conform themselves to the mode adopted by you.

"They have therefore, given instruction to their agent, and enjoined his attention on the subject of the petition." And it concluded, "the house have directed me to assure you, that they are desirous to keep up a correspondence with you, and to unite with the colonies, if necessary, in further supplications, to His Majesty, to relieve his distressed American subjects." Pursuant to these sentiments, the house, May 7th, 1768, adopted a petition to His Majesty, in which, after recounting the perils and labors of the primitive settlers, they declared that "the subjects thus emigrating, brought with them, as inherent in their persons, all the rights and liberties of natural born subjects within the parent state. In consequence of these, a government was formed, under which they have been constantly exercised and enjoyed by the inhabitants, and repeatedly and solemnly recognized and confirmed by your royal predecessors, and the legislature of Great Britain.

"One of these rights and privileges vested in the people of

this colony, is the privilege of being exempt from any taxation but such as are imposed on them by themselves, or by their representatives; and this they esteem so invaluable, that they are fully persuaded no other can exist without it."

In their controversy upon the stamp act, the colonists found their most effectual weapon in their non-importation agreement. Recourse was again had to them. But as New Jersey had but little direct commerce of importation, she could not express her sense of injury adequately, by this mode; but she was not precluded from giving to her commercial neighbors, the stimulus of her approbation.

Accordingly, at the October session of 1769, her legislature resolved unanimously, "That the thanks of the house be given to the merchants and traders of this colony, and of the colonies of New York and Pennsylvania for their disinterested and public spirited conduct in withholding their importations of British merchandise, until certain acts of parliament, laying restrictions on American commerce, for the express purpose of raising a revenue in America, be repealed."

Efforts having been made in Rhode Island to break through the non-importation agreement, the freeholders, merchants and traders of the county of Essex, convened at Elizabethtown on the 5th of June, 1770. and resolved, that such agreement was a legal and constitutional method of discovering their sense of the acts of parliament for raising a revenue in the colonies; and therefore, should be firmly adhered to until such acts were repealed. That they would not themselves, or by others, receive, purchase, sell or otherwise use any of the manufactures or merchandise imported from Great Britain, contrary to the agreement; and that they would not trade, nor have any commercial intercourse with such persons who should import goods or cause them to be imported, or with any person who shall purchase goods so imported; but would use every lawful means to hinder the sale of such goods in any way whatever. That they highly approved the spirited behaviour of their Boston, New York and Philadelphia brethren, in renouncing all commerce and intercourse with the traders and inhabitants of Newport, in Rhode Island, who had perfidiously deserted them in this struggle; and that they would observe the same rules of conduct they had so properly adopted, with respect to the traders and inhabitants of Newport. And at a meeting held at the same place, on the 16th of July, when having learned that "the merchants and traders of the city of New York, had lately thought proper, contrary to their own agreement and in violation of their public faith, to break through the only measure that could have obtained redress, they declared that the signers to the late non-importation agreement at New York, had perfidiously betrayed the common cause, deserted their countrymen in their united struggles for the removal of ministerial oppression; and that every person who, contrary to the non-importation agreement, shall import, ought, by the friends of their country, to be treated, not only in like manner as they themselves set the example in the late case of the merchants and traders of Newport, but be held in the utmost contempt by all the friends of liberty, and treated as enemies to their country. And they would strictly adhere to their resolutions adopted at a former meeting. The conduct of the New York importers was condemned by the inhabitants of Woodbridge and New Brunswick and other places, in terms still more energetic. Some of these importers, venturing soon after, to New Brunswick and Woodbridge with their goods, were severely handled by the populace.

The assembly of Virginia passed resolutions unanimously asserting the exclusive right of that assembly to impose taxes on their constituents. They also resolved, that all persons charged with the commission of any offence, within that colony, were entitled to a trial before the tribunals of the country, according to the known course of proceedings therein; and that to seize such persons and transport them beyond the seas for trial, derogated in a high degree, from the rights of British subjects; as thereby, the inestimable privilege of being tried by a jury from the vicinage, as well as the liberty of summoning and producing witnesses in such trial, would be taken from the party accused.

On the 6th of December, 1769, this last resolution was adopted in terms, by the assembly of New Jersey.

The remonstrances of the colonies was so great that Great

Britain was compelled to modify their import act by reducing it one-half.

The period of four years succeeding the modification of the revenue act, contains few incidents of historical interest. The late war, by the great expenditure of money and consumption of agricultural products, had caused an extraordinary appearance of prosperity in New Jersey, as in other colonies. A ready market and advanced price for grain increased the value of lands, and seduced the enterprising into improvident purchases. The causes of this excited state ceasing with the peace, great depression of prices, and contraction of business ensued. Debtors were unable to pay; bankruptcies and suits at law were numerous, and the prosecuting creditor and his attorney became odious to the debtor and his sympathizing friends.

In January, 1770, many citizens of Monmouth county assembled at Freehold, on the stated day for holding the county court, and violently deterred the judges from executing their office; compelling them to return to their respective homes; and a similar riot in Essex was suppressed, only by the spirited conduct of the sheriffs, magistrates, and the better disposed citizens.

The cause alleged for the unwarrantable proceedings, was oppression by the lawyers, in their exorbitant charges for costs. The governor, by the advice of his council, issued a special commission for the trial of the defendents, adding to the justices of the supreme court, some gentlemen of distinguished character. In Essex, the rioters were immediately tried, convicted and punished; but, in Monmouth, they were screened from chastisement by the sympathy of their fellow-citizens.

In suppressing these seditions, Mr. Richard Stockton was highly instrumental, supporting with dignity the authority of the government, mildly assuaging the temper of the people.

In the intercourse between Governor Franklin and the assembly, considerable harmony prevailed. But, occasionally, differences of opinion led to intemperate altercation. Thus, a war of words grew out of the application of the King's troops, for supplies and accommodations greater than the house was disposed to grant.

The statesmen of New Jersey did not take the high ground of Massachusetts; upon this subject they were reluctant to expend any thing more than the strictest construction the act of parliament required. A lengthened discussion was finally terminated by mutual concession. But, another dispute soon after arose, on the application of the assembly, for the removal of the treasurer of the eastern division of the province. With singular policy a treasurer was retained and located in each of the ancient divisions of the colony.

Mr. Stephen Skinner was treasurer of East Jersey, and resided at Perth Amboy. On the night of the 21st of July, 1768, his house was broken open, and the iron chest in which he kept the provincial funds, was robbed of sixty-six hundred pounds, chiefly in bills of credit.

This robbery was supposed by some to have been caused by carelessness on the part of the treasurer, and the assembly called on the governor to remove him, which he refused to do, alleging a royal instruction, forbidding him to displace any officer or minister in the province, without sufficient cause, to be signified to the King; an instruction, he said, wisely calculated to guard against that arbitrary, despotic temper, which sometimes actuated governors, as well as that levelling, democratic disposition, which too often prevails in popular assemblies.

The subject caused an angry discussion between the governor and assembly, for nearly two years longer; in which the former was encouraged, by the discovery of a gang of counterfeiters and forgers, one of whom it was probable, from the evidence of his accomplices, had perpetrated the robbery of the treasury.

Governor Franklin seems to have been truly solicitous to promote the welfare of the colony, by increasing the agricultural and commercial products. At his instance, which in the present season of political quiet, he earnestly renewed, the assembly established bounties for the growth of hemp, flax and silk. Considerable efforts were made to diffuse the culture of the mulberry tree, and had not this simple branch of industry been prostrated by the war, silk would soon have become a staple commodity of the country. At the suggestion of the governor, also, means were taken by the assembly, to obtain a full census, and statistical account of the province; but these were rendered ineffective by the scenes of political disquiet which soon after arose.

Previous to the year 1772, the house of representatives consisted of twenty members. The cities of Perth Amboy and Burlington, and the counties of Middlesex, Essex, Somerset, Bergen, Gloucester and Cape May, each sent two representatives, while Salem and Cumberland jointly, sent only two, and Hunterdon, Morris and Sussex, jointly, sent the same number. But in that year, an act of assembly, for increasing the number of representatives, had been approved by the King, and seems to have been a cause of congratulation between the governor and assembly. By this act, each county was entitled to two representatives, and the whole number was increased to thirty. This representation appears to have been based upon territorial divisions merely, without regard to the essential principle of population, and was continued, upon an erroneous basis, which was not fully corrected, until the adoption of the present constitution in 1844, which specifies, that the senate shall be composed of one member from each county, and the general assembly shall be apportioned among the different counties, as nearly as may be according to the number of their inhabitants, to be regulated according to the United States census every ten years, but that each county shall always be entitled to one member, and the whole number in the house shall never exceed sixty.

Governor Franklin on the part of the province, contrary to the policy which it had hitherto pursued, attended two conferences with the northern Indians.

The first was in 1769, at Fort Stanwix, at which he was accompanied by the chief justice;[*] and where the *Six Nations* having agreed upon a general boundary *line between them* and the northern colonies, (the object of the meeting) publicly acknowledged the repeated instances of the justice of the province, in bringing murderers to condign punishment; and declared that they had no claim, whatever, upon the province, and in the most solemn manner conferred upon the government of New Jersey, the distinguishing name of *Sagorighwiyogstha*, or the great arbiter, or doer of justice.

It is not our purpose to detail all the remote causes and

---

[*] Frederick Smyth.

immediate motives that led to the revolution, which culminated in the dissolution of the connection between Great Britain and her North American colonies; but to keep up such a connected narrative of circumstances pertaining to that great event, as will enable us to exhibit the part New Jersey bore in the contest.

The honor of originating the legislative committees of correspondence in the several colonies, which afterwards became so essentially useful, is claimed, by Mr. Jefferson, for Virginia.

The general state of quiet which had been induced by the prudence of the European and American parties, the one forbearing to ship, and the other to purchase teas, was, after three years' continuance, terminated by the unpolitic avarice of the British ministry. The East India Company became pecuniarily embarrassed in consequence of the American quarrel. They proposed to the government the abolishment of the duty on teas imported into the colonies, which was rejected by the administration.

The export of tea to America, under these circumstances, was, in itself, sufficient to arouse opposition.

But the occasion was eagerly seized by those whose interests would be promoted by popular resistance.

The cry of endangered liberty was again heard from New Hampshire to Georgia. Town meetings were held in the capitols of the different provinces, and combinations formed to obstruct the sale of the fatal weed.

The most determined spirit of resistance displayed itself in New Jersey, upon the first favorable opportunity. On the 8th of February, 1774, the assembly on the proposition of Virginia, appointed from its members, a standing committee of correspondence, consisting of James Kinsey, Stephen Crane, Hendrick Fisher, Samuel Tucker, John Wetherill, Robert Friend Price, John Hinchman, John Mehelm and Edward Taylor, whom they instructed to obtain the most early and authentic intelligence of all the acts and resolutions of the parliament of Great Britain, or to the proceedings of the administration, which might effect the liberties and privileges of His Majesty's subjects, in the British colonies of America; to maintain a correspondence with the sister colonies, respecting these important considerations, and to inform the speakers of the several continental assemblies of this resolution, that they would submit them to their several houses. They returned thanks, also, to the Burgesses of Virginia, for their early attention to the liberties of America. Thus, while Virginia was the first to move in a determined manner against the unjust acts of the mother country, towards her children on this continent, New Jersey was the first to second their action.

These two colonies were the first that struck for liberty.

Upon the approach of ships loaded with tea, and destined for Philadelphia, the Delaware pilots were warned not to conduct them into harbor; and their captains apprized of the temper of the people, deeming it unsafe to land their cargoes, consented to return without making an entry at the custom house; the owners of goods on board, cheerfully submitting to the inconvenience of having their merchandize sent back to Great Britain. The captains of vessels destined to New York, wisely adopted the same resolution. The tea sent to Charleston, was loaded and stored, but was not offered for sale; and being placed in damp cellers, became rotten, and was entirely lost. The ships for Boston entered that port, but before the tea could be landed, a number of colonists, amounting to about fifty, disguised as Mohawk Indians, boarded the vessels, and while the dense crowd silently watched the proceedings, they drew up from the holds of the vessels three hundred and forty-two chests of tea, deliberately broke them open, and emptied their contents into the water. This occupied between three and four hours. No damage was done to anything else, and when the tea had been destroyed, the crowd dispersed, without further noise or trouble, to their homes.*

All this occurred on the night of the 16th of December. Previous to the destruction of the tea, a meeting had been held in the old South Meeting house. The owner of the ships was sent for, and requested to obtain from the collector of the port, the necessary clearance for their departure, but he refused to comply. These three ships were moored near each other at Griffin's wharf.

---

* See Bancroft, Vol. VI. pp 465-489.

Josiah Quincy harangued the crowded and excited assembly, with great solemnity of manner, and in his peculiar fervid style of eloquence said: " It is not the spirit that vapors within these walls that must stand us instead. The exertions of this day will call forth events which will make a very different spirit necessary for our salvation. Look to the end. Whoever supposes that shouts and hosannas will terminate the trials of this day, entertains a childish fancy."

" We must be grossly ignorant of the importance and value of the prize for which we contend ; we must be equally ignorant of the power of those who have combined against us ; we must be blind to that malice, inveteracy and insatiable revenge which actuates our enemies, public and private, abroad and in our bosoms, to hope that we shall end this controversy without the sharpest—the sharpest conflicts ; to flatter ourselves, that popular resolves, popular harangues, popular acclamations and popular vapor will vanquish our foes. Let us consider the issue. Let us look to the end. Let us weigh and consider before we advance to those measures which must bring on the most trying and terrible struggle this country ever saw."*

This appeal at once aroused the assembled multitude, and the question was put, " Will you abide by the former resolutions with respect to not suffering the tea to be landed ?" The reply was a unanimous shout, and the excitement was terrible. It was now growing dark, but still the multitude refused to disperse but called for candles. At this stage of the proceedings, a man disguised as a Mohawk Indian, seated in the gallery, raised the war-whoop, which was instanly responded to in the street. The sound was at once taken up, and another voice suddenly shouted, " Boston harbor, a tea-pot to night! Hurrah for Griffin's wharf!" At which the meeting adjourned at once, and the people hurried down to the harbor, to witness the result.

It was a fine still evening, and about six o'clock. It was then that the boarding the vessels above described, commenced.

The military and naval force offered no resistance. Admiral Montague, was at this time, at the house of a friend, and as the

---

*" Memoir of the life of Josiah Quincy, Jr.," pp 266—267.

party marched from the wharf, he raised the window and said, 'Well boys, you've had a fine night for your Indian caper, haven't you? But mind, you've got to pay the fiddler yet." Pitt, one of the leaders, shouted, "O, never mind, squire, just come out here, if you please, and we'll settle the bill in two minutes!" The admiral wisely shut down the window, and the crowd went on its way, without further demonstration of popular feeling.

In April of the next year, a vessel having on board eighteen chests of tea, arrived at Sandy Hook. The pilots, under instructions from a "Vigilance Committee," refused to bring the ship up to New York until they were assured there was no tea on board, and when it was discovered there was tea on the ship, they were thrown into the river; the captain was cooly put on board of his ship, the anchors were weighed, and he was sent to find his way back to England.

Such was the unanimity of sentiment among the people of the colonies, and so systematic their opposition, that not a single chest of the cargoes, sent out by the East India company, was sold for their benefit.

By one act of parliament, the port of Boston was closed, and the custom house transferred to Salem, until compensation should be made to the East India Company, and the king satisfied of the restoration of peace and good order in Boston. By another act, the charter of Massachusetts was subverted, the nomination of counsellors, magistrates and other officers, being vested in the crown, during the royal pleasure. By a third, persons indicted in that province, for any capital offence, if an allegation was made on oath to the governor, that such offence had been committed, in aid of the magistracy in the suppression of riots, and that a fair trial could not be had in the province, might be sent to any other colony or to Great Britain, for trial. A bill was also passed for quartering soldiers upon the inhabitants. But these penal bills were not wholly unopposed in either house of parliament; in the house of lords, the minority entered their protest against each.

By a resolution of the assembly of Virginia, the first of June, the day the Boston port bill was to take effect, was adopted as a day of fasting, humiliation and prayer, throughout the continent, to implore the divine interposition of providence to avert the heavy calamity which threatened destruction to their civil rights, and the evils of civil war, and to give one heart and one mind to the people, firmly to oppose every invasion of their liberties.

Early in the month of July, the inhabitants of the several counties of New Jersey, assembled at their respective county towns, and adopted resolutions strongly disapproving the course of the ministry, and of the late acts of parliament, in closing the port of Boston, invading the charter rights of the province of Massachusetts, subjecting supposed offenders to trial in other colonies and in Great Britain, and sending an armed force to carry these injurious measures into effect. They nominated deputies to meet in convention, for the purpose of electing delegates to the general congress, about to convene at Philadelphia. The convention, consisting of seventy-two members, selected from the most intelligent and respectable citizens of the colony, among whom were many members of the assembly, met at New Brunswick on the 21st of July, 1774. Stephen Crane was chosen chairman and Jonathan D. Sergeant, clerk: James Kinsey, William Livingston, John DeHart, Stephen Crane, and Richard Smith were chosen to represent them in the congress; and William Peartree Smith, John Chetwood, Isaac Ogden, Joseph Borden, Robert Field, Isaac Pearson, Isaac Smith, Samuel Tucker, Abraham Hunt and Hendrick Fisher were appointed as a standing committee of correspondence.*

The delegates from eleven provinces assembled in Carpenter's Hall, Philadelphia, on the 4th of September; those from North Carolina did not arrive until the fourteenth.

Congress approved and endorsed everything that had been done by the colonies, and adopted resolutions prohibiting the importation, purchase, or use of goods from Great Britain or Ireland, or their dependencies, after the first day of the succeed-

---

*Kinsey left congress in 1775, refusing to take the republican oath of allegience, and on the 22d day of November, his resignation, as well as that of Mr. DeHart, was accepted by the assembly; the three remaining ones continued to act and to represent the colony in congress.

December; and directed that all exports to Great Britain and the West Indies, should cease on the 10th of September, 1775, unless American grievances should be sooner redressed. An association, embodying these resolutions was then formed, and they were signed by every member present, and as Mr. Marshall says: "Never were laws more faithfully observed, than were the resolves of Congress, at this period, and their association was, of consequence, universally adopted."

To enforce these resolutions, Congress recommended the appointment of committees in the several counties and towns, which was accordingly done, and they became efficient instruments in aiding the progress of the revolution.

On the 11th of January, 1775, the New Jersey delegates reported the proceedings of Congress to the assembly of the colony, who unanimously approved of the same.

They also resolved, that the same gentlemen should represent the colony in the future Congress, and report their proceedings to the assembly at the next session. That they should propose and agree to every reasonable and constitutional measure, for the accommodation of the unhappy differences subsisting between the mother and her colonies.

The joint action of the colonies was especially obnoxious to the royal government; and the governors of the respective colonies threw every obstacle in their power in the way of its accomplishment. To this end, Governor Franklin refused to summon the assembly of New Jersey, notwithstanding the petitions of the people; and the first delegates to Congress instead of being appointed by the house, were elected by the people in convention. Although not legally elected they nevertheless acted, and had a powerful influence in the legislation of the state.

On opening the assembly in January, 1775, Governor Franklin observed. "It would argue not only a great want of duty to His Majesty, but of regard to the good people of this province, were I, on this occasion, to pass over in silence, the late alarming transactions in this and the neighboring colonies, or not endeavor to prevail on you to exert yourself in preventing those mischiefs to this country, which, without your timely interposition, will, in all probability, be the consequence."

He further set forth that it was not for him to decide on the particular merits of the dispute between Great Britain and her colonies, and that he did not intend to censure those who, conceiving themselves aggrieved, had aimed to redress those grievances. He adverted in severe terms against the convention of the people, who had appointed the delegates to the Congress, that they had usurped the powers which alone belonged to the assembly, and that it was the duty of that body not to allow such things to go unrebuked.

That any grievances they might feel disposed to set before the King would be properly attended to, and have greater weight coming from each colony in its separate capacity, than in a channel, the propriety and legality of which there might be much doubt.

He goes on further to say: "You have now pointed out to you, gentlemen, two roads—one evidently leading to peace, happiness, and restoration of the public tranquillity—the other inevitably conducting you to anarchy and misery, and all the horrors of a civil war. Your wisdom, your prudence, your regard for the interests of the people, will be best known, when you have shown to which road you give the preference. If to the former, you will probably afford satisfaction to the moderate, the sober and discreet part of your constituents. If to the latter, you will perhaps give pleasure to the warm, the rash and inconsiderate among them, who, I would willingly hope, violent as is the temper of the present times, are not even now the majority. But, it may be well for you to remember, should any calamity hereafter befall them from your compliance with their inclinations, instead of pursuing, as you ought, the dictates of your own judgment, that the consequences of their returning to a proper sense of their conduct, may prove deservedly fatal to yourselves."

These persuasions were powerless with the assembly, who unanimously approved and adopted the very measures condemned by the governor, and in their address to him they were unequivocally set forth.

The language of the council, however, was in a different tone, and as loyal as the governor himself could desire.

When the proceedings of the congress was received in Lord don, it appeared to have a momentary beneficial effect upon their cause.

The administration was staggered, and the opposition triumphed in the truth of their predictions, that the measures pursued by the ministry would unite all the colonies in resistance. The petition of congress to the King, was declared by the secretary of state, after a day's perusal, to be decent and proper, and was received graciously by His Majesty, who promised to lay it before his two houses of parliament. But the ministry had resolved to compel the obedience of the provinces.

In vain did the merchants of London, Bristol, Glasgow, Norwich, Liverpool, Manchester, Birmingham, and other places, by petition, pourtray the evils which must result from such determination, and predict the dangers of the commercial interests of the kingdom. In vain did the planters of the sugar colonies, resident in Great Britain, represent, that the profits on British property in the West India Islands, amounting to many millions, which ultimately centered in Great Britain, would be deranged and endangered by the continuance of the American troubles. In vain did the venerable Earl of Chatham,[*] raised from a long retirement, by the danger of losing these colonies, which his own measures had protected, and, seemingly, assured by the parent state, apply his comprehensive mind, and matchless eloquence, to arrest the fatal course of the administration. In vain, from a prophetic view of events, did he demonstrate the impossibility of subjugating the colonies; and urge the immediate removal of the troops collected by General Gage, at Boston, as a measure indispensably necessary to open the way for an adjustment of the differences with the provinces. In vain, when undiscouraged by the rejection of the motion, did he propose a bill for settling the troubles in America.

The period of American emancipation had approached, and the power which might have delayed it, was providentially stultified.

---

[*] William Pitt.

The King in his opening speech to the newly elected parliament, declared "that a most daring spirit of resistance and disobedience to the laws, unhappily prevailed in the province of Massachusetts, and had broken forth in fresh violences of a very criminal nature; and that these proceedings had been countenanced and encouraged in his other colonies. Parliament put forth an address, echoing the royal speech, which was carried by large majorities in both houses, against which lords Richmond, Portland, Rockingham, Stamford, Stanhope, Torrington, Ponsonby, Wycombe, and Camden, from the minority, issued a spirited protest.

But both houses joined in an address to the King, declaring, "that they find a rebellion actually exists in the province of Massachusetts." This was followed by an act for restraining the trade and commerce of the New England provinces, and prohibiting them from carrying on the fisheries on the banks of Newfoundland, which was subsequently extended to New Jersey, Pennsylvania, Maryland, Virginia, South Carolina, and the counties of Delaware.

Before the continental congress again met on the 10th of May, 1775, hostilities between the colonists and the British troops in America, had commenced. The battle of Lexington was fought April 19th, and Ticonderoga captured May 8th, and soon after, June 17th, the ever memorable battle of Breed's Hill, gave confidence to the colonists; and the British army, under General Gage, was besieged in Boston.

Peyton Randolph was chosen president of congress, but being speaker of the House of Burgesses of Virginia, John Hancock, of Boston, was unanimously elected his successor.

Congress promptly proceeded to further measures of offence and defence. They prohibited exports to such parts of British America, as had not joined the confederacy; forbade the supply of provisions or other necessaries, to the English fisheries on the coast; to the army and navy in Massachusetts, and to vessels employed in transporting British troops and munitions of war; and interdicted the negotiation of bills of exchange, drawn by British officers, agents or contractors, and the advance of money to them, on any terms whatever.

To secure the colonies against the forcible execution of the late obnoxious acts of parliament, they resolved to put them immediately in a state of defence, reccommending to them, severally, to provide the munitions of war; to prepare the militia, so classing them, that a fourth of their number might be drawn into action, at a minute's warning; and to form a corps for continual service; authorizing each colony, apprehensive of attack, to levy one thousand regulars at the expense of the confederacy. They organized the higher departments of the army, framed regulations for its government, and issued three millions of dollars, in bills of credit, for its maintainence. In an address to the army and the people, they reviewed the conduct of Great Britain, exposed the enormity of her pretensions and the dreadful alternative she had created, of unconditional submission or resistance by arms, in which they asserted the justice of their cause, and the competency of their means to maintain it, with their free determination to employ, at every hazard, the utmost energy of the powers granted them by their Creator, in order to preserve their liberties.

They concluded this stirring appeal in the following language: "In our native land, in defence of the freedom which is our birthright, and which we always enjoyed until the late violation of it, for the protection of our property, acquired solely by the honest industry of our forefathers and ourselves, against violence offered, we have taken up arms; we shall lay them down when hostilities shall cease on the part of the aggressors, and all danger of their being removed, and not before."

In the congress, Colonel George Washington, of Virginia, was nominated by the delegates of Massachusetts, as the most proper person for commander-in-chief, and was unanimously elected to that important position. He was at that time, a delegate in the congress, a man of high character, and splendid fortune, who had pledged his life in the contest.

He was at that time, of mature age, and well known for his military talents, his sound judgment, firm temper, spotless integrity, and dignified person and demeanor. The southern and middle districts possessed no man having superior claims to public confidence. His commission, dated June 15th, 1775, gave him full power and authority to act as he should think best for the country and welfare of the service, subject to the rules of war and the orders of congress. They also passed a resolution declaring, "that for the maintenance and preservation of American liberty, they would adhere to him with their lives and fortunes."

The reply of Washington, when apprised of his appointment by the president of congress, showed in a high degree, his modesty, devotion to the cause of the country, and that disinterestedness for which he was in the most eminent degree distinguished. And to show that it was not out of any pecuniary motive that he assumed the dangerous honor, he declined all compensation for services, and declared that he would accept only the reimbursement of his actual expenses.

Congress, soon after the nomination and appointment of the commander-in-chief, created and filled the offices of subordinate generals. Artemus Ward, Charles Lee, Philip Schuyler and Israel Putnam, were appointed major generals; Horatio Gates, adjutant general, and Seth Pomeroy, Richard Montgomery, Daniel Wooster, William Heath, Joseph Spencer, John Thomas, John Sullivan and Nathaniel Green, brigadier generals.

Although determined upon resistance to the uttermost, against the tyranny of the parent state, the colonies had given no public indication of their desire to become independent of her government, though among many, it was thought the result of the contest would be independence; while perhaps, some wished it and sought for it, none publicly avowed it The American people were proud of their descent from Great Britain, and exulted in being connected with a country so great. And even while they were making warlike preparations, they determined to put forth renewed efforts to propitiate the British government and people, and it was determined to send another petition to the king, which met with some opposition by several members of congress, under the supposition that it would be of no avail. But, through the influence of Mr. Jonathan Dickinson, who proposed and wrote the petition, it was adopted.

This address was filled with professions of duty and their attachment to the mother country and His Majesty, and stated, "that they not only most fervently desired the former harmony between Great Britain and the colonies, to be restored, but that a concord might be established between them upon so firm a basis, as to perpetuate its blessings uninterrupted by any future dissentions, to succeeding generations in both countries. They therefore, besought His Majesty to direct some mode by which the united applications of his faithful colonists to the throne, in pursuance of their common counsels, might be improved to a happy and permanent reconciliation." These professions of three millions of his subjects, were treated with contempt by the king. The petition was presented through the secretary for American affairs, on the 1st of September, by Messrs. Richard Penn and Henry Lee, and on the 4th, Lord Dartmouth informed them, that "to it, no answer would be given."

Finding they could get no redress from the king, and while preparing for the contest, from respect to their fellow subjects, congress deemed it proper to put forth their motives in addresses to the people of Great Britain and to those of Ireland, as well as to the assembly of Jamaica. They also published a declaration to the world, setting forth the necessity of assuming arms and reiterating the injuries they had sustained. They said: "We are reduced to the alternative of choosing an unconditional submission to the tyranny of irritated ministers, or resistance by force. The latter is our choice. We have counted the cost of this contest, and find nothing so dreadful as voluntary slavery."

General Washington, immediately after his appointment to the chief command, repaired to the army before Boston. With his small army he found it difficult to maintain a show of force to confine the British troops to that town from the month of June until the following March, when the Americans, having seized and fortified Dorchester Heights, which overlooked and commanded the place, General Howe, who had succeeded General Gage, on the 10th of October, abandoned it and sailed with his command for Halifax.

The provincial congress of New Jersey re-assembled on the 5th of August, 1775, and engaged in devising further means for the collection of the tax they had imposed and for the organization of the militia. They directed fifty-four companies, each of sixty-four minute-men, making in all three thousand four hundred and fifty-six effective men, to be organized; and to each they allotted a specific number, and to the respective county committees, the duties were allotted of appointing their officers.

The following engagement was entered into by them:

"We, the subscribers, do voluntarily enlist ourselves as minute-men in the company of———, in the county of ———; and do promise to hold ourselves in constant readiness, on the shortest notice, to march to any place where our assistance may be required, for the defence of this and any neighboring colony; as also, to pay due obedience to the commands of our officers, agreeable to the rules and orders of the continental congress, or the provincial congress of New Jersey, or during its recess, of the committee of safety."

These troops were formed into ten battalions; in Bergen, Essex, Middlesex, Monmouth, Somerset, Morris, Sussex, Hunterdon and Burlington, one each; in Gloucester and Salem, one, while in the counties of Cumberland and Cape May, were independent light infantry and rangers. They took precedence of the other militia, and were entitled to be relieved at the end of four months, unless in actual service. Congress also, resolved, that two brigadier generals should be appointed, but named at the time, only Mr. Philemon Dickinson to that command; Mr. William Livingston, soon after received the other command.

In regard to the Quakers, a number of whom resided in the province, who were opposed to bearing arms, they declared that they intended no violence to their religious scruples, but earnestly recommended them to contribute the more liberally to the relief of their distressed brethren, and to do all other services to their oppressed country, consistent with their religious profession.

They ordered that the inhabitants in each county, qualified to vote for representatives in the general assembly, should meet together, (at places designated,) on the 21st day of the following September, and elect, not exceeding five substantial freeholders, as deputies, with full power to represent such county in provincial congress, to be held at Trenton, on the 3d day of the following October. That during the continuance of the present unhappy disputes between Great Britain and America, there be a new choice of deputies in every county, yearly, on the third Thursday of September; that on the said Thursday in every year, such inhabitants shall choose a sufficient number of freeholders, to constitute a county committee of observation and correspondence, with full power as well, to superintend and direct the necessary business of the county, as to carry into execution the resolutions and orders of the continental and provincial congresses; that the inhabitants of each township so qualified, do immediately choose a sufficient number of freeholders, to constitute a township committee, and that on the second Tuesday of March, thereafter, they make a like choice, to act as a committee of observation and correspondence, in the townships respectively, with power within their precincts, similar to that conferred upon the county committees.

CHAPTER XVIII.

1775—1776.

Appointment of provincial treasurer—Committee of safety—Acts passed preparing for war—Delegates to continental congress—Provincial congress of New Jersey—Governor Franklin's proclamation—Governor Livingston's prediction—Virtual declaration of independence—Governor Franklin's arrest—Opposition to the measures of congress.

THE provincial congress appointed Jonathan D. Sergeant, the treasurer, and a committee of safety, to act during the recess, after which they adjourned to the 20th of September.

The committee of safety were Hendrick Fisher, Samuel Tucker, Isaac Pearson, John Hart, Jonathan D. Sergeant, their treasurer, Azariah Dunham, Peter Schenk, Enos Kelsey, Joseph Borden, Frederick Freelinghausen and John Schureman. The council of safety of 1777, was composed of a number of gentlemen selected from different parts of the state, to advise with the governor, in order that the state might the better be enabled to meet the exigencies of war, the calling together of the assembly being too tedious and difficult. And from this council of safety, came the council of the state, afterwards the state council. It first met at Haddonfield, March 18th, 1777, and consisted of twelve persons and the governor. The first selected were judge John Cleves Symes, William Patterson, (afterwards governor,) Theophilus Elmer, Silas Condict, John Hart, John Mehelm Samuel Dick, John Combs, Caleb Camp, Edward Weatherby and Benjamin Manning, all of whom afterwards held prominent positions in the state.

A number of prisoners taken to Salem were ordered transferred to Bordentown, and hundreds of suspected persons were examined, but most of them took the oath of abjuration and allegiance, while a few were sent to different prisons, for treason against the state.

The council finally found it necessary to summon the members of the general assembly on the 7th of May, in order to address them upon the importance of filling the prescribed quota of men. This was their first meeting with the general assembly and the original joint meeting of the New Jersey legislature.

During the year 1777, flags of truce were respected, and parties in this state were permitted in certain cases, to visit their sick relatives within the British lines.

The council was possessed of full powers to send guilty persons to jail, and ordered respectable persons to keep within one hundred yards of their respective houses.

The order to send dangerous persons into the enemy's lines, was issued July, 11th, 1777. By this order nearly fifty families were transported as disaffected, the wives and children of most of them following by a similar order. The disaffected district was about Hackensack, South River and Tappan neighborhood. We forbear to mention their names, as their descendants now comprise some of the most respectable people of the vicinity, they having returned (most of them) after the close of the war. At a subsequent meeting of the council, citations were issued to about one hundred persons, who were summoned to appear to take the oath of abjuration.

At the session held in September, no business of importance was transacted. The council met again in October and appointed as the committee of safety, Samuel Tucker, president; Hendrick Fisher, vice president; Abraham Clark, secretary; Azariah Dunham, Ruleoffe Van Dyke, Augustine Stevenson, John Pope, John Hart,* Joseph Holmes.

At this session, they modified the act regulating the militia, and an act was passed for collecting such munitions of war as could be found in the country, to be ready for the struggle which they saw was inevitable. Persons who were accused of disaffec-

---

*John Hart was one of the signers of the declaration of independence.

tion to the country, were summoned before them, fined, imprisoned, or held to bail; and if an officer of the government, he was suspended. In order to transact other business, they summoned the congress to meet at New Brunswick, on the 31st of January.

To procure arms and ammunition, was a labor of great difficulty, in consequence of the continental congress in their war with the ministry, having prohibited the importation of these indispensable articles, the consequence of which was, the country was almost bare. On the 6th of February, 1776, the convention appointed William Livingston,* John Hart, Richard Smith, John Cooper and Jonathan Dickinson Sergeant, as delegates to the continental congress.

This congress, like the previous ones, exercised the whole power of the state, controlling its funds and directing its armies. Their first endeavors were to protect such points as were most exposed to the ravages of the British ships of war, and supposing New York to be well protected, they concentrated their forces for the protection of Perth Amboy and Swedesborough, on the Delaware. They were requested to procure two battalions and two companies of artillery to guard these exposed points, but congress was unable to procure more than twelve small cannon, and two companies of artillery. They modified their act in regard to bearing arms to meet the religious scruples of the society of friends, by enacting that all whose religious scruples would not allow them to bear arms, could sign with the following proviso: "I agree to the above association, as far as the same is consistent with my religious principles."

Those who refused to sign this, it was ordered that all arms be taken from them, and they were required to give security for their peaceable behaviour. They were empowered to arrest all persons who might prove dangerous to the common cause.

All persons between the ages of sixteen and fifty years, were required to attend in proper accoutrements, and bear arms, at the times and places appointed for general muster, and for failure so to do, a fine of ten shillings was imposed, to be recovered by war-

---

* Afterwards governor of the state.

rant of distress. And to encourage enlistments, the soldiers were granted exemption of person and goods from execution for small debts.

Upon the invasion of New York, that city was filled with alarm, and many of its inhabitants fled into the neighboring counties of New Jersey. This emigration became so numerous that congress passed an act requiring all who were able to bear arms, and who had fled from other colonies, to immediately return to the same, and aid in its defence, unless they had permits from the committee of the precinct from which they removed to reside in this colony, or unless such residence appeared necessary for the support of the resident's family, or he had no visible means of support from whence he came and could procure such support in this colony.

This body also, resolved to dissolve itself, and directed an election to be held on the fourth Monday of May, following, and thence annually, for the members of the provincial congress; and they extended the right to vote for delegates, to all persons who had signed the general association, and who had been residents of the colony one year previous to the election; were of full age and worth fifty pounds in personal estate.

Governor Franklin convened the legislature on the 16th of November, 1775. In his address, he set forth where he thought the colonists had made their mistake in taking up arms against the mother country. He said: "I have indeed, the stronger inducement to run this risk and to use my influence with the other crown officers to do the same, because our retreat would necessarily be attributed to either the effect or well grounded apprehension of violence, and of course, subject the colony to be more immediately considered as in actual rebellion, and be productive of mischiefs, which it is my earnest inclination and determination to prevent as far as may be in my power. Let me therefore, gentlemen, entreat you to exert your influence likewise, with the people, that they may not by any action of theirs, give cause for bringing such calamities on the province. No advantage can possibly result from the seizing, confinement or ill treatment of officers, adequate to the certain damage, such acts of violence must occasion the province to suffer."

The governor seemed to fear his own personal safety, and therefore made that subject the prominent feature of his address, as well as to obtain a disavowal from them, of any desire for independence. And the house at this time, concurred in his views, and disavowed all sentiments for independence, or any act that would have a tendency to encourage such a measure.

The dread of independence seems at this time, to have occupied the minds of others besides the governor, and several petitions were presented from the freeholders of Burlington, praying the house, by resolutions, to discourage an independency on Great Britain. The house disclaimed any such idea, and recommended the delegates of the colony to use their utmost endeavors to obtain a redress of grievances, and for the restoration of the union between the colonies and Great Britain, upon constitutional principles, and not to give their assent, but to reject any propositions that should be made to separate this colony from the mother country or change the form of government.

The governor communicated to the legislature the royal assent to the act, for issuing a loan on bills of credit to the amount of one hundred thousand pounds. This the assembly had labored hard for more than twelve years to obtain, but had always before met with opposition from the crown, and now the name of the king was no longer potent to open the purses of the people, they therefore, declared it inexpedient at this time, to go into any increase of salaries of the officers of government, or expedient to erect buildings at present, for the better accommodation of the members of the legislature.

The governor, on the 6th of December, 1775, finding himself unable to carry his point, prorogued the house until the 3d of January, 1776, but it never re-assembled, and thus terminated the provincial legislature of New Jersey.

For more than a year, the whole country had been, not only in open rebellion against the king, but its inhabitants had made war against those who had preserved their loyalty.

In the first half of the year 1775, among the great mass of the people, these sentiments were real. But the more daring and ambitious, had not only foreseen that the continuance of political connection with the mother country was not much longer possible, but had successfully sought to inspire the people with the desire of independence. And every reflecting man believed that the severance of the ties that had formerly bound them, was now inevitable, though many, from various causes, were disposed to postpone the event.

William Livingston, afterwards governor of New Jersey, in 1768, wrote in the *American Whig*, of New York, of which he was the editor: "The day dawns in which the foundation of this mighty empire is to be laid, by the establishment of a regular American constitution. All that has hitherto been done seems to be little besides the collection of materials for the construction of this glorious fabric. 'Tis time to put them together. The transfer of the European part of the great family is so swift and our growth so vast, that before seven years roll over our heads, the first stone must be laid. Peace or war, famine or plenty, poverty or affluence, in a word, no circumstances, whether prosperous or adverse, can happen to our parent; nay, no conduct of hers, whether wise or imprudent, no possible temper on her part, will put a stop to this building. What an era is this to America! And how loud the call to vigilance and activity! As we conduct, so will it fare with us and our children."

Thomas Paine, of Bordentown, in his pamphlet styled "Common Sense," boldly pronounced a continued connection with England unsafe and impracticable, and ridiculed her constitution, which had hitherto been deemed a masterpiece.

This pamphlet was read everywhere, and made friends to the cause of independence, and the general belief now was, that a reconciliation was impossible, and that the colonies must strike for freedom; that mutual confidence could never again be restored; that jealousy, suspicion and hate, would take the place of that affection which would be necessary to a beneficial connection; that the commercial dependence of America upon Great Britain, was injurious to the former, and beneficial to the latter; and that incalculable benefit would be derived to the colonies from a full liberty to manufacture her raw material and to export her products to the markets of the world; that further dependence upon a nation or sovereign, distant three thousand miles, ignorant and regardless of their interests, was intolerable in the present rapidly increasing strength and power of the colonies; that the hazard in prolonging the contest was as great as in the declaration of independence. The people were at once aroused, upon finding that they were declared to be in a state of rebellion; that foreign mercenaries had been employed against them; that the tomahawk and scalping knife were engaged in the British service, and that the slaves were to be seduced and armed against their masters.

Congress, during the contest, was governed altogether by the wishes of the people. On the 15th of May, 1776, they declared that his Britanic Majesty, with the lords and commons, had, by act of parliament, excluded the united colonies from the protection of the crown; that, not only had their humble petition for redress and reconciliation been received with disdain, but the whole force of the kingdom, aided by foreign mercenaries, was about to be exerted for their destruction; that, therefore, it was irreconcilable with reason and good conscience for the colonists to take the oaths for supporting any government under the crown of Great Britain; and it was necessary that the exercise of every kind of authority under the crown should be suppressed, and that all the powers of the government should be exercised by the people of the colonies for the preservation of internal peace, virtue and good order, and the defence of their lives, liberties and properties, against the hostile invasions and cruel depredations of their enemies. At the same time they resolved, "That it be recommended to the respective assemblies and conventions of the united colonies, where no government sufficient to the exigencies of their affairs has been hitherto established, to adopt such government as shall, in the opinions of the representatives of the people, best conduce to the happiness and safety of their constituents in particular, and America in general."

This was virtually a declaration of independence.

It was renouncing allegiance to the British crown, and establishing a government by the authority of the people, all hope of reconciliation having been abandoned, as well as all desire of reunion with the parent state.

Old parties forgot their animosities and united to oppose a common oppression. The Quakers, opposed to every form of war, and strongly attached to the parent state and to their church, and family connections therein, shrunk with deep sensibility from the unnatural contest, and with horror from permanent separation and independence. While the royal officers and their dependents and connections, (a large portion of whom were wealthy and distinguished in the province,) beheld in a change of government, the loss of official emoluments and influence.

While these parties opposed the separation, the great body of the people were opposed to oppression, and saw in independence successfully maintained, bright visions of glory and wealth, and hailed with rapture, the recommendation of congress, were anxious to take the first irrevocable step towards political emancipation.

The provincial congress of New Jersey, elected on the fourth Monday of May, in accordance with the act of the preceding congress, met at Burlington on the 10th of June, 1776, and was organized by choosing Samuel Tucker, Esq., president, and William Patterson, Esq., secretary.

Before the 21st of the month, numerous petitions were received from East Jersey for and against the formation of a new government; at which time the convention resolved, that a government be formed for regulating the internal police of the colony, in accordance with the recommendations of the continental congress of the 15th of May. This recommendation was adopted by a vote of fifty-four against three.

Messrs. Richard Green, of Hunterdon; John Cooper, of Gloucester; Jonathan D. Sergeant, of Somerset; Lewis Ogden, of Essex; Jonathan Elmer, of Cumberland; Elijah Hughes, of Cape May; John Covenhoven, of Monmouth; John Cleves Symes, of Burlington; Silas Condict, of Morris, and Samuel Dick, of Salem, were appointed a committee to prepare a constitution on the 24th of June, and on the 26th, two days after their appointment, they reported a draft of the same, which was confirmed on the 2d of July, and continued as the fundamental law of the state until the adoption of the new one on the 29th of June, 1844.

Congress, impelled by the tide of public opinion, had gone far beyond their resolutions of the 15th of May, and had actually resolved on declaring the colonies independent states, thereby severing forever all political ties which had connected them with Great Britain. The convention of New Jersey even yet had not abandoned all hope of a reconciliation, and therefore, they made a provision in the last clause of their constitution, that if reconciliation between her and the colonies should take place, and the latter be again taken under the protection and government of the crown, the constitution should be null and void. This door of retreat was kept open by the fears of the president of the convention,* who, in a few months after, claimed the clemency of the enemy with whom this clause gave him an interest. Other clauses of the constitution show also, that it was made for the colony. The laws were to be enacted, and all commissions, writs, and indictments, were to be in the name of the colony. But on the 18th of July, 1776, the provincial congress assumed the title of the "Convention of New Jersey." And after the declaration of independence, the commissions and writs were made in the name of the state ; the indictments concluded "against the peace of the state," and an act of assembly of September 20th, 1777, substituted the word state, in all such cases, for the word colony.

There was a difference of views between the continental congress and the New Jersey convention, which was condemned by some of the latter, who even went so far as to move to defer the printing of the constitution for a few days, that the last clause might be considered by a full house. It was negatived when not more than half the members were present. Notwithstanding this, New Jersey was not backward in engaging in the contest. She had kept pace with the foremost, and her spirited conduct was the more meritorious because it had less of the excitement of immediate interest, inasmuch as she had felt no burden, and was not irritated by the vexations of commercial restrictions. She had no ships, no foreign commerce. She instructed her delegates in congress, to join in declaring the united colonies independent of Great Britian.

The constitution above named was formed in great haste, less

---

* Samuel Tucker.

than two days being consumed in framing the draft, and less than six days in adopting it, and the people never having a voice in the matter at all, as the whole thing was devised by the delegates and by them adopted; notwithstanding all this, it remained the fundamental law of the state for sixty-eight years. In the old constitution, the office of the governor could be vested in one individual for life or made hereditary; the judges may be appointed for months, for years, or for life—their number increased or diminished—and their compensation varied, and the courts continued or abolished, at the will of the assembly; in a word, all the other branches were dependent on and at the mercy of the legislative branch of the government.

Under the old constitution, the legislative branch of the state was vested in a council and assembly; under the new, in a senate and general assembly.

The minimum number of the assembly was fixed at thirty-nine, three members to each county, without regard to territorial extent and population; in the new constitution, they are apportioned among the several counties as nearly as may be, according to the number of the inhabitants, the whole number of which shall never exceed sixty. In the old constitution, no regard was paid to territorial extent and population. But the legislature was empowered to diminish the number or proportion of the representatives in the assembly for any county.

The qualification for a member of council was, that he should be worth one thousand pounds proclamation money, and for assembly, five hundred pounds. Neither mature age, citizenship, nor oath of allegiance, were required in the old constitution. In the new all property qualification is abolished. Under the present constitution, members of the senate are required to be not less than thirty years of age, and a citizen and inhabitant of the state for four years, and of the county, one year before his election; and for assembly, he must have attained twenty-one years of age, and been an inhabitant and citizen of the state two years, and of the county, one year; and no person can be elected to either house, who is not entitled to the right of suffrage.

All electors were required to be of full age, worth fifty pounds, clear estate, and a resident of the county twelve months previous to the election, under the old constitution. This qualification was found to be too broad, as it admitted all inhabitants of the proper age and estate, whether they were bond or free, white or black, native or foreign, male or female.

Under the new constitution, this was remedied, as it provided that none should be electors except *white male citizens* of the United States, of the age of twenty-one years, residents of the state one year, and of the county five months; and by an act of congress in 1869, the right of suffrage was extended to include negroes.

Under the old constitution, the council and general assembly in joint meeting assembled, elected the governor annually; the judges of the supreme court and inferior courts, justices of the peace, clerks of courts, the attorney general, secretary of state, state treasurer, and all general and field officers of the militia. Under the new constitution, the governor is elected by the people for three years; the judges of the supreme court and chancellor are nominated by the governor, and confirmed by the senate, and hold their offices for seven years; the justices of the peace are elected by the people in their several districts, and hold their offices for five years; the attorney general, prosecutors of the pleas, clerk of the supreme court, clerk of the court of chancery and secretary of state, are nominated by the governor and appointed by him with the consent of the senate, and hold their office for five years. The state treasurer is appointed annually by both houses in joint meeting.

The clerks and surrogates of counties, are elected by the people every five years.

Sheriffs are elected annually by the people, and cannot be re-elected for a longer term than three years, respectively.

Captains, subalterns, and non-commissioned officers are elected by the members of their respective companies. Field officers of regiments, independent battalions and squadrons, are elected by the commissioned officers of their respective regiments, battalions or squadrons. Brigadier generals are elected by the field officers of their respective brigades. Major Generals are nominated by the governor, and appointed by him, with the advise and consent of the senate.

Brigade inspectors are chosen by the field officers of their respective brigades. The adjutant general, quartermaster general and all other militia officers not provided for in the constitution, are appointed by the governor.

Major generals, brigadier generals and commanding officers of regiments, independent battalions, and squadrons, appoints their own staff officers of divisions, brigades, regiments, independent battalions and squadrons, respectively.

The old constitution of New Jersey vested in the legislature to an alarming degree, all the powers of government. The incumbents of chief executive offices, including the judiciary were not only dependent upon the legislature for their commissions, but for the amount of their salaries, which they could enlarge or diminish at their pleasure. Those, therefor, who held position moved by ambition or avarice, whether governor, judges, secretary, treasurer, clerks, or chief officers of the army, were creatures of the assembly, and not of the people, and from it they received life and their daily sustenance.

By the old constitution, the governor was the supreme executive power; was captain-general of all the militia and other military force; was chancellor, ordinary and surrogate general, hence, none but a man well versed in the law, was competent to occupy the post; he was also president of council, and judge of the court of appeals in the last resort, and in council had the casting vote in their proceedings in case the house was evenly divided,

Under the old constitution, seven members constituted a quorum in either house, under the new, it requires a majority of the members of either house to constitute a quorum, and a majority of all the members are necessary to pass a bill, and it does not then become a law until approved by the governor.

Under the new constitution, the executive formed a part of the court, and the court consisting of members annually chosen, and perhaps as often changed, and whose education as well as pursuits did not always qualify them to determine legal questions, yet these same gentlemen sat to revise, and perhaps to reverse decisions given by the best legal authority of the land.*

While the old constitution guaranteed to all, the right to worship God, according to the dictates of their conscience, and that they should not be compelled to attend any place of worship that did not accord with their own faith and judgment, and that they should not be compelled to pay tithes, taxes or any other rates for the purpose of building or repairing any church, or place of worship, or to maintain any minister or ministry, contrary to what they believed to be right, or had voluntarily engaged themselves to perform. No establishment of any one religious sect, in preference to another, was allowed; no *protestant* inhabitant was to be denied the enjoyment of any civil right, merely on account of his religious principles; but all persons professing a belief in *the faith of any protestant sect*, whose conduct under the government was peaceable, was capable of being elected to any office of profit or trust.

This last clause was much less liberal than were the concessions of the proprietors; it was modelled on the laws of England, and excluded Catholics from office. While this intolerance had ceased in England, it was here continued under the constitution, and the Catholic christian, with all others who did not profess a belief in the faith of a protestant sect, were excluded from full participation in civil rights. This remained a foul blot on the country, until the adoption of the new constitution in 1844, which not only set forth in its broadest sense, the liberty of conscience, and the right of all to worship God, according to the dictates of their own consciences, but it also enacted—" That there shall be no establishment of one religious sect, in preference to another; no religious test shall be required, as a qualification for any office or public trust; and no person shall be

---

* Members of the bar were frequently elected to council, to whom the foregoing remarks were not applicable. The business of this court might render it necessary that the councillors should all be lawyers, as it was required the governor should be, no one else being competent to perform the duties of the office.

denied the enjoyment of any civil right, merely on account of his religious principles.

The first council and assembly, under the constitution adopted in 1776, met at Princeton.

The revolutionary period has been truly termed, "the time that tried men's souls." The breaking of the ties that had kept them as a nation more than a century were hard to sunder, but they were forced to do it, in consequence of the oppression of the mother country. The declaration of independence had broken the unanimity that had previously existed against resistance to the unjust measures of the parent state. A large majority of the people had adhered to their professions of loyalty to Great Britain, with a religious tenacity, concientiously believing that their political happiness and salvation existed only in the British empire. Besides many were bound by the tenderest ties of blood and affinity. They had emigrated from there to the foreign wilds of the western continent, had left behind them their kindred and friends, to seek an asylum in a country where they could enjoy undisturbed all the privileges of religious, as well as political freedom.

Opposed to American independence, there was also men of desperate character, who confiding in the strength and success of Great Britain, availed themselves of their protection to prey upon the country, and while pretending loyalty to the mother country, and their desire to punish treason against it, used this method to gratify their own evil passions, and to revenge themselves upon those who opposed them. Bands of these marauders infested the forests and shores of the eastern part of the state, particularly in the county of Monmouth, and the mountains of Morris and Sussex counties. New York, one of the largest, richest and most powerful of the royal colonies, was the most divided upon the question of independence. The tories were there protected by the English forces.

They were numerous, wealthy and active, and had many friends and dependents in East Jersey, over whom they exercised a dangerous influence. New Jersey being a frontier state, was exposed to all the dangers and miseries of border warfare. At one time the enemy lay upon the northern and southern boundaries, and her losses in proportion to her wealth and population were probably greater than those of any other state, except South Carolina.

Upon the arrival of the British army in 1776, the disaffected in New York and New Jersey were collected into a body, under officers selected from among themselves.

Mr. Courtlandt Skinner, late attorney general of this state, his brother, the late treasurer, together with every member of the family, adhered to the enemy. Courtlandt, was, also, appointed a brigadier, and directed to raise two thousand five hundred men, but he was unable to raise more than five hundred.

On the 18th of July, an ordinance was adopted removing the pains and penalties of treason from all who should take up arms in defence of the colonies against the mother country.

Governor Franklin at once joined with those who were opposed to taking up arms. He sought to control the torrent of public opinion, but he found it too strong for him to attempt to turn its course, and was, therefore, compelled to stand by, an almost idle spectator, while it swept away all the powers which lately pertained to him, the abandonment of which he used his utmost endeavors to prevent, but in vain. Before the new government had been formally adopted by this state, the whole political power had passed, by the voice of the people, to their delegates in convention, which became the government *de facto;* and the powers of royal authority were at once suspended, by the exercise of those derived from the people. The governor strove to prevent this, by endeavoring again to set in action what little was left of His Majesty's government.

Of the thirty members of the assembly, only seven were members of the convention, and the governor knowing that some of these were distinguished as royalists, sought to array one popular assembly against another. He therefore, on the thirteenth of May, issued a proclamation, in the name of the King, summoning the house to meet on the twentieth of June.

As soon as this proclamation was issued, the provincial congress saw the mischief it was likely to accomplish, and at once prepared to defeat it, and resolved by a vote of thirty-eight to eleven, that the proclamation of William Franklin, late governor, ought not to be obeyed, and on the sixteenth of June, they resolved by a vote of thirty-five to ten, that by such proclamation, he had acted in direct contempt, and violation of the resolution of the continental congress of the fifteenth of May, and had proved himself an enemy to the liberties of the country, and by a vote of forty-seven to three, they further resolved, that all payments of money, on account of salary, or otherwise, to him, as governor, should thenceforth cease; and that the treasurers of the province should account for the moneys in their hands to the provincial congress, or to the future legislature of the colony, and that measures should be immediately taken to secure his person.

Congress immediately issued an order to Colonel Nathanial Heard of the first battalion of the Middlesex militia, to cause his arrest, at the same time enjoining upon him, to conduct the necessary business, with all the delicacy and tenderness which its nature could possibly admit. A written parol was sent to Colonel Heard, with a blank space for him to fill up, and at the choice of Mr. Franklin, with the name of Princeton, Bordentown or his own farm at Rancocas, as the limits in which he was to abide. In case he signed the parol, congress was willing to depend upon his honor for its faithful performance. But in case he refused to sign, he was to be put under strong guard, and kept in close custody until further orders.

On the seventeenth, Colonel Heard and Major Jonathan Deare, waited on the governor at Amboy, to get him to comply with the order of congress, and sign the parol. This he refused to do, upon which they surrounded his house with a guard of sixty men, and immediately sent a messenger to report their proceedings, and receive further instructions from congress, then in session at Burlington, who ordered that Mr. Franklin should be immediately brought to that place.

The further proceedings relative to his case, and the final action thereon, has been more fully detailed in a previous chapter.

The patriots at first manifested the most lenient measures toward the disaffected, and all taken with arms, were treated as prisoners of war, and those not in arms but who were known as opposed to the measures inaugurated, were treated with no more severity, than was sufficient to prevent them from committing the mischief they meditated. On the 2d of January, 1776, congress passed resolutions recommending to the several township and county committees, as well as other friends of the cause, to explain to the honest and misguided, the nature of the controversy, as well as the many, but fruitless efforts that had been made to bring about a reconciliation, but to proceed vigorously against all active partizans from whom danger might be apprehended, disarming them, and keeping them in safe custody, or binding them with sufficient sureties for their good behaviour. Congress had great faith in the power of reason and gentle treatment, on the presumption, that those who were among the disaffected, were generally misinformed.

In New York and New Jersey the British were received in open arms by the disaffected, as their deliverers from oppression.

The articles of association of 1775, was the entering wedge of division, between the parties of New Jersey, as well as in other parts of America. Those who refused to sign, or after having signed, disobeyed their requirements, were considered as enemies to their country, and as such, where not only denounced by the township and county committees, but were fined and imprisoned by the order of such committees, as well as that of the provincial convention and committee of safety. Notwithstanding these measures, counter associations were attempted, who resolved to pay no tax levied by order of the provincial congress, nor to purchase any goods distrained for such taxes, or for non-attendance at militia musters.

These, as well as other demonstrations of a like measure, manifesting hostility, induced the committee of safety of the province, on the 15th of January, 1776, earnestly to recommend to the several county and town committees, the prompt execution of the resolutions of the continental congress, adopted on the 2d of that month, recommending due moderation and prudence, and requesting all officers of militia to lend their assistance.

In accordance with this resolution, several persons from different parts of the state, were brought before the committee of safety, and the continental congress who continued their sitting from the thirty-first of January, to the second of March, 1776. Most of the prisoners confessed their faults, craved pardon, and were either dismissed without further punishment, or subjected to a small fine, or ordered to give security in various sums for their future good behaviour.

Congress again assembled on the 10th of June, at which time memorials were presented from several counties, complaining of the hostile intentions and proceedings of the disaffected, particularly in Monmouth, Hunterdon, Bergen and Sussex counties, at which the county committees were ordered to summon those charged to appear before the convention. Having heard on the 26th of June, of several insurgents in the county of Monmouth, who were using all their endeavors to contravene the acts of congress, and to oppose the cause of American freedom, thereupon they directed Colonel Charles Reade, to take to his aid two companies of Burlington county militia, and proceed without delay, to the county of Monmouth, and apprehend such insurgents as were designated to him by the president of the committee.

At the same time information was received of persons in the county of Hunterdon, who had united together to oppose the measures of congress, and had even gone so far as to commence acts of open daring and violence, that they had plundered the house of a Captain Jones, beaten, wounded and in other ways abused the friends of freedom in the county, and publicly declared, that they would take up arms in behalf of the King of Great Britain.

To effectually check this combination, which assumed so hostile and dangerous a character, Lieutenant Colonel Abraham Ten Eick and Major John Berry were directed, with the militia of the counties of Hunterdon and Somerset, to apprehend these insurgents, and on the first of July the provincial congress resolved, that the several colonels of the counties, should, without delay, proceed to disarm all persons within their district, who, from religious principles, or other causes, refused to bear arms. Two days after, an additional order was given to Colonel Charles Reade, Lieutenant Colonel Samuel Forman and Major John Haight, to take two hundred militia of Burlington, and the same number from Monmouth county, and proceed without delay, to quell an insurrection in Monmouth, and to disarm and take prisoners all whom they should find assembled, with the intent to oppose the friends of American freedom, and to adopt such measures as they should think necessary to accomplish the object.

On the 4th of July, congress resolved, " that as divers persons in the county of Monmouth, who had embodied themselves in opposition to its measures, had expressed their willingness to return to their duty, upon assurances of pardon, alleging, that they have been seduced and misled by the false and malicious reports of others; such persons as should, without delay, return peaceably to their homes, and conform to the orders of congress, should be treated with lenity and indulgence, and upon their good behaviour, be restored to the favor of their country; providing, that such as appeared to have been the leaders and principals in these disorders, and who, to their other guilt, had added that of seducing the weak and the unwary, should yet be treated according to their demerits."

The refugee royalists frequently perpetrated their outrages against the persons of the distinguished patriots of the state. Among their first successful attempts, was that on Mr. Richard Stockton, of Princeton. On the entrance of the British army into New Jersey, after the capture of Fort Washington, that gentleman withdrew from congress, in order to protect his family and property, at his seat near Princeton. He removed his wife and younger children into the county of Monmouth, about thirty miles from the supposed route of the British army.

On the 30th of November, he was, together with his friend and compatriot John Covenhoven, at whose house he resided, dragged from his bed at night, stripped and plundered, and carried by way of Amboy to New York.

At Amboy he was exposed to severe cold weather in the common jail, which, together with subsequent barbarity in New York, laid the foundation for disease, that terminated his existence in 1781. His release was probably owing to the interference by congress in January.

From the actual assumption of political independence, to that of a formal declaration, the interval could not be long. The same day the resolution recommending to the colonies a change in their form of government, was adopted, the convention in Virginia resolved unanimously, that their delegates in congress should propose to that body, to declare the united colonies free and independent states, absolved from all allegiance to, or dependence on the King and parliament of Great Britain. The public mind was now fully prepared for the measure, in fact were looking forward anxiously for it.

The assemblies of Maryland, Pennsylvania and New York, which had displayed the greatest reluctance and held out the longest, at length assented to it. The proposition was made in congress, on the 7th of June, 1776, by Richard Henry Lee of Virginia, and seconded by Mr. John Adams, of Massachusetts, "that the united colonies are, and of right ought to be, free and independent states, and that all political connexion between them and the state of Great Britain, is and ought to be totally dissolved." The resolution was referred to the committee of the whole congress, where it was daily debated. Messrs. Lee and Adams were the most distinguished speakers in favor of the resolution. Adams had been characterized as "the ablest advocate," of independence. Mr. John Dickenson, author of the "Farmers Letters," which had signally served to awaken the resistance of the people to British oppression, opposed it. Mr. Dickenson's views were those of a sincere, yet timid patriot.

He afterwards discovered that his fears were groundless, and was among the most ardent in aiding to mature and perfect the institutions of independent America.

In resisting the declaration of independence, he was honest in his views, being apprehensive for his country. At this period, no man could be more obnoxious to British statesmen, than the author of the Farmers Letters, who was now in possession of a colonel's commission, and was, in the month of July, 1776, upon the lines of New Jersey and New York.

The same thing which weighed upon his mind affected the minds of others; among whom were Wilson of Pennsylvania, R. R. Livingston, of New York, E. Rutledge and R. Laurens of South Carolina, and William Livingston of New Jersey, who, although they did not doubt the absolute inexpediency of the measure, considered it premature.

On the first of July, the resolution declaratory of independence, was approved by the committee of all the colonies except Pennsylvania and Delaware. Seven of the delegates from the former were present, four of whom voted against it. Mr. Rodney, one of the delegates from Delaware was absent, and the other two, Thomas McKean voted for and George Read against the resolution. The further consideration of it was postponed until the next day, when the resolution was finally adopted and entered on the journals.

Pending this memorable discussion, a committee, consisting of Messrs. Thomas Jefferson, John Adams, Benjamin Franklin, Roger Sherman and R. R. Livingston, was appointed to prepare the declaration of independence. A sub-committee, consisting of Messrs. Jefferson and Adams, were appointed, whose special duty it was to prepare the draft, which was made by the former. It was adopted by the chief committee without amendment, and reported to congress on the twenty-eighth of June. On the fourth of July, having received some slight alterations, it was sanctioned by the vote of every colony.

The delegation in congress from New Jersey, was Messrs. William Livingston, John DeHart, Richard Smith, John Cooper and Jonathan Dickenson Sergeant. These were elected by the convention on the 14th of February, 1776. After the proposition of May 15th, for organizing provincial governments, it would seem that nearly all these gentlemen were reluctant to assume the responsibility of adopting measures, which eventually led to independence. On the twelfth, Richard Smith, by alleging indisposition resigned his seat; on the 13th, John DeHart resigned, and on the 21st of June, Mr. Sergeant resigned. Mr. Cooper does not appear to have taken any part in the proceedings, although his name with that of Mr. Sergeant, appears on the minutes of the state convention, from the 10th of June to the 4th of July. Mr. Livingston was withdrawn on the 5th of June, being appointed brigadier general of the militia of New Jersey.

Messrs. Richard Stockton, Abraham Clarke, John Hart,

Francis Hopkinson and Dr. John Witherspoon, were substituted for the previous delegation, on the 21st of June, and were all of them present at the time the final vote was taken upon the resolution, and the declaration of independence, and affixed their signatures to that important document, by instructions from the provincial congress of New Jersey, empowering them to declare the united colonies independent of Great Britain.

On the 17th of July, the provincial congress resolved, that, "Whereas, the honorable, the continental congress have declared the united colonies free and independent states. 'We, the deputies of New Jersey, in provincial congress assembled, do resolve and declare, that we will support the freedom and independence of the said states, with our lives and fortunes, and with the whole force of New Jersey.'" And on the succeeding day they changed the style and title of the "provincial congress of New Jersey," to that of the "Convention of the state of New Jersey."

CHAPTER XIX.

1775—1776.

Our people divided on the war question—First blow at Lexington—Opposition to the claims of the British parliament—Capture of the Hessians—Death of Colonel Rahl—Washington recrosses the Delaware.

WE have now arrived at the most serious and important part of the history of our country, when without a government, and with no money, or munitions of war, and when even the people themselves were divided in sentiment upon the expediency of the measure, it was resolved to take up arms against the best organized, most powerful and wealthiest nation in the world, and to either carry out the principles of the declaration of independence, adopted in Independence Hall, Philadelphia, on the 4th of July, 1776, or perish in the attempt.

The first blow had been struck at Lexington in Massachusetts, on the 19th of April, 1775, which had aroused the whole country, and at which eight Americans had been slain by the British army, under Major Pitcairn, with a large body of the flower of the English army, against only seventy minute-men. This occasioned intense and burning indignation, throughout the length and breadth of the land. On the 17th of June of the same year, was fought the ever memorable battle of Bunker Hill, on the Heights of Charleston, which caused the people in every direction to fly to arms. The husbandman, changed his plow for a musket, and about 15,000 men from Massachusetts, New Hampshire, Rhode Island and Connecticut, at once rushed to the vicinity of Boston, and placing themselves under General Ward, were ready to cope with the disciplined and well equipped British troops, under Generals Gage, Howe, Clinton, Burgoyne, Pigot, and others, then occupying Boston.

"Blood had been shed at Lexington, and cried aloud from the ground for vengeance, and volunteers had hastened hither, towards the scene of action, and within a few days Boston was besieged by the outraged people. Stark of New Hampshire, in ten minutes after the news reached him, was on his way to join the patriot force. Israel Putnam, of Connecticut, at this time in the sixtieth year of his age, was peacefully occupied in plowing, when the tidings of the battle arrived; he left his plow in the field, and without even going to his house, sped on his way to the camp."*

"Early in July, 1775, Georgia entered into the opposition made to the claims of the British parliament to tax America, chose delegates to congress, after which the style of 'The thirteen united colonies,' was assumed, and by that title the English provinces, confederated and in arms, were thenceforth designated."† Ticonderoga, in the state of New York, was captured by Ethan Allen and Benedict Arnold, with a force of eighty-three men, on the morning of the 10th of May, taking the whole garrison of the fort prisoners, before they had even time to array themselves in their clothing, having been aroused from their beds, by three hearty cheers from the Green Mountain boys, as they hurried up the sally-port. Captain DeLaplace, who was in command of the fort, was still in bed. Allen knocked at the door with the hilt of his huge sword, and in stentorian voice, ordered him, instantly to appear, or his entire garrison would be put to death. He made his appearance at the door, half dressed, his pretty wife peering over his shoulders in affright, and gazing at Allen in bewildered astonishment, half awake, inquired by whose authority he acted; whereupon, that veteran flourishing his long sword, and with an oath exclaimed: "In the name of the Great Jehovah, and the continental congress."

Seeing there was no other alternative, DeLaplace surrendered,

---

* Spencer's history of the United States, p. 352.
† Ibid. p. 365.

and in two days after, Crown Point, twenty miles distant, was surprised and taken, by which more than two hundred pieces of artillery, with a large and valuable supply of powder and munitions of war, which was greatly needed, fell into the hands of the Americans.

The second continental congress met on the 10th of May, in Philadelphia, and in order to meet the expenses of the campaign, voted three million dollars in continental money, to bear the inscription of "THE UNITED COLONIES," the faith of the confederacy being pledged for the redemption, and towards the close of June they issued an additional sum of three millions. At this time the actual force of the American army was about fourteen thousand.

"The American army with about fourteen thousand men were posted on the heights around Boston, the British occupied Bunker and Breed's Hill, and Boston Neck."* Montreal was surrendered by the British on the 3d of November, and was soon after occupied by the American troops.

General Montgomery, with three hundred men, then marched upon Quebec, expecting to meet Arnold there with his detachment, who were to penetrate that province by the way of Maine.

Arnold had started with one thousand men about the middle of September, and after sustaining almost incredible hardships, he arrived on the 9th of November, at Point Levi, opposite to Quebec, crossed the St. Lawrence on the night of the 13th, but from the hardships he had endured during the march, his army was reduced to seven hundred men. He then marched towards Quebec, intending to surprise it, but being convinced that the enemy were ready to receive him, he was obliged to retire, and on the 18th he marched to join Montgomery, at Point aux Trembles.

Montgomery was killed on the 31st day of December at Quebec, Captains Cheesman and McPherson, his aides-de-camp, as well as several soldiers in front of the army, were wounded. Seeing the odds were so strongly against them, the continental army were obliged to retreat. Arnold advanced to the attack with

---

* Spencer, p. 362.

desperation, and in assaulting the first barrier, he received a severe wound in the leg, obliging him to quit the field. Had this wound have been mortal, and the brave Montgomery saved instead of Arnold, the latter instead of being disgraced, as subsequently occurred, would have died a martyr to his country, and found a soldier's and a patriot's grave, beneath the rock-built walls of Quebec; but it was ordered otherwise—the patriot Montgomery was slain, and the traitor Arnold was spared.

And as Mr. Irving says—"His name, like that of Montgomery, would have been treasured up among the dearest, though mournful recollections of his country, and that country would have been spared the single traitorous blot that dims the bright page of its revolutionary history."

After this defeat the American army was driven out of Canada, Carleton having surrendered, Morgan, upon whom the command fell after Arnold was wounded, and four hundred and twenty-six of Morgan's command were obliged to surrender, Carleton having with his detachment got in his rear, there was no other alternative left him.

On the first of January, 1776, Norfolk, in Virginia, was bombarded by the British fleet, under Lord Dinmore, and property to the value of three hundred thousand pounds was destroyed.

Sir Henry Clinton attacked Charleston, South Carolina, on the 28th of June, but was unsuccessful, and was obliged to retire with his fleet, from whence he sailed to New York.

Our army was in no condition at this time to cope with so powerful an enemy. They had met with several reverses, the most serious of which was on Long Island, from which place they were compelled to withdraw for want of means to render their position tenable. After frequent remonstrances from the commander-in-chief, and soon after the defeat on Long Island congress became awake to the condition of affairs, and proposed a permanent army, enlisted for the war, to be composed of eighty battalions, to be raised by the states, in proportion to their ability; these were apportioned as follows: New Hampshire, three; Massachusetts, fifteen; Rhode Island, two; Connecticut, eight; New York, four; New Jersey, four; Pennsylvania, twelve; Delaware, one: Maryland, three; Virginia, fifteen;

North Carolina, nine; South Carolina, six; and Georgia, one; making a total of eighty-eight. They also held out as inducements to enlist, a bounty of twenty dollars to each recruit, and portions of vacant land was promised to each officer and soldier. To a colonel they promised five hundred acres; lieutenant-colonel, four hundred and fifty; major, four hundred; captain, three hundred; lieutenant, two hundred; ensign, one hundred and fifty; and to non-commissioned officers and privates, one hundred acres of land.

General Washington established his army at Forts Washington and Lee, on the Hudson river, for the purpose of preserving the navigation of that stream.

By having possession of both sides of the river, it essentially checked the movements of General Howe, who lay above that point, and who deemed the complete possession of the entire island of New York an object of great importance, and determined to effect it at the first favorable moment.

General Washington wrote to Governor Livingston, that in the movement General Howe was then making, he would not content himself with investing Fort Washington, but would invade the Jerseys. He urged the governor to put the militia of New Jersey in condition to reinforce the continental army, and to take the place of the new levies—a body of men between militia and regulars—whose term of service expired on the first of December, and who could not be depended on to continue with the army a longer period than that for which they had engaged. Intelligence of this movement was also given to General Nathaniel Greene, who was in command in New Jersey, and his attention was particularly directed to Fort Washington. He was advised to increase his magazines around Princeton, and diminish those near New York. He was also apprehensive that Howe would attempt to cross at Dobbs' Ferry, and envelope the troops about Fort Lee, as well as those in Fort Washington.

General Greene was also advised of this, and drew his men from Amboy—a body of whom he posted on the heights to defend the passage at Dobbs' Ferry.

At this time General Washington had his headquarters at Hackensack.

The garrison of Fort Washington was under the command of Colonel Magraw, a brave and intrepid officer. General Howe, with his army, crossed the Hudson river in boats, and on the 15th of November he summoned the garrison to surrender on pain of being put to the sword; upon which Colonel Magraw replied that he should defend it to the last extremity. This summons was immediately communicated to General Greene, at Fort Lee, and by him to the commander-in-chief at Hackensack. Washington immediately rode to Fort Lee, and though late in the night, was proceeding to Fort Washington, where he expected to meet Generals Putnam and Greene, when, in crossing the river, he met those officers, returning from a visit to that post, when, having a good report from them, they returned together to Fort Lee.

But although the place was extremely strong, the British carried it by storm about ten o'clock in the morning, the British being reinforced by the arrival of a detachment which had crossed the Harlem river; they were overpowered and compelled to abandon their lines and retreat towards the fort. This retreat having been conducted with considerable confusion, a part of the men were intercepted by the division under Colonel Stirling and made prisoners. The British general having carried the lines and all the strong ground adjoining them, again summoned Colonel Magraw to surrender. While the capitulation was in progress, General Washington sent him word to hold out until evening, when he would endeavor to bring off the garrison; but Magraw had already proceeded too far to retract. It is not likely, however, that the place could have resisted an assault from so formidable a force as threatened them on every side, as the first division, consisting of two columns of Hessians and Waldeckers, amounting to about five thousand men, under command of General Knyphausen, had invested them on the north; the second, consisting of the first and second battalions of British light infantry and two battalions of guards, under Brigadier-General Mathews, supported by Lord Cornwallis, at the head of the first and second battalions of grenadiers and the thirty-first regiment, was on the east; while the third division, under Lieutenant-Colonel Sterling, crossed the river higher up;

and the fourth, under Lord Percy, accompanied by General Howe in person, was to attack the lines in front and on the south side.

The attacks on the north and south by General Knyphausen and Lord Percy, were made upon Colonel Rawlings and General Cadwalader at about the same instant, who maintained their ground for a considerable time; but while General Cadwalader was engaged in the first line against Lord Percy, on the south, the second and third divisions dispersed the troops fronting Harlem river, together with a detachment sent by Cadwalader to support them.

The fort in which they had taken refuge being too small, to contain all the troops, and their ammunition being nearly exhausted, they were compelled to surrender as prisoners of war.

The prisoners taken on this occasion was reported by General Howe to have been two thousand six hundred, exclusive of officers, but General Washington reported them at two thousand.

This was the greatest loss the Americans had yet sustained, and their cause bore a hopeless aspect, but General Washington, having full confidence in the justness of the cause and of their final success, at once set about to concert measures that would ultimately accomplish their overthrow, and after the surrender of Fort Washington he made arrangements to evacuate Fort Lee and remove the stores to the interior of New Jersey, but on the 19th of November, before this could be accomplished, a detachment of the enemy, commanded by Lord Cornwallis, amounting to about six thousand men, crossed the North River below Dobbs' ferry, and by a rapid march, endeavored to hem in the garrison, between the Hudson and Hackensack rivers, and with great difficulty the safety of the garrison was accomplished by crossing a bridge over the latter river. Our army lost at Fort Lee all their heavy cannon, except two twelve pounders, together with a large quantity of provisions and military stores, which fell into the hands of the enemy.

He then posted his troops along the western bank of the Hackensack river, but he was unable to defend his position, having only three thousand effective men, who were exposed to the inclemency of the weather, without tents, in a level country without an entrenching tool, and among people who were in no wise zealous in the American cause; and being still enclosed by two rivers, the Hackensack and Passaic, his position was thereby rendered more dangerous. The position of affairs was now gloomy indeed, and no reliance could be placed on reinforcements from any quarter.

He directed General Schuyler to hasten to his assistance from Ticonderoga the troops of Pennsylvania and New Jersey, who had remained stationed there until General Carlton had retired from that position. But the march was long, their term of service nearly expired, and they refused to re-enlist. General Mercer, who commanded part of the troops stationed at Bergen, was called in, but these troops had engaged to serve only, until the first of December, and like other six months men, had abandoned the army in great numbers.

General Washington, with Beal's, Heard's and part of Irvine's brigades, crossed at Acquackanonck bridge, and posted themselves at Newark, on the south side of the Passaic river.

Washington now endeavored to collect such a force as might preserve the semblance of an army, to accomplish which, he sent General Mifflin to Pennsylvania, and Colonel Joseph Reed, his adjutant general, who was well known and highly valued in New Jersey, to Governor Livingston, to urge upon him the absolute and immediate necessity of making further exertions to prevent the whole state from being overrun.

In this perilous state of things, he found it necessary to detach Colonel Foreman of the New Jersey militia, to suppress an insurrection which threatened to break out in the county of Monmouth, where great numbers still clung to the royal cause.

The British now crossed the Passaic river, and General Washington, unable to make an effective resistance against them, abandoned his position, and on the 28th of November, as Lord Cornwallis entered Newark, he retreated to New Brunswick.

December 1st was the time when the Maryland and Jersey troops in the flying camp were entitled to their discharge, and General Washington had now the mortification of seeing his small army still more enfeebled by the abandonment of these troops almost in sight of an advancing enemy. The Pennsylvania militia of the same class had engaged to serve until the first of January, but so many of them deserted, that it became necessary to place guards on the roads and ferries over the Delaware to apprehend the fugitives.

While at New Brunswick, the commander-in-chief again urged upon Governor Livingston, that the intention of the enemy was to pass through New Jersey to Philadelphia, and that it was necessary to adopt some measure which would effectually call out the strength of the state to his support, and for its own defence. But the governor was unable to furnish the aid required.

The legislature had removed from Princeton to Trenton, and from Trenton to Burlington, but had now adjourned, and the members had returned to their homes to look after their own interests. In the middle counties, those who were in favor of the cause of the patriots were compelled to remain quiet by the British army, then in their midst. In the lower counties, they were continually overawed by the tories, or paralyzed by the non-combating Quakers. Not that this class of the population were less patriotic than others, but their religion forbade them to take up arms. And in Morris and Sussex counties, the militia turned out slowly. Washington in this crisis again urged General Lee to hasten to his assistance.

Washington kept his troops in constant motion for the purpose of concealing his weakness, and to endeavor to retard the advance of Cornwallis, creating an opinion that the Americans meditated an attack upon him, but as the British approached the opposite side of the bridge, he was compelled to retire from New Brunswick. He left Lord Sterling in Princeton, with two brigades from Virginia and Delaware, in all twelve hundred men, for the purpose of watching the enemy, while he continued his march, with the residue of his army, to Trenton. He had directed to collect and place under sufficient guard all the boats on the Delaware river, from Philadelphia upwards, for seventy miles in order to stop the progress of the enemy at this river, hoping that in the meantime reinforcements would arrive, sufficient to enable him to dispute its passage. He then with, great labor transported his few remaining military stores and baggage across the Delaware, determining to remain there as long as possible with the small force that still adhered to him.

In his retreat into and through New Jersey, he met with every circumstance that could embarrass and depress him, which commenced immediately after the heavy loss he had sustained at Fort Washington. In fourteen days after, the whole flying camp claimed its discharge, as well as other troops, whose time of service expired about the same time, were leaving him daily. Every man of the two New Jersey regiments, which had been forwarded by General Gates, and were under General St. Clair, left as soon as they entered their own state, and nothing was left of them but a few officers. Those who were with Washington, composed mostly of the garrison of Fort Lee, had no tents, blankets or shoes, and were without the necessary utensils to cook their provisions.

Scarce any one joined him during his retreat, which occupied nineteen days to march ninety miles, while numbers daily flocked to the royal army, to make their peace with them, and crave protection. The British army was well appointed, well clad, brilliant and imposing, while that of our own was in tatters, and were reproached by the tories, as ragamuffins. While our army was in this condition, the King of Great Britain issued a proclamation to all persons assembled in arms against his Majesty's government, to disband and return to their homes, and to the civil officers to desist from their treasonable practices, and give up their usurped authority. A full pardon was offered to all, who, within sixty days would appear before an officer of the crown, claim the benefit of the proclamation, and subscribe a declaration of submission to the royal authority. A great many took advantage of this and craved the protection of their conquerors, upon the plea that they were opposed to the measures adopted, and were at all times opposed to independence.

Washington having secured his baggage and stores, and learning that Cornwallis had stopped at New Brunswick, detached twelve hundred men to Princeton, on the 6th of December, hoping by his appearing to advance, he might not only delay the progress of the British, but reanimate the people of the state.

General Mifflin having been highly successful in raising troops in Pennsylvania, and particularly in Philadelphia, where a large proportion of the inhabitants of that city capable of bearing arms, had associated in defence of the country, fifteen hundred of whom now marched to Trenton; congress also ordered a German battalion to the same place. Washington immediately upon receiving this reinforcement, commenced his march to Princeton, but before he had reached it, he learned that Cornwallis was rapidly advancing from New Brunswick by different routes, with the intention of getting in his rear, and he was obliged to retreat across the Delaware, and establish himself in Pennsylvania.

Washington having secured the boats, and broken down the bridges on the roads leading along the Jersey shore, posted his army on the west bank of the river, to guard the fords by which the enemy might pass, and as his rear guard crossed the river, the glistening bayonets of the enemy came in sight. The main body halted at Trenton, and stationed detachments above and below, so as to render it uncertain where they might attempt to pass.

Cornwallis attempted to seize a number of boats at Coryell's ferry, which were guarded by Lord Sterling, but was unsuccessful; he then repaired the bridges below Trenton, and sent a strong detachment of his troops to Bordentown, six miles below, evidently showing his design was, to cross the river both above and below Trenton, and in two columns to march directly to Philadelphia, or to completely envelop the American army.

General Washington in his endeavors to counteract this plan, stationed four brigades under Generals Lord Sterling, Mercer, Stephens and DeFormoy, from Yardley's to Coryell's ferry, in such manner as to guard every suspicious point of the river, and to assist each other in case of attack. General Irvine,[*] with a portion of the Pennsylvania flying camp, and some New Jersey

---

[*] In Spark's Life of Washington, this officer is called Ewing ; in Marshall's Irvine, and in Wilkinson's, Irving—all evidently meaning the same officer.

militia under General Dickenson, were posted from Yardley's ferry down to the ferry opposite Bordentown. Colonel Cadwalader, with the Pennsylvania militia was stationed on the Neshamony as far as Dunk's ferry, at which place was also Colonel Nixon, with the Philadelphia battalion. Strict orders were given these officers as to their line of conduct, in case he should be driven from his post, and forced from the river, to rendezvous on the high grounds at Germantown.

General Lee having been frequently directed to join the rest of the army, but being desirous of retaining his separate command, was slow to obey, desiring rather to threaten the rear of the British army, than to strengthen the army in front of them. In opposition to the judgment of Washington, he established himself at Morristown. Being again urged to march, he proceeded reluctantly toward the Delaware.

Information of his march having been communicated to the British, General Harcourt, with a body of cavalry, while he was passing through Morris county, near Baskingridge, and about twenty miles from the British encampment, stopped at a house about three miles from his troops, and early in the morning of the twelfth of December, reached Lee's headquarters, and surrounding the house, Lee became a prisoner, and was borne off in triumph to the British army, where for some time he was treated not as a prisoner of war, but as a deserter from the British service.

This misfortune made a painful impression throughout America. No officer except the commander-in-chief himself, had so large a share of the confidence of the army and country; his capture therefore was universally bewailed, as the greatest calamity that had befallen the army.

After the capture of Lee, the command fell on General Sullivan, who obeyed the orders promptly, and on the twentieth of December, he joined Washington by the way of Phillipsburg. General Gates arrived the same day with some northern troops. These with other reinforcements increased the American army to about seven thousand men.

The British were unable to obtain boats, and were therefore, unsuccessful in crossing the river as they had anticipated to do;

he therefore determined to close the campaign, and retire into winter quarters. He disposed his army of about four thousand men, on the Delaware at Trenton, Bordentown, White Horse and Mount Holly, the remainder he distributed from the Delaware to the Hackensack rivers. Washington supposing that the object of the enemy was to attempt to gain Philadelphia, in case the ice became sufficiently firm to bear them.

In order to counteract this, three regiments marching from Peekskill, were halted at Morristown, and there consolidated with about eight hundred New Jersey militia under General Ford. This whole command was placed under General Maxwell, of this state.

He was to watch the movements of the enemy and harass their marches, and to communicate intelligence as to their movements, particularly such as might be made from New Brunswick towards Princeton or Trenton, and to prevent the inhabitants from going within the British lines for protection.

At this perilous juncture Washington labored to impress upon congress the necessity of making still greater exertions to form a permanent army, particularly to increase the cavalry, artillery and engineers, and also to extend his own powers, which were not sufficient to meet cases which daily occurred.

His army at this time, except a few regiments from Virginia, Pennsylvania, Maryland and New York, leaving him an effective force of only about fifteen hundred men, would dissolve in a few days. New Jersey had in a great measure submitted, but the militia of Pennsylvania had not displayed as much alacrity as had been expected, and, in case the ice on the Delaware proved sufficient to bear them, it was feared that General Howe would capture Philadelphia, which would have a dangerous effect on the contest.

But General Washington saw a ray of hope in the dispersed situation of the British army, and determined to strike a blow, which if successful might recover the ground he had lost, and retrieve his cause. He therefore formed the daring plan of attacking all the British posts on the Delaware. This plan was suggested by General Joseph Reed.

" In the present alarming position of affairs in America, it was of great moment that something should be done to rouse the spirit of the country, which had been so greatly depressed by the retreat through the Jerseys. Washington devoted anxious thought and prayerful attention to a plan, which he determined at the earliest moment to carry into effective action. At the time the Americans crossed the Delaware, winter was fast setting in, and the British general determined not to carry on active operations, during the inclement season of the year. He seemed to have lost all fear of a feeble enemy, whom he had so easily driven before him, and whom he confidently expected soon to annihilate; he therefore cantoned his troops with a view to the convenient resumption of their march, rather than with any regard to security against a fugitive foe.

"As he entertained not the slightest apprehension of an attack, he paid little attention to the arrangement of his several posts, for the purpose of mutual support. He stationed a detachment of about fifteen hundred Hessians at Trenton, under Colonel Rahl, and about two thousand at Bordentown, under Count Donop, the rest of the army was quartered over the country, between the Hackensack and Delaware rivers. Howe felt perfectly secure in his winter quarters, for so far as appearances went, he had no cause to fear anything from the Americans; for with an over-powering force, well disciplined, and flushed with victory, he felt quite justified in treating with contempt the small and broken army of Washington.

"He did not suppose the commander-in-chief would dare venture upon offensive operations. But Washington determined to anticipate the movements of Howe, and to strike a blow which should be felt, and which should demonstrate to the enemy, as well as the people of America, that the cause of independence was by no means hopeless. He therefore formed his available forces into three divisions, and accompanied by Greene and Sullivan, proposed to cross the river at McConkey's ferry, about nine miles above Trenton, and fall upon the Hessians in that town.

"The second division, under General Ewing, was to cross over at Trenton ferry, and taking charge of the bridge over the Assanpink, were to cut off the enemy's retreat; while the third, under General Cadwalader, was to cross lower down, from Bristol, about ten miles below Trenton, over to Burlington. Had the plan been executed at all points it must have resulted in the capture of the whole line of the British cantonments, but owing to a variety of obstacles it was but partially successful. The evening of Christmas day was selected, because it was known to the commander-in-chief, that the Germans held that day as a general holiday, and he knew they, feeling secure in the town, would give way to more than ordinary indulgence and festivity, and would not be on their guard for the approach of an enemy.

"The night was intensely cold; the Delaware was choked with floating masses of ice; the current was strong; and the wind blew keenly and sharply.

"He exhorted the soldiers to be firm, and they remembered, with indignation, the outrages and injuries inflicted upon the people of New Jersey by the insolent foe, and the no less insolent and vindictive tories. They were now ready to do or die for their homes and their country.

"Washington had expected that the passage of his division might have been effected by midnight, but the dreadful weather, the encumbered state of the river, and the difficulty of getting the artillery across, occasioned so much delay, that it was four o'clock before the whole body were in marching order on the New Jersey shore.

"The darkness of a winter morning was still further deepened by a heavy fog, and the road was rendered slippery by a frosty mist. The snow and hail beat upon them during the whole march.

"As it would be daylight before they could reach Trenton, a surprise of that post was now out of the question; there was, however, no alternative left but to proceed. Washington took the upper road, while Sullivan commanded the lower; and about eight o'clock in the morning, both parties encountered the pickets of the enemy, who, keeping up a fire from behind the houses, fell back upon the town, and aroused their comrades.

"The Americans followed them up so closely that they were able to open a battery at the head of King street, the principal street of the town, before the astounded Hessians could offer any effectual resistance."*

While the two armies were in and around Boston they suffered severely from the small pox; the enemy, in order to avoid the pestilence, and finding it a more favorable place as their base of operations, removed to New York, which necessarily led to the breaking up of the American camp at the former place. A portion of the enemy's force proceeded to Charleston, South Carolina, where they met with the memorable defeat at Fort Moultrie. Acting upon the presumption that New York was the objective point of the British commander, Washington ordered his troops in that direction.

The brigade of General Nathaniel Greene was despatched to Long Island, where he arrived about the middle of April, and established his headquarters at Brooklyn; the remainder of the American troops were put in possession of New York, while the enemy were encamped on Staten Island, in New Jersey.

To Greene was assigned the command of the troops in New Jersey, and he established his headquarters at Fort Lee, on the Hudson, about nine miles above New York, or at Bergen, as events required his presence at either place, in order to keep open a communication with the main army east of the Hudson river, and secure for Washington a retreat, should circumstances render it necessary.

Overwhelmed by the enemy, the army abandoned this part of the state, and made their retreat through New Jersey, and continued across the state until they had arrived upon the Pennsylvania side of the Delaware river.

They remained here until Washington had conceived that the auspicious moment had arrived to strike a blow in Trenton, and either perish or accomplish this desired object. And at a moment of the greatest seeming prostration, the columns of Washington were set in motion for the surprise of Trenton, which was eminently successful, and at once aroused the nation into hope and confidence. In this enterprise the affair was decided in a few minutes, by the defeat and surrender of more than a thous-

---

* Spencer, Vol. 1, p. 458.

and Hessians, who were considered among the best troops of the British army.

At dusk on the night of the 25th of December, 1776, the continental troops, commanded by General Washington in person, amounting to two thousand four hundred men, with twenty pieces of artillery, began to cross at McConkey's ferry. The troops at Yardleyville and the stations above, had that day assembled at this ferry. Among the prominent and active men who were employed ferrying over the troops, were Uriah Slack, William Green and David Lanning.

It was between three and four o'clock in the morning before all the artillery and troops were over and ready to march.

Many of the men were very destitute, as regarded clothing. The ground was covered with sleet and snow, which was falling at the time, although the day before there was no snow, or only a little sprinkling of it, on the ground

General Washington, (who had sat in silence on a beehive, wrapped in his cloak, while his troops were crossing,) as they were about to march, enjoined upon them all *profound silence* during their march to Trenton, and said to them: "*I hope you will all fight like men.*"

The sun had just risen as the tents of the enemy appeared in sight. Washington, rising in his stirrups, waved his sword and exclaimed: "*There, my brave friends, are the enemies of your country; and now, all I have to ask is, to remember what you are about to fight for. March!*"

The army marched at a quick step, in a body, from the river up the cross-road to the Bear Tavern, about a mile from the river. The whole army then marched down this road to the village of Birmingham, about three and a half miles distant.

There they halted, examined their priming, and found it all wet. Captain Mott, notwithstanding he had taken the precaution to wrap his handkerchief around the lock of his gun, found the priming wet. "*Well,*" said General Sullivan, "*we must fight them with the bayonet.*"

From Birmingham to Trenton, the distance by the river road and the Scotch road is nearly equal, being about four and a half miles.

The troops were formed in two divisions. One of them, commanded by General Sullivan, marched down the river road; the other, commanded by General Washington, accompanied by Generals Lord Stirling, Greene, Mercer, and Stevens, filed off to the left, crossed over to the Scotch road, and marched along until they entered the Pennington road about one mile above Trenton.

Scarcely a word was spoken from the time the troops left the ferry (except what passed between the officers and guides,) till they reached Trenton; and with such stillness did the army move, that they were not discovered until they came upon the outguards of the enemy, who were posted in the outskirts of the town, at or near the house of Colonel David Brearley,* when one of the sentinels called to Laning,† (who was a little in advance of the troops,) and asked, "Who is there?" Laning replied, "A friend!" "A friend to whom?" "A friend to General Washington." At this the guard fired and retreated.‡

The American troops returned their fire and rushed upon them, driving them into the town. At the head of King street, (now Warren,) Captain T. Forrest opened a six gun battery, under the immediate orders of General Washington, which commanded the street. Captain William Washington and Lieuten-

---

* This was just after daybreak, according to the testimony of several persons who lived in the town or neighborhood at the time.

† This Laning had a few days before been taken prisoner by a scouting party, in the Scudder neighborhood, near the Delaware river, carried to Trenton and confined in a house on Tucker's corner (Greene and State).

Watching an opportunity, when there was a little commotion among the guard, he slipped out of the back door, sprang over a high board fence, and escaped to the house of Stacy Potts, who took him in, and concealed him that night. The next morning, Laning dressed in an old ragged coat, and flapped hat, put an axe under his arm, and went with his head down, limping along, and so passed the enemy's sentries in safety, in the character of a wood-chopper, but when he got where the Pennington and Scotch roads meet, he looked in every direction, and seeing no person, threw down his axe, and took to Dickinson's swamp, and so escaped.

‡ At the commencement of the engagement, when Washington with his sword raised, was giving his orders, it is said a musket ball passed between his fingers, slightly grazing them. He only said, " that has passed by."

ant James Monroe, (afterwards president of the United States,) perceiving that the enemy were endeavoring to plant a battery in King street, rushed forward with the advance guard, drove the artillerists from their guns and took from them two pieces, which they were in the act of firing. These guns are now in the State Arsenal. Captain Washington and Lieutenant Monroe were both wounded in this successful enterprise.

A part of this division marched down Queen street (now Greene) and extended to the left, in order to cut off the retreat of the enemy towards Princeton.

The division of the army which came down the river road, under the command of General Sullivan, fell upon the British advance guard at Rutherford's place, in the northwestern part of the town, at about the same time that Washington entered it on the north.

Both divisions pushed forward, keeping up a running fire with small arms,* and meeting with but little opposition until the enemy were driven eastward in Second street, (now State,) near the Presbyterian church, where there was some fighting, the enemy having made a momentary stand; but finding themselves hemmed in and overpowered, they laid down their arms in the cornfield back of the Presbyterian church.

Colonel Rahl, the Hessian commander, whose headquarters was at the corner of Warren and Bank streets, was mortally wounded during the early part of the engagement, being shot from his horse while endeavoring to form his dismayed and disordered troops.

When, supported by a file of sergeants, he presented his sword to General Washington, (whose countenance beamed with complacency at the success of the day,) he was pale and bleeding, and, in broken accents, seemed to implore those attentions which the victor was well disposed to bestow upon him. He

---

* When the firing commenced on the morning of the battle, a daughter of Mr. Stacy Potts was at Miss Cox's, opposite the Episcopal church, and as she was running to her father's house a musket ball struck the comb from her head, slightly injuring her.

was taken to his headquarters, where he died on the third day after the battle.

The number of prisoners taken at that time was twenty-three officers and eight hundred and eighty-six privates. Four stand of colors, twelve drums, six brass field pieces, and a thousand stand of arms and accoutrements.

The British light-horse and four or five hundred Hessians escaped at the beginning of the battle over the bridge across the Assanpink, at Trent's mills, and fled to Bordentown.

If General Ewing, whose division of the army was opposite Trenton, had been able to cross the Delaware, as contemplated, and take possession of the bridge across the Assanpink, at Greene street, all the enemy's troops which were in Trenton would undoubtedly have been captured. But there was so much ice on the shores of the river that it was impossible to get the artillery over.*

Immediately after this victory—which greatly revived the drooping spirits of the army—General Washington commenced marching his prisoners up to the Eight Mile Ferry (McConkey's), and before night all were safely landed on the western shore of the Delaware. But Washington would not let a man pass more than was necessary, until all the prisoners were over.

Among the Americans but two men were killed, while the Hessians lost seven officers and about thirty men. Twenty-four of the latter were buried in one pit, in the Presbyterian burying ground, by the American troops.†

It has been reported that after taking the Hessians, while the American army were marching their prisoners to the ferry, that two of our men were frozen to death. But the cause of their death can be accounted for in this way. The night after the capture, December 27th, several of the American soldiers, who were worn down with fatigue, being poorly clad, took refuge at

---

* New Jersey Hist. Coll., by Barber and Howe, p. 296.

† Some years after this battle, several skeletons and coffins were found where the Assanpink empties into the Delaware river, which many supposed were Hessians killed in this battle, but it has since been ascertained that they were English, quartered at White Hall barracks, during the French war, about the year 1760.

the house of a Mrs. Scudder. Several of them became very sick in the night and two or three died, and it is not, therefore, unlikely that these were the persons mentioned as having frozen to death. Although the American army suffered great privations and underwent very many hardships, still it is extremely doubtful that the two men above mentioned did actually freeze to death.

Washington, in his report to Congress, under date of December 27th, 1776, from his headquarters at Newtown, Pennsylvania, the next day after the battle, gives the following account of it :

"I have the pleasure of congratulating you upon the success of an enterprise which I had formed against a detachment of the enemy lying in Trenton, and which was executed yesterday morning. The evening of the 25th I ordered the troops intended for this service, to parade back of McConkey's ferry (now Taylorsville), that they might begin to pass as soon as it grew dark—imagining that we should be able to throw them all over with the necessary artillery by twelve o'clock, and that we might easily arrive at Trenton by five o'clock in the morning, the distance being about nine miles.

"But the quantity of ice made that night, impeded the passage of the boats so much, that it was three o'clock before the artillery could all be got over, and near four before the troops took up their line of march.

"I formed my detachment in two divisions—one to march up the lower or river road, the other by the upper or Pennington road.

"As the divisions had nearly the same distance to march, I ordered each of them, immediately upon forcing the outguards to push directly into the town, that they might charge the enemy before they had time to form.

"The upper division arrived at the enemy's advanced post exactly at eight o'clock, and in three minutes after, I found from the fire on the lower road, that that division had also got up. The outguards made but a small opposition ; though, for their numbers, they behaved very well—keeping up a constant retreating fire from behind houses. We presently saw their main body formed, but from their motions, they seemed undetermined how to act.

"Being hard pressed by our troops, who had already got possession of their artillery, they attempted to file off by a road on their right, leading to Princeton; but, perceiving their intention, I threw a body of troops in their way, which immediately checked them.

"Finding from our disposition, that they were surrounded, and they must inevitably be cut to pieces if they made any further resistance, they agreed to lay down their arms.

"The number that submitted in this manner was twenty-three officers and eight hundred and eighty-six men.

"Colonel Rahl, the commanding officer, and seven others, were found wounded in the town.

"I do not know exactly, how many they had killed; but I fancy not above twenty or thirty—as they never made any regular stand.

"Our loss is very trifling indeed—only two officers[*] and one or two privates wounded.

"I find the detachment of the enemy consisted of three Hessian regiments of Landspatch, Kniphausen and Rahl, amounting to about one thousand five hundred men, and a troop of British light-horse; but immediately upon the beginning of the attack, all those who were not killed or taken, pushed directly down the road towards Bordentown.

"These, likewise, would have fallen into our hands could my plan have been carried into execution.

"General Ewing was to have crossed before day at Trenton ferry,[†] and taken possession of the bridge leading to the town,[‡] but the quantity of ice was so great, that though he did everything in his power to effect it, he could not cross.

"This difficulty also hindered General Cadwalader from crossing with the Pennsylvania militia from Bristol. He got part of

---

[*] These were Captains Washington and Monroe.

[†] Just below where the old Trenton bridge now stands.

[‡] The bridge across the Assanpink in Greene street, which post he was to have taken to prevent the escape of the enemy to Bordentown.

his foot over, but finding it impossible to embark his artillery he was obliged to desist.

"I am fully confident, that, could the troops under Generals Ewing and Cadwalader have passed the river, I should have been enabled, with their assistance, to have driven the enemy from all their posts below Trenton. But the numbers I had with me being inferior to theirs below, and a strong battalion of light-infantry being at Princeton above me, I thought it most prudent to return the same evening, with the prisoners and artillery we had taken. We found no stores of any consequence in the town.

"In justice to the officers and men, I must add that their behaviour on this occasion reflects the highest honor upon them. The difficulty of passing the river on a very severe night, and their march through a violent storm of hail and snow, did not in the least abate their ardor—but, when they came to the charge, each seemed to vie with the other in pressing forward; and were I to give a preference to any particular corps I should do injustice to the other. Colonel Baylor, my first aid-de-camp, will have the honor of delivering this to you, and from him you may be made acquainted with many other particulars. His spirited behaviour upon every occasion requires me to recommend him to your particular notice."

Spencer says *—"It is said, that on the morning of the surprise, Rahl, who had been carousing all night, after an entertainment, was still engaged at cards, until aroused, at length, by the roll of the American drums, and the sound of musketry, he started to his feet, hurried to his quarters, mounted his horse, and in a few moments was at the head of his troops, vainly attempting to atone for his fatal neglect. In a few moments he fell to the ground mortally wounded, and was carried away to his quarters. All order was now at an end; the Hessians, panic-struck, gave way, and endeavored to escape by the road to Princeton; but were intercepted by a party judiciously placed there for the purpose, and compelled to surrender at discretion,

---

* Spencer's History of the United States, Vol. I., p. 459.

to the number of about a thousand men. Six cannon, a thousand stand of arms, and four colors, adorned the triumph of Washington. In this moment of brilliant success, purchased at the expense of others, he was not unmindful of the duties of humanity; but, accompanied by Greene, paid a visit to the dying Hessian leader, and soothed his passage to the grave, by the expression of that grateful and generous sympathy, which one brave man owes to another, even when engaged in opposite causes."

END OF VOL. I.

www.ingramcontent.com/pod-product-compliance
Lightning Source LLC
Chambersburg PA
CBHW021233300426
44111CB00007B/526